The Incomparable Guru Golwalkar

The Incomparable Guru Golwalkar

Ranga Hari

Translation by
Ratan Sharda

PRABHAT PRAKASHAN

Published by
PRABHAT PRAKASHAN PVT. LTD.
4/19 Asaf Ali Road,
New Delhi-110 002 (INDIA)
e-mail: prabhatbooks@gmail.com

ISBN 978-93-5266-778-9
THE INCOMPARABLE GURU GOLWALKAR
by Ranga Hari

Edition
2025

Price
₹ 600.00 (Rupees Six Hundred only)

Printed at
Narula Printers, Delhi

Preface

Time and history have proved that among the modern India's organisers of men and movements, Shri Guruji Golwalkar occupies a place in the topmost few. For more than three decades till his death, he, with no respite and rest, covered the entire length and breadth of this vast country on wheels, wings or legs with no unfortunate occasion to cancel any scheduled programme. Never in his life did he reach a programme late. With a diligent team as unfailing as himself, he built up the largest organisation of our times, Rashtriya Swayamsevak Sangh, with a very wide network. With an absolutely self-reliant structure and a unique working system evolved out of native genius, this organisation today is nothing short of a phenomenon; comparable only to itself.

Any inquisitive mind, candid and unprejudiced, would like very much to delve deep into the lives of men who built up such a movement. In case of Shri Guruji, the attention is bound to be more compelling due to the fact that here was person maligned and cursed all through by the powers that be; but who, despite them, unflinchingly and relentlessly, paced towards his cherished goal. Golwalkar was truly 'Goal Walker', come what may.

It is more to satisfy such aforesaid minds that I had penned a rather comprehensive biography of Shri Guruji soon after his birth centenary. Now that my colleague and comrade-in-arms Ratan Sharda has come forward to render the Hindi original into English, I feel truly happy, naturally at the personal level; but much more so, because Ratanji has opened the doors wider to facilitate its reach to a larger section. Hence, my purpose of presenting Shri Guruji to the public would be served even better. So more than happy, I feel gratified.

—Ranga Hari

15-3-2018
Kochi

Contents

1
Golwalkar Family Tree

Supreme Lord Shri Krishna says in the *Gita* that a person, disrupted during yoga, takes birth again in a pious and yogi family to complete his interrupted effort. If one goes through history, one feels that the Golwalkar family had this quality including a high level of spirituality. Roots of the Golwalkar lay spread in a small isolated village called Golwali, which was situated on the Mumbai-Kanyakumari highway in Konkan, 51 kms. south of Ratnagiri and 41 kms. north of Chiplun. This village was donated by the Naval commander of Shahu Maharaj, who was a descendent of Shivaji Maharaj, Kanhoji Angre to 'Vedmurti' Kashi Upadhyay, a well-wisher of the king due to a sense of obligation, on 4th October, 1725. He is considered to be the head of the family which was engaged in the study and teaching of the *Shruti*, the *Smriti* and the *Puranas*. Over a period of time, the surname 'Upadhyay' got abbreviated to 'Padhye' and to 'Golwalkar Padhye' as the family tree extended. Over time, even Padhye got dropped and only Golwalkar remained.

Kashi Padhye had two sons, Yagnyeshwar and Anant, with the elder Yagnyeshwar taking *sannyas* at a young age and the second taking to *grihastha ashram* or family life. To fulfil his family obligations, Anant Shastri Padhye left Golwali to settle down at Bhaivkunth Pandharpur, where religious rituals like *upanayan* (sacred thread ceremony) and upbringing of his son Kashinath took place in a highly religious atmosphere. Kashinath was a die-hard devotee of Lord Pandharinath. He fulfilled his religious duties and served the Lord with the highest degree of commitment and was enriched with invaluable experiences. He wrote a scriptural tome titled *Dharmasindhusar* in Sanskrit, laying down the rules of religious rituals. It was renamed later as *Dharmasindhu*. Even today, scholars consider this to be their scripture and consider it a beacon during debates on any religious policy. During this time, Kashinath sired another son, who was named Sakharam. Taking a view that his worldly duty was over with birth of son and creation of the scripture as his crowning achievements, Kashinath took *sannyas* like his paternal uncle Yagnyeshwar and left for his pilgrimage, taking *samaadhi* finally in year 1806.

Nurturing his family values, Sakharam came to the famed pilgrim town Paithan, from Pandharpur, to earn a decent living by teaching Sanskrit. His son Balkrishna was born there. Taking forward this chain of migrations, Balkrishna left Paithan and reached Nagpur, the capital of Bhonsales and took up a job in government even as he carried on with his Vedic activities. Silent epoch-changing events were taking place there at that time. Balkrishna was blessed over time with two sons named Sadashiv and Ramchandra but met an untimely death on the outskirts of Nagpur during an official administrative tour. Both the sons grew up in Nagpur, bereft of their father's care. According to the customs of the time, Sadashiv Golwalkar became the son-in-law of Raikar family at the age of 15 and as the wheels of time turned, this couple was blessed with a son in the year 1906. It is this son who is the central personality of this narration – Madhav Golwalkar, who came to be known famously as Guruji Golwalkar. Coincidentally, it was the centenary year of the *samaadhi* of his great grandfather, Kashinath!

This is a brief account of the Golwalkar family's seven generations.*

□

* Based on introduction to *Dharmasindhu* and *Maa. Sa. Golwalkar – Vyakti va Kaarya*

Golwalkar's Genealogy (Seven Generations)

Kashi Upadhyay

Yagnyeshwar Upadhaya

Anant Shastri Padhye

Kashinath Padhye (Dharmasindhu's creator)

Sakharam Golwalkar Padhye

Bal Krishna Golwalkar

Sadashiv Golwalkar

Ramchandra Golwalkar

10 Short-life Child

Madhav Golwalkar

Vasudev Golwalkar

4 Sisters

2

Shri Guruji's Father

Mother and father leave a deep imprint on the life of a child. No child brought up in a family atmosphere can negate it. Clear and pure pronunciation, decent behaviour, disciplined life, easy-going nature of interacting with people – all such individual and group characteristics bloom in a child blessed with the desire to observe and learn. Loving nature and strict check by elders on unruly behaviour contribute to this evolution. This is the reason why our religious texts place mother and father at par with the Supreme Creator. Development of Guruji's personality cannot be an exception to this social regulation. So, let us look at the lives of his mother and father from this viewpoint.

With luck veiled behind the misfortune of untimely demise of father Balkrishna, Guruji's father Sadashiv Golwalkar had to take up the government job on compassionate grounds as Balkrishna's heir even before he passed the tenth class. He had to shoulder the responsibility of his family in his teens at the age of 15. As stated, he was married into the Raikar family and there was an age difference of six years between the husband and wife. Sadashiv did not succumb to adversity, but carried on with the job, taking care of his family and also continuing with his studies. As a result, he passed the tenth class in 1893 at the age of 19. The importance of a person passing tenth was like that of a graduate in those days and with this, Sadashiv got promoted to higher posts in his job. At the young age of 17, he was posted to the postal department at Kaamthi, near Nagpur. Even at that time, his extreme hunger for knowledge continued unabated. He passed intermediate in 1903.

By this time, he had fathered a child. The child was named Amrit after a lot of thought, and this apple of his eyes gradually grew up well. Madhav was born three years after Amrit. Meanwhile, the ever-eager student, Sadashiv picked up his B.A. degree in 1910. At that time, his age was 36.

While working at Kaamthi, Sadashiv Golwalkar received information that the state government planned to open schools in new regions for dissemination of education. The dormant desire to teach in the Golwalkar family lay buried deep before bursting like a fire within. Immediately, he sent an application for 'any suitable appointment in any suitable school' without delay. This application remained buried like a seed planted in the soil. After a passage of time, a written message arrived one day, saying: "It is hereby notified that if you are ready to go to Saraipalli, you can be appointed with immediate effect in that department."

Sadashiv's heart filled with happiness, but where was Saraipalli? It was a small tribal village hidden like a shy village belle deep within a forest area, 145 kms from Raipur and 100 kms from Raigadh. There were hardly any facilities available from the government, as compared to those available in Kaamthi. This village, situated in the north-east corner of the then Central Province, had hardly any transportation facility. The administration had opened a new school there. He resigned immediately from the postal department and reached Raipur with his family.[2] He took up the post of a teacher (Upadhyay, the profession of his elders) on 1st October, 1908 at the Saraipalli Government School. He got his elder son Amrit Sadashiv Golwalkar admitted to Standard One the same day.[3] After two-three months, two-and-half-year-old toddler Madhav also began sitting with his dear brother enthusiastically in his class. In the old days, there were no nursery school, no L.K.G. or U.K.G. schools. Children could sit with their elder brothers informally in their class on the designated benches. Madhav also went through this exercise. Therefore, the Saraipalli School register does not show registration of Madhav's name, but it is true that his education began there.

Teacher Sadashiv's stay in Saraipalli was not long. Within seven months, on 30th April, 1909, he was transferred. From then on, his cycle of transfers continued for twenty years till he retired as a headmaster after teaching serially in different places – Durg, Raipur, Chandrapur, Bhandara, Balaghat, Narsinghpur, Hushangabad, Chandrapur, etc. He came to Nagpur after retirement, arranging for his own house at Ramtek, 50 kms away from Nagpur. He settled down there in 1932. Coincidentally, at the sacred time of *griha pravesh,* that is, house-warming function on entering a new home, Dr. Keshav Baliram Hedgewar happened to be present.[4]

Sadashiv, with an insatiable hunger for studying, experienced spiritual bliss in the task of teaching. He did not attach much importance to the salary he received. He would invite backward students and teach them without charging any fee. To hone the innate talent of students, he used to encourage self-study. He was a strong opponent of guide books. His subjects were Mathematics, English and Sanskrit, but he also taught Hindi and Marathi, if required. He was a strict disciplinarian. In the matter of forgiving anybody, he was like Sage Durvasa, but sans his nature of cursing anybody. A seeker of truth and knowledge, Sadashiv Golwalkar abhorred sycophancy. This could be one of the reasons behind his long series of transfers. He was not well versed in worldly affairs. Therefore, he had more people who admired him than he had friends. He loved discussions. He spoke like a scholar and in the true spirit of a teacher. His submission was always clear and logical. He loved taking walks. He was an object of respect due to his honesty and internal and external purity, so much so that he came to be called Bhauji.[5]

□

Endnotes

1. *Bhagyotkarsh Visheshaank*, 2006, Raipur
2. Ibid
3. Ibid
4. *Lekhanjali* pp. 118
5. Ibid

3

Mother and Son

While talking about Guruji's mother, one tends to wonder whether the chapter's title is correct or not. On the one hand, one feels 'Mother and Sons' is the right title, but on the other, it seems that the above is appropriate where the word 'son' is in singular form. There is an important reason for this.

Raikar family's young nine-year-old daughter, who became wife of Sadashiv Golwalkar, grew with time and became a mother eleven times, but misfortune took away lives of all the earlier six children. The seventh son was Amrit, about whom we have mentioned in the earlier chapter. He was highly intelligent. His religious initiation (*brahmopadesh*) took place at Pune in 1915, but, at the age of 15 in 1918, while studying in tenth class at Balaghat, he fell prey to an attack of severe fever with delirium and left this world. What could the poor twelve-year-old Madhav do? With his eyes shut, he kept crying in a corner. There was left a vacuum in his life. He was the eighth offspring. God had gifted the family with three brothers and a sister after him. The youngest among them was Tara. She too left the world at the young age of only 5. The other two also faced untimely deaths. At the end of this all, only Madhav survived, without any elder or younger brother or sister. He was now the only child of his parents.[1] He was the centre of his family, and referred to as *Madhu*, i.e., honey. His parents started calling him Madhu. The maiden name of Madhu's mother was Sakhubai, who had one brother and two sisters. Her brother had died in his childhood. So, the heir of the family was a paternal cousin brother Balkrishna, alias Aba Raikar. He became Madhu's guardian and as per tradition in Maharashtra, when Sakhubai came to her husband's home, she was renamed Lakshmibai. Over time, she came to be called 'Tai' (elder sister) of Madhu by the neighbours and everybody around.[2]

In those days, the Vedic tradition of teaching females had been discontinued. Thus, Lakshmibai was illiterate, though it did not mean that she was uneducated. The reason for this was the exceptional system of education in this land. It was undoubtedly necessary to learn the alphabets, but receiving or giving knowledge was not dependent on it. In the oral tradition of the time, more importance was given to perfect pronunciation and to hearing than to writing. This is the reason that *shrut* (heard) became synonymous with knowledge. The synonym for scholar was *bahushrut*, meaning one who has been heard by many. This means that in this country, nobody was called uneducated for being illiterate or not knowing how to write. Happily married, Lakshmibai belonged to this league. She had 'heard' a lot in her parent's house and in-law's house, memorised it, sung it, so much so that she had learnt many *shlokas*, hymns, *kirtans* by heart. Taking advantage of various transfers of her husband, she had memorised many verses of *Ramcharitmanas.* Apart from this, she would make her sons Amrit and Madhav read out from religious scriptures like *Pandav Pratap*, *Ramvijay*, *Harivijay*, etc. and would hear them with full attention. Progressing in the same direction, she later became an ordained disciple of Paramhamsa Punyatma Gulabrao Maharaj, Vedant Kesari Babaji Maharaj and followed various rituals of this sect unerringly. She also participated once in an 1800 kms.-long religious pilgrimage. This pilgrim's walk was from the sacred town of Prayag (Allahabad in Uttar Pradesh) to the place of *samaadhi* of Gyaneshwar at Alandi (in Maharashtra), carrying pots of Ganga water on one's person. One was prohibited from visiting one's relatives and near ones on the way during this pilgrimage (*yatra*). The walk also touched Nagpur, but Tai did not go to her home, nor did her family members visit her. So strong was the understanding and spirit of all the family members.

God makes plans that test his devotees. Something similar happened in this case too. During the pilgrimage, boiling water fell on Tai's back due to somebody's carelessness and she developed boils. But she continued with her pilgrimage uninterrupted. She moved on with deep faith after putting some ointment on her boils.[3] Tai used to conduct prayers and rituals everyday and the name of her special worship was *parthiv pooja*. She would not take food without completing this *pooja*.

Quite opposite to her respected husband, Tai was like Mother Earth in the matter of forgiving people. She was a picture of serenity in her speech and behaviour. Very few people would have seen Tai getting angry. Lord Krishna has said that animosity towards none, piety for all, friendship with all, lack of selfishness, absence of ego – all these qualities existed in Tai.

In short, the Golwalkar couple belonged to such a class. Their belief in 'got one, even if lost ten' was totally philosophical. While thinking about it, one is reminded of Khalil Gibran's poem, in which an enlightened person tells his mother, "O Mother, your son is not yours. He did not come from you, but he came through you. He is an arrow in the hand of the Supreme Lord. You are the other arm that is forced to bend when he stretches the bow to pierce his target." Similar was the thinking of this couple. "O Lord, he is yours," and with this sentiment, this couple nurtured this jewel of a son.

□

Endnotes

1. *Lekhanjali*, pp. 118.

   Dr. Shridhar Bhaskar Varnekar gives detailed information about the offsprings of Golwalkar couple in this book published in 1990. In the article written after a lot of enquiries with the close relatives, he tells that first child was a daughter, and after her came five short lived children; the seventh was Amrit, Eighth was Madhav, ninth and tenth were sons while last girl Tara survived only for five years. Title of the article is *Teerthroop Tai Shri Guruji*, published in 1950. According to writer Gangadhar Indurkar, the total was nine children.

   N.H. Palkar, in his book, *Maa. Sa. Golwalkar*, published in 1956, writes there were nine children.

   H.V. Date in *Aarti Aalok ki,* published in 1964, repeats Indurkar's views.

   After scrutinising all this information, this author concludes that Varnekar's details are authoritative and correct.
2. *Lekhanjali*, pp. 115
3. *Maa. Sa. Golwalkar*, pp. 8

4

Auspicious Start of Education

The eighth offspring of Sadashiv-Laxmibai came in this world on *Yugabd* 5007, *Magh Krishna Ekadashi* (*Pushya* in North India) in *Moolnakshatra* and on *Brahm mahurtam*. As per the Gregorian calendar, it was 19th February, 1906, Monday. Considering the date and *nakshatra,* etc., the boy was named Madhav.

Toddler Madhu undertook his first journey at a delicate age of two-and-a-half years at the end of the monsoon in 1908 to a distant place called Saraipalli. This travel, sitting on his father's shoulders and, at times, in his mother's arms, was like an inaugural run that marked the beginning of an unending journey throughout his life. Not only that, this was also a symbolic experience of 'upper berth' and 'lower berth' in Indian Railways! Who could have imagined that this journey would continue uninterrupted for the next sixty-five years! This willful boy would walk some distance, catching his elder brother Amrit's fingers on this long journey that ran into scores of miles. Tai, his mother, recalled years later that little Madhu didn't cry even once during that long journey. It seems the Almighty had created and prepared this person for countless journeys in his life.

Both Bhauji and Amrit entered school on the same day – one to teach and the other to study. From that day, Bhauji also began teaching enthusiastic Madhu at home to keep him happy. He was unhappy with the old hand-me-down slate of his elder brother. He was adamant about a new slate and started dancing when he got it. He began writing alphabets immediately. He started going enthusiastically to his big brother Amrit's class on his own.

Madhu's education began in right earnest under the watchful eyes of Bhauji. After imparting knowledge about alphabets, he brought home the book, *Ram Raksha Stotra* to help him practise reading. Within no time, Madhu understood that this book contained the same *shlokas* that his mother recited everyday. It was difficult for him to read conjoined words from the book. So, he told his father, "*Pitaji*, please speak these words slowly to me, I will grasp them. Then, I will recognise them in the book." Bhauji was very happy with this suggestion from his child. Madhu learnt all the 38 *shlokas* in a few days. His pronunciation was very clear.

Bhauji was firm about regular religious practices. His day would not begin without a daily bath, *pooja* and related rituals. During the *pooja,* he would make both his sons sit with him. He would recite the *mantras* slowly and loudly, with both his sons following him enthusiastically, like the young *Pauranic* sages, Ashwini Kumars, in all these activities. Therefore, both of them got interested in religious practices even before the formal *upanayan samskaaras*. They got trained in the good practice of distributing and then eating *prasadam* at a young age. It is true that *samskaaras* can be imparted and cultivated, but they cannot be handed down as instructions or transplanted.

Bhauji had a novel way of imparting education. When he sat down for food, he would ask both his sons to sit beside him and give them different questions in mathematics. Both of them were supposed to give answers orally through mental calculations. Not only mathematics, he taught even English poems, Sanskrit *shlokas,* Hindi and Marathi poetry during lunch and dinner with easy-flowing chats. This artful way of teaching imbibed while partaking food became a part of Madhu's style. During snacks, lunch and dinner with his colleagues, this style of inculcating ideas in informal discussions became virtually an enjoyable wisdom fount from which people could sip loads of knowledge.

Madhu completed his primary education in Raipur, Chandrapur, Bhandara and Khandwa. He was not only enthusiastic about giving prompt answers to a teacher's questions, but capable too. Therefore, like any knowledgeable student, he used to be the leader. An experienced teacher advised him to give his answers in whispers close to him or in his ears so that the other students would not feel jealous and unhappy about his knowledge. Thus, a way out was found that kept everybody happy.

Tai saw that both her children were growing up the way their parents wished. Both could study on their own. This mother felt blessed and very happy. She initiated both of them into reciting religious texts while she would sit in front, listening to them, absorbed in devotion. Naturally, both the parties – children and mother—benefited from this effort. After the sad demise of Amrit, Madhu was left as the sole practitioner of this art for his mother.

Madhu was aged nine when he was studying in fourth standard in Khandwa. There was going to be a school inspection. The date for the inspector's visit was fixed. Both the teachers and students were preparing diligently. Madhu was the miracle child of the school. He was famous for being capable of answering any kind of straight or tricky question, but he fell sick on the given day and was absent from school. After understanding the situation, the teacher took special permission from his parents and brought Madhu to school on somebody's shoulders to be in the class. Everything worked out fine as per the plan. That year, Madhu came first in Narmada division, to which the Khandwa school was affiliated.

During the same period, when Madhu was around eleven years old, Tai and Bhauji planned on holding the sacred thread ceremony (*upanayan samskaar*). The sacred ceremony was blessed with the presence of relatives, who came to Khandwa for this e-programme. From that day, the ordained *brahmachaari*

Madhu began his *trikaal sandhya* (regular ritual of prayers), a practice he followed diligently and without a break till his very last day. Years later, while speaking at a conference of young *brahmachaaris* in Pune's Narad Temple, he recounted his experience thus, "Nurturing inner and physical strength through *Gayatri Mantra* and *Surya Namaskar* through *sandhya* has given me a healthy body as well as a healthy mind."[1]

Students have been trained in extra-curricular subjects for personality development since ages, and parents and teachers encouraged students in these activities. Madhu too got his major chance in life when he was eleven years old. While he was studying in Balaghat, a large congregation of people met on the banks of River Wainganga, where various competitions for different age groups were to be held. Child Madhu was very keen on taking part in this programme. He persuaded his father to help him prepare a speech. Madhu presented his speech so well in the competition, presided over by Barrister Malana that he stood first! Barrister Malana was so impressed with this talented boy that he specially patted him on his back. When he visited the school in Balaghat for some work again a few days later, he specifically called Madhu and asked him to deliver his speech again. So, happy was he with his speech and presentation.

There is a delightful anecdote of those days. Amrit and Madhav were in the same school in Baitul. Bhauji prepared Amrit for a speech to deliver during the annual function of the school. Amrit memorised a well-prepared English speech to render at the right speed, intonation, accent and voice training. Amrit proved himself well during the practice sessions. Organisers felt sure that the programme would go down very well, but alas, Amrit fell sick just three to four days before the function. There was no chance of his recovering in three days. The organisers became worried. Intelligent Madhu grasped the situation and approached his father: *"Pitaji,* can I go in place of Bhaiyya?" He recited the whole speech to him, with the right intonation, accent, and speed just like his elder brother. Father was astonished. Actually, he had been observing and absorbing various nuances of the proposed speech while Amrit was practising. With due permission from the organising committee, he made his presentation without a trace of stage fright. He went on to win accolades for his performance.[2]

Madhu entered the English High School in 1919. He received a princely scholarship of four rupees per month on winning the 'high school entrance and scholarship exam' after class seventh. Unfortunately, his loved Bhaiyya was not there to share this joy as he had left this world by then.

His school friends could see his strong inclination towards reading during those days. He had already read the entire *Ramcharitmanas* before completing higher secondary. In his own words, "When I was studying in the secondary school, I liked those excerpts from the *Ramcharitmanas* very much. I read the entire sacred book and also memorised a few of its parts."[3]

Apart from reading story books and novels, Madhav also started reading books on history and literature. His father encouraged him in this passion for books. He used to study and finish the school syllabi at home with help from his father. His reading speed was above normal and he felt that he was wasting his time in the class. So, he continued with his out-of-course reading during the class. A teacher once noticed that Madhav was reading some other book. He objected to this and scolded Madhav. Madhav replied calmly, "Sir, yesterday night I had already studied the subject being taught in the class. I am reading something else so as not to waste time." The teacher was more upset as he thought that the student was trying to give excuses and befool him. He asked many difficult and tricky questions to expose Madhav, but he gave correct replies to all of them. He sat down after this small cross-examination and got busy with his reading again! The teacher's suspicion under normal circumstances would not be considered unnatural. But, understanding this individual's nature, he felt quite satisfied and Madhav went on to become one of his most loved students.

It was Madhav's nature to study a subject in depth. Like his father, he also abhorred 'guides'. Once a new teacher started teaching from a guide in the class. The clarification given in the guide was not correct, so Madhav refuted it! A debate ensued between the teacher and the student. The teacher couldn't refute the arguments of the student satisfactorily, but insisted, "I am your teacher; you are only a student." The student agreed politely that he indeed was his student, but added, "Nevertheless, your explanation is wrong, sir." Finally, the matter reached the principal, who calmed down both of them. But, behind the scene, the principal pointed out the mistake to his teacher. In spite of this episode, Madhav showed the same respect for the teacher as if nothing had happened.[4]

Madhav used to read with deep concentration to satisfy his insatiable thirst, but he was not a bookworm. He was equally enthusiastic about sports as he grew into a teenager. His first love was hockey. The *malkhamb* exercise, which he exhibited during his tenth class in Jubilee School of Chandrapur, was of the highest standard. His physique was quite attractive and was a gift of his genes. A physical instructor was so impressed with his physical prowess that he wished to keep him in the school for another year, but, Bhauji was against this. Madhav passed his class tenth in 1922 at the age of sixteen. He, thus, became a matriculate in the colloquial language.

□

Aum Shree Ganeshaay Namah
Guruji Golwalkar – Jeevan Charitra

Endnotes

1. *Aalok ki Aarti*, pp. 13
2. Ibid, pp. 10-11
3. *Avismaraneey Guruji*, pp. 24
4. Ibid, pp. 15-16

5
Student of Nagpur College

Passing matriculation was like reaching a crossroad and deciding one's direction. His parents, perhaps, pondered over it even more intensely. The year 1922 was an important landmark for young Madhav as he had to decide about his further education. Bhauji, his father, dreamt of making his son a doctor. The son too thought the same way. So, Bhauji went ahead with this idea. He arranged for an application from Pune's Fergusson College and posted it. He had shown his annual income in the application form as 10,000 rupees. Expectedly, Madhav got admission in Fergusson, but there was an unexpected glitch. A new government regulation came into effect allowing only local students to get admission in educational institutions. As per this regulation, the student of Mumbai Presidency from the Central Provinces was disqualified and his admission nullified. The disappointed young man returned to Nagpur. He took admission in Hislap College in the Department of Zoology. Imagine the irony of fate that the Mumbai Presidency regulation was withdrawn within two months of his return from Mumbai.

There is a natural change in the mental makeup of a young person as he leaves high school to enter a college. He starts feeling that he is on his own now. He wants to take his own decisions and realising that he is no more a child, he wishes to break free from his parents and elders. He talks to his teachers as an equal. His attendance falls as compared to his attendance in school. In short, self-realisation dawns on him and he wishes to untie and re-tie the bonds of his childhood on his own terms. This is a normal cycle in life, though there are some exceptions too.

Madhav became a college student in 1922. A *shloka* in Sanskrit says: '*Praapte tu shodashe varshe putram mitravadaacharet*', i.e., a son should be treated by his father like a friend on his reaching age sixteen. As an experienced human being, Sadashiv Golwalkar left his budding young son Madhav to flower on his own. Madhav, however, took care to preserve the '*samskaaras*' or value systems imbibed in him since childhood.

His urge for deep and multifarious studies further got honed in college. He became a regular visitor to the college library. He would be found absent many a time from his regular classes as he sat buried in books, studying varied subjects. He was, however, never careless about his syllabus. He had read many celebrated novels of the time, including the biography of Napoleon written by Abbot. His intellect was all-encompassing. Though he was a student of science, he was awarded in a competition on English literature.

Hislap College was run by Christian missionaries and study of Bible was compulsory. Principal T.W. Gardiner used to take these classes himself. Young Madhav would make it a point to be present in the class. Once the principal cited a wrong reference, which the student Madhav immediately pointed out. But the principal, being an authority on the Bible, would not accept his mistake. Without crossing the fine line of respect, the young student stood his ground. Finally, the principal requisitioned an authorised copy of the Bible and after due reference, it was found that young Madhav was right. Large-hearted principal Gardiner, pleased with the sharp intellect of his student Golwalkar, patted him with love and congratulated him.

Apart from studying the subjects relevant for his intermediate examination, reading voraciously and doing necessary exercises, Madhav loved wandering about all alone. He would go for walks many times and keenly observe things around him. He covered the whole of Nagpur in this manner. There is an interesting anecdote about his keen sense of observation. In his own words, "I used to wander in lanes and bylanes of Nagpur in my earlier days. When I was studying in college, the discussion once turned to a specific plant. Then the question arose, where could this plant be found? I told my professor and student friends that it could be found in a *nullah* that ran behind the respected Doctorji's home, near Shukrawari Road under the bridge. When I showed the plant, everybody was amazed and wondered how I had noticed it. Then I told them that I had virtually scanned the whole of Nagpur."[1]

This small anecdote proves that this wandering of young Madhav was not day-dreaming. Even as he enjoyed his walks, he would remember the subjects discussed in class. Secondly, he would make a note of people who came his way, otherwise how could he have recognised Doctor Hedgewar's home? Maybe this wanderlust ran in his family or maybe, this inherent love for travel and wandering gave him the inner strength to tour Bharat at least sixty to sixty-five times as a Sarsanghchaalak or head of RSS. He surprised all with his early warning about Communist China's incursions in 1962.

Madhav's love for fine arts also blossomed during his student days in Nagpur. When he learned about the famous flautist Pandit Sawlaram, who had been blind since birth, he began to take lessons in playing the flute. From this initial contact, the relationship blossomed into a friendship that became a deep bonding of hearts. The training in music went ahead as per plan and Madhav became expert in many *ragas*.

Our ancient texts tell us that the relation between a teacher and a student or a seeker of truth is built on previous practices. This student of intermediate came in touch with Vasudev Muley, Superintendent of Nagpur City School. They did not know each other previously. Madhav introduced himself, referring to his father. When asked about the purpose of his visit, Madhav told him, "I heard that you have a copy of *Panchdashi*.[2] *Panchdashi* is not available anywhere these days. So, I want to make a copy of this rare book. Please help me. I am told you have many other rare *Vedanta*-related books." The quest for learning stayed alive and Madhav became a regular guest at his home to study *Vedanta*. There was a big gap in their ages, but both became thick friends because both were on the same wavelength. Madhav kept getting guidance from Muley even later in life.

Two years of study for intermediate just flew past. Madhav studied subjects both within and outside his syllabus. His goal was not just to pass the examinations. This point comes to the fore when we hear it in his own words, "I was preparing for my intermediate examination. I had not studied much. There were many reasons for this. When I sat down to write answers from the question paper, I looked upwards in between as I tried to think. The supervisor came to me and said, 'Don't copy.'"

"I told him, 'I am not copying.' But, he said, 'Still, don't even try.' I told him, 'Sir, my subject is science and the student sitting in my front is an Arts student. Even if I were to copy him, it won't benefit me at all.'"

"The supervisor stuck to his argument nevertheless and said, 'I still believe that copying is not a good act.' I told him, 'Sir, I know how to copy. If you wish to see, I will show you.' Then, I took a piece of paper from him, wrote a paragraph and handed him the paper, telling him to find out from which student I had copied it. The supervisor couldn't tell anything. Then I told him, 'I copied it from the student sitting in front in the fourth row. Please check it.'"

"The supervisor was highly surprised. He went and checked it out. He was flabbergasted because I had copied each and every word of that student. I told him, 'In spite of this talent, I dislike copying strongly. I won't mind failing or losing out once in a while, but not at any cost would I stoop to a despicable act like copying.' "[3]

"It was clear that I had not prepared well and I was not ready to copy. I still appeared for the exam and passed with good marks."

Madhav Sadashiv Golwalkar's studies till intermediate got over. Now where would he go and what would he do?

□

Endnotes

1. *Shri Guruji Samagra*, Vol. 5, pp. 73
2. *Panchdashi* is a spiritual text written by Bharati Teerth Vidyaranya Swami.
3. *Avismaraneey Guruji*, pp. 10-11

6

In the Lap of Kashi

A place can sometimes be as effective in imparting the right *samskaaras* as a person. Kashi is one of those renowned cities that have such a strong influence on people. The sacred Ganga flows northwards in Kashi and is, therefore, held highly sacred in this region. Kashi is considered the religious capital of Bharatvarsh. Through all the ups and downs of history, she has survived as one of the oldest cities in the world. Nothing could destroy it. It was a centre for a variety of fine arts and sciences. People hungry for knowledge about normal and paranormal knowledge used to come here to take a dip in the vast river of knowledge that flows through this city. Lord Buddha too gave his first sermon in this region. Adi Shankara presented his exposition of *Advaita* on its banks. Maharishi Dayanand also began his restatement of the *Vedas* in line with the new age thinking here. It is here that Madan Mohan Malaviya laid the foundation stone of Kashi Hindu Vishwavidyalaya (Banaras Hindu University) on the auspicious day of Vasant Panchami in 1916. The inscription on the walls of Vishwanath Temple in its campus, says, "*Prasaadat Vishwanaathasya kaashyaam Bhaagirathee tatey. Vishwa Vidyaalayah shreshthah Hindunaam manvardhanah*", meaning, "With the blessings of Lord Vishwanath, an excellent university has been established here that will raise the self-esteem of the Hindus." It was a residential university that reminded one of the ancient *gurukul*. Spread over three-and-a-quarter kilometres by two kilometres, this campus, in the words of Malaviya ji, is "Amaraavati of Mother Saraswati".

Madhav Golwalkar came to this campus in 1924 to pursue his studies for Bachelor in Science, with Zoology. Room number 309 in Boracha Hostel was his address up to 1928, till he finished his M.Sc. It was his great fortune that Malaviya ji was the Chancellor of the university and he could stay in the campus. He used to have close contact with teachers as well as students and offered valuable advice to them. His advice to students was in the form of a *shloka, "Satyen brahmacharyen vyayaamenaath vidyayaa. Deshbhaktyayatmatyaagen sammanaarh, sadaa bhav."* This means, "O' student! Acquire respect by following the qualities like truth, celibacy, exercise, education, patriotism and self-sacrifice."[1] His exhortation during the convocation was, "The education that you have received is a waste if it has not motivated you with the deep urge to free your nation and see it self-ruled."[2] It is clear that the Chancellor aimed at developing a golden combination of personal and national character. Young Madhav came into such a character-building environment. All his colleagues started calling him Golwalkar. His life as a college student began in Kashi.

His old habit as a voracious reader continued here too. He was overjoyed to see the grand library of the university and his mind was filled with enthusiasm. He delved into the library like a swimmer diving in a lake. He did not limit himself to studying the subjects of his syllabus. He would get into a subject like fire taking to wood. His natural power of concentration and sharp memory were of great help. Thus, his intellectual wealth kept on multiplying over time.

Not that he remained cocooned in Room Number 203. He was a friendly soul and an extrovert who loved meeting people. He was equally adept at fun and games with friends. His love for hockey continued and he started playing tennis too. He also took lessons in the flute once in a while from Sawalaram. He took to learning the *sitar* now. His skill in *malkhamb,* acquired at Nagpur, came to the fore again. Along with all these activities, he kept up with his studies along with his colleagues.

Here we also get an idea about the compassionate side of his personality. A student from a Scheduled Tribe came to his room one day. His tuition fee had been waived, but, he had difficulty in even paying for the mess bill. He told Golwalkar about his problem. Golwalkar sent him back to his hostel, promising some help. He immediately called some people from the mess and a couple of friends to discuss this colleague's problem. All of them agreed to share his expenses. This student was able to go through the two years of education without stress. He also took the Bachelor's degree with them.[3]

Kashi was the main centre of the Theosophical Society. Well-known leader, Annie Besant, had established the Central Hindu College there and merged her college with the Hindu Vishwavidyalaya on request from Malaviya ji. As a result, Theosophical Society was considered a highly respected body in the campus. Golwalkar came in touch with it and in its inspiring atmosphere, studied its philosophy under the guidance of its senior members.

He also got an opportunity to take part in the religious rituals of Arya Samaj in Kashi. Speaking at an Arya Samaj meeting in Ajmer in 1963, he said, "When I was in Benaras, one of my teachers was a volunteer of Arya Samaj. He used to do *yagna* every week. I also used to take part in it."[4]

The sacred Ganga flowing past the banks near the university attracted the young Golwalkar, prompting him to sit on its banks in deep silence of the night many a time. He would lie down on its sands, and during festivals, go to the river for a bath and *sandhya pooja*. Sharing his experience, he says, "I don't know whether any one of you has experienced the sanctity of Gangaji, but I have experienced it. I have spent many nights sitting on the banks of the Ganga. Small waves keep playing on the surface of the river. This play is so beautiful that on watching it, all sinful thoughts are washed away and the heart brims over with purity. I am telling you this from my own experience."[5]

This way the small seed of spiritualism that lay deep in the heart of Madhav Golwalkar was nurtured and strengthened in the garden of wisdom laid by Malaviya ji. After watching him on his return to Nagpur during the summer vacations, his maternal uncle, Mama Raikar, told his relatives, "His nature has undergone a revolutionary change after studying in Kashi Hindu Vishwavidyalaya; his demeanour has become more sober. His inclination towards spirituality is clearly visible. He has started giving more time to meditation and spiritual practices."[6]

His uncle, a worldly man, had made the right observation. His nephew's pronounced inclination towards spirituality had indeed strengthened. Examinations for M.Sc. were drawing near. This student realised quite late that he was much behind in his studying of his course material, but he didn't give up. After a lot of pondering over, he decided that it was better to appear next year rather than appear and lose out. It is rightly said that troubles don't come alone. He fell ill and had high fever and lost three weeks and became very weak. He informed his uncle about his problem and about his decision to appear in the next session. His uncle was mighty upset at these developments and unhappy about Madhav's decision. He was more concerned about his examination than his illness. He immediately sent a message to him that it was immaterial whether he succeeded or failed, but he had to appear for the exams. Madhav could sense that this message was influenced by his father's views. He had never disobeyed his elders' decisions. So, he decided to go ahead and succeed in exams inspite of his health problem, come what may. Once he had taken the decision, he went about preparing for the exams in a meticulous and professional manner.

From that night onwards, the lamp never switched off in Room Number 309. His friends could see that apart from daily chores, like taking a bath, etc. Golwalkar was always focussed on his studies. During this period, a scorpion stung him once. Without getting frightened, he simply filled a bucket with water, added some chemical to it, lowered his feet in it and went back to his studies, as if nothing had happened! No secrets remain hidden in hostels. The news immediately spread. His friends came and advised him to take rest. Shrugging off their suggestion, he said, "Brother, the scorpion has stung me in the legs and I am reading from my head. Let both of them do their respective jobs." He carried on with his studies without any apparent disturbance.[7]

The letter sent by his uncle had hit the nail right on the head. The nephew passed his examination with first class marks. M.S. Golwalkar was now a postgraduate in science.

□

Endnotes

1. *Mahamana Madan Mohan Malaviya*; pp. 162
2. Ibid, pp. 161
3. *Organiser* weekly, dated 8th March, 1969
4. *Shri Guruji Samagra*, Vol. 5, pp. 35
5. *Avismaraneey Guruji*, pp. 9
6. *Guruji – Indurkar*, pp. 17
7. Ibid, pp. 7

7

Unfinished Research in Chennai

After discussions with professors and his father, Madhavrao Golwalkar joined the Chennai aquarium to do research in fisheries. He took a room on rent in Triplicane. His father used to send him fifty rupees from his limited income. He adjusted his life according to these limitations. The aquarium was not very far off, so he walked to his institute.

Golwalkar made some good friends in Chennai too. Most of his friends were from South India. He visited a restaurant regularly and became friendly with the owner of the place too. Once he was sitting with his friends when he noted that the table was made of glass and wondered aloud, "How many days will it survive the pushes and shoves of this place?" The owner, who stood in the vicinity, heard this comment and told Golwalkar, "This is a very thick glass and it cannot be broken easily." Madhavrao took it as a challenge and asked him if he was prepared to check out its strength. On getting his consent, Madhavrao raised his fist and the next moment it was shattered into pieces. The spectators were dumbfounded. One cannot tell if it was his will power or his strength that shattered the thick glass sheet.[1]

Within two to three months, Golwalkar's health started deteriorating. Brought up in the dry weather of Nagpur and Kashi, his body couldn't adjust to the humid conditions of the seaside. He began being troubled by cough, headache, cold and fever; but his research continued unabated.

He recounted his experience of those days, "While studying in the Madras aquarium, we used to go to sea to catch fish. Once we were sitting together in a boat. I had put both my feet in the water. There was another boat next to ours. Suddenly, the owner of the other boat shouted something aloud in Tamil language. I couldn't understand his words, but, someone with me asked me to pull back my feet immediately. I immediately complied. Then we saw a shark just next to our boat."[2] Rushing in of a shark and then turning back on missing the prey was an entirely new experience of his post-graduate studies. Maybe, it proved useful to the students in their research.

Research was progressing well under the guidance of expert guides. The

Chennai aquarium was famous all over India and spectators came from all over India to see and enjoy the large variety of aquatic creatures. The students took care to guide the visitors around and providing scientific answers to their queries. One day the news about a possible visit of the Nizam of Hyderabad and his family to the aquarium reached them. Naturally, there was plenty of excitement. They wondered if the visitor could be charged a fee or not. Golwalkar's view was, "He should also pay the fee and enter with a valid ticket. This is a public organisation. If we have to give free admission, we should give it to the poor." Though he was correct, who would bell the cat? Finally, when the day arrived, Golwalkar went to the secretary, put forward his opinion boldly and the family was welcomed but upon paying the fee. The whole group was very happy with this principled approach of the students. The initial fear of the authorities proved to be unfounded.[3]

Golwalkar's daily routine, like religious rituals etc. went on regularly as usual. He used to get up at 4.30 in the morning. After morning ablutions, he would do yoga, *Surya namaskar,* exercises, etc. He studied and understood *Thirukkural,* considered a prime religious text of the Tamils, with the help of his Tamil friends. Years later, while addressing the students of Sangh Shiksha Varg at Swami Vivekananda College in Chennai, he said, "*Thirukkural* is the king of sacred books. This great scripture is more than two thousand years old. Great saint Thiruvallura is the father of this book. Its proposition is the eternal four *purusharthas*; the only difference is that *moksha* comes first in this book and the other three *purusharthas* are analysed in detail with reference to this." During an informal chat after this programme, he added, "Poet Kamban's Bharat is spiritually even more elevated than the Bharat of Valmiki." He smiled at the Sangh state general secretary (*prant kaaryavaah*), advocate A. Dakshinmurthy, who was looking at him with wonder and said, "I had grasped all this while I was studying in Chennai."

Speaking at a religious conference (*dharma sabha*) in the sacred town of Pandharpur in 1966 in Maharashtra, he said, "My birth chart seems to have gifted me the good fortune of being in the company of great saints. This may be the reason I keep meeting saints regularly and I receive their blessings. This has been the case with me since childhood."[4] He had a similar experience in Chennai. Three monks wearing saffron robes came to his room once. Two of this group seemed ordinary to him, but the third one looked quite different. He found that his story was extraordinary. His current persona as a saint was as different from his previous life as day and night. There was only one exception – He had been an alcoholic in his early worldly life. But, he never spoke untruth when intoxicated. This was his special quality. Once he sat down in a bylane to relieve himself. This act was prohibited there. A policeman accosted him immediately and started abusing him. Then he whispered in his ears, "Give me my share I will let you off, or else, get stuck in the police station." Upon hearing these golden words from the policeman, he caught hold of the police and beat him black and blue till he bled from his nose. He was prosecuted. He recounted the whole episode to the honourable judge when he was produced in the court. He asked bitterly, "Do these people get salary from the government to force people to lie?" He was burning with rage. But, in the court of justice, there is analysis of justice and injustice, not truth and untruth. The accused was asked to pay a fine. He had to go through a prison term as he had no money. Only God could answer how this person had become a mendicant after this incident. Observing his meditative power, knowledge and behaviour, knowledge-hungry Golwalkar was highly impressed. He remembered the profound declaration of the Supreme Lord, who has said, "If even an evil person worships me honestly with devotion, he is to be considered a saint because he has keen devotion to me." Golwalkar wrote this whole episode from Chennai in a letter to his friend Baburao Telang in Kashi. He didn't mention about the mendicant's mother tongue or his place of residence in the letter. It is said that one should not look at the source of a river or a saint. Golwalkar may have acted on this dictum.[5]

Golwalkar's health deteriorated during the last year of his studies. His young heart was disturbed at the killing of Saunders by revolutionaries, the Brahmin and anti-Brahmin agitation and happenings in different parts of the nation. His mental state was like a whirlpool. He wrote to his friend, thus, "…My heart was shaken badly. I was deeply upset. This situation continued for many days. It led to high fever and severe headache. I used to talk a lot about *Vedanta* but my health didn't improve. I started smoking those days to console my heart. It led to bouts of cough, heaviness in the eyes, darkening of my face and overall weakness. The situation so deteriorated that the supervisor of the aquarium, who used to observe my condition daily, took me to a doctor. The body that could tolerate cough and fever in Nagpur routinely had become so weak that it couldn't bear this new kind of high fever now. The doctor told us that if proper care was not taken, this could turn into T.B. This information didn't perturb me that badly, but I started taking injections to fight my sickness. I also started taking egg after reciting *Ram-nam*."[6]

He must have realised the futility and foolishness of smoking to console the heart. He did not speak about it later in life, but, he analysed the compulsion of eating eggs later on.

He presents his analysis in just six sentences. He writes to a close friend of his, "How do I explain how unhappy I feel and undergo mental agony when I eat an egg? Religious scriptures tell us, '*Ahimsa paramodharma*' (non-violence is the highest *dharma*) On the other hand, they also tell us '*naymatma balheenen labhyah*' (a weak body cannot realise *aatman*) and '*shareeramadyam khalu dharmaasadhanam*' (healthy body is necessary for performing *dharma*). In this mental struggle, I said to myself, '*Aushadhi jaahnaveetoyam vaidyo naaraayano harih*' (medicine is akin to Ganga and *vaidya*, medical man, is like God) and dedicated every act to the Supreme Being. I cannot judge whether this is *punya* (pious act) or *paap* (sin). *'Kim karma kimkarmeti kavayopyatra mohitaah'* (What is act, who is the doer…). Then, who am I to judge this act?" He reaches the highest levels of universe while analysing his act of eating an egg![7]

While he was going through various experiences, his father Sadashiv Golwalkar came to Chennai in June 1929 to stay with him for a couple of weeks. He had retired in March and had come to know about the deteriorating health of his son. He was distressed and wished to take care of his only child. There was another delicate matter. How could he take on the responsibility of his son's fee in the limited income after his retirement? The only way out was to try for a scholarship or a loan. He took the trip to Chennai as he thought that it would be ideal and more practical to explain this problem to his son personally while staying with him.

The father and son stayed in the same room. Madhu would work in the kitchen to prepare food, but there arose another problem in this situation. Madhu got scalded with hot oil from hand to shoulder while frying some food. He developed boils all over his arm. Therefore, the father had to take care of the kitchen and feed his son. He stayed there for about three weeks and left on 23rd June.

Madhav had already understood the situation. The problems enumerated by his father were not unexpected. He had already been trying for some scholarship for two to three months. He writes to his friend Telang on 23rd June, "Respected Bhauji left by the morning train for Nagpur…. Now let us talk about the scholarship. The person who could provide it came only in March. He had gone to America, Europe, etc. due to vacations. He did not stay in Chennai for more than 15 days. He has been on tours since then. Therefore, I have not been able to contact him and to get the scholarship."[8]

Bhauji reached Nagpur on 24th June. His son too returned by the end of June or July, abandoning his research half way.

□

Endnotes

1. *Maa. Sa. Golwalkar*, pp. 19
2. *Avismaraneey Guruji*, pp. 5
3. *Maa. Sa. Golwalkar*, pp. 19
4. *Shri Guruji Samagra*, Vol. 1, pp. 76
5. *Shri Guruji Samagra*, Vol. 6, pp. 230
6. Ibid, pp. 179
7. Ibid, pp. 180
8. Ibid, pp. 234-235

8

Churning of Ideas in Chennai

Madhavrao Golwalkar did not come up with any scientific research work during his one year in Chennai, but he had come up with an interesting body of ideas unknowingly. This was in the form of long letters he used to write to his dear friend Baburao Telang. He had touched upon wide-ranging subjects in these letters. Subjects like child marriage, custom of *sati*, etc. are out of date now and not relevant here, but there are many subjects that are topical even today and relevant. He was hardly 23 years old at that time. Thus, analysis of his thoughts at that time is very important to understand his personality.

We need to remember another fact here. Every age has a tone and tenor of its own. Honesty and truthfulness are the tenor of childhood, a high sense of being constitutes the musical notes of youth that emerge out of the flowering of one's self-reliant nature. A youth is eager to find direction for self at that age. He finds himself entangled in his own web of thoughts woven like a spider from his own strands of beliefs. It doesn't mean that these ideas are bereft of humane feelings. Twenty-three-year-old Madhav was also no exception to this aspect of young age. The chain of Chennai letters is a set of documents that reflect his wishes, expectations, ambitions and doubts.

The decade between 1920 and 1930 was a critical phase for the country. Entry of Gandhiji on the national stage, underground armed revolutionary movement in state after state, the rise of national consciousness in the hearts of the common man, the churning of ideas about the right or wrong path to national independence, and suppressive and exploitative conduct of foreign rulers – this decade was the centrestage to all these actions and thoughts. The revolutionaries of this period killed British officer Saunders, blaming him for poor and vindictive governance. This action echoed across the length and breadth of the country, from Indian Ocean to the Himalayas. Young Madhav's mind too couldn't remain immune to all this. His thoughts ran thus: "My hot-headed nature comes from my hot-headed father. Pure blood runs through my veins. I heard of Lahore explosion in such a state of mind. Words like 'God bless, God bless' came on my lips thrice. There was deep satisfaction that revenge, even if incomplete, had been finally taken. If I was there, I too would have done the same. I have discussed with you thousands of times serious subjects like universal brotherhood, equality and peace. I fought with you against the idea of murder, mayhem, violence, jealousy and revenge. I have put the blame on you many times. I am the same person now writing this to you. You may be surprised at this change in stance."[1]

At another place, we find him discussing the problems of society's weakness, selfish and unhelpful attitude, etc. with his friend. He writes, "*Agrataschaturo vedah, prishthatah sashram dhanuh, idam braahmam, idam kshaatram, shaapaadapi sharaadapi*" (the four *Vedas* on the front, bow and arrow at the back, power of Brahman to protect from evil intentions of enemies, the strength of *Kshatriya* – spirit of warriors – to save from arrows of others) – we shall be able to work for the welfare of the universe by attaining such a paramount position. Therefore, it is necessary to tell people that friends, let us work for the upliftment of the nation, earn wealth, gain strength, organise ourselves and end the animosity arising out of differences in castes. Let us serve our motherland and Hindu *dharma*."[2]

Madhavrao spoke in English when he went to Chennai after graduation. He did this well. After all, he had won a prize for elocution in English at Hislap College of Nagpur. This use of English was for day-to-day work, but, for him, language was not just a medium for interaction. It was also the carrier and medium of growth for the culture of a society suppressed over time. He wrote, "Why do I insist on purity of language? The answer is very simple. Among the various means that we adopt to keep our culture and heritage alive, purity of language is a critical component. After pondering over it, I believe I am putting efforts to this end."[3]

Dharma is eternal and *dharma* of a particular period is also a part of this. Describing the duality of extremes of the period of peace and period of conflict, Madhav does an interesting critique that underlines the moral values that he holds dear to his heart. "Now, should one beat somebody after evaluating a person's evil or good nature or beat everyone without discrimination between the two qualities? This question is highly sensitive. Howsoever good an idea it may be in times of peace, it would be stupid to go through this choice at the time of conflict, even though it would look unjust and cruel. Howsoever good or just and kind a person may be, still he would need to take the blame for the shortcoming of that system, the system he represents, and be ready to bear the penalty for it if that system turns out to be horribly wrong. If it were not so, Shri Krishna would have told Arjun, 'O' my brother, Bhishma, Drona, Shalya and Vikarna have been arguing with Duryodhana on your behalf. So, don't fight with them; leave them alone and attack wicked Duryodhana, Duhshaasana and Shakuni. If killing Bhishma and Drona was just a duty, even then it was due to circumstances prevailing at that time, not due to any animosity. When such an action is undertaken, moist wood also gets burnt with dry wood. It should be considered its bad fortune or the result of its bad association...If somebody says that we are fighting for *dharma,* God and country, which is a pious action, then how does it matter if the action is undertaken with animosity or some other feeling? I consider it incorrect because to take up a fight with a sense of animosity is *adharma*. In such a mental state, there is no greatness if one fights for *dharma*."[4]

There is a paragraph about the unique quality of the Hindu way of life in a long letter of Madhavrao. One is reminded of Swami Vivekananda when one reads it. He notes, "Our Hindu people have qualities that mark us apart from others. Our mental make-up is also different. Our thinking and actions are also different. Worshipping beauty was the major point of reference in Greece, Vedanta was less important. In Rome, physical and political virtues (which cover speech, arts, writing, etc.) were supposed to be great qualities. Years before this, spirituality, worship of gods and acquiring noble virtues were supposed to be major obligations for a human being. And these thoughts got reflected in the creation of our great *Vedas*, *Upanishads* and *Samkhya* philosophy. From these thought processes were born Manusmriti and many other social sciences and writings. This viewpoint of life led our people to look beyond this world and aspire for enlightenment. These aspirations are our unique quality. We should take up such actions that nurture these aspirations."[5]

Varied types of thoughts were popular in our country due to Western imperialism. Some people openly said that the British are angels sent by God to liberate us; that their culture can be accepted and that our orthodox culture needs to be abandoned totally. People at the other end of the spectrum said that Western culture is libertine and promotes a luxurious lifestyle. So, it is destructive for us. There were a third kind of people who believed in the middle path. They said that no culture is completely wrong or right. Every culture has negatives and positives. Therefore, we should use our own intellect in tune with the changing times. Young Madhav thought on the same lines. His thinking was, 'Should we close our doors to other cultures, claiming our culture to be ideal and behave like a frog in the well? We must accept that we should absorb any idea that doesn't weaken our culture, but helps in making it more effulgent. Along with this, we also must take care to teach our culture to the others in the world. This is possible only if we preserve our purity.'

"We should take care that whatever we bring in from outside should be brought in carefully so that it should not damage our roots. Rather, it should nurture them further – that's the way it should be utilised. Till the time this world becomes one in the true sense, we should take care to preserve our culture's purity till this golden day dawns."[6]

Madhav chose the middle path, but he was firm in his belief that we should remain alert to the fact that our culture has great significance for the world.

The young generation even today discusses the mode of dressing up, specially in hostels. Students, be they boys or girls, wish to look good. There may be differing opinions only on how to do so. A Sanskrit *subhashit* tells us that the Ocean, father of Laxmi, gave her away in marriage to Vishnu who came in nice clothes (*peetaambar*) and gave Shiva poison as he had come wearing animal skin. Such discussions must have taken place even between Madhav and Telang as friends. The friend from Chennai writes, "You know about my views on clothes. Our behaviour and character should be spotless, but it would be wrong to show your back to the changing social mores. If we do not respond to the demands of times, we may have to disappear from the face of Earth, because nature is a merciless teacher."[7]

"When a person absorbs his culture totally, nothing is lost even if somebody wears any kind of clothes. Once spirituality overpowers a person, then outer appearances do not affect him. But, till then, one should be careful."[8]

Since his student days, Golwalkar had no inclination to present a detailed analysis of various problems facing the society and the country and then stand back with a neutral stance. Affirming his commitment to his view, he says, "Now I have decided on the direction. I have resolved to arouse the national conscience in the cowardly people, explaining the relationship between Hindus and Muslims and a Brahmin and non-Brahmin divide. It is not that I am a leader or a worker, but every person must contribute his might. Even if each of us brings five to ten people under the national flag, it would be good enough."[9]

Madhavrao Golwalkar's spiritual proclivity in his life had been visible since his childhood. This spirituality got further enhanced in the serene environment of Chennai. He had discussed this issue with friend Babu Telang, who was already married by then. He took this issue further in his letter. He said, "Does following one's *dharma* in worldly affairs only mean getting married and producing children? Is there no higher meaning in it? Then, how can you say that I have not accepted this *dharma* in its elevated sense? Can I not stay aloof from the world even while staying within it? Surely it can be done. It is not necessary to get married to follow the worldly path. As per our religious texts, marriage may be a duty, but a person decides on it, based on his or her own inclination. Getting married may be ideal, but even if one doesn't get married, nothing is lost."[10]

He clears his concept of *pravritti marg* (involvement in worldly affairs) further, "Earlier my thought of going to the Himalayas was a negative one. I am trying to achieve *sannyas* for life while staying in this world, braving vicious attacks from people and carrying out the duties expected of me as a part of this society. Now, the Himalaya, as also the solitude is within me. No need to go anywhere."[11]

An interesting and memorable anecdote needs to be recounted here. When Madhavrao was in Chennai, the Rashtriya Swayamsevak Sangh had come into existence nearly three-and-a-half years prior to it. Though Babu Telang had become a swayamsevak by that time, Madhavrao knew very little about the Sangh. With little understanding of the Sangh at that time, he wrote, "If you keep talking and working for Sangh, then it will be stupidity. It is good to be part of the Sangh, but, you should not forget that passing your examinations successfully and making life of the family worthwhile would be even better than that. You cannot complete the duties given by our forefathers successfully and here you talk of doing your duty to the entire Hindu society! You don't know how to serve four members of the family and you wish to serve the whole Hindu society! It is meaningless. Still, please do what you deem fit. I have presented my views to you. It depends on you whether to accept them or reject them."[12] It is a strange play of God that later when he became the Sarsanghchaalak, speaking in the language of Jesus Christ, he said, "I have come to take away children from their mothers."

In short, the letters written by the postgraduate Madhavrao from Chennai give a glimpse of the inner core of his personality. They are reflections of his views on different facets of life. Without doubt, they show that he believed in a purpose of life and had a definite spiritual bent of mind. There was a specific direction to his life. Be it in solitude or in company of others, knowingly or unknowingly, the course of his life was flowing gradually like Mandakini (river Ganga at its source) in that direction.

□

Endnotes

1. *Shri Guruji Samagra*, Vol. 6, pp. 78
2. Ibid, pp. 181
3. Ibid, pp. 192-193
4. Ibid, pp. 184
5. Ibid, pp. 196
6. Ibid, pp. 199-200
7. Ibid, pp. 184
8. Ibid, pp. 207
9. Ibid, pp. 179
10. Ibid, pp. 222
11. Ibid, pp. 210-211
12. Ibid, pp. 236-237

9

The Interregnum in Nagpur

Madhavrao returned to Nagpur in the middle of 1929, leaving his research midway and became a teacher in Kashi after two years in 1931. He spent this period of two years in Nagpur with his maternal uncle, Mama Raikar. His parents were staying in Ramtek in a rented house at that time.

Mama Raikar used to run a coaching class called 'Raikar Coaching Classes'. So, nephew Madhav too started teaching there. Raikar needed a postgraduate person like Madhavrao to prove the institute's credibility and capability. At the same time, Madhav too was without a job. Thus, both needed each other.

When Golwalkar was in Chennai, a story used to float around in his friends' circle that he was going to become a professor there itself. When he heard about it, he immediately refuted this rumour. In his letter dated 23rd June in 1929, he wrote clearly that he was trying for a job in Kashi Vishwavidyalaya (Banaras Hindu University). Studying his life minutely, we realise that there was another reason behind this deep urge to go to Kashi. This urge was to spend some time in the august company of Mr. Desai.

There was a gentleman named Mr. Desai in Kashi Vishwavidyalaya. He knew him and had been in touch with him since 1924. Desai was senior to Golwalkar and a student of M.A. from Mumbai. He was a great poet, musician, singer, expert in reciting hymns and playing musical instruments. He was a simple man, always ready to support weak students. He used to stay in the outskirts of the university and was a follower of Theosophy.[1]

Noble qualities like pure character, deep spiritual knowledge, a heart full of devotion, compassionate behaviour – all these qualities had earned deep respect of the young student Golwalkar for Desai sir. He was in Kashi during all these years while Golwalkar finished his studies, took up teaching and passed law. Golwalkar mentions Desai at least ten times in the long letters he wrote to Baburao Telang. When he was in inner turmoil, he wrote to the same Desai to seek peace of mind. This part of the letter says, "I get into a depressed mood time and again. I do *sheershasana*, Gayatri recitation, etc. to escape from it. Generally, it helps, but if it doesn't, I write to Shri Desai. He sends me an answer. It is not that he writes anything specific in it, but I consider him near to me and feel calm. I cannot tell why it happens, but, it is true that I never feel despondent when he is around."[2]

More important than this is his statement, "If I were to tell you in brief, what makes my life worth living and enjoying is the presence of Shri Desai, respected Mataji, Bhauji, you and other friends. I have not counted Shri Desai amongst friends because I look upon him as my guru. If I have any capabilities, it is due to his influence. If you were to ask him about it, he will simply refuse to acknowledge it…." [3] It seems Shri Desai had the same importance in the life of Madhavrao that Shri Lele had in Shri Aurobindo's life. Inspite of lot of efforts, it has not been possible to fathom the deep bond they shared. We must admit that both self-abnegating brothers were able to maintain their confidentiality.

During this interregnum in Nagpur, Madhavrao could re-establish his old relationship with the school supervisor, Vasudevrao Muley. He had nurtured this relationship from time to time and kept it alive since the days of his intermediate studies. During his stay in Kashi, he would send totem (*ganda*) of God Kalbhairav to Vasudevrao either by post or through some person. He loved gifting these totems to members of the family and treated it as a pious deed. Vasudevrao's house was in the same area where the Raikar family stayed. So, it was possible for both to meet once in a while. This blossoming afresh of the relationship was helpful in Golwalkar's journey towards his destined path.

During this period, Madhavrao went to Mumbai for some work given by his Mama Raikar. His eyes fell upon a blind young man in the milling crowds at the station. With some unfathomable pull, he went near him and introduced himself. This gentleman was Raobahadur Narayanrao's son, Vamanrao Wadegaonkar and he was from Nagpur. Vamanrao had been blind since birth. He had completed his B.A. through sheer will-power. He had also started practising music. He became an expert in this discipline within no time. He did not stop at that, but went on to establish a school for other unfortunate blind comrades. Here was a self-made person with whom Madhavrao had established contact at the railway station that day. This introduction developed into a deep emotional bonding over time. Madhavrao became an active supporter of Vamanrao's school for the blind. They would move around together on a bicycle to collect donations for the school with Madhavrao taking along his blind friend on the cycle's carrier. Sometimes the short-tempered Madhavrao would get angry when he witnessed callous attitude of rich people. At that time, Vamanrao would calm down his friend and save the situation by explaining to him about the helplessness of social service. In free time, Madhavrao would recite scriptures like *Panchdashi* and the *Vedas* for his blind friend. Both of them had grasped the essence of the great scripture, *Gyaneshwari*. We recall that this habit was ingrained in dear Madhu's mind by his mother, Taiji, years back.

Later in life, there was an occasion to put this knowledge of *Vedanta* to use in real life. Vamanrao required a major operation. One had to go to Mumbai for such a treatment in those days. He was in two minds due to his blindness as it would require him to be dependent upon others for his care during the time. Madhavrao motivated his friend by promising him that he would take care of him and went to Mumbai with him. The operation was conducted successfully and postoperative care was taken too. Madhavrao had to take every kind of care of the patient like a mother takes of a child. When the patient exclaimed in sorrow, "What a distressing condition I am in!", caretaker Madhavrao would say lovingly, "Vamanrao, if I can clean my dirt, why can't I do the same for this body?" as he caressed his head with love. Vamanrao's eyes filled up with tears. His eyes couldn't see but they could reflect love. While thinking over this flow of love between the two souls, Madhavrao wrote during the last leg of his stay in Nagpur, "My dearest friend Vamanrao, I had never even dreamt that I will meet you on the Mumbai platform. But, it is true that I was attracted to you at that very moment. Though I cannot find any reason for this attraction, it is not just a play of emotions. There is inexplicable and unknown inner flow in the human heart behind it."[4]

The date given on the letter is 3rd August, 1931. He landed up in Kashi to teach in the Zoology Department after thirteen days, i.e., in August 1931.

□

Endnotes

1. *Maa. Sa. Golwalkar*, pp. 29
2. *Shri Guruji Samagra*, Vol. 6, pp. 203-204
3. Ibid, pp. 224
4. Ibid, pp. 238

10

Seventh-Generation Heir of Kashi Upadhyay reaches Kashi

"I came suddenly to Department of Zoology of Benaras Hindu University on 16th of the last month. I have got a temporary job here. I received a telegram from the office of the university in Nagpur and had to start off immediately. I am working as a demonstrator in the Department of Zoology here. This is a temporary appointment for a vacant post."[1] This is the first half of the letter Madhavrao Golwalkar wrote to Vamanrao Deshpande, a C.A. in Mumbai, on 2nd September, 1931. Thus, the seventh generation heir of Golwalkar clan that was initiated by Kashi Upadhyay, became an Upadhyay (teacher) in Kashi as if it were a plan set up by destiny. He received his appointment in writing on 22nd August. This assignment was given due to long leave taken by a demonstrator, B.L. Pawar. Madhavrao was selected on the basis of his being an ex-student of the university. His salary was 100 rupees. He stayed in the Gajanand Lodge that was outside the university campus. People start calling a teacher a 'professor', classification he may fall into. Thus, this new appointee also came to be known as Professor Golwalkar.

In those days, there were very limited graduation-level colleges in the whole country. Therefore, becoming a professor was as prestigious as riding an elephant. Thus, Professor Golwalkar also received a lot of complimentary letters, amongst them was a message from C.A. Deshpande quoted above. He responded to everybody, clarifying his position. Writing in a lighter vein, he wrote to Vamanrao, "It is not that I have grown big with this job. I am the same person that I was earlier. Because my weight is still 106 pounds and I am still five feet six inches tall, there is no reason for all these compliments on this job. If you think I am acting smart, then you are mistaken."[2] He had taken up this assignment without any ego hassles and without any sense of attachment.

The new teacher became instantly popular amongst the students. He had a straightforward nature and was always ready to meet and mingle with everybody. He would not give advice easily, but share his experiences, if asked for. His age was also such, he was hardly 25 at the time, that he would look like one of them. He would go out to play hockey and tennis with students and sometimes for a swim in river Ganga.

Kashi Hindu Vishwavidyalaya was, indeed, a mini India. It was necessary and also expected that one would have the willing-ness to live together with different people and have the ability to understand the other without any pre-conceived notions. Hostels had intelligent students right from Punjabi to Tamil, that is, nearly all linguistic groups. It was not only essential but also desirable to have a positive and inclusive approach towards all the languages. With God's grace, Professor Golwalkar had the opportunity to get exposure in this regard since childhood. His young ears had heard Oriya language in Saraipalli; he had sung Saint Tulsidas's Awadhi through his young lips; he was not a stranger to Telugu in Jubilee School of Chandrapur. This young man also had to understand a little of Tamil when he reached Chennai. He had inherited Marathi while he was a suckling child in his mother's lap. Thus, his settling down in Kashi was like a duck taking to water.

The students learned about the multifarious talents of their Professor Madhavrao within no time. They witnessed his readiness to teach any subject. Therefore, students of different disciplines also started flocking to him to clear their doubts. No student had to return disappointed. If he didn't know the subject, he would ask the concerned student to come the next day. He would study the subject at night and wait for the student the next day with the right solution. Once he explained how a teacher's conduct should be in these words, "I recall an incident when I was the Sanghchaalak of Kashi Sangh Shakha. We had a karyakarta (senior volunteer) who studied in B.A. The exams for the final year were just round the corner. He had worked very earnestly for the Sangh during his two years, day and night. His friends began telling him, 'You should study hard or you will fail, and people will point fingers and say that senior karyakartas like you failed in the exams.'

"These discussions reached my ears. I too thought that if he failed, people would carry a very negative perception of the Sangh work. It will affect the rapid growth of the Sangh negatively. So, I had a talk with him. He also understood the issue and got ready to study hard. But, he didn't even know where his books were. Not only this, he began by asking me about the subjects he would need to appear in.

"I found out the details about his subjects. When he saw the big pile of books, he exclaimed, 'I will not be able to study so much!' I told him, 'Don't worry, I will teach you and you will pass out successfully.'

"That karyakarta was very hardworking, studious and intelligent. I remember that when I started teaching him, not only would he not move or fidget around, but would not even take his eyes off me. He would listen to me with full concentration. He had to prepare for three subjects in the exams. A

Professor of Economics was a friend of mine. I told him to explain Economics in simple terms so that he could pass the exam.

"Similarly, a student of M.A. was also a good friend of mine. I also asked him to help this student. We divided different chapters of Political Science between us. We decided that we will study for him and impart the essential information to him.

"The studies began, that is, our learning and his studies. I would learn from his books the whole day and after the evening Shakha, he would sit with me the whole night to study. We would sit down at around eight or nine in the evening and continue till four in the morning. We would take a break of around 15 minutes, and then study hard till half-past five in the morning.

"This way, I would study the whole day and teach him the whole night. Finally, when the results were declared, he had passed. He had studied all the subjects very honestly and prepared what was necessary for the exams. He was successful and I felt a great sense of satisfaction."[3]

He would provide books to poor students. Major part of his salary would get consumed in this. He would make do happily with whatever was left for him. This young professor became an object of loving respect from the students. The students brought up in this atmosphere started calling him "Guruji". When he left his temporary job and returned to Nagpur after some time, this loving way of calling him "Guruji" became a prefix to his name even after he returned.

His dressing sense during his teaching days in college was quite up-to-date. He was resolute about it like a soldier. He never agreed with the idea that messy clothes are a sign of simplicity in life. He also never agreed that clean, well-ironed clothes were a show off. People graduating out of Kashi at that time tell us that he used to be very well-dressed when he went to take classes and dress in *kurta-pyjama* otherwise. He had his own views on clothes too.

Once, while he had gone out for a walk, there was a heavy downpour and he got drenched. He went to a friend in a hostel close-by. Seeing him all wet, his friend gave him a fresh, clean set of clothes. He changed his clothes, sat down in a relaxed posture on the floor mattress and got into a general discussion. But, the owner of the clothes was not enjoying the discussion. He would keep staring at the spoilt crease of the trousers worn by Golwalkar. His face reflected his worry lines clearly. Madhavrao understood his discomfort and stood up suddenly to say, "Brother, please take back your trousers and its crease." He took off the trousers and *kurt*a and ran down to his room in his underwear.[4]

There is another incident that took place in his own room. Once he returned after a visit to his friends and his *pyjama* had become dirty. He changed into a freshly ironed *pyjama*. His friend asked him, "Where is the need to change the *pyjama* as you are going to sleep anyways?" He responded, "Dear friend, one must change the dirty cloth immediately, whether it is daytime or night."[5]

These two incidents seem to be two extremes, but there is no conflict between the two. They are the two sides of the same way of thinking. The basic question for Madhavrao was "Are clothes meant for a person or is a person meant for the clothes?" The second was "Is cleanliness and purity meant for one's own satisfaction or to show one off? What has it got to do with light or darkness?" He knew the answer to these fundamental questions and conducted his life on these principles.

Anybody can make a mistake. However, a cook's mistake is a sin, but the owner's mistake is only an oversight – this is the normal thinking of any boss. But, Madhavrao didn't go by this dictum. Ram Sevak was a servant in Gajanand Lodge. He was from a distant village and miles away from the mores of modernity. Once he dropped the tray in which he was carrying tea for a group of friends and the whole tea drained off; some cup-saucers were broken too. On hearing this shattering noise, Madhavrao came to him and the first thing he asked him was, "Have your hands and feet got scalded with hot tea?" Once the servant recovered from his embarrassment, he joked, "What is the use of this huge body? You could break only a couple of cups and saucers!" The friends laughed and the servant shrank back in embarrassment. His master's sentence displayed love, concern and a sense of humour.[6] Guruji maintained this way of conversation throughout his life.

The room of Guruji at Gajanand Lodge was always open to students. Looking at the age of the visitors, neighbours would doubt whether the room belonged to a teacher or student – so easy-going was the atmosphere there. But, it was not easy to find a place to sit in the room. Piles of books took up space in every possible corner. Annaji Pandaripande, who was a student during those days, writes in his memoirs, "There was a jungle of books there. In the corners, on the table, on tripod – there were books all around. Piles of books. One would wonder if a library was being shifted here. If my colleague Raghuvir Dhongdi, who became a *sannyasi* later, spoke about these books, Guruji would carry on with his subject without responding to his query. Strands of serious issues and humorous jokes would intermingle during these moments. He never showed himself off as a great intellectual. Looking at his easy-going nature, nobody could even judge that here was a soul always thirsty for more knowledge. He knew by heart, the speech of Mark Antony in the death scene of *Julius Caesar* written by the great dramatist, Shakespeare. He had memorised *Ekachvyala* of Marathi dramatist, Gadkari. He had read the complete works of Swami Vivekananda in Kashi. He used to narrate stories of Vivekananda to us."[7]

Guruji lived a life that saw him mingling with ease with both teachers and students. But, he was not careless about his own life. This was his inherited capital (*dharohar*). There was a big conference in the university in 1932. It was held in the assembly hall of alumni association. Guruji was in-charge of all the arrangements. He had prepared the plans very carefully. There was separate entry for men and women. Volunteers were advised strictly about this.

A large number of people started turning up for the conference. Things were going fine because of well laid-out plans. At such a time, a professor named Mukutbihari Lal tried to enter through the gate meant for women. Volunteers stopped him politely. He was the son of a great friend of Govind Malaviya, son of Mahamana Malaviya. He insisted on entering through the same gate. Young volunteers also stuck to their guns. Finally, these young people pushed him out of the gate. The programme got over, but, the unpleasant experience remained in the air. Office-bearers led by Govindkant decided to suspend Dr. Sadgopal and a few volunteers. On hearing about this, Guruji met the officer-bearers concerned and said, "Whatever Dr. Sadgopal ji did was under my directions. I am fully responsible for his actions. Therefore, if there is any penal action, it should be taken against me." The whole affair got settled after the intervention of the respected founder, Malaviya ji and the atmosphere returned to normal.[8]

After some days, Prof. B.L. Pawar returned to his post and the temporary posting of Golwalkar came to an end. He returned to Nagpur in February 1933 after getting relieved from his responsibility.

□

Endnotes

1. *Aarti Aalok ki*, pp. 16
2. Ibid, pp. 17
3. *Avismaraneey Guruji*, pp. 2
4. *Maa. Sa. Golwalkar*, pp. 27-28
5. Ibid, pp. 27
6. Ibid, pp. 31
7. *Annaji Pandaripande Smritiyan*, (unpublished, Nagpur Documentation Centre)
8. Ibid

11

Induction into Sangh at Kashi

Madhavrao Golwalkar was inducted into the Sangh when he landed at Kashi as a teacher. Before this, many of his friends and contacts were already swayamsevaks, but, he had never shown any keenness about the Sangh, and, therefore, had no more than a passing knowledge about it. He had not even met the founder of the Sangh.

Dr. Keshav Baliram Hedgewar, an organiser par excellence, had brought about the growth of Sangh into a powerful organisation that carried an impact. There were more than 100 Shakhas (branches) and over ten thousand swayamsevaks. Once he established a foothold in the region, he decided to take the next step, that is, to spread it across Bharat. The place chosen for the next stage of growth was the city of pilgrimage, Kashi. There was a specific rationale behind it. Kashi had an important place in his scheme of things from the organisation's point of view. Dr. Hedgewar had come to the conclusion that if one were to present an idea in Kashi, it would get broadcast across the nation because Kashi was the pre-eminent centre of convergence for ideas in this nation. His conclusion was based on historic experiences. For example, Lord Buddha's first sermon, Adi Shankaracharya's first session to explain Advaita, Swami Dayanand Saraswati's first campaign about Vedic thoughts, etc. – all had taken place there. These great souls had deliberately chosen Kashi for propagating and broadcasting their views. Having got a direction from these historical incidents, he decided to sow the seed of Sangh philosophy in Kashi and sent a select team of swayamsevaks from Nagpur. The leading light among them was Prabhakar Balwant Dani alias Bhaiyyaji Dani, belonging to the Malgujar clan of Umred. Nagpur being a city of dual languages, all the students knew Hindi well apart from their mother-tongue Marathi. Other colleagues of Bhaiyyaji Dani were Tatya Telang, Babu Telang, Tatya Lokhande, Anna Pandaripande, Balwant alias Abba Gunde. Their goal was to start a Shakha in the university while pursuing graduation or post-graduation studies. All of them were intelligent, talented and action-oriented youth.

Dr. Hedgewar had sent his friend Babarao Savarkar, elder brother of the famous revolutionary Barrister Savarkar, to Vyankatesh Damle of Kashi for improvement in health. He had, then, invited Dr. Hedgewar with a strong urge to start Sangh work in Kashi. As per this plan, Dr. Hedgewar stayed in Kashi from 11th March till April for around three weeks. A Shakha was started in the temple of Dhanadhaneshwar at Brahmaghat with the help of contacts established by Babarao. The Shakha was established at the beginning of the academic year, as soon as the students arrived in the university. We may recall that all this happened prior to Golwalkar's appointment as a teacher. He had been appointed in August.

Bhaiyyaji Dani contacted the new teacher Golwalkar immediately after arriving from Nagpur. This contact grew slowly into a strong bonding and they became good friends. His close friend Baburao was already there. Within no time, other students of Nagpur also became his friends. The Sangh Shakha began functioning in the university campus and he got to know about this in a routine manner. But, Professor Golwalkar would play hockey or tennis while his other friends attended the Shakha. They used to chat with each other on the road as they went their ways. During this time, as noted earlier, many students began to take help from Golwalkar. Among them were the above-mentioned Lokhande and Pandaripande. Bhaiyyaji had got an idea about Golwalkar's spiritual bent of mind quite early. He had also realised that this person went to the bottom of things in any subject. Gradually, Golwalkar began going to Shakha once in a while, even as he kept up with his hockey and tennis. During the weekly holidays, he also went a couple of times for a swim with these students. All the swayamsevaks (volunteers) of Shakha used to call him Guruji.

An outing to Sarnath was organised for the Kashi Shakha in the last week of December. Nearly 40 volunteers participated in this picnic. Guruji also took part in it from morning till evening. In one session, Guruji narrated the history of Sarnath to the other participants. He threw light on the historic, philosophic and global importance of Bhagwan Buddha in a very impressive way in Hindi that flowed smoothly like river Ganga. Swayamsevaks talked about it for many days even after the programme. Apart from this, there was a lecture by Raghuvir Dhongdi and the concluding speech by Bhaiyyaji Dani. This picnic was the turning point in the history of Kashi Shakha. Guruji also started coming regularly to the Shakha after this. He began taking more interest in physical programmes. He would remove his coat and tie after the Shakha and learn wooden stick (*laathi*) from Tatya Telang and Tatya Lokhande.

Bhaiyyaji must have been sending report about Sangh work to Sarsanghchaalak Dr. Hedgewar as per Sangh's way of working. These reports must have talked about Guruji becoming a swayamsevak. Bhaiyyaji must have received the right directions from there. Be as it may, Bhaiyyaji Dani declared Professor Golwalkar the respected Sanghchaalak of Kashi Shakha and

Dr. Sadgopal ji the General Secretary on an auspicious day before the Sangh *prarthana* (prayer) before the most sacred (*param pavitra*) *bhagwa dhwaj* (saffron flag).[1]

Guruji used to practise his favourite *ragas* on the *sitar* or the flute, sitting on the floor before sunrise or after sunset, in his room in Gajanand Lodge. Other music lovers or friends would also join in many a time. Once some of his friends found him tense and immersed in deep thought. When asked the reason, he didn't say anything. He rose silently, brought out his *sitar* and handing it over to a friend, said, "That's it. Now, the music of life is going to be different." He never touched the *sitar* or flute after that day.

The entry of Guruji in the Sangh became a subject of discussion among his teacher colleagues. It seems that the birth chart (*janma kundli*) of the Sangh is under the influence of strong opposing planets. A few of the great intellectuals who considered themselves modern and progressive, asked him, "What is your 'ism'?" Guruji gave a thoughtful answer, "Our 'ism' is 'Sanghism'. You people would have to study it in future." Those people lost the courage to go into a debate.

Gradually, Sanghchaalak got more busy with regular Sangh Shakha. It was normal to see him enter the rooms of old and new swayamsevaks, especially the sick. If required, he would arrange for his proper care. swayamsevaks considered him their personal guardian. During these days, an idea got floated that the university Shakha should have its own band. There were no two views about this and there was a lot of enthusiasm among the young swayamsevaks. But, who had the resources? Everybody became quiet when faced with this question. A parcel with desired equipment for the band arrived in Bhaiyyaji's name in about ten to fifteen days. When asked about it, Guruji said, "Isn't our work God's own work? He must have sent it." Intelligent youngsters understood whose deed it was.

Guruji came to the university on 16th August. Around this, time Malaviya ji left for the Round Table Conference on 29th August, 1931. He returned after four-and-a-half months. The university Sangh Shakha had started functioning during this period. On his return, as soon as he had spare time, Guruji went with senior volunteers to pay respects to him and get his blessings. Subsequently, some meetings were held on and off. When Malaviya ji came to know that the Sangh Shakha has been set up in the university, he was very happy. There is story behind his pleasure.

Pandit Malaviya had taken part in the annual conference of Hindu Mahasabha held at Belgaum in Karnataka in 1924. He had spoken in the conference thus: "If Hindus were not cowards and weak, many Hindu-Muslim riots could have been averted. The nation is facing a debilitating situation because of these riots for which Hindus' weakness is responsible to a large extent. Therefore, it is necessary to get rid of this weakness."[2] Five years after this speech, Malaviya ji had come to Akola in Maharashtra on 20th April, 1929 to preside over the All India Plenary Session of the Hindu Mahasabha. The founder of the Sangh, Dr. Hedgewar was also present in this session. Pandit Malaviya was among the people with whom he had discussions about the Sangh. Impressed with this exchange, he dropped in at Nagpur while returning from Akola to see this work himself. All the swayamsevaks welcomed him in a grand manner in the Shakha at Mohite grounds. At that moment, Pandit Malaviya turned towards Dr. Hedgewar to say, "People call me a royal beggar. If you allow me, I can collect some funds for the Sangh from a few people." And, like the humble disciple Kautsa of Raghuvansha, Doctorji said humbly, "Pandit ji, I am not worried about money. I only need blessings from people like you."[3] He had this first encounter with the Sangh that considered money to be secondary and put all its energy in building human beings with character. Now, after two years, the Sangh had reached his place of contemplation in the university. Therefore, this information gladdened his heart.

Once Chancellor Malaviya went for a walk in the morning with Guruji. The informal discussion on way was like that between a father and son. He told Guruji, "Never go after petty goals in life; always aim for the supreme objective. I have always kept a goal for myself of establishing a great university." For Guruji, a mere child in worldly experience at that time, these sentences were like sacred *shlokas* from the *Veda*s. Later, whenever Guruji talked about this episode, he would become highly emotional.[4]

One evening, Malaviya ji saw some swayamsevaks carrying a flag-pole, band equipment and *lathis*, etc. to their hostels while he had gone out for a walk. He obtained more information from his sources and called Bhaiyyaji Dani and Dr. Sadgopal one day. He told them, "I know that you require a place to store your Sangh-related material and for your meetings, etc. I will give you such a piece of land. You can collect funds from your well-wishers and construct a building there." Thus, a Sangh office came up there in due course of time. It had two rooms and a wide verandah in the front – a small but clean and nice place. The Shakha would be conducted daily in front of this place. Swayamsevaks would chat for long hours in an enjoyable atmosphere in the verandah. Guruji, Bhaiyyaji, Sadgopal ji also used to participate in these joyful informal discussions.[5]

* * * * * * *

It is essential to go back in time at this stage from the point of view of history. The sad demise of Pandit Malaviya ji also saw the eclipse of his idealistic liberal mindset. Vested interests in the institution rose in its wake. Politics too took a dominant position. The presence of the Sangh became a sore point in the eyes of many a powerful person. They kept creating hurdles in its path. Finally, when the Emergency was declared in 1975-77 and certain people made a bonfire of the fundamental rights, Chancellor Kalumal Shrimali's henchmen destroyed the Sangh building completely on a dark night. They removed the debris, levelled the site and put up a grass lawn overnight. Even the portrait of Malaviya ji was not spared and was made part of the debris.[6]

****

Guruji came to Nagpur in the summer of 1932. He met Dr. Hedgewar for the first time during this visit. He noticed Dr. Hedgewar coming towards him while he was going somewhere from Mama Raikar's house. Dr. Hedgewar came and stood before him and enquired, "Are you Madhavrao Golwalkar?" This was their first direct introduction. "Come home in a day or two, whenever possible," he added. He went his way after this brief conversation. There is no further information about when Guruji went to his house and what they talked about, but, surely, Guruji must have gone to Dr. Hedgewar's house, and have had a heart-to-heart talk. Dr. Hedgewar, a brilliant organiser, must have observed and judged Guruji. He must also have enquired about him, directly and indirectly, with senior workers of the Sangh in the university like Bhaiyyaji Dani. The founder of Sangh must have seen some unusual qualities in Guruji. Why would he have invited a twenty-six-year-old young demonstrator in a science laboratory as a chief guest for the function at the RSS headquarters, otherwise? We get an answer to this question later in a letter written by Dr. Hedgewar.

The most important festival of RSS is Vijayadashami. Large- scale preparations were underway for the occasion in Nagpur. Doctorji was on tour of western Maharashtra. His ideas became clear from a letter he had written at that time to the swayamsevaks in Nagpur. He wrote, "Dussera (Vijayadashami) festival that we celebrate in Nagpur is a manifestation of the life force of the RSS. We judge our strength based on this programme. People who love our work will feel a wave of happiness sweep through their hearts when they witness this programme. We should always remember that this deeply felt happiness about Sangh work is a tower of strength for the Sangh. Many important people, not only from Nagpur, but also from other states, are coming to see this festival in Nagpur this year. As per our vision, if we wish to see expansion of the Sangh Shakhas in other states of Hindustan, then our guests must feel a surge of energy in their hearts when they see this festival."[7]

The festival on 9th October, 1932 was a grand success as per the wishes of the Sangh founder. The physical drills presented by 1,200 uniformed swayamsevaks were highly impressive. Military-like marchpast with a music band thrilled the hearts of the audience. *Param poojaniya* (highly revered)

Sarsanghchaalak offered garlands to both Professor Madhavrao Golwalkar and Dr. Sadgopal. He introduced them by saying, "Both of them are dedicated workers of the Kashi Sangh Shakha." After the programme, Doctorji guided these two guests to observe the Shakha work in Umred, Bhandara, etc. He also wished to accompany the guests, but could not do so due to ill health. He had to be satisfied with deputing office-bearers with them.

For the Sanghchaalak and *Karyavaah* (General Secretary) of Kashi, this Nagpur tour was highly inspirational. They talked of their energising experiences at the Shakhas in Kashi. Sharing of these experiences had a positive impact on the local Shakhas. The Sangh work began striking deep roots in Kashi.

In short, Guruji Golwalkar became a swayamsevak in Kashi and also a senior office-bearer. He had stayed in Kashi for nearly five-and-a-half years to study for four years and one-and-a-half years to teach. It is interesting to note that in his 67 years, apart from Nagpur, he stayed for the longest period in Kashi. That too at an age when both mind and heart are evolving, growing and absorbing *samskaaras.*

Guruji's Hindi became more refined, beautiful and he expressed his thoughts powerfully. Those were the days when Pandit Malaviya's movement for propagation of Hindi had become very strong in the whole of Sindh-Gangetic belt. Kashi was the epicenter of refined Hindi. The huge well-stocked library of Kashi Vishwavidyalaya was the right place for development of intellect. To his great fortune, he was privileged to be in the august company of the revered founder, Chancellor Malaviya ji. His righteous *sattvik* nature got nurtured and blossomed in the rarified company of Malaviya ji. He was influenced till his last days by the pious discourses of this noble soul. Malaviyaji's enlightened directions were put together in the following *shlokas*:

Hitaaysarvalokaanaamnigrhanay cha duskirtaam
Dharmasansthaapanaarthaaypranamyaparameshwaram ||1||
Grameygramey sabhaa kaaryaa graamey graamey kathaa shubhaa
Paathshaalaa mallashaalaa pratiparvamahotsavah ||2||
Anaathavidhavaarakshyaahmandiraani tathaa cha gauh
Dharmasanghatanamkritvaadeyamgaayam cha tadhitam ||3||
Streenaamsamaadarahkaryahduhkhiteshudayaayatathaa
Ahimsakaahnahantavyaah aatataayee vadhaaharnah ||4||
Uttamah sarvadharmanaam hindudharmoyamuchyate
Rakshyaah prachaaraneeyashcha srvabhoothite ratah ||5||

Meaning: "May the entire humankind enjoy welfare, may evil forces be destroyed, rule of law (*dharma*) be established. Towards these objectives, praying to God Almighty, let us come together from village to village, narrate pious tales in villages, open schools in villages for development of the mind and body, start gymnasiums and wrestling pits in villages to make bodies strong. Orphans, widows, temples, sacred religious centres and Mother Cow must be protected. Let us organise our *dharma* to impart life-elevating knowledge. Women be given respect and let there be piety for the deprived. Non-violent creatures are not to be killed, but, enemies of the society deserve to be eliminated. This Hindu *dharma* is superior to all other religions. It spells the welfare of all the living beings. Let this be protected and propagated."[8]

Guru Golwalkar returned to Nagpur from Kashi Hindu Vishwavidyalaya (Banaras Hindu University) with these noble thoughts embedded in his heart. □

Endnotes

1. *Annaji Pandaripande Smritiyan* (unpublished, Nagpur Documentation Centre)
2. *Dr. Hedgewar*, pp. 136
3. Ibid, pp. 205
4. *Shri Guruji Uttar Pradesh Mein*, pp. 5
5. Ibid, pp. 6
6. Ibid, pp. 6
7. *Dr. Hedgewar,* pp. 264
8. *Hindu Dharmopadeshah* – created by Malaviya

12

In Search of a Guru

Guruji reached Nagpur in the first week of March 1933 after bidding farewell to the Banaras Hindu University (Kashi Hindu Vishwavidyalaya) in the last week of February 1933. He went straight to the house of his maternal uncle, Mama Raikar. Immediately after this, he went to his own home in Ramtek. After paying respects to his mother and father, he apprised them of his job-related issues, about which they had learnt from the letter their son had sent from Kashi. The parents had some plans about his future accordingly. There was no dearth of opportunities for graduates, specially postgraduates in those days, but a person taking up service was obliged to go anywhere in the country. Sadashiv Golwalkar knew about this fact from his own experience. He had to go through transfers from north to south and east to west in different regions. With the idea that he and his only son should not be separated, he had planned to make his son, Madhu, a graduate in law, to make him a lawyer. One morning, Taiji disclosed his wish to Madhu and added, “Bhauji also approves of this idea.” It was as if the patient had received a medicine he wished for. Madhu agreed to it immediately. Dr. Hedgewar had also made the same suggestion when he was going to Ramtek!

Guruji became a student of the Law College at Nagpur. He became a teacher again in his uncle’s coaching classes and became self-reliant. Both the activities went together without any hitch. However, there were two outstanding things in this new *avatar* of a student. One was that he had become a Sangh swayamsevak now; secondly, his friend from the university, Raghuvir Dhongdi had become his classmate. Dhongdi belonged to Nasik, so he was staying in the hostel of Shri Ramakrishna Ashram situated in Dhantoli. Golwalkar, an ex-student of Kashi, visited the place once in a while to meet him.

“For a Sangh swayamsevak, all Sangh Shakhas are his own; no Shakha is alien to him.” This was a part of the teachings of the founder of the Sangh. With this training, the ex-Sanghchaalak of Kashi also became active in Nagpur. The Sangh Shakha at Mohitewadi had to be shifted to Tulsibag due to some unexpected reasons and the Shakha was called Tulsibag Shakha. As per the plan,

Guruji used to give a lecture generally on all Sundays in this Shakha. Later, revered Dr. Hedgewar made him the General Secretary (Karyavaah) of Nagpur Shakha in 1934. This was the first responsibility he was given in Nagpur. Dr. Hedgewar sent him later to Mumbai to establish the Sangh there. There was no well-structured system of Prachaaraks those days. Doctorji used to send Dadaji Paramarth or Babasaheb Apte as per the necessity. He sent Guruji to Mumbai with a similar purpose. Guruji stayed there for a couple of months and returned to Nagpur when he was asked to come back.

Sangh work went well in the state of Vidarbha in 1933. Therefore, O.T.C. (Officers' Training Camp) had to be organised in Mehkar in addition to the Nagpur camp. The situation was equally compelling in 1934. So, plans were made for setting up two camps again – one at Nagpur and the second in Akola. Sangh founder Dr. Hedgewar used to stay for the whole duration in those training camps till 1932 and guide the participants through interactions as well as his personal conduct. When the number of camps doubled, the arrangements had to be modified. Keeping these facts in mind, Doctorji decided to hand over all the responsibilities of the Akola camp to Shri Guruji as a 'Sarvadhikari', that is 'Chief Officer'. He acquitted himself commendably with his sharp intelligence. He gathered all the details pertaining to the participants in the first two days and guided each one of them personally during the duration of the camp.

The Sangh encourages a positive approach in discussions. Guruji had this innate nature of positivity. People looking after the arrangements at the Akola camp had a direct experience of this quality. Around eight senior people involved in arrangements of the camp went to the bungalow of Bhaiyyaji Dani in Umred immediately after the completion of the camp to take a little rest for four to five days. Apart from Guruji, the others included Annaji Pandaripande, Bhau Kulkarni, Somnath Pandit, etc. During the leisurely discussions one day, the subject veered around to 'Goswamis'. The discussion became heated due to the differing opinions that society had about this sect. Seeing the discussion taking a negative direction, Guruji stopped everybody with a raised voice and then went on to explain the etymology of the word 'Goswami', the history of this tradition, its contribution to the society, etc. Then, closing his talk, he instructed the others that one should not get stuck in the muck created by others.[1]

When Guruji was appointed the Chief Officer of the camp, he was a law student in the first year. He began his studies for the final exams immediately with the end of the summer vacations. Sessions judge Wadegaonkar, who was a relative of his friend Vamanrao Wadegaonkar, used to help him in his studies. His famed power of concentration came in handy at this time. Once he took a bus from Nagpur to Ramtek and started reading the 'Hindu Law'. The bus reached Ramtek in a few hours stopping at various places. He was not aware of this at all. He carried on with his reading. He realised that he had reached his destination when another passenger brought this to his notice.[2] He passed the exams, standing sixth in the college. Now he had become M.Sc., LL.B. His mother, father, Mama and Doctorji were satisfied with this achievement. On being persuaded by his friends, he put up his name plate as a lawyer few days later in a room in Devji building in Badkas Chowk (named Bachcharaj Chowk now). A little later, he changed his office to Walker Road (named Ruikar Road now) when he decided to take up practice with his friend Dattatreya Deshpande.

It is often said that self-experience is the most powerful guide. His experience told him that he was not fit to be in this profession. Let us hear about this in his own words, "I had also practised law for a short period. A plaintiff came to me once. He told me that he had given some loan to a person who he didn't want to return now. There was no written proof about this transaction. I took advice from some senior lawyers. All of them advised me to put up two witnesses who would say the right thing. That would be enough. That is, I should prepare false witnesses and train them to tell the court that the loan was given in their presence. But, it was not possible for me to do it. I refused to take the brief and bid goodbye to law."[3] This self-confession was done in front of highly respected lawyers of Punjab-Haryana High Court on the festival of Baisakhi in 1969!

While law and Sangh work were going on one side, his parents began to worry about his family life. But, just as the parents of various saints – Samarth Ramdas, whose original name was Narayan, Narayan Guru, whose original name was Nanu, Ramakrishna Paramhamsa known as Gadadhar, were reluctant to talk about these matters with them, knowing their nature and inclination. Bhauji and Taiji also faced a similar reluctance. Still, not to be derelict in his duty as a father, Bhauji came to the room of his son after prayers one day and asked him frankly, "Madhu, it is about your marriage. We think this is the right time. What is your opinion?" Madhu too gave a frank reply, "I don't wish to get married. I will not be happy with it. But, beyond saying this, I will do whatever you wish." The loving father was not upset at all. Deep in his heart, he had gauged his son correctly. He never raised this subject again. But, a mother is a mother. She is an ocean of love and waves do rise in oceans. Mother and son shared a different kind of bond. Therefore, she would not leave Madhu alone on any occasion over this issue. Madhu's defence in such cases was to treat such interactions with humour and laugh off the matter. Still his mother sent him with some relatives to meet a girl. He went there and returned. Mother asked him, "Did you see the girl?" He said, "No, my eyes were closed."[4] This mother finally got the message that day. But, still, the saintly lady's heart was upset. One day she explained to him the importance of raising a family to carry the family name. Madhu became serious now. He told his mother clearly, "Tai, don't tell me about the continuity, damage or disappearance of our family name. If this society around us has to survive and remain united, it would be imperative that many other families also lose their family name, not just ours. I am not unhappy at all about it." What choice his mother had but to remain silent after this conversation?

Guruji used to go to the hostel of Shri Ramakrishna Ashram to meet his colleague Raghuvir Dhongdi while studying in the Law College. His heart was inclined towards spiritualism since childhood. That is why he had chosen the Ashram hostel during his student days. The two birds of the same feather would roam around in the sacred atmosphere of the Ashram for hours together. Swami Bhaskareshwaranandji was the head of this Ashram. The chairman saint of Shri Ramakrishna Ashram, Swami Akhandananda had a soft corner for him. When he was going from Mumbai to Nagpur, he broke journey at Nagpur on a special request of Swami Bhaskareshwaranandji. This incident took place in the middle of November in 1934. Some spiritual seekers had received *diksha*[5] from venerable chairman Swamiji. Many other college students had also put in their request to receive *diksha* from him. Swamiji asked all of them to come to his resident headquarters in Sargachhi. God alone knew what Swamiji had in his mind. The fact remains that he did not impart *diksha* to any student in Nagpur. He, then, returned to his headquarters.[6]

Raghuvir Dhongdi was one of the students who wished to be ordained as a *sannyasi,* i.e., receive *diksha*. He disclosed his desire to go to Sargachhi. Guruji also longed to become a *sannyasi,* but he had kept this thought to himself. He raised this subject with Raghuvir and said, "I also wish to take *sannyas* but I will need to talk to Desai ji." This is the same Desai whom Guruji considered akin to a guru. Guruji wrote to him immediately and got his reply saying, "Such an auspicious occasion arises rarely in one's life. Don't let it pass. Go to Sargachhi at the earliest." Accordingly, Guruji began his preparations quietly. He told of his heartfelt desire to Swami Bhaskareshwaranandji. Swamiji sent him to Amitabh Maharaj *alias* Anand Chaitanya, who used to look after the management of the Ashram, for discussions. He had seen the young lawyer come to Ashram many a time in the company of Raghuvir. Relations between the two became closer after they met personally.

Bhagwan Ramakrishna Paramhamsa was a person who could recognise sterling qualities in a person like a jeweller sifts for a diamond. He had accepted his disciples after testing them thoroughly. Shri Ramakrishna Ashram also follows similar practices. Only after being together in close contact, over discourses and discussions, etc. was it possible to receive the *mantra*, the oath of celibacy and *diksha* for *sannyas*. A person who had internalised the *mantra*, "*Sthaapakaay cha dharmasya sarvadharmaswaroopine. Avataarvarishthaay Raamkrishnaay te namah*" (meaning – my salutations to Ramakrishna who manifested to establish *dharma* in all its glory) would be blessed with *diksha*. Swami Bhaskareshwaranandji knew both Dhongdi and Golwalkar quite well. He wrote to Swami Akhandananda about the desire of these two to receive *diksha* and he received the green signal from him. But, these brothers-in-arms didn't leave Nagpur together. Raghuvir Dhongdi reached Sargachhi immediately upon receiving the requisite permission in May/June 1936.

For Golwalkar, it was not that easy to leave for Sargachhi. Dhongdi was from Nasik. He had already left his home and village. Therefore, he did not face the difficulties that Golwalkar faced in leaving Nagpur. He belonged to Nagpur. His centre of life was Nagpur and all his relatives were in Nagpur. So, he had to make his plans more carefully.

He spent the time during Dussera at his home in Ramtek. He must have come for the Vijayadashami *utsav* of the Sangh. He began his preparations to leave for Sargachhi after this. He finalised the date of journey and the train, etc. in consultation with Swami Bhaskareshwaranand and Amitabh Maharaj. He told his lawyer friend Dattatreya Deshpande about these plans. He wrote a letter to his father giving him complete information and asked his friend Deshpande to send it by post to Ramtek. He got into the train for Kolkata before Diwali after receiving an introductory letter from Amitabh Maharaj. The Ashram had instructed him to go to Sargachhi immediately on reaching Kolkata. He reached Sargachhi in November, about four days before Deepawali. Raghuvir led him into the hallowed presence of Swami Akhandananda. Remembering the traditional *samskaar* that one should not have a *darshan* of Guru with empty hands, Golwalkar had kept with him a handful of *shamipatra*. He offered these at the revered feet of the Gurudev on meeting him and offered *sashtaang namaskar,* i.e., lying prostrate before him. “You are Gowalkar, isn’t it? Was the journey pleasant?” Gowalkar[7] of Baba had now become the resident member of Sargachhi Ashram.

□

Endnotes

1. *Annaji Pandaripande Smritiyan*, (unpublished, Nagpur Documentation Centre)
2. *Maa. Sa. Golwalkar*, pp. 39
3. *Shri Guruji Samagra*, Vol. 1, pp. 198
4. *Jeevan Prasang*, Vol. 2, pp. 4
5. “*Diksha* is a process of acceptance of a disciple by the Guru, gifting him a *‘gurumantra’* and ordaining him as a sannyasi in his lineage or his order.”
6. *Swami Akhandanand* (Hindi), pp. 265
7. *Swami Akhandanand* used to call Golwalkar as Gowalkar.

13
The Monk of Sargachhi

Gangopaadhyay of Jasaur district in Bengal passed his Tarkratna examinations while practising celibacy. He roamed around the whole country for nearly seven to eight years as a *vairagi* (one who has given up worldly possessions). Finally, he returned to his village to lead a normal family life. It was the outcome and sacred gift of his pure spiritual life that this Gangadhar later became Swami Akhandananda. Gangadhar's inclination towards spirituality had been evident since his childhood. He had seen Bhagwan Ramakrishna Paramhamsa at the age of 13 with his friend at the home of Dinu Basu. At the age of 16, he went off with an unknown *avdhoot* (spiritual seeker) without informing or asking anybody. Members of the family were quite worried and they found him after great many efforts. At the age of 19, he went to Dakshineshwar temple and met Paramhamsa again. He was successful in speaking a few words to him. This was his first sacred meeting (*darshan*) with Paramhamsa. Not only this meeting had a great impact on him, but he also became a devotee. He became a regular visitor to Dakshineshwar after this and as a result, a dear friend of Narendra Nath too. Watching Shri Ramakrishna with devotion, grasping the deep meaning of his folk stories, he morphed into an enlightened soul like a salt idol melting into water. He became one of the pet disciples of this noble soul. Gangadhar was amongst the fortunate disciples whom Shri Ramakrishna loved like his sons and blessed with saffron clothes (*bhagwa vastra*) before he left this world and went on his eternal journey.

It had been a year since the passing away of Thakur (Shri Ramakrishna). Gangadhar left the Ashram as a roaming mendicant a week before Maha Shivaratri in 1887 wearing the saffron clothes that Gurudev had blessed him with, as if receiving a directive, without informing his *guru-bhais* (disciples of the same Guru). He told of these plans only to his father because he understood his heart. As planned, the father-son duo met at a pre-decided time at the railway station. Both of them stood silent, the son's hand etched with the sacred soil from his father's feet and eyes directed at his feet! The train gave a whistle to indicate its readiness to leave. Father came forward, and putting his hands on his son's shoulders, said, "Go, my dear son, go. Accomplish your work. World is meaningless. I bless you that may you have unshakeable faith at the feet of God Almighty." The son preserved this invaluable blessing of his spiritual father deep in his heart as a treasure.[1]

Charaiveti, *Charaiveti* (keep walking, keep walking). Gangadhar went as his heart ruled. He went around Varanasi, Himalayas, Kashmir, Trivishtap (Tibet) and many other places. He returned back to his Ashram after four long years in 1890 June, as if he had re-incarnated. His brother-*sannyasis* couldn't recognise him easily. There was a festival that day in Varaahnagar Mutt. Within a short time, in the first week of July, he officially took *sannyas* during a religious function that took place under the stewardship of Vivekananda. He was ordained with the *sannyasi* named 'Akhandananda'. He was twenty-six-years old at that time.

Swami Vivekananda had a different *sannyasi* name at that time. He and Akhandananda went to circumambulate the Himalayas. After some months, they went roaming separately on their own for their self-evolution. Akhandanand ji reached Jamnagar in Gujarat. He came in touch with the famous top-ranking Ayurveda expert, Jhandu Vitthal Bhattji. He was highly impressed with the service-oriented nature, readiness to help others, ever-flowing energy, humility, philanthropy, etc. of the wealthy Bhattji. He says, "I could really absorb the lesson that loving a human being and serving them is the best thing one can do, when I saw the life of Bhattji."[2]

During this circumambulation, Swami Akhandanand gained many new experiences. He came face to face with many apparent and not so apparent facts of this world. These experiences affected his heart in a new way. Sitting the whole night, he wrote this letter to his brother-*sannyasi* (*guru-bhais*), "Seeing that countless million human being toil hard to produce wealth that is wasted away to fulfil the sensual desires of a handful of rich people, I have lost peace of heart forever. I believe that dedicating my life to serve the common people who are exploited, oppressed and deprived of justice by the powerful should be the prime duty for me."[3]

Talking of this searing pain in Swamiji's heart, the writer of his biography, Swami Anadanand Maharaj says, "The change in Swami Akhandananda's perception of pain was not sudden. It was a gradual evolution of his heart as he walked the path of self-discovery indicated to him by his Gurudev." He first gave up everything, chanting *'Neti, neti'* (neither this, nor that). Then, achieving the desired vision for his soul, he accepted all with *'Iti, iti'* (this is it, this is it). This was the vision of God being present in all living beings."[4]

Swamiji started various social service projects in different parts of Rajputana region. From there, destiny took him back to Bengal. Moving slowly along the banks of the Ganga, towards north he reached Murshidabad. The deathly dance of famine was in full force there. Akhandananda's soul was shaken to the core. His grief burst forth, "I felt sad and frustrated to call God merciful. I could not fathom for what reason the merciful God was punishing these small children dying of hunger. I felt like running away from his empire of so-called mercy. But, someone was telling me, 'Where will you go? You have lot of work here. You are on the banks of Ganga.... you will have to stay here...."[5]

Finally, he received the directive. Swami Akhandananda began famine relief work in Mahula village near Murshidabad. He distributed rice to 18 families on 15th May, 1897. This marked a historic beginning of social service for Shri Ramakrishna Ashram. Coincidentally, with God's grace, Swami Vivekananda had founded Shri Ramakrishna Mission just a fortnight prior to this, on 1st May, 1897. What a heartwarming coincidence!

Swami Akhandanand's next phase in life as an action-oriented *sannyasi* commenced from here. He became famous in the area as 'Baba'. Everybody, from the common man to the elite and government officials, fell under his spell due to his compassion and efforts for an equitable society. Even the British district collector, judicial officers and others started coming to the service centre. Everybody gave him open-hearted co-operation. Even the administration was not far behind. After sixteen years of hard, sustained effort and penance, he established an Ashram in 1913, 10 kms south of Behrampur town, at Sargachhi on a 50-*bigha* piece of land. He set up a temple of Ramakrishna Paramhamsa in 1929 and started many multi-disciplinary social service centres. In a short time span, this place became a centre for penance, brimming with the spiritual consciousness of Swami Akhandananda. His was a life of penance and action-oriented spiritual exertion. He was an enemy of sleep and indolence. He did not like the afternoon sleep at all. "This is a house fully awake... I am a sixty-year-old man, but even now I feel like I can catch hold of the Sun and Moon and swallow them..." Reminiscing about old memories with his co-workers in the Ashram, he said, "I used to dig earth in the morning, work in the garden and eat rice soaked in lemon juice in the afternoon. I didn't even think of sleeping during the day. I used to read the whole night after hard labour during the day. I used to sleep after a gap of two to three days."[6]

Swami Akhandananda was a monk, with meditative power that gave him perpetual bliss. He would give highest importance to Swami Vivekananda's views. After taking a round of the orphanage, the temple and other places in the Ashram, Swamiji, looking at his *guru-bhai*, told his disciple Sharat Chakraborty, "Just see what a man of action he is. He doesn't worry at all about fear or death, etc. He is working assiduously for '*bahujanahitaya, bahujanasukhaya*' (maximum benefit of maximum people)".[7]

Golwalkar, a disciple eager to gain *diksha,* had by now reached the feet of this fiery monk.

□

Endnotes

1. *Swami Akhandanand* (Hindi), pp. 24
2. Ibid, pp. 83
3. Ibid, pp. 86
4. Ibid, pp. 87
5. Ibid, pp. 115
6. Ibid, pp. 254
7. Ibid, pp. 136

14

The Spiritual Seeker of Sargachhi

Global headquarters of Ramakrishna Mission was on the banks of River Ganga in Belur. Golwalkar went directly to distant Sargachhi rather than going there. Two reasons are attributed to this. During those days, the highest authority to give *diksha* was the Chairman of the Mission. Swami Akhandananda became the Chairman of the Mission on 4th March, 1934. Sargachhi was the hub of his activities, though Belur was the main centre of the organisation. Akhandananda ji visited Belur only rarely. Therefore, disciples like Dhongdi Golwalkar, etc., who wished to be ordained as *sannyasis,* had to go to Sargachhi to be blessed with *diksha*. Shri Babaji was in Sargachhi from 1912 to 1937, i.e., for 25 years, till he attained *mahasamadhi*. This was his place of penance and meditation. Just a week before his *samadhi*, he had noted in his memoirs, "Solemn vow to serve (*sevavrat*) was taken in Jamnagar, though it took roots and grew in Khetadi and reached its maturity in Murshidabad."[1] This seed of serving the humanity blossomed in Gujarat, flowered in Rajasthan and bore fruits in Bengal. Describing Sargachhi with a deep sense of spiritual fulfillment, he noted, "One year of famine relief in 1897, an Ashram on the roadside for 14 years and after that, this Ashram at Sargachhi was established."[2] It was this sacred piece of soil where Golwalkar arrived.

In this sacred place of meditation, brothers-in-arms (*guru-bhais*) were Param Chaitanya, Vibhuti Chaitanya, Anand Chaitanya, Raghuvir and Gopal. Param Chaitanya was an aeronautical engineer from Austria and had taken part in the First World War. He had settled down in America. His beloved had lost her life in the floods resulting from a dam burst in California. He had sought refuge at Vedanta Ashram in Boston for acquiring peace of mind. Swami Paramananda, who headed the centre there, sent him to Belur Mutt. He came to Sargachhi to enjoy the company of Swamiji. His name by birth was Phillips. Swami Akhandananda blessed him with *diksha* as a *brahmachari* (a spiritual seeker who has taken the vow of celibacy) in front of the sacred *yagna* fire on the occasion of the *pooja* ceremony of the Mother of the Universe. Phillips was given the name 'Param Chaitanya'.

Raghuvir Dhongdi became Tureeya Chaitanya and went on to become Swami Raghavananda later; Vibhuti Chaitanya became Swami Niramayananda. Amitabh Maharaj was called Anand Chaitanya as a *brahmachari* and was named Swami Amoortananda on being ordained a *sannyasi*. We could not get more information on one more disciple – Gopal inspite of researching hard.

According to Hindu *dharma*, spiritual practices and its path are not something to be publicised or made an exhibition of. Not only this, it has to be kept confidential too. It is said that the essence of *dharma* is secretive or to be kept under wraps. Even in modern times, during the sacred thread ceremony (*upanayan samskaar*), which is celebrated with much pomp, the preacher and the young student both are covered with a new cloth when the student is being preached and bestowed with the *mantra*. If this is the tradition, how could we get detailed information on the spiritual practices of people like Golwalkar?

This author had the great fortune to be in touch with him from 1944 to 1973. Many others have shared this luck. None of us ever heard Guruji mentioning the name of his Guru, Akhandananda ji. So, where was the chance of hearing about anything else on the subject? It is said that a venerable person's name is not to be spoken, but only indicated. He, perhaps, followed this religious etiquette. But, he had written about his experiences in Sargachhi for his own personal fulfilment. He kept these writings confidential for 36 years till his death. These memoirs lay quiet in a corner of his cupboard for nearly 30 years, even after his death. When the desired material was being researched for his comprehensive collected works in 2003, these writings came to light rather unexpectedly. This literature, though not much, is vital for understanding the path Guruji traversed in his spiritual quest. The notes, written in English, are undoubtedly written by him. This material can be found in Volume VI of *Shri Guruji Samagra* published in *Yugabd* 5106, on pp. 269-280.

In addition to this, we chanced upon some more sources. Swayamsevaks gathered some information in bits and pieces from brother *sannyasis* (*guru-bhais*) Amoortananda ji, Raghavananda ji and Niramayananda ji. Even these noble souls were a little miserly in giving information, but, as a Malayalam proverb goes, "a morsel dropped by an elephant is a lavish dinner for an ant." There was another crack in the wall during this time. A Bengali periodical, *Udbodhan* published the memoirs of Swami Niramayananda as a series of articles. Shri Ramakrishna Ashram published a Hindi translation of these memoirs under the title *Akhandananda ke Sannidhya Mein,* i.e., 'In the August Company of Swami Akhandananda'. Even such small nuggets gave a thrust to our journey of discovery.

Golwalkar spent time with Vibhuti Chaitanya, Tureeya Chaitanya, and Anand Chaitanya in Sargachhi for only about four months, but, it was an eventful period that left a deep mark on them. Some celebration or festival followed another during this period. Bhagwan Ramakrishna's centenary, Deepawali celebrations, Durga *pooja*, Jagadhatri *pooja*, one of the most important days among the disciples of Shri Ramakrishna – January 1, the Kalpataru day, Mother Sharada's birthday on January 4, Swami Vivekananda's birthday on February 2 – all these followed one after another. It was as if the gods were joining in one after another in a marriage procession of Lord Shiva and Goddess Parvati!

Guruji Golwalkar kept his luggage in the storeroom as per the directions of the Ashram and began to understand the working and ethos of the place. On the first night, he slept soundly, totally unaware of his surroundings, due to exhaustion after the long journey. Next day, Shri Babaji woke up at four in the morning as usual and asked Raghuvir, "Where is Gowalkar?" Raghuvir replied, "He is sleeping." "What will such a sleepy person achieve?" Shri Babaji said on a serious note. Raghuvir told his friend about this quip. Such a critical comment on the very first day? He was very upset and regretted his lethargy. "I will not let this happen again," he resolved. Shri Baba used to keep an eye on the conduct of each person in the Ashram. He would delegate responsibilities to different people and not allow anybody to sit idle. He put Gowalkar also to task while he too worked untiringly as was expected of him. Within a few days, it was time for *Ashwini Amavasya* and *Kali pooja*. Baba wished to celebrate these with great fanfare since it was the centenary year. He gave the responsibility of *pooja* and religious ceremonies to Vibhuti Chaitanya and preparatory arrangements to Golwalkar. His job was to prepare everything for the *pooja* and clean and clear out everything after the *pooja*. The job included scrubbing and washing of temple and cleaning the kitchen utensils. Vibhuti and Golwalkar accomplished the jobs given to them successfully.

Shri Babaji generally used to sing hymns and give informal sermons in the night after the evening *mangal aarti*. Nearly all the residents of the Ashram would attend it. They would get to hear pearls of wisdom at this sacred time from Guruji. One day, Shri Baba said, "Every act connected with worship is real worship. Undertake every act with dedication of worship; whether it is sweeping the worship room, wiping the floor, cleaning utensils, picking flowers or arranging fruits. Chant the *mantra* for your favourite God and focus your heart on God."[3] Golwalkar, squatting on the floor with others, felt as if Gurudev was talking to him. He felt fulfilled. After three to four days, Shri Baba asked Vibhuti, "How is the advocate volunteer?" Vibhuti replied, "Very good. He forgets himself when he works. He polishes all the instruments of *pooja* spotlessly. I feel embarrassed to imagine whether I can do this as well." Shri Baba had also made this observation. Not many days had gone, when he called Gowalkar and said, "*Arrey*! My body is getting weak. Take its care." Golwalkar's heart leapt with joy. He thought, this must be the fruit of my previous pious deeds. He started serving the master with full dedication.

It is said that the wise masters speak in riddles to test their disciples. They take a measure of their disciples every moment and thereby mould them.

They are expert psychologists in today's parlance. While serving his master, Golwalkar slipped down once and broke a cup that Shri Babaji liked a lot. Babaji said immediately, "Be cautious, don't be in a rush. That was a good cup. Are you hurt?" These words offered solace, indicated direction and caused embarrassment at the loss of Ashram's property.[4] At another time, Golwalkar's feet hurt badly when he was in a hurry to enter the stores. He started bleeding, but, Babaji didn't show any sympathy this time. He said, "Why don't you see where you are going? See your fault first."[5] These words were a little harsh and the caretaker also understood the lesson well.

It was natural for Golwalkar to be totally absorbed in his duty as an attendant. People had seen this same quality when he was taking care of his friend Vamanrao in hospital at Mumbai earlier. Shri Baba was also looked after in the same manner. While talking of King Dilip serving mother cow Nandini, poet Kalidas notes that the king followed the cow like a shadow. Similar was the manner in which Golwalkar nursed Shri Baba. At the time, keeping in mind his failing health, Shri Baba called Amitabh Maharaj, who was previously a resident of Sargachhi Ashram, from Nagpur Ashram to help him. So, the triumvirate of spiritual seekers –Dhongdi, Golwalkar and Amitabh came together again in December.

The path of a seeker is not simple. Sages of *Upanishads* have pronounced that it is tough; not easy. This proved to be true in case of Golwalkar too. He received a letter from his Mama in Nagpur, "Mother has fallen sick at the shock of your running away from home." He was highly perturbed with this news. He informed Shri Baba about it, who made a short observation, "These are bonds of *maya* and in *maya* is misery." The seeker got his direction from this pithy comment and went back to his duties.

Shri Baba's health kept deteriorating. Distressing thoughts began troubling people around him. Amitabh also thought of Golwalkar's *diksha*. He knew that his friend hadn't received his *diksha* yet. One day he cautioned his friend during the morning prayers, "Take a little time out to request Shri Baba for *diksha*. You may repent any delay." It is not that Golwalkar didn't realise this. He had surrendered his weighed down heart in the hands of his Guru. Now, a nudge from *guru-bhai* set him rethinking. His written notes throw light on his state of mind. "I couldn't calm my mind on Tuesday night and whole of Wednesday because I lacked courage. 'O my heart!' Then I said to myself, 'If only I get a few moments, when I can find him alone.' Generally, I could be a little bold after early morning duties of taking his care; and then I could beseech him for his blessing. He heard my silent prayer and called me at 03:45 in the morning. I got busy with his care. He then said, 'If you are not inconvenienced, I would like to wash my face now.' How careless of me! I immediately arranged for it. After completing the cleaning up, I brought a lamp as desired by him, since Raghuvir had, fortunately, gone out for jogging and Gopal was asleep, and so was Param Chaitanya. I gathered every ounce of courage at my command and entered his room. He was sitting in a contemplative mood. He had sung one hymn beautifully. Before he could begin singing the next hymn, I uttered words that were stuck in my mouth with full force as I sat down near his knees, 'Maharaj ji!' Every bit of my body was tremulous and tears were streaming down my eyes. He asked me, 'What is it?' Aah! Words failed me again. Swallowing my tears and sobbing hard, all I could utter was, 'Maharaj ji, when will I receive your blessings?' Because he couldn't understand my words, I repeated the same words again. Then, he spoke with immense mercy, 'It will happen. There are ten to twelve days of holidays and some more people will come for *darshan*. It will happen with them. I will tell you; go now.' Unable to cope with this moment of sheer bliss, I kept saying, '*Jai Prabhu*' again and again and I came out.'

"He began reciting a *shloka*. I cried because out of my unrestrained happiness and looking at him from the window, I bowed down to him with a deep sense of gratitude. What peace that salutation gave! That day was extremely blissful because he is great, he is merciful."[6]

All this had happened on the night of 24th December, the sacred birthday of Jesus Christ. Just as he was ready to retire for the day on Sunday, after finishing his chores, Shri Baba asked Gowalkar to come near him and said in a low voice, "Disciples coming from outside are putting excessive pressure on me. Let them leave first. Ramlal from Meerut is here. Let him go. Then, you, Jagdish and Robin will receive *diksha*." I noted that my heart felt fulfilled and my soul reached a state of absolute peace. I only said, "*Jai Prabhu,*" bent my knees and bowed before him. He put his kind hands on my head. How joyful that touch was! Now, I began waiting for that moment of bliss."[7]

Shri Baba kept delivering his late evening discourses despite his progressively failing health. All the students were recipients of his priceless thoughts during this period. He said once, "*Paropakaar* – favouring others! Why do we say so? Who is the 'other'? After all, everybody is our own. Only God can show favours. What is *Parahit vrat* – pledge for doing good to others? Say, *Lokahit vrat* – pledge to do good to people."[8]

One evening he said, "Vivekananda's *deshprem* (love for country) is not easy. It is not just *deshprem*; it is *deshatmabodh* (understanding the soul of the country). Normal people have *dehatmabodh* (knowing about one's physical self); therefore, they are involved only in taking care of their body. *Deshatmabodh* is to ponder over the past, present and future of this country. Above this understanding is *vishwatmabodh* (realising the soul of the universe) and worrying about every human being."[9]

Year of 1936 passed by in sipping the droplets of nectar of wisdom of the Guru and the year 1937 arrived. 1st January is celebrated as '*Kalpataru* Day' by the residents of Ashram. 4th January being the birthday of pious and revered Mother Sharada, it was celebrated with profound devotion. All this while, the eager disciple, waiting to be ordained as *sannyasi*, spent these days with fervent anticipation. Finally, the sacred day of 12th January dawned. He completed his daily chore of taking Baba's care. Shri Babaji said, "Tomorrow is your *diksha*. Observe fast today." He was thrilled to the core. To be in close proximity of one's God in every way – one's heart, speech and action – is the true way of fasting or sacrificing. Golwalkar, born of the pious lineage of the creator of sacred text, *Dharmasindhusar*, observed a fast on that day. Next day, 13th January, was the sacred day of *Makara Sankranti*, birthday of Swami Vivekananda and the first day of *Uttaraayan* that spells well-being of human kind. At the exact sacred moment – *mahurtam* – the disciple sat down in front of the Guru and was ordained as a *sannyasi* as per ancient religious tradition. In the words of the newly anointed *sannyasi*, Golwalkar, "For me, it was the greatest day, a day to be written in golden letters, because, great fortune accrued through ages with countless births, had finally smiled on me and I was the recipient of an indescribable bliss from the kind hands of *Gurudev*. Experience of that day is literally most sacred. Words fail to describe that sense of sanctity. I can never forget those moments. The look in the eyes of *Gurudev*, his affection, his overpowering presence; the way he kindly bestowed upon me that luminous joy – I think and hope I will never forget all this. Every atom of my body was tremulous. I experienced my transformation. I was no more the person I was a few moments earlier."[10]

Diksha he did receive, but he had to undergo extraordinary experiences for the next whole week. He writes on 18th January, "I experienced a kind of shock (*thaska*) for nearly three minutes in the afternoon. When I felt an unbearable pain during this time." On 19th January, he writes, "I have received shocks repeatedly since last evening. I am feeling a little uneasy. Why?"[11] Great sages tell us that a dedicated seeker has to go through such experiences many times. It is described as *asht sattvik bhava* – eight spiritual experiences. These are *Svedasthambhoti romanchah swarabhangothi vepathuh vaivarnamashrupralayah ityasttau satvika matah* – sweating, stiffening of the body, getting goosebumps, voice becoming hoarse, trembling, changing colour of the face, crying, falling unconscious – these are called eight *satvik bhavas*. Golwalkar's indescribable pain, uneasy feeling, experiencing shocks, etc. may be part of this process.

Shri Baba sat one day in a meditative mood after cleansing his face with warm water, as he usually did. Then, after dawn, he sat on a wheel chair, gifted by his two female disciples from America – named Annapurna and Bhakti – and took a tour of the Ashram campus. Raghuvir or Golwalkar used to push around this chair. That day, Golwalkar prepared and offered breakfast for him as usual. Shri Baba looked quite cheerful. As he looked at the face of his dear Gowalkar, he noticed that his hair had grown long during the past two-and-a-half months. He called him with great affection near him, asked him to sit down next to him and stroking his soft hair with his fingers, said, "These hair look beautiful on you. Remember, never cut them." This was not an order from the Guru, but his heart's wish that just flowed with noble affection from his mouth. The newly ordained disciple Gowalkar accepted this wish in a true sense – figuratively and literally. And till his death, his face carried this look.

13th February, 1937 was the last day of the birth centenary of Shri Ramakrishna Paramhamsa. Shri Baba's attention was fully focussed on the centenary celebrations as soon as *Makar Sankranti* got over. During the same time, his physical condition deteriorated further. This may be the reason why he started talking to his disciples in his evening sermons about surrendering to the Supreme God, to repay his worldly debts. On one of those days, he insisted on calling everybody around after evening *aarti* and told them, "Being in close contact with a *sadhu* is necessary. Is anything possible without the good company of a *sadhu*? Who is a *sadhu*? Only that person, who always thinks about Him, always depends on Him, egoless, pure and unselfish. *Naaham*, *naaham*, *Tu hee, tu hee…*' (Not me, not me, Thou art, thou art). Are we actually doing something? Everything is happening only with His wish. I am telling you the truth – I have experienced this at every step in my life. Without His kindness and wish, does anyone have the power to do anything? O Lord, *Naaham naaham*, *tu hee, tu hee*' – this is the magnificent sentence uttered by Thakur Ramakrishna Paramhamsa. You can attain supreme power by reciting this *mantra*."[12]

This magnificent eight-word sentence etched an everlasting impression in the deep recesses of Golwalkar's heart as he sat in those discourses, savouring each sentence with a highly focussed mind. This guiding philosophy of his life echoed again after 17 years like a bugle on the shores of Sindhu Saagar (Arabian Sea) in Mumbai. Renowned editor of weekly *Dharmayug*, Satyakam Vidyalankar had requested national-level leader to send him one sentence on what had guided their lives. Revered Guruji also received this message at Hedgewar Bhavan in Nagpur. The following grand noble sentence just poured out of his heart: "Not me, only thou." He sent it in his own handwriting to Satyakam Vidyalankar on 29th September, 1954.[13]

Shri Babaji went about his life's mission inspite of being very frail. Six young spiritual seekers had arrived at the Ashram on 22nd January from Manikganj. He bestowed *diksha* to all of them.[14] Two more devotees came from Behrampur on 31st. He offered *diksha* to them inspite of his trembling hands.[15] During this time, he suddenly called Golwalkar one day. Seating him beside himself, he spoke spontaneously, "May you have the best of everything, may you achieve self-realisation. This is my only prayer to my Guru Maharaj. I am passing on to you anything that may be good in me. May you be the recipient of any goodness that I may have and may all your poor qualities come unto me.

Do hand over your bad qualities to me. I do not wish to be happy, I yearn for unhappiness. I pray to God to give me unhappiness so that I never forget him. What is happiness? It is not good. Look, even our God has suffered so much pain. Shri Krishna could not drink his mother's milk even once upon his birth because he had to stay with cowherds, away from his mother. He grew up there, but he could not enjoy happiness even there. He was always under attack from evil forces. He suffered all that with forbearance. What are our pains compared to his? Therefore, I seek unhappiness. So, do pass on all your bad qualities to me and may all my goodness be yours. Go now. This is my blessing to you. Remember this every evening, always. Go, may good things always happen to you. What better blessing can there be other than this?"[16] Was this a transfer of power at spiritual plane? Who knows?

2nd February was the birthday of Narendra. Shri Baba was in an emotional trance that day. His health deteriorated rapidly on the next day. It was decided to move him to Kolkata on 6th February, which fell on a Saturday. He was put on a camp-bed to be taken to station to catch the train coming at 5 in the evening. The train arrived. He was transferred on to a berth in first class and Golwalkar was also asked to accompany him to attend to him. Raghuvir and Amitabh sat elsewhere. Vibhuti had been sent to Kolkata a day earlier to make proper arrangements in advance. Shri Baba lost his outer consciousness by the time the train had covered a distance of 10 kms and reached Bel Danga. He gained consciousness again after two hours near Shanaghat. His attendant Golwalkar got him to drink a glass of lemon juice while stroking his forehead gently. His eyes closed after a little while. He was taken down at 11 in the night at Sealdah station of Kolkata and brought to 'Udbodhan' office in an ambulance. He was not taken inside but taken directly to Belur Mutt from the main gate itself as advised by the doctors. Golwalkar briefed his senior brothers who waited anxiously. By this time, it was 2 in the night. On 7th, Sunday morning, doctors tried to give him oxygen, but nothing worked. Finally, Swami Akhandananda left for eternal bliss (*akhand anand*) in the afternoon at 3:07. The same night his physical body was cremated as per the Ashram's traditions.

Now what? Golwalkar wondered. Shri Ramakrishna's centenary's last programme was scheduled for 13th February, after six days. He took part in it as a duty. He, then, returned to Sargachhi, paid silent respects with a heavy heart in front of the respected chair of his revered Guru and picked up all his belongings from the storeroom. Golwalkar left for Nagpur, carrying with him the sacredness (*punya*) he had accumulated so far and the rare wealth he could collect. And, what was this wealth? It consisted of a life-size photograph of Shri Baba that carried the signature "Akhandananda", woolen sheet of *Gurudev*, sacred yellow fabric used for worship, two white towels carrying the impressions of right and left feet, two saffron handkerchiefs, a dress worn by Guruji, a teaspoon and his pocket watch. Apart from these items, there were four to five pieces of burnt bones and ashes recovered after cremation and 20-25 hair stands of Ramakrishna Paramhamsa.[17]

Golwalkar, an ordained *sannyasi* now, returned to Nagpur with these valuables.*

□

Endnotes

1. *Akhandanand ke Sannidhya Mein*, pp. 125
2. Ibid, pp. 123
3. Ibid, pp. 83
4. *Shri Guruji Samagra*, Vol. 6, pp. 274-275
5. *Akhandanand ke Sannidhya* Mein, pp. 123
6. *Shri Guruji Samagra*, Vol. 6, pp. 274-276
7. Ibid, pp. 275
8. *Akhandaanand ke Sannidhya Mein*, pp. 66
9. Ibid, pp. 72
10. *Shri Guruji Samagra*, Vol. 6, pp. 278-279
11. Ibid, pp. 279
12. *Swami Akhandananda* (biography), pp. 271
13. *Shri Guruji Samagra*, Vol. 7, pp. 202
14. *Akhandaanand ke Sannidhya Mein*, pp. 113
15. *Swami Akhandananda*, pp. 279
16. *Shri Guruji Samagra*, Vol. 6, pp. 279-280
17. *Vivekananda Kendra Patrika*, Vol. 35, No. 2, pp. 96-99

* These sacred objects are in the pooja room of Vasudev Golwalkar in Pune and this author has personally seen them.

15

In August Company of Dr. Hedgewar

There was a noticeable difference between the Golwalkar who had left for Sargachhi and the Golwalkar who returned from there. But this difference was not about change; it was about evolution, progression. Golwalkar definitely gained spiritually in Sargachhi, but Sargachhi was not just a uni-dimensional centre of spirituality. It was planned as a centre for serving the society. Fired by eagerness to serve, it was established by its founder to serve the people; for nothing is greater than service to mankind. Therefore, the seekers who stayed at the centre needed practical knowledge and skills to run it properly. It is possible that Golwalkar did not know of this dimension when he went to Sargachhi. In his words, "I shouldn't say this but I admit that I had gone there to think of God. He told me, 'Forget about God, first clean the utensils.' I cleaned the utensils with full sincerity. He, then, said, 'Now take up dusting and cleaning.' Then he ordered, 'Water the garden.' I never showed my disinterest in all these tasks. I did whatever I was asked to do. Then, he finally said, 'Ok, now think of God.'"[1] Thus, he learned the lesson of true *karma yoga* there. He had internalised it.

Golwalkar, a person dedicated to his goal, stayed in the company of four to five young dedicated, selfless people there. This group had people like foreigner Param Chaitanya, Vibhuti Chaitanya, etc. All of them were ordinary people embodied with the selfless spirit of *paropakararth midam shareeram*, i.e., 'this body is meant for helping others'. This spirit also had left a mark on the Golwalkar returned from Sargachhi. His personality was evolving from 'me' to 'we'.

All this while, founder of Rashtriya Swayamsevak Sangh, Dr. Hedgewar's eager eyes were waiting for Golwalkar to return. Since the time he came in touch with Golwalkar in 1932, he had high expectations from him. Just as Shri Ramakrishna had tested Narendra's mettle, Dr. Hedgewar had tested Guruji's mettle. It is said that sages who organise people have sharp observant eyes. Whenever Dr. Hedgewar met advocate Dattatreya Deshpande, he would ask, "When is your friend returning?" Finally, when he got the news that he had returned, he immediately re-established contact that had been broken since the past four to five months. Thus, Guruji's relations with Sangh Shakha were renewed. Now, he had no personal dreams. Anything that might have been his own had been annihilated in the sacrificial fire (*yagna*) of Sargachhi.

Madhu went to his Mama Raikar immediately after alighting at Nagpur. Seeing his nephew's bearded countenance and long hair, he felt a sense of respect rather than surprise. After getting acquainted with the latest situation in the family and freshening up, Madhu proceeded to Ramtek without further delay. He called out to his mother lying on the sick bed. Hearing her dear Madhu's voice, she got up as if she had received the elixir of life. Her eyes welled up. Said she, "So, you have returned? It is God's grace." When he enquired about her health, she said, "My dear, the reason for my ill health was nothing else but not being able to see you. Remember, you went away without informing me?" Those words carried within them her unhappiness, pain and compassion. Madhu felt guilty at hurting her. He said with a deep sense of regret, "Ma, I will never go anywhere without informing you from now onwards." It was not just a light assurance; it was a pledge of conduct for himself. Later, when Madhu became the Sarsanghchaalak and began his endless journeys, he would always tell his mother about his programme before he left for a tour. Madhu stayed in Ramtek till his mother recovered, both physically and emotionally. He then returned to Nagpur.

Doctorji began visiting Guruji regularly in Nagpur. He also began attending the Sangh Shakha regularly. He would visit the Dhantoli Ashram often. He never felt any mismatch in these activities. Not only this, he went ahead and translated Swami Vivekananda's globally renowned Chicago lectures in Marathi when staying at his Mama's home. It was like an emotional homage to the noble memories of Sargachhi and Belur. He submitted it to Swami Bhaskareshwaran and on the monthly *shraaddha* (religious ritual of paying respect to a departed person) of his Guru. The day was Monday, 8th March, 1937. Coincidentally, it was also his own birthday, i.e., *Vijaya Ekadashi*. The submission of this translation was his silent *Guru Dakshina* – respectful offering to a Guru to acknowledge his teachings.[2]

Swami Bhaskareshwaranand published it in February 1938. The book was titled, *Chicago Parishadeteel Swami Vivekanandanchi Vyakhyaney*. In his preface, Swamiji wrote, "This translation clearly illustrates that the translator has identified himself absolutely with the inherent emotions of the words of that great personality."[3]

Howsoever short a period it might have been, but we sense a phase of literary creativity in Golwalkar's life. During this phase he translated in English the letter written in Persian by Shivaji to Raja Jaisingh of Rajasthan. Later, he translated *Rashtra Mimamsa* in English. It was a book written in Marathi by Babarao Savarkar, elder brother of great revolutionary Vinayak Damodar Savarkar. During those risky days, Babarao misplaced that translation. The 32-year-old Golwalkar had been highly impressed with that book. So, he wrote a book that was like a sequel to this particular book. It was titled *We or Our Nationhood Defined*. Preface to this 67-page booklet was written by a top-ranking Congress leader of Central Province, M.S. Aney. Aney expressed his differing opinion clearly in this preface. At the same time, he also appreciated sincerity and honesty of the author. He wrote, "This creation is a scientific exposition about nationalism. But, I would like to say that the strong vituperative language used by the writer against those with whom he doesn't agree, crosses the fine line of civility."[4] ".....this book is, perhaps, a necessary and much-desired response against the 'blank cheque' mentality of Mahatma Gandhi and people like him."[5] This view of the author in this preface is bolstered by the words of dedication written by the author, "To the memory of those noble martyrs who, despite ignominy, calumny and contempt at the hands of their own undeserving brethren, have kept the flame of true nationality burning in our land."[6] It is worth acknowledging and complimenting the honesty of both the leader and writer of the preface Aney, who wrote critically and the young author Golwalkar, who unhesitatingly incorporated it in its entirety in the book.*

We find that this young writer lost interest in creating literature in the later period. Today, he is not remembered as a writer.

Guruji once said with a tinge of pride, albeit in a lighter vein, "Doctor Saheb caught me like a cat catches a mouse when he accosted me on the road and introduced himself." In a sense, this observation was right, because he had come in closer contact with Doctorji after returning from Sargachhi. Doctorji began focussing more attention on him. Doctorji had developed a short term *vistaarak* plan in 1938 to spread Sangh work in *tehsils* around Nagpur. He included Guruji also in this plan. There was a possibility of more students joining the Sangh Shiksha Varg (Officers' Training Camp). It was not just this anticipation; students from states like Karnataka, Bengal, Bihar, Uttar Pradesh and Punjab were also expected to join the camp. Thus, the training camp of 1938 was going to be a multi-state, multi-lingual camp. It was necessary to have an officer-in-charge (*sarvaadhikari*) of the camp, so that he would mingle easily with people and who would ideally be a polyglot. Doctorji had his eyes on Guruji. He knew Hindi, English and Bengali apart from Marathi. He had experience of staying with students in a hostel. He had also experienced *ashram* life that inculcated the right *samskaaras*. Doctorji concluded that he was the right person for the post and he was appointed to this important post accordingly. The camp used to be conducted for 40 days during those times and Guruji stayed full time at the camp for 40 days,

---

* It would be ideal to note here that in the changed post-independence scenario, Guruji himself had said, "Forget 'We'. It is outdated now." (*Sangh, Beej se Vriksha*, pp. 108, Devendra Swaroop)

discharging his duties. The camp became his universe for those 40 days. He got a detailed introduction from each participant. His phenomenal memory was also a great help. He used to address each student by name like the head of a family. In every way, the camp's environment bristled with a sense of idealism and dedication. The Sangh founder's heart felt a great sense of fulfilment on seeing the atmosphere at the camp.

The Nagpur camp got over in June; Lahore camp was to follow it immediately. Since summer vacations in the north-west region used to be in July-August, the camp at Lahore was to take place in August. This was the first camp in north Bharat; and the head of the organisation, the highly revered Doctorji was naturally expected to be present in this camp. Inspite of his ill-health, Doctorji left for Lahore with Babasaheb Apte and Guruji on 15th August. All the three travelled by third class. They broke journey at Kashi and stayed there from 17th to 20th August. Guruji gave a lecture at the town-level meeting of Sangh Shakha on directions of Doctorji. Second programme, which was in the form of a question-and-answer session, was held in the university. It was also conducted by Guruji. Both these programmes in Kashi were in Hindi. Therefore, the senior workers had organised a third programme for non-Hindi-speaking students. Guruji spoke in that programme in English. 19th August happened to be the auspicious day of Krishna Janmashtami. Students of Varanasi Sanskrit College had decided to hold a festive meeting on the day. All the three 'special guests from Nagpur' attended this programme on invitation. Apte ji and Guruji addressed this gathering. When Guruji reached Nagpur after concluding his Lahore tour, he shared his experience of this Janmashtami programme in a humorous vein. He said, "…I had to speak unexpectedly at the Shri Krishna *Utsav*. The principal was thrilled to see my long hair and beard and thought that he would receive a good deal of information on *dharma*. I spoke for about 15 minutes. The theme of my lecture was "'We are not 'Brahmins', but 'Chaandaals'. Because our religious texts tell us that a person becomes a Chaandaal upon staying in the homes of a 'malechh' (foreigner) for three days. And, that we should follow the *dharma* of Kshatriyas.'"[7]

They reached Lahore from Kashi via Delhi on 22nd August. The lecture of the Sangh founder took place on 3rd August, followed by a lecture by Guruji on 24th. It was the turn of Doctorji again on 25th, but, he could not speak because of fever. So, Guruji spoke as a substitute.

The brethren from Maharashtra, staying in Lahore, had established Maharashtra Mandal there. When they found that the Hindu leader Dr. Hedgewar was coming from Maharashtra, they met the local Prachaarak Rajabhau Paturkar and requested him to ask Doctorji to speak in front of their members. A programme was fixed accordingly for 28th August, but, Doctorji could not attend this programme because of fever. Doctorji, again, sent Guruji. Guruji spoke on the subject 'Individual and Society'. Office-bearers of the *mandal* met Doctorji after the programme and were full of praise for Guruji's speech. They thanked Doctorji, specially for sending the right person for the programme.

Doctorji's backache worsened during the Lahore camp. So, he had to discontinue his programme and return to Nagpur via Delhi in September. He got sufficient time during that 20-day-long tour to observe Guruji from close quarters and also mould him to some extent. The founder of the Sangh was conscious that the fire that spewed forth in his speech was the result of the vigour of his young age and aggressive commitment to the cause. He realised that this fiery nature was not a desirable trait for somebody who wishes to organise people. Therefore, like a great Ayurveda physician, he uprooted this disease from within the patient without even talking about it with him. Guruji was also an intelligent person, so it is difficult to say that he could not understand this situation. This becomes clear what he spoke on 6th September at the Nagpur Shakha while sharing his experiences about the tour. He said, "One thing that has made its mark on my psyche is that it is necessary to have a balanced mind if one wishes to organise and bring people together. Doctorji has the skill to perceive someone's thoughts, putting it together in a sentence to convince him and weave together diverse opinions of people into a unified thread to end their antagonism. We cannot find this skill in people like us. Therefore, we should always keep the ideal example of the revered Sarsanghchaalak before us."[8]

Doctorji's scheduled programme was to visit Gujarat, Mumbai, Pune, Sangli, etc. to observe the growth of Sangh and guide swayamsevaks in these places to finally return back to the Centre in the last week of September. So, he had written a letter to Abaji Hedgewar from the Lahore camp in the last week of August. The subject was preparation for the arrival of the Vijayadashami festival. He had written, "Doctor Sir Gokul Chand Narang is a highly respected and well-established, knowledgeable gentleman who takes pride in Hindutva and likes the Sangh. He has agreed to preside over the Vijayadashami function this year. If this programme creates the desired impression on him and brings him nearer to the Sangh, the state of Punjab will see the Sangh everywhere. He has great influence in Punjab. He is very popular in various groups of Hindus. By motivating him, the Sangh will grow very easily and rapidly in Punjab on a strong foundation. The central committee has a major responsibility in celebrating this Vijayadashami *utsav* (festival) with pomp and vigour this year… please read this part of this letter out to other senior workers and capable swayamsevaks and enthuse them to put all their energy and time in recruitment and training."[9] Arrival of this letter written on 31st August and of Doctorji after abandoning his programme –both these incidents may have occurred around the same time. Still, relevance of this letter is important in the way views were expounded. Doctorji had written in a very similar way to the senior colleagues in Nagpur six years back. The only difference was that Guruji was the expected Chief Guest then and now the awaited person was Dr. Gokul Chand Narang. Apart from this, the tone, tenor and flow of the letters were the same. Yes, there is another small difference. The former carried the signature 'K.B. Hedgewar' while the latter had the signature of M.S. Golwalkar.

Dr. Hedgewar became busier after Vijayadashami. His health, too, was going downhill. There was some relief in January 1939. He organised a special meeting immediately in mid-February at Sindi near Nagpur. This meeting is considered a milestone in the history of Rashtriya Swayamsevak Sangh. This was a 10-day *chintan* or brainstorming workshop. This was necessary from the organisational point of view. A young Sangh had turned into a pan-Indian organisation over the last 18 years. It was essential to review and improve its organisational structure and working methodology. The founder of the Sangh had called for this meeting with this objective in mind. The people invited for this meeting did not fall into any particular category by way of experience, organisational responsibility and years with the organisation. Attendees included Doctorji's colleagues Appaji Joshi, Nanasaheb Talatule, while the younger generation was represented by Balasaheb Deoras, Tatyarao Telang, Vitthalrao Patki, Babaji Salodkar, Krishnarao Moharir, and a comparative newcomer, Madhavrao Golwalkar. Discussions went on for eight hours daily for 10 days. In-depth discussions encompassed the Sangh's systems, methodology, orders, oath, prayer, hierarchical structure, official festivals of the Sangh, etc. After thorough all-round discussions, the final responsibility for taking decisions on any subject used to be left to Doctorji. The current Sanskrit prayer, orders in Sanskrit, state-wise organisational structure, regular management systems for Sangh Shiksha Varg, etc. are all an outcome of this historic meeting. All the participants noticed Guruji's highly analytical intellect, logical approach, sharp focus, strong ideological clarity. At the same time, his *sattvik* or spiritual nature in taking a detached view once a decision was left to Doctorji and move on to the next subject was also well received. During an informal discussion in private with Appaji Joshi, Doctorji asked him, "Appaji, if we were to nominate Madhavrao Golwalkar as the next Sarsanghchaalak?" Appaji Joshi responded immediately with one word, "Excellent." This incident has been described in one of the articles in Appaji Joshi's memoirs. This means that another achievement of Sindi meeting in February 1939 was that Doctorji had scrutinised Guruji fully well. In the words of Yadavrao ji Joshi, "Keshav had perceived Madhav."

Guruji and Vitthalrao Patki went to Kolkata to begin the Sangh work there on directions from Doctorji on returning to Nagpur from Sindi. Both of them stayed in Room No. 1/1 in Sarkari Gali of Simulia area near Swami Vivekananda's home. They founded the Sangh Shakha in Maniktola on the 22nd of the same month, i.e., on the auspicious day of *Varsh Pratipada* (*Gudi Padwa*). They stayed there till the end of April. Guruji then returned to Nagpur on instructions of Doctorji to take charge of Sangh Shiksha Varg of that year as its sarvaadhikari. While going to Kolkata, *vyavasthaa pramukh* (person in-charge of finances) Krishnarao Moharir had given him 20 rupees. Guruji handed over the balance of 3 paise to him while submitting the expense account to him on return.

The 40-day camp was over in the month of June. A memorable programme after this was the release of a film, '*Bhagwa Jhenda*' in Minerva Theatre. The invited honorary guest for this inauguration was Doctorji. He took along Guruji with him. Dadasaheb Torane was the producer of this film. Idealistic Dadasaheb wished that a film that depicted the great organising skills of Shivaji's guru Samarth Ramdas of bringing people together should be released at the hands of Dr. Hedgewar, whom he considered a great organiser of people in the modern times. A photograph taken at that time in Saraswati Photo Studio turned out to be a historic one, because it is the only photograph that has Doctorji and Guruji in the same frame.

Doctorji appreciated Guruji's Hindi during a meeting with Sangh workers on this stay in Pune and also asked him to narrate two stories in Hindi. There was a get-together of Sangh swayamsevaks and well-wishers one day in Tilak Smarak Mandir. Doctorji had told the office-bearers that Guruji would speak before him. So, Guruji spoke first. People were surprised to hear the subject of his talk, which was 'Sarsanghchaalak'. People were thrilled by the way Guruji analysed Doctorji from that point of view. As a person with deep knowledge of science of organisation, Doctorji's purpose behind this talk was clear. He wished that workers of a potential high-growth Shakha like Pune should see the sterling qualities of a rising senior worker like Guruji and understand him. This process was critically important in an organisation like the Sangh.

Senior workers of the Sangh in Nagpur were anxious about the rapidly deteriorating health of Doctorji. Even the weather in Nagpur was unbearably hot. Giving due regard to feelings of the workers, Babasaheb Ghatate pressurised Doctorji to accompany him to Deolali and rest there for four to five weeks. Taking advantage of his relationship, Doctorji was able to cut down this recuperation period before he agreed to this proposal. Make-shift arrangements were made in 'Jay Villa' at Deolali. Plan was to take rest for two weeks, but Doctorji fell prey to double pneumonia there. He had to stay there for nearly a month. Guruji took up the nursing responsibility again. He must have recalled nursing Babaji. He served him with full dedication. But, it must be said that Guruji himself was also cured in a way during this nursing. Where was the chance of not listening to the mutterings of the patient in his semi-conscious state? He never heard a word from Doctorji that deviated from the flow of his emotions. There was only one passionate emotion that flowed through his thinking – it was about the nation and his organisation. Pieces of thoughts about Shakha, Swayamsevak, future plans, pain at increasing growth, eagerness to take part in programmes, plans for independence, etc. would rise and fall like waves. This attendant would listen to them very carefully. He observed and understood that there was not an iota of selfish interest in any of these utterances. Here was a live example of ruthlessly egoless existence. He experienced a real-life example of a '*naaham tuhi, naaham tuhi*'. This was the steadfast loyalty to a cause that runs through inner and outer core of a person – a searing amber that burns through a body and soul. This condition of a goal-driven unconscious patient was more soul awakening than the conscious state of that person. Just as Doctorji had understood Guruji in Sindi, Guruji discerned and understood Doctorji in Deolali. Here, in Deolali, Madhav had perceived Keshav.

Doctorji returned to Nagpur on 6th August after recovering from his sickness in Deolali. Nagpur Shakha's Raksha Bandhan festival (*utsav*) and concluding programme of *gurudakshina utsav* were held on 13th August, Tuesday. Doctorji made two announcements on that day. One was declaration of Babasaheb Ghatate as the Sanghchaalak of Nagpur city; the second was appointment of Madhavrao Golwalkar as the respected Sarkaryavaah (General Secretary) of Rashtriya Swayamsevak Sangh. Guruji bowed before the retiring general secretary, Appaji Joshi and touched his feet immediately at the end of the programme. The response of the swayamsevaks participating in the programme was natural; not as if this change of guard was a revolutionary change for the Sangh. The atmosphere was full of camaraderie and joy.

The Sarkaryavaah's first tour programme was to begin in Punjab. Sangh Shiksha Varg for northern states had commenced in the first week of August at Lahore. Nearly 150 participants had come from nearly thirty places. Sarkaryavaah had stayed in the camp for one week. He gathered information about each participant during introductions (*parichay* in Sangh terminology) as was his nature. He offered knowledge about the fundamental principles of the Sangh to the participants of the camp through three lectures during his stay. He also disseminated critical knowledge about the science of organisation during discussions and meetings. His view was, "An individual cannot carry out all the work related to organisation. If there were to be even a germ of negative feelings about our colleague, it will prove harmful for the organisation and the nation. If we cannot co-operate with each other, then it will be difficult to claim that we have learnt even the primary lesson about organising people."[10]

Talking about Doctorji, who couldn't be present in the camp, he said, "The science of organisation is manifest before us in the form of Doctorji. You can see the complete science of organisation in his person. Just as we can learn how to live a life with ethical values when we study the life of Lord Rama, we can understand how to organise people and what is the science of organisation when we study the life of the founder of the Sangh."[11]

In his last lecture in the camp, he told the students, "The means of organising for us is the daily Shakha. Our duty is to bring together more and more Hindus everyday and imbibe an urge to get organised. You are returning from here after learning about the Sangh and going out as a worker now; that is, you are expanding your area of work. Work hard to bring our goal nearer at the earliest."[12]

Guruji returned from Lahore and at the time, the Second World War had begun in Europe on 1st September. Its ripple effect was also felt in the imperialist atmosphere prevailing in Bharat in those days. There was also a strong resonance of national and political thoughts in our country. Analysing the scenario, Doctorji asked all his colleagues and senior workers to accelerate Sangh work with full effort. So, Babasaheb Apte, Guruji and Dadarao Paramarth went about their endless tours tirelessly, but Doctorji himself couldn't accompany them. His complicated health turned more complex. He had to agree to the affectionate insistence of his colleagues to visit *Saptarishi Kund* that has seven hot water springs, to soak his body thoroughly in those springs. He left Nagpur with Appaji and a few other friends on 31st January, 1940, Wednesday and returned back after two-and-a-half months on 20th April. His health had improved a little by then. He was satisfied to find that the Sangh work had grown well even in his absence.

Time for Sangh Shiksha Varg, that used to take place in May every year, was also coming closer. Decisions taken in the Sindi brainstorming workshop in 1939 were to be implemented from this camp. It was important to prepare well for putting new Sanskrit orders and new prayer in Sanskrit in place. Guruji, as Sarkaryavaah, began preparations in April itself. For example, he wrote to the Prachaarak, Yadavrao Joshi, on 22nd April, 1949, "Revered Doctorji has returned from Rajgir two days back. We have to release our new Sanskrit prayer beginning with this Sangh Shiksha Varg. Responsibility of reciting this prayer is upon you. I am sending the written prayer to you. Please memorise it well. You should prepare to sing it well with full rhythm."[13]

From the time the first Pune Sangh Shiksha Varg took place, highly revered Sarsanghchaalak used to stay there for fifteen days. It had become a customary practice. So, Doctorji stayed in Pune camp from 27th April to 15th May. The commendable aspect of this camp was that it had the highest member of participants compared to all previous camps. More than 800 participating students from 120 places all over Maharashtra were present in it. State-level meeting of Maharashtra team was organised on 11th and 12th May to take advantage of his presence. Sarkaryavaah Guruji had also arrived to participate in it. The report collated at the time shows that there were 250 Shakhas with a total attendance of 18,000 volunteers. Eastern Maharashtra was a separate state named Vidarbha at that time. The founder of Sangh presented a target for the workers in this meeting, "We should expand our work to the extent of three per cent of the population in cities and one per cent of the population in villages."[14] Next day, Guruji addressed the state-level workers thus, ".....Our work today hasn't reached a stage that we should be satisfied. A tendency to feel satisfied and happy can be fatal to the growth of organisation. It is nurtured only with a sense of dissatisfaction. Therefore, we should never feel satisfied with our work."[15] Guruji returned to Nagpur after this meeting on 4th while Doctorji returned on 15th May.

People were waiting eagerly for the arrival of Sarsanghchaalak on 16th May in the Nagpur Sangh Shiksha Varg. So, Guruji was there at Nagpur station with a garland to welcome him. Bihar Krishnavallabh Prasad Narayansingh alias Babuaji alighted just behind Doctorji. On seeing the garland, Doctorji introduced Babua ji immediately and said, "He is our Chief Guest." Guruji got the message and offered the garland to Babua ji. Doctorji's face lit up with pleasure.

The story at Nagpur was similar to Pune's. They had also crossed all previous records. It was, literally, an all-India camp. It had representation from the Himalayas to Indian Ocean. The participating students numbered 1,400, but they were not blessed with the good fortune that the Pune camp was. Doctorji fell sick again upon reaching Nagpur. He could not stay even for one night in the camp. His health turned critical as days passed. The public function of the camp was scheduled on 8th June. It was impossible for him to participate in it. He could be present at the valedictory function the next morning only through sheer will power. His words of deep fulfilment were, "I see before my eyes today a miniature form of entire Bharat." The entire participant community of the camp was thrilled to hear these words. Actually, it was the declaration of a dream having taken concrete shape. It was also the swan song of an austere monk who had led a deeply dedicated life.

It was 7 in the morning on 20th June. Doctors came to do medical check-up of Doctorji. They were of the opinion that his health had turned worse. Dr. Sharma suggested removal of liquid from his spine. Doctorji understood the nature of his problem when he heard about the suggested line of treatment. He was sure that he had been left with only a few moments of his life. Calling doctors nearer, he said, "I need a little time before you carry out any procedure." He seemed to be lost in deep thought. He called Guruji urgently to his room and told him in front of all the people present in the room, "Time has now come to carry out lumbar puncture. If I am saved, it would be fine, otherwise, please take over the whole responsibility of Sangh work. Guruji exclaimed in deep grief, "Doctorji, what are you saying? You will be alright very soon." Doctorji smiled on hearing these words and said, "That is alright, but do remember what I have told you."[16]

Another day. At 9.27 a.m. on 21st June, Friday, the world saw the physical existence of Doctorji come to an end, but he had appointed his successor before this happened.

□

Endnotes

1. *Shri Guruji Samagra*, Vol. 2, pp. 200
2. *Aarti Alok Ki*, pp. 55

3. *Maa. Sa. Golwalkar*, pp. 53
4. *We or Our Nationhood Defined*, pp. viii
5. Ibid, pp. 5
6. Ibid, pp. Dedication
7. *Dr. Hedgewar*, pp. 350
8. Ibid, pp. 352-353
9. *Shri Guruji Samagra*, Vol. 8, pp. 5
10. *Shri Guruji Samagra*, Vol. 4, pp. 9
11. Ibid, pp. 11
12. Ibid, pp. 15-16
13. *Shri Guruji Samagra*, Vol. 8, pp. 6
14. *Dr. Hedgewar*, pp. 412
15. Ibid, pp. 411
16. Ibid, pp. 425-426

16

The Second Sarsanghchaalak

It is said that words spoken at deathbed spread very fast. Thus, the words spoken by Doctorji on 20th June in his room in the presence of Krishnarao Moharir and Yadavrao Joshi were conveyed to the core team members. From there, the news spread rapidly that Madhavrao Golwalkar is the new Sarsanghchaalak. Official pronouncement had not been made so far, but people who understood the Sangh work didn't find it abnormal. Highly revered Doctorji's wish itself was enough, irrespective of any official announcement being made or not. In the following days, while recalling that propitious moment, Yadavrao Joshi had commented, "At that moment, I perceived Keshav in Madhav." This was the very emotion that the brethren brought up on Sangh culture went through. But, it is important in public life to give due consideration to views of people outside the organisation. Thus, respected Sanghchaalaks came together as required by Sangh's code of conduct and social norms. This group had also come together nearly a decade back on 10th November, 1929 to declare the founder of the Sangh, Dr. Hedgewar, as the Sarsanghchaalak. It was decided to follow the same process again. A meeting was convened on 30th July in Akola. Among those present were Nagpur Sanghchaalak Babasaheb Ghatate, Vardha district Sanghchaalak Appaji Joshi, Vidarbh state Sanghchaalak Bapusaheb Sohoni, Maharashtra state Sanghchaalak Kashinath Limaye and others. The information confirmed by Yadavrao Joshi and Krishnarao Moharir, who were present during the meeting, tells us that everybody accepted the last wish of the late Sarsanghchaalak solemnly without any discussions. It was decided that a formal declaration about the newly appointed Sarsanghchaalak would be made in the meeting to be held at the time of the religious rituals related to the 13th day of the death on July 3 and the special public meeting scheduled for the month-end *shraaddha* (memoriam) day on 21st July.

Guruji was very busy during those days. He had to acknowledge countless condolence messages. Like in any family, he also had to inform people who had strong bonds of affection with the Sangh and Doctorji, in writing. As the General Secretary (Sarkaryavaah), these responsibilities fell on his shoulders.

He discharged his duty in an exemplary manner. He wrote to each addressee according to his standing in the organisation, society, relationship and place that person belonged to. He wrote to hundreds of brethren spread from Chennai to Lahore. A point worth noting is that in none of the letters did he use the words like 'a void that cannot be filled'. Rather, these letters had a spirit of self-dedication, urge for even more co-operation from the swayamsevaks and well-wishers than received so far and a firm commitment to realise the dream of the departed soul. For example, he wrote to Vinayakrao Apte in Pune on 27th June, "Growth of this Sangh work of revered Doctorji will be the eternal memorial to him. Now this is the only job that is left to be done...What could not be achieved while he was alive, we have to take that living work of his to its successful conclusion; to make it a success with strength of our action and sacrifice in his sacred memory... please motivate everybody to jump into the field of action with competitive spirit and enthusiasm."[1]

Guruji sent an advisory note to all the Shakhas on 24th June, on the fourth day after the demise of Doctorji. The first paragraph contained information about Doctorji's death, the second paragraph had the condolence message and the third contained instructions from the organisational point of view. He notified the recipients, "The thirteenth day of the death of Doctorji falls on 3rd July. It should be celebrated in all the Shakhas. All the swayamsevaks should be brought together on the Shakha ground in the evening; flowers should be offered to the *dhwaj* (flag) and picture of highly revered Doctorji, followed by talks with pride about his qualities. Plans for an overview of the national organisation created by him and ways of strengthening it through talks by responsible senior workers should be made. Then, there should be prayer and salutation to the flag. Finally, the programme is to be concluded with the order – Sarsanghchaalak *pranaam* 1-2-3."[2] It is important to make a note here that the order to be given on the Sangh ground on that day was to be 'Sarsanghchaalak *pranaam*' and not '*Adya* (first) Sarsanghchaalak *pranaam*'. It was a clear-headed view of Guruji that using the term '*Adya* Sarsanghchaalak' would be improper till there was a formal decision by senior office-bearers about the new Sarsanghchaalak. We should understand the importance of the meeting to be held at Akola six days after this in this context.

There was a large gathering (*saanghik*) on 3rd July, Wednesday at 6 in the evening at Reshim Bagh. The flag was hoisted right opposite the place of cremation. A well-decorated picture of Doctorji, prepared for the day, was kept at an appropriate designated place. More than 3,000 swayamsevaks in uniform stood in military-like formation. The group playing the band stood in a specially designated area. A large gathering that was present at the right time took up the specified spot and pointed to the immense popularity that departed soul enjoyed. Dignitaries present on the simple neat stage were Sanghchaalak of Nagpur, Babasaheb Ghatate, Vidarbha state Sanghchaalak Babasaheb Padhye, elderly paternal uncle of Doctorji – Abasaheb Hedgewar and Guruji. Sarsanghchaalak *pranaam* was not offered at the end of the programme as directed in the earlier notification. It was offered at the beginning of the programme with a musical tribute from the band. Other activities followed after this. The first speech was made by respected Padhye ji. Telling people, he said, "Our supreme duty is to fulfil the unfulfilled ambition of Doctorji." He then added, "Doctorji had taken care to make complete arrangements in every aspect for future work before he left this world due to his concern for the Sangh. Being an organisation that believes in following one leader (*ek chaalakanuvartitva*), we in Rashtriya Swayamsevak Sangh accept his every wish whole-heartedly without any reservation. Just a day before his death on 20th June, Doctorji had passed on the entire responsibility of Sangh to most revered Madhavrao Golwalkar. As the first Sarsanghchaalak, he had handed over all his rights to highly revered Madhavrao. Thus, I declare today that highly revered Madhavrao ji Golwalkar has become the Sarsanghchaalak as per the last wishes of our first Sarsanghchaalak. For us, he has taken the place of Doctorji. I offer my first salutation (*pranaam*) to the new Sarsanghchaalak."

Immediately, after this declaration, respected Abaji Hedgewar offered his words of blessings, "Doctorji has set before you an ideal for work. He has also given you thousands of colleagues. So, get down to work and do not grieve about his departure. Please note that our Doctorji hasn't left us. Today, we can see him in the person of Madhavrao ji Golwalkar. We should respect his orders as orders from Doctorji. That's all I would like to say in the end."[3]

There was no clapping after the two speeches. There was no sloganeering. Now was the time for the first address of the newly appointed Sarsanghchaalak. Swayamsevaks were all ears to hear him. Words that came out of his mouth were, "Highly revered Doctorji has handed over a responsibility that is huge beyond imagination. But, this is the throne of Vikramaditya. Even a shepherd's boy sitting on it is going to dispense proper justice. An average person like me has the opportunity to sit on this throne. But, Doctorji will make it possible for me to speak what is right. There is no doubt that due to the pious deeds of this noble leader, I would do what is right. If there were to be any mistakes, then I would be guilty."

"Now, let us move ahead with our work with absolute devotion. Let us take forward Sangh work with the same loyalty as before but with double the enthusiasm and more momentum. Doctorji had departed bequeathing this wonderful organisation. Now, many preachers are likely to come forward to sermonise us, but I would like to tell all such preachers with all humility and very clearly that our Doctorji has not left for us a soft pulpy organisation that may get lost in the chaos of different views and ideologies; our organisation is an invincible fort. People trying to peck at its embankments will only end up breaking their beaks. So strong and unyielding is the fortification that Doctorji has built. He has set the clear path for us and we have firmly resolved to move ahead on his path. Herein lies the ultimate welfare of this nation and Hindus are going to attain the blissful days of great prosperity of yesteryears through this path. Let us be steadfast on this path without bothering about any kind of opposition and without getting stuck in the whirlpool of differences. We shall achieve the desired results from this work of Doctorji through co-operation of all our friends and brethren."[4] Thus, he expressed the wondrous greatness of Doctorji in a few eloquent words.

The monthly *shraaddh* arrived after another eighteen days. The programme that stood out in these celebrations was the military salute offered by thousands of swayamsevaks to the first Sarsanghchaalak. There is a small history behind it. There were two points of opinion over Doctorji's death. Senior office-bearers of physical and military training department like Anna Sohoni and Martandrao Jog were of the opinion that the last rites of the supreme leader of an organisation like Sangh should be given military honours. Leaders like Appaji Joshi, Babasaheb Padhye felt that the funeral ceremony should be conducted in a traditional manner. The final decision was left to Guruji and his decision was in favour of conducting normal traditional funeral. While giving his decision, Guruji said, "Ultimately, Sangh is a big family, not a limited militarist organisation. For us, Doctorji is the head of this family and like a father." Therefore, the last rites were conducted in a traditional manner. But, in the huge public meeting that day, it was important to display the distinguishing character of the Sangh so that the spirit of virility and unity was aroused in the society. Therefore, the programme on 21st July saw an exhibition of physical drills from the swayamsevaks.

For nearly a month after the demise of the Sangh founder, there had been a feeling of uncertainty, specially in Maharashtra. Conflicting reports floated around. The theory behind these rumours could be understood from the views expressed by the 19th century philosopher, Schopenhauer. According to him, "Any truth passes through three phases – first is of ridicule, second is of opposition and third is of acceptance." The Sangh had entered the second phase in 1940.

The new Sarsanghchaalak's speech on the occasion of the first *shraaddh* was conducted in such an environment. He began in the calm voice of a young *yogi*, "I ascended to this post due to the highly revered Doctorji's wish and order. Whatever has been said so far about me, I believe, is the result of the pious deeds of Doctorji. The organisation of Rashtriya Swayamsevak Sangh is immortal. Though the founder and first Sarsanghchaalak of this organisation has left this world, this organisation will keep growing... Some people had alleged that we swayamsevaks idolise worship of an individual. We are not saddened at this allegation. But, isn't it the fact that all the swayamsevaks are working as before which shows that Doctorji has taught us not to be blind followers?...

"...People have been asking various questions about our organisation. People even raise questions about the direction that Sangh will take in future. Actually, the goal and work of Sangh are clearly defined. The vision of Sangh is steadfast and there is no reason for us to deviate in future…

"…What will happen to the Sangh after Doctorji? Such doubts rise in many hearts. The truth is that there is no reason for such questions to arise. There is no doubt at all that the Sangh will always march forward on its well-defined course bravely, overcoming all types of hazards and without bothering about them. Find its way in every adverse situation... Our strength will keep rising, crossing all hurdles and one day it will spread throughout this entire nation."[5]

Madhavrao completed his speech – his first public speech –enlightening the hearts of the common people, swayamsevak brethren, critics and supporters alike. This is how Madhavrao Golwalkar became the second Sarsanghchaalak of the Rashtriya Swayamsevak Sangh.

□

Endnotes

1. *Shri Guruji Samagra*, Vol. 8, pp. 8-9
2. Ibid, pp. 7-8
3. *Maa. Sa. Golwalkar*, pp. 75
4. *Shri Guruji Samagra*, Vol. 1, pp. 5-6
5. Ibid, pp. 7-8

17

Unending Circumambulation

"Each swayamsevak joins the Sangh only after taking oath to surrender his all for the nation. Because of the importance of the post I hold, I am obliged to own much higher moral responsibility. I remember this well. I am fully charged to take up this duty."[1] Speaking thus in front of a large number of people standing on the grounds where Doctorji's last rites were conducted, he organised his life to transform these respectful sentiments of devotion expressed by him into a plan of action that would take his life into a phase of total action. The transformation of any age (*yuga*) lies within us, says a Sanskrit *mantra*. While we sleep, it is *Kaliyuga*, when we are awake, it is *dwaapar*; when we stand up, it is *Tretaa*; and when we begin walking the age of action, *Kritayuga,* is created. Keeping this in mind, he resolved in his heart that it will be *Kritayuga* for him. With such a goal, he circumambulated Bharat 60 times in 33 years – non-stop, continuously, untiringly, without break or rest, from the Himalayas to the Indian Ocean.

Guruji once had said, "The train is my home." But, during this unending travel, his stay used to be of four types. One, the train bogey as he had said; second, the Sangh camps as he always stayed with the swayamsevaks in camps; third, stay with Sangh workers, sympathisers or office-bearers and fourth, in the Nagpur Central Office of the Sangh, Hedgewar Bhavan. These journeys throughout his life can only be termed as 'on-the-move' austere practices of an ascetic. Not only this, he never stayed in a hotel or a *dharamshala*. The credit for this practice also goes to the organisation. Actually, this culture of staying with families began with the founder of the Sangh. Guruji converted this into an arrangement and a part of the Sangh's system of working. This arrangement is still prevalent in the Sangh.

When we think about Guruji's journeys, we shall have to go back six to seven decades. Air travel was not as common as it is today. The Railway bogeys used to have first, second and inter-classes apart from the third class, but, reservations were available only for the first class. There was no reservation apart from this; there was no facility of air-conditioning in the country so we can't imagine it in the Railways. Five decades back we only had coal-fired engines and a person alighting from a train after a long journey looked virtually like a demon (*kaal bhairav*). Then came the diesel engine and people had to, compulsorily, end up smoking. Guruji used to travel with a companion during those days. Arrangements for snacks and food on the way used to be made from swayamsevaks' homes. Nagpur office or assistant of Guruji never used to send 'menu cards' to the swayamsevaks. The swayamsevaks were informed well in advance about the train, date, class of travel, etc. The swayamsevaks and their families would arrive with enthusiasm at each station to have the privilege of meeting him and have the joy of offering him home-made food. The food could be cooked in coconut, groundnut, cumin seeds or mustard oil as per that region's culture. Guruji used to take this food happily, saying, "*Annam Brahma*". He never depended on the station canteens.

Earlier we had mentioned about Guruji saying, "Train is my home." This was not a light-hearted comment. He used to take all the necessary precautions during a journey. On one occasion, he reached Vijaywada from Vishakhapatnam. He had to change trains to go to Chennai. So, the travelling group went and sat down in the Chennai-bound train straight away. It was morning time. Prant Prachaarak Bapurao Moghe informed him that the train toilet was free for use. Guruji didn't get up to use it. He asked Moghe, "Haven't you read the notice inside the toilet? It says, avoid using the toilet in a stationary train." Both Guruji and Moghe ji just sat waiting. Only after the train had left the platform did Guruji get up to complete his morning ablutions. Similarly, he would take care to get all the switches in the train switched off while alighting from the train. He would never leave behind even a scrap of litter in the bogey. He treated the train bogey just like his home.

Journeys became a part of his life. He had used all the means of transport – from the airplane to the bullock cart, only exception was the rickshaw. He would never get on to a rickshaw as its puller used to be a human being. Guruji had gone to Ernakulam in 1944. He was to visit his Kashi University-friend Dr. B.G. Abaji Gunde after a programme in Tatapuram that was about four kms away from that place. Abaji had come to the programme on his cycle. Swayamsevaks had arranged for a rickshaw to go to Tatapuram. When he saw it, he promptly said, "Let it be, the rickshaw is not required. We shall walk together, chatting on the way," and both of them went walking.

It was customary for Doctorji to stay at swayamsevaks' or well-wishers' homes. Guruji developed this into a systematic arrangement. This proved highly effective in building strong brotherly bonds within the organisation. Hotels were not that common during those days. There used to be inns. But, avoiding those comforts, both Doctorji and, later, Guruji preferred to stay at swayamsevaks' homes without worrying about the lack of amenities in some homes. Many homes did not have electricity or proper bathrooms in those days. There were no toilets with flushing arrangements. Nor all the houses had beds. Telephones were considered a means to display superiority!

Only restriction about Guruji's diet was that it should be vegetarian. His rule was, "Home food is my food." He stayed at Bangalore for three to four days. The host was a well-known writer. During this time, a Sangh worker invited Guruji to partake food at his home. He also invited Guruji's host. The gentleman said, "Thanks, but my difficulty is that I don't eat others' food." Guruji, on hearing this, shot back loudly, "Oh, I am also like that. I have never eaten others' food to this day." The host said, "How is it possible Guruji? You are going to this gentleman's house tomorrow." "That's right. But how can food from his home be an outsider's food? Can this colleague of mine be 'other' for me?" said Guruji. The host, an intelligent and a large-hearted person, got the message, took it as a guiding principle and made a new beginning. He immediately said, "I am also coming tomorrow." Everybody laughed together. Such was Guruji's nature. How many houses he must have stayed in during his life-time? How many types of waters from countless wells would he have drunk? It may be a world record.

The life in camps is an experience in community living on a large scale. It is nearly impossible and impractical to give attention to an individual. But, swayamsevaks used to take care that Guruji should face the least of difficulties in the camps. Guruji used to be present during the physical activity sessions in the morning and evening on the ground in the camps, especially in the Sangh Shiksha Varg. He used to take lunch in the afternoon sitting in rows (*pangat*) with other student swayamsevaks. He was insistent that one should honour time not only on the Sangh ground but even in every other programme – whether small or big. Therefore, he used to enter 10-15 minutes earlier in the dining section from one end of rows and move on, chatting with the swayamsevaks, refreshing old contacts, and enquiring about the well-being of other local brethren. He would then take his place in time. Once, while passing through a line, he stood in front of two students who were together and said smilingly, "Have you recognised the *sadhu*? He has come for *bhiksha*." Those swayamsevaks stared at the ground in embarrassment. They also had a little smile on their faces. There is an interesting tale behind this incident. Guruji was travelling in the same train in which these students were travelling, but, they hadn't seen him in person. Therefore, when they saw a bearded *sadhu*, they passed a light remark between themselves, "Who knows where will this *sadhu* go? Perhaps he will reach the camp in time for *bhiksha*." Guruji had made note of the remark and had recognised them sitting in the rows. One of the two became a very good responsible worker of the Sangh later on and used to talk about this incident with pride.

There is another incident that took place in Uttar Pradesh. Many dignitaries had been invited to take lunch with Guruji in a camp. There were very few leading swayamsevaks like Atal Behari Vajpayee also in this group. After lunch, to make it convenient for the guests, the person in-charge of lunch distribution instructed, "Till the whistle blows, swayamsevaks will remain seated, the guests can please get up and leave." All the guests including Atalji got up to wash their hands. Guruji didn't leave his seat. The row in-charge told him immediately, "You can get up, please." Guruji replied, "How can I? Am I not a swayamsevak? Didn't you hear the instructions?" The distribution in-charge got the message and blew his whistle immediately. This playfulness of Guruji with words did embarrass the guest swayamsevaks a little. Working while playing and playing with work – Guruji was an expert in this art of informal training.

Guruji was like Bhrigu-Ram regarding discipline. This may be the reason that the creator of Sangh, Doctorji chose to make him *Sarvaadhikari* continuously for three training camps in 1938, 1939 and 1940 to further sharpen the qualities of a swayamsevak in him. He could never tolerate indiscipline. He once sent back a swayamsevak from the camp when he got up from his lunch seat to take photographs in 1966 at Calicut (Kerala). He was livid at that time.

He didn't even spare himself from the firm grip of discipline. There was a camp of young boys (*baal*) in Nagpur. There was strict rationing on rice and wheat flour during those days. One had to seek special permission for organising a camp. Therefore, there were instructions to participants in the camp to bring their own ration. Three young boys from Guruji's home in Nagoba Lane had also joined the *Shivir*. He went home for his morning bath and *pooja* as per his routine and while leaving the house, he told his mother, "*Tai,* I have to attend the *baal shivir* today. I will come back tomorrow now." Mother, in her affectionate humour, said, "It is fine. But, remember Sarsanghchaalak's ration has not reached there." The people accompanying him laughed at her humour. Exclaiming, "Ok, ok," Sarsanghchaalak went to the *shivir*. After the programme, he told his driver, "Let us go." He went straight to Hedgewar Bhawan and took his afternoon rest. Krishnarao Moharir used to pay minute attention to details and he realised that Guruji had not taken the afternoon lunch. He also understood the reason behind it. On the second day, when Guruji was leaving home after the morning prayers, he remarked, "Ration has been taken to the camp." Their eyes met and Guruji simply smiled. He didn't say anything. He took lunch with everybody that day in the camp. This was the discipline of the head of the organisation that could impress any observer deeply but it was never meant to show off. Spiritual, self-imposed discipline without any ulterior motive!

With this conscious approach, he would have hardly ever adjourned or changed his preplanned programmes. Sardar Patel's death in Mumbai, Prime Minister's invitation for discussions during war with Pakistan, untimely death of Pandit Deendayal Upadhyay, sudden passing away of his revered father, etc. are a few examples of such exceptions. Guruji always reached in time for any programme, whether personal or public. It is very difficult to find an example to the contrary. He would remind his colleagues about these fine points when his tour programme was being planned. Therefore, even the common people used to reach his public meetings before time.

This was the kind of perennial cycle of his circumambulations. This journey was not like the well-propagated programme of a public figure, but it was a pilgrimage of a *karmayogi* to fulfil his mission. Let us understand his feelings in his own words, "I had the great fortune to traverse the whole of Bharat, from the Himalayas to the Indian Ocean. I have gone to Kashmir and also to Kanyakumari. I have literally travelled across Bharat many times over, to the extent that I have reached the smallest of places in remote parts of our nation for prolonged periods. It would have been nearly impossible, but I have tried to meet people and understand their lives from close quarters. And, I have reached the conclusion that actually there is no difference between the people of this country at individual level in real sense. They have similar strengths and similar weaknesses. They are similar from every angle. Therefore, when I go to any place, I feel that I am in my own home. I have never felt otherwise after getting to know a person. Then, that person may be a Tamil-speaking person, or Marathi or Bengali or Punjabi language-speaking person. The lesson that this mission has taught me makes me see all these people as one."[2]

□

Endnotes

1. *Shri Guruji Samagra*, Vol. 1, pp. 8
2. *Shri Guruji Samagra*, Vol. 9, pp. 210-211

18

Challenge and Expansion

In 1940, when the Sangh Shiksha Varg held at Nagpur, Doctor Hedgewar had spoken with a sense of satisfaction, "I see a miniature Bharat in front of me." What he meant at the time was that the seed that was sown in 1925, had blossomed and one could see its flowering. From 1937, while he was grooming highly capable workers (*Karyakartas*) like Guruji, he had sent young people like Bhaurao Deoras to Lucknow, Digambar Paturkar Munje to Lahore, Krishna Joshi to Sialkot, Moreshwar Munje to Rawalpindi to study and also begin and organise Sangh work there. He had sent Vasantrao Oke to Delhi, Narahari Parkhi to Bihar, Bapu Diwakar to Patna, Vitthalrao Patki to Bengal and Gopalrao Yekuntwar to Mumbai as full-time workers. Apart from this, he used to send out Dadaji Paramarth and Babasaheb Apte for tours to different places, depending upon the circumstances and requirements. Thus, he had set up well-planned activities to spread Sangh work all over Bharat, though the organisation was still limited to Central Province (C.P.), United Provinces (U.P.), Punjab and Bombay Presidency (B.P.). In other places, only the seeds had been sown. This was the capital that Sangh had collected when Guruji was appointed Sarsanghchaalak; this was the capital this 34-year young person started off with to take the organisation forward.

After the public programme held in Reshim Bagh on 21st July; Sanghchaalaks, Kaaryavaahs, full-time workers and the newly appointed Sarsanghchaalak came together for a meeting to chalk out the future programmes. Their first priority was to further strengthen the present organisation. Programmes were planned with this in mind. Three new programmes were expected to be organised every day: get-togethers of all old and new swayamsevaks, meetings and workshops for workers and inclusion of parents and well-wishers in the scheme of things. Of these, the first programme was to give proper direction to the swayamsevaks; second programme was meant to know the workers better at a personal level, understand them and guide them and third programme was to further reinforce the social base of the Sangh. Keeping these objectives in mind, the workers at the local levels could change the programmes based on the local factors.

In Sangh terminology, the speech to stimulate the volunteers' thoughts and guide them is called *Bouddhik*. This is not just a dry speech; there are other dimensions to it. This idea can be elaborated on the basis of the thoughts Guruji had on this subject. In the first year after his appointment, a well-known scholar asked Guruji, during his Bombay tour in 1941, "Are you opposed to publish literature on the Sangh? Why don't you publish various kinds of literature to spread Sangh ideology?" Guruji's response was, "I hope that a great scholar like you would be well aware of the tradition of this country. We give more importance to spoken word, '*shruti*'. As long as one can manage with the spoken word, one should work through this system only. Sangh swayamsevaks make contacts by visiting homes and meeting people face to face and move forward on the basis of *shruti*, that is share what they have experienced in their own life. While doing this, based on our experience regarding the growth of the organisation, if we feel it is no more possible to work without *smriti*, i.e., written word, we shall not hesitate to create *smriti* or put our thoughts and philosophy in writing. Is it not correct to say that in our own country, the code of conduct – *aachaarsamhitaa* – was written only after *shruti* had been established?"[1] *Bouddhik* in Sangh falls under this classification of *shruti*. This is not an exhibition of one's intellect, but a radiation of the emotions of the heart.

Workers' meetings – *baithaks* – are a special working methodology of Sangh in the same way. Leaders do not deliver sermons, nor are appeals or orders invoked; workers are moulded in these meetings. You might call it a dialogue between a teacher and a student or *satsang,* a place where noble ideas are discussed. People would come out of these *baithaks* with smiling faces, hearts radiating with positivity. Let us see an example. Place – Mahavir Dharamshala, person conducting *baithak* – revered Guruji. Guruji asked a Karyavaah, "How many swayamsevaks attend your Shakha?" "How many of them have memorised the prayer?" "How many of these would be reciting the prayer correctly?" "How many swayamsevaks would know the meaning?" After getting satisfactory replies to all these queries, Guruji asked him, "How many swayamsevaks would be trying to assimilate its meaning into their lives?" Questions about life, hidden behind simple questions about facts and figures! What could be the reply from Karyavaah? How could he respond to it? But, he could perceive a new direction, a new vision. He understood the core of his responsibility.[2] This is how Guruji conducted meetings or *baithaks*.

Even the third type of programme – meeting with parents and well-wishers – used to have its own unique quality. Guruji would speak only for about 15-20 minutes in those meetings. Then he would meet people personally, have introductions and one-to-one chat with them. Such discussions would throw up many interesting viewpoints and information. During such meetings, Guruji used to understand traditions and culture of different regions, their background, specialty of the respective languages, etc. from these interactions. For him, this two-way conversation used to be a pleasant occasion. Guruji would *share* his knowledge of, say, South by meeting people of other regions, "The best Indian-word for English word 'junction' is *sandhi* in Tamil. Similarly, another word for food is *saadam* which has roots in *prasaadam*; Malayalam word *chor* is a modified version of the Vedic word *charu*. He would urge senior brethren not to forget the sentiments of integral unity of our nation even when joking about something. While speaking to senior citizens of Ernakulam Bharat Tourist Home, he said, "Even knowledgeable people sometimes slip up due to carelessness." He gave an example about a highly respected and intelligent bureaucrat of South who had said, "There are only two great epics in Hindi – *Ramcharitmanas* and Railway Time-Table." In a similar vein, a well-known Marathi litterateur had said, "Put seven to eight pebbles in a brass mug and shake it. What you hear then is Tamil." "Will such cheap satire enhance the sense of national unity?" he asked the senior citizens sitting in front of him. Such were Guruji's meetings with senior citizens. Elite citizens of society used to gain a national and social perspective and become more active in social life.

Guruji commenced his tours, adopting this approach in his work. His supreme goal was to expand the Sangh and make it strong at the earliest. Towards this end, he focussed his attention and ignited a sense of dedication for the mission among the ordinary swayamsevaks. He resolved to make the Prachaarak system bigger and stronger from the seed of this system that Doctorji had sown. His policy was 'more work from more hands'. He was also well aware of the shortage of various resources. He began his journey, keeping all these issues in mind. Some young swayamsevaks met him at the Wardha station and requested him to give them a message for their handwritten magazine. Guruji promptly wrote a message on the manuscript of their magazine. "*Kriyasiddhi satve bhavati mahatan nopakarane*," meaning, success of our work depends on us, not on other resources.[3] This comment tells us about the intensity of his thoughts. His appeal to young swayamsevaks in 1941 and 1942 was, "We need Prachaaraks…we need Prachaaraks. This is the demand arising from all directions. We must fulfil this demand." He further said, "Karyakartas don't fall from heaven. For this, we will have to make efforts ourselves and create Karyakartas from amongst ourselves. We will have to walk the path of duty with firm resolve and austerity by giving up all thoughts about our personal lives...the mission before us is enormous with very little time in hand. But do not worry. If we decide even now, we can do as much work as we wish and create as many Karyakartas as we want. The question is of just bringing about a little revolution within our hearts. Just one revolution of hearts and our lives will see unprecedented changes and we shall see the gateway of hope...Let us close all the doors of our personal lives and take a pledge to put in concerted effort. Let us become *sannyasis* for one year."[4] This was the tone and tenor of his appeal during those days.

These thoughts found echo in the hearts of hundreds of youths. Remembering those days, 94-year-old Prachaarak, Thakur Ram Singh says proudly, "48 Prachaaraks came out just from Lahore in 1942. Of these, 10 were M.A., two doctors, 14 *shastris* and others were B.A. and above matric. Prachaaraks joined in from other towns. 52 Prachaaraks from of Amritsar city and out of these there were four doctors…."[5]

On the homage-paying day, 22 Karyakartas became Prachaaraks in Nagpur. Many Prachaaraks joined in from Vidarbha and Maharashtra. Guruji and Balasaheb Deoras appointed these people in different states of the country with the strategic expertise of Napoleon. Year 1942 was literally a year of comprehensive transformation in the history of the Sangh. In Maharashtra's tradition, Vijayadashami of that year literally and in every way was a year of *seemollanghan*, i.e., crossing the borders.

But, in this period there was an indication of an evil omen. The Central Government came out with a gazette on August 5, 1940. As per its Sections 56-58, private organisations were prohibited from giving army training or wearing army uniforms. There was no mention of the Sangh in it, but people understood the reason behind it. Wicked, crafty British knew very well about the political background of Dr. Hedgewar. So, they used to keep an eagle's eye on Rashtriya Swayamsevak Sangh founded by him. This is the reason that the Central Province government had issued a gazette eight years back on 15th December, 1932 that termed participation of government servants in the Sangh as illegal. History is witness to how this notification failed. The Sangh rose out of all such birth-pangs very successfully. They felt that they had got their chance now that a person like Dr. Hedgewar, who was well versed in public life, was gone and his successor Golwalkar seemed to be raw, lacking such an experience. So, this seemed to be the right time to strangle it. This was the intention behind this government order.

Guruji's reaction was not against the government but against the opposition to the Sangh. He took a step that would help swayamsevaks work undisturbed for their goal without being bothered about this order. He worked on the principle that 'even if my road is uneven, my horse should not be hurt' and took the Sangh on a new expansion path. Keeping this government gazette in mind, he wrote ten days later on 16th August to Professor Malkani in Sindh, "Our purpose is not to raise an army. We believe firmly in an organised society. Our goal is to generate a sense of unity in the Hindu society."[6] Similarly, he wrote a detailed letter with even more clarity to the Chief Prachaarak of Delhi, Vasantrao Oke. There was a hidden purpose behind it. The intelligence bureau used to read all the correspondence of the Sangh stealthily. In this letter, Guruji wrote, "You know it well that we are not bound by any specific type of programme. We are not hindered by any situation and we modify our programmes and come up with plans for new programmes, keeping in mind our core objective. With this view, we had given up that part of our training syllabus in our programmes that was based on military terminology, keeping in mind the restrictions imposed by the notification issued in August 1940. Earlier too, we used to impart only the training that would equip a person with qualities of discipline, etc. so that they acquire better capabilities to handle their daily lives. Actually, we never thought that such programmes had any importance from the militarist point of view. We had given this training section in Shakha a 'military' type of name for lack of better words. But, we have stopped the training named as 'military education' from August 1939.

"...Today, now that this department has lost its utility, we have decided to dissolve it fully. So, the chain of command structure that we used to create in this department, with designations like 'Commander', etc. should be completely disbanded. We have removed these posts from our organisational planning. So, it is necessary to say that this system of command has effectively ended by itself."[7]

Guruji had sent notifications with similar contents from Nagpur central office to all the states. The report sent by the Central Police Intelligence Department on 13th December, 1943 speaks about the impact of these communications. "It is not possible to create a case for banning the Sangh. But, it is equally clear that Golwalkar is creating a strong organisation at a rapid pace so that would obey the orders, maintaining confidentiality and jump into any activity of sabotage or of any other type whenever required as per their leader's orders. The structure of this organisation looks superficially like that of *khaaksaars*. But, the fundamental difference between the two is that the leader of *Khaaksaar*, Inayatullah, is a big-mouthed imbalanced lunatic, while Golwalkar is a very cautious, crafty and much more capable leader."[8]

When the Sangh was growing at such a pace, the August Kranti (Quit India movement) of 1942 exploded on the scene. This was the second freedom struggle in the life-time of the Sangh. First one was the Salt Satyagraha of 1930. Dr. Hedgewar had taken part in that movement in his personal capacity after handing over the responsibilities of Sarsanghchaalak to Dr. L.V. Paranjape. Appaji Joshi of Vardha and Dadarao Paramarth had also gone to prison with him. A circular was sent to all the Shakhas that ordinary swayamsevak can take part in the *satyagraha* in his personal capacity after taking permission from the local Sanghchaalak. After twelve years now, Guruji faced the question of taking part in the 1942 movement. During these twelve years, strong hunger for Independence had awakened the entire society across all sections of the populace. On the other hand, the condition of the British was deteriorating rapidly in the fierce war. Feeling that their poor position implied our strong position, ordinary people of the country believed that Delhi was not far off – Independence was round the corner. The situation for the Sangh had also changed a lot for the better. A number of experienced workers had risen. Though the growth was not very balanced, the Sangh had expanded geographically in large areas. But, it was also true that this expansion was limited to Mumbai Presidency and Central Provinces. In other places, its presence was more like a seedling; still the tone of organisation was that of growth. Guruji had to decide about the role of the Sangh in this background, and his age at that time was only thirty-six!

Guruji convened a meeting of state-level workers and held discussions with them. It was decided to evaluate the state of the movement dispassionately. The famous revolutionary, Dr. Pandurangrao Khankhoje (who earned his fame in Mexico) and Sangh strategist Balasaheb Deoras were sent to meet underground leader Jaiprakash Narayan ji with this objective in mind. Guruji was keen to get satisfactory answers to seven questions. The questions were:

- Part of 'dying' is clear in the slogan 'Do or Die'. But what is to be 'done'? Has the Congress Working Committee given any directions about it?
- What is the immediate and long-term goal of the movement? That is, what do we want to achieve without fail?
- What is the working methodology of the movement and how is it going to work?
- How long will the movement run?
- You must have estimated your strength; how big is this strength?
- What is the next move after the movement is successful?
- If it is unsuccessful, then what is to be done next?[9]

Dr. Khankhoje and Deoras came back after meeting Jai Prakash ji. Dr. Khankhoje's opinion was that "none of the answers by Jai Prakash ji was satisfactory. Not only this, there was no clear direction about what was to be done or not done by the people, next in line, after the front-line leaders were arrested". In the light of this information, Guruji held discussions with his colleagues. He was aware of the Sangh's strengths and limitations as an organisation. He had also discovered the actual state of movement. In spite of all this, he had no two opinions about the lofty goals of this movement. Under the circumstances, Guruji decided, "The agitation is being conducted for the freedom of the country. Therefore, swayamsevaks, as citizens, can take part in this agitation in whichever part of the country they are. But, as an organisation, the Sangh will keep working for the national cause, that is organising the society, without getting involved in the agitation directly."

There is another direct source of information on this subject. That is the personal interaction of Dattopant Thengadiji at that time. It would be ideal to mention it completely. "Guruji had to go to Chennai after his programme in the port city of Mangalore in September 1942. Swayamsevaks and Prachaaraks were deeply upset and were in a state of dilemma due to the impact of the movement that was shaking up the whole nation. Questions like – why is the Sangh inactive in these times? What is the use of its strength? – hurt their souls hard. I was Prachaarak in Calicut, in Kerala those days. Brethren there insisted that we should meet Shri Guruji and inform him of these ground realities. With this objective, I met Shri Guruji in Mangalore. Summary of his detailed response is as follows:

- The Sangh has its own code of conduct in such matters. According to these, when the Sangh, founder Doctorji took part in the *satyagraha*, he kept the Sangh out of the agitation and urged swayamsevaks to keep their Sangh work going without any disruption.
- However, if we were to reach near the goal of Independence by leaving aside this tradition, then we are not bound by it because our work and traditions have the same goal and Independence is definitely our immediate goal.
- It would have been desirable if the Congress had taken the other parties and the Sangh into confidence before initiating the agitation. But, it did not do so. Still, there is no reason to be upset. Independence gained through this movement will be for all, not just for the Congress. So, it would not be right to show any ego in this matter.
- It is a worrying prospect that Congress leaders have not made any preparations before launch of this agitation. People had to face and fight the British rulers directly. There was no planned arrangement for this. Though it is true that in a period of revolution, things won't go as per plans, it is equally true that there should be some element of planning and leaders should be alert to take advantage of any situation that might arise. It is also true that policies and directions depend only on *josh* – energy of the people and leaders cannot do much about it. But, we must remember that it is fatal not to have any plans during a movement or revolution.
- In spite of all this, if the country was to gain Independence with the Sangh jumping into the agitation, we would have not been averse to it. But, when I took a comprehensive view, it was my firm belief that we would not be able to reach anywhere near the goal.
- Many people have overestimated the Sangh's present strength. It is a situation where people who are in a place where the Sangh is strong believe that the Sangh is equally strong in other places too. But, this is not the reality. To be victorious in a struggle, many other things need to be favourable apart from your strength. Of these, first is support from the common people and their co-operation. Second is dissatisfaction among police, armed forces, etc. Attitude of these sections of the government is crucial before one takes the path of struggle. Even if these things were favourable, still chances of success of our struggle would be bleak. This is my assessment. I believe our strength will be limited from Belgaum to Gondia. Will

we be able to achieve our objective with these limitations?

- Truth is that our influence is confined to the central region of our country. Even if the struggle was to be successful in this limited area, it would be possible for our enemy to post its army from all the directions. People will get frustrated with such a development. But, if the zone of struggle were to be near the borders, it would be easy to put up a fight and would be more useful from the strategy point of view.
- In such circumstances, I believe it would be fruitless for the Sangh as an organisation to get involved in this movement. It doesn't mean that we wish to save our skin, but the truth is that people will end up disappointed with this agitation."[10]

In short, Guruji comprehended the inherent inertia of this battle, the practical view of Sangh's status across India, the society's mental state and permitted swayamsevaks to take part in this national struggle as patriotic citizens and extend whole-hearted co-operation to it. As a result, many swayamsevaks jumped into this battle and took part to the best of their abilities along with the common people, as a part of the society. In Vidarbha, swayamsevaks of Chimur launched an agitation under the leadership of Ramakant Deshpande. Breaking the bounds of non-violence, it turned violent. A few British were also killed in an encounter. This encounter became famous in the history of this movement as 'Chimur Ashti episode'.

Similar was the heroic story of Hemu Kalani of Sakkhar town in Sindh. He was busy removing fishplates from the railway tracks with his brave colleagues. Their objective was to frustrate the plans to move forces to suppress the struggle in various areas. Unfortunately, Hemu was arrested. His friends escaped and were saved. Hemu was awarded death sentence by the Army Court in 1943. Sindhi brethren in Mumbai celebrate the memory of martyr Hemu Kalani in Mumbai to this day.[11]

Apart from such activities, many swayamsevaks also helped the underground leaders of the movement. The house of Sanghchaalak of north-east, Lala Hansraj, was the secret place of stay for Aruna Asaf Ali. She herself speaks about it in an interview published in Hindi daily *Hindustan* in August 1967. She says, "I was underground in 1942 agitation, Delhi Sanghchaalak Lala Hansraj provided me refuge in his house for 10-15 days and arranged for my complete safety. He saw to it that nobody got information about my stay at his house. Since underground workers should not stay for long at the same place, I moved out of his house dancing '*Bhangra*' in an embroidered *ghagra* and *chunari* in a *baraat* (marriage procession). This dress was given to me by Lalaji's wife. When I went to return it in due course, she refused to take it back, saying, keep it with you as our gift with our best wishes."[12]

"When famous Vedic scholar, Pandit Shripad Damodar Satavalekar was the

Sanghchaalak of Aundh, he had given asylum for many days to the revolutionary underground leader, Nana, Patil who had experimented with the novel idea '*Patri Sarkar*'. Nana Patil's colleague, Kisanveer had stayed at the house of Satara Sanghchaalak in Wai while working underground there. Famous Socialist leader, Achyutrao Patwardhan had stayed at many Sangh swayamsevaks' homes when he used to work underground and change places according to circumstances. Not only these people, but even the life-long bitter opponent of the Sangh and follower of Gandhiji, Sane Guruji used to stay at Pune Sanghchaalak Bhausaheb Deshmukh's house secretly."[13]

To give more clarity to this subject, it would be a good idea to quote an episode that took place about six years later. The Congress Committee member of Solapur, Ganesh Bapuji Shinkar had taken part in the *satyagraha* to press for the removal of ban on the Sangh in 1948. He had resigned from the Congress on grounds of democratic ethics before joining the *satyagraha*. He issued a statement clarifying his stand and it was published on 12th December, 1948. He says, "I had participated in Bharat *Chhodo* (Quit India) movement in 1942. The capitalist and agrarian community was scared of the government at that time, therefore, we were not offered safe haven in their homes. We had to stay in Sangh workers' homes to work underground. People from the Sangh used to help us happily with our underground work. They also took care of all our requirements. Not only this, if someone from amongst us fell sick, the Sangh swayamsevak doctors used to treat us. Sangh swayamsevaks, who were advocates, used to fight our cases fearlessly. Their patriotism and value-based lifestyle was undisputable."[14]

While the anti-national Communists were acting like fifth columnists and getting agitating patriots arrested, the Sangh was doing its bit for the struggle. Eventually, the agitation cooled down after 75 days by the end of October. Scattered and weak leadership and disorganised agitation on one side and highly well-entrenched ruling set-up of British on the other, led to the death of a well-intentioned (*satprerit*) movement in its infancy.

As noted earlier, Prachaaraks were sent out in nearly all the states of Bharat after the Sangh Shiksha Varg of 1942, and they had begun Sangh work in different places. Thus, when the August Kranti exploded on the scene, Sangh work was in its infancy. Guruji's big worry as Sarsanghchaalak was how to guard this young lamp in this storm. His tours were organised without discriminating between small and big Shakhas where he met swayamsevaks and took careful stock of their work. During this time, his correspondence with nearly all the senior Prachaaraks continued. He wrote to Prachaarak Madhukar Rao Bhagwat, who had been sent to Ahmedabad to plant the Sangh seedling there, ".......It is quite possible that we shall have to face many difficulties while carrying on with our work because people's minds are highly agitated with many thoughts. But, we have to carry on with our work through our own methods and techniques.

If we are worried about expanding this work very fast, even then we should not hurry. All our swayamsevaks should increase the number of Shakhas with patience in their areas. They should not get unnecessarily over-enthusiastic in their work…."[15]

That the British rulers were alert was well known. They had kept a sharp eye on every activity of Guruji. The CID kept sending reports about him regularly. The report of 30th December, 1943 says, "Rashtriya Swayamsevak Sangh is moving ahead rapidly towards building a highly significant all-India organisation. Spokesmen of the Sangh keep saying that the basic goal of the Sangh is to achieve Hindu unity...In a programme in November 1943 at Lahore, M.S. Golwalkar declared that the Sangh's objective is to remove the feeling of untouchability and weave together all sections of Hindu society in a single unifying thread.

"…It is clear that the Sangh is bent upon expanding its area of influence and this year it has been able to bring on board the famous religious saint Sant Tukadoji Maharaj from Central Provinces for spreading its message...

"Membership of the Sangh is swelling continuously. In Central Provinces, membership has increased from thirty-two thousand to thirty-three thousand three hundred forty-four. It has reached twenty thousand four hundred seventy-six from eighteen thousand twenty-nine in Mumbai and fourteen thousand from ten thousand in Punjab…

"A new dimension to their growth is their efforts to gain entry in the villages. M.S. Golwalkar laid a lot of stress on this aspect in the winter camp of Wardha – that the Sangh should expand into villages…

"The Sangh office-bearers from its head office are touring the Shakhas in remote areas continuously, so that they can heighten interest of the swayamsevaks in Sangh work, give them secret directions and strengthen the local organisation. We can see the recent well spread out tour of the present chief of the Sangh, M.S. Golwalkar as an example of such efforts. In the last month of April, he was in Ahmedabad; in May, he was at Amravati and Pune. In June, he was at Nasik and Benaras. He toured Chanda in August, Pune in September, Madras and Central Provinces in October and Rawalpindi in November..."[16]

If one were to read this report carefully, one fact comes out clearly. All the places mentioned in it are situated north of Chandrapur, with the exception of Chennai. There is a specific reason behind this. Sanjeev Kamat of Chennai was present in the open valedictory function of the 1940 Sangh Shiksha Varg due to his personal relationship and efforts of Sangh founder, Dr. Hedgewar. Taking this contact forward, Guruji had taken the initiative to expand the Sangh in southern states by undertaking a special tour of the South. Under this plan, he had sent English-speaking Prachaaraks from Mumbai Presidency and Central Provinces to South in 1942. Mention of Dattopant Thengadiji having gone to Calicut in Kerala has been made earlier. Similarly,

Yadavrao Joshi was sent from Jhansi to Belgaum. Gold medalist Shivram Joglekar from Pune was sent to Chennai. Shivram Shankar alias Dada Apte, who became General Secretary of Vishwa Hindu Parishad twenty-five years later, was sent to Tiruchirappalli in Tamil Nadu. Narhari Parkhi was sent to Andhra region of Madras Presidency. Anna Shesh and Babu Telang reached Mangalore and Thiruvananthapuram, respectively. This is not the complete list but only a representative one. Guruji used to visit major cities of the South to strengthen the newly launched expansion programme that had begun in 1941-42, and to be in close touch with the young committed Prachaaraks.

On 21st September, 1942, when Guruji was leaving for his next programme after getting free from a Bengaluru Shakha programme, the police of Mysore state arrested him and kept him behind bars for one night. The police officers believed that he had come there to spread the word of August Kranti. He was released next morning due to intervention of famous litterateur, Sitaram Shastri and advocate of Mysore High Court K. Venkatranga Iyengar. The police had realised its mistake.

During these days, he had appointed a leading advocate V. Rajagopalachari as the Sanghgchaalak of Chennai city after a personal meeting. He also declared popular advocate of Mangalore, Karakalaa Sadashivrao as the Sanghchaalak of Mangalore. Some other worthies were also appointed in the same way. Work in South thus struck roots, resulting in Prachaaraks coming out of the southern states from 1945 onwards.

After appointing him as the General Secretary in 1939, Doctorji had realised that Guruji may not be able to visit his parents in Ramtek like earlier days. To get over this problem, he had requested Guruji's father to move to Nagpur with his family. Bhauji had also agreed to this suggestion. Unfortunately, before a proper arrangement could be made, Doctorji had left this world. After Guruji became Sarsanghchaalak, elders like Appaji Joshi, Babasaheb Ghatate and Abaji Hedgewar took this responsibility upon themselves and requested Bhauji again. Accepting this request happily, he let out his house in Ramtek on rent and came to Nagpur to stay with his dear son. He became a tenant in Pachpore's house in Shukrawar Peth. He shifted to Ghatate's house in Nagoba Lane after 1942. Till 1945, the central meetings of the Sangh used to take place in this house just as they used to take place in Doctorji's home during his lifetime. After Mohitewadi, an area around it was purchased and Dr. Hedgewar Bhavan was constructed. These meetings shifted to the central office.

People, specially the knowledgeable elite of Vidarbha and Maharashtra, were well aware of Doctorji's experience, his public life and wide contacts. His successor, Guruji, was an unknown, inexperienced innocent-looking *sadhu*. Therefore, many intellectuals expressed their doubts, asking, "What can this *sannyasi* do?" Guruji satisfied all such people with his intense and duty-bound work. When he reached Calicut in the southern corner of the country, during his all-Bharat tour in 1946, a reporter of popular daily *Mathrubhoomi* asked him, "Guruji, are you satisfied with the growth of the Sangh?" The answer was, "Yes, as a worker, I am satisfied. But, as an idealist, I can never be satisfied." Second question was, "How many Shakhas do you have currently?" His response was in the form of a riddle, "If I were to visit each of our Shakhas, it would take me around 12-15 years to complete the tour." Then, after a brief pause, he added smilingly, "If new Shakhas are not added during this time." This was the intense enthusiasm of the topmost worker of the Sangh who had taken up this responsibility only six years back.

□

Endnotes

1. *Jeevan Prasang*, Vol. 2, pp. 124
2. *Madhya Bharat Mein Guruji*, pp. 29
3. *Jeevan Prasang*, Vol. 1, pp. 313
4. *Shri Guruji Samagra*, Vol. 3, pp. 11-14
5. *Shri Guruji Punjab Mein*, pp. 29-30
6. *Shri Guruji Samagra*, Vol. 8, pp. 9
7. Ibid, pp. 21-22
8. *Sangh Beej se Vriksha*, pp. 60-61
9. *Rashtray Namah*, pp. 83-84
10. *Pioneer of New Era*, pp. 54-55
11. *Rashtriya Swayamsevak Sangh – Sindh ka Pravas* pp. 71
12. *Rashtray Namah*, pp. 85-86
13. Ibid, pp. 86
14. *Pehli Agnipariksha,* pp. 140-141
15. *Shri Guruji Samagra*, Vol. 8, pp. 19
16. *Sangh Beej se Vriksha*, pp. 63-66

19

The Period During Country's Partition

Bharat was partitioned in 1947. Debate is still on whether the Partition was right or wrong; it will carry on for long. For intelligentsia it is a topic for intellectual gymnastics. Be as it may, it is an undeniable fact of history that Bharat was divided into pieces. Every person who appeared on stage was a part of this tragic drama. One: Mohammad Ali Jinnah, supreme leader of Muslim League who passed a resolution on 23rd March, 1940, at the Lahore session with the demand "Divide Hindustan into pieces and hand us over our Pakistan." Second: Lord Mountbatten who acted like the proverbial monkey claiming to be a fair judge of distribution of bread between two quarrelling cats. Third: Triumvirate of Gandhi-Nehru-Patel. Of these, Jinnah had the whole Muslim community behind it. He was accepted as the official spokesperson of this community. On this side, Hindu community accepted Gandhi-Nehru-Patel triumvirate as its spokesperson, ignoring the Hindu Mahasabha and its leader Savarkar. These three leaders had earned the confidence of nearly the entire Hindu society. The rationale behind this acceptance seemed to be correct. In 1946, the Congress had passed a resolution that it stood for United (*akhand*) Bharat. Iron Man Sardar Patel had roared: "The sword will be met with sword." Jawaharlal Nehru's pet song was: "Pakistan is a fantastic nonsense." Mahatma Gandhi had written in '*Harijan*' on 6th April, 1949 and 13th April, 1949 thus, "Two-nation theory is a baseless falsehood. My conscience abhors this very idea. Division of Bharat is a scenario that is worse than anarchy. It is unbearable to chop-off limbs. Cut me down before you divide Bharat." These words had a huge impact on the people. The populace had put their faith in leaders whom they looked upon as angels due to their selfless sacrifice throughout their lives in the cause of freedom. But, Muslim League waved its 'green flag' for 'Direct Action' on 16th August, 1946 when the Muslims butchered thousands of Hindus mercilessly, with indescribable cruelty. The Congress was shaken to the core due to this act. The Congress showed bankruptcy in the 'Kshatriya' spirit of putting up a fight and not running away from battle ground as commanded by Bhagwad Gita that says, *"Yuddham apalaayanam"*.

In this disastrous scenario, Guruji took up the responsibility of keeping the morale of the common people high. He also sent a message across to people to conserve their energies and build up their strength to face the looming disaster ahead. Criticising this 'weakness in action' of the leadership at that time, in his speech during the Vijayadashami festival on 5th October, 1946, he said, "Arjun had suddenly faced a mesmerising dilemma when his chariot stood between the forces of Kauravas and Pandavas. There stood before him, Gurus, brothers, fathers and sons. Arjun was not a coward; he was brave. He did not wish to run away from the battle-field, but wished to lay down his life by dropping his arms and turning his face away from worldly affairs (*nivritti*). Our nation is facing the same situation today. Like Arjun, the Hindu society finds itself gripped by the dilemma of action versus non-action, doing duty or not doing duty."[1]

Analysing the talk about 'reaction', his blunt response was, "There is a lot of talk about not picking up arms and not taking revenge. But, I cannot agree with this current language of not reacting; it is not something arising out of courage. It is nothing but cowardice and about fooling ourselves. It is *adharma*, that is, immoral to inflict pain upon self."[2] Appealing to be ready for self-defence, he affirmed unhesitatingly, "It is our firm belief that every individual has a natural right to self-protection and the society made of such individuals also has the same right. I had read a bizarre statement in newspapers that said, "An individual or society does not have the right to defend self, only the government has this right, and a person should take law unto his hands even if he is attacked." Only law has the right to defend an individual and society. Does it mean that we should sit quietly and wait for the police if somebody attacks us? Should there be no attempt for self-defence? How far can this be justified? Right of self-defence is a right endowed by Nature to every individual and society."[3]

With this clear sense of direction, the central leadership of Rashtriya Swayamsevak Sangh began moving around the country. Prominent among them were Guruji, Babasaheb Apte and Balasaheb Deoras. Hundreds of young men and middle-aged people began joining the Sangh. The Hindu brethren started coming together with self-confidence in cities and villages of Punjab like Rawalpindi, Lahore, Peshawar, Amritsar, Jalandhar, Ambala, etc. Witnessing this atmosphere, the *English Tribune* wrote, "Punjab is the sword arm of Hindustan and R.S.S. is the sword arm of Punjab." Perturbed at this development, the mouthpiece of Muslim League, *Dawn*, wrote, "If Congress leadership wishes to receive co-operation from Muslims, then it must ban the Sangh immediately."[4]

This kind of talks went on making rounds, but, Guruji had strong faith in Gandhiji. He had reverence for Gandhiji's spiritual persona. He had gone to Multan during his tour of Punjab in November 1946. His stay was arranged at the home of District Sanghchaalak Dr. Baldev Burman. During conversation over tea, Dr. Burman asked, "There is lot of noise about Pakistan. Is there a possibility that it might be created?" Guruji replied, "I have full faith in Mahatma

Gandhi. He will never agree to this proposal of Pakistan. It is possible that he may agree to many of Jinnah's proposals to appease the Muslims, but, he will never allow Partition of the country."[5]

Guruji went to Sialkot and Montgomery after touring Multan. A swayamsevak asked in the Montgomery meeting, "Should we not collect arms to defend ourselves against the Muslims?" Guruji asked him, "Have you read the Gita? The Gita says, '*Atman* is immortal.' Then what are we afraid of? Collecting weapons is a sign of fear." Quoting a proverb, he added, "A person who does not terrorise others nor does he fear for self, the world is afraid of such a person. Understand this very well that fearlessness is the strongest weapon."[6] It is notable that Guruji used to describe factual scenarios objectively in his lectures, meetings and discussions. But, he was always cautious that it should not result in anarchy.

Guruji entered Sindh from Punjab. Sindh had around 80 Shakhas at that time. There were 52 Prachaaraks and included Lal Krishna Advani and Hashu Advani. Guruji was a guest of Barrister Khanchand Gopaldas in Karachi and advocate Hotchand Gopaldas in Hyderabad. The head of Shri Ramakrishna Ashram, Swami Ranganathanand Maharaj was present in the front row at the huge public meeting held at D.B. High School grounds on Bunder Road of Karachi that Guruji addressed.[7]

Around this time, Pandit Nehru had also reached Hyderabad in Sindh. The Muslim League supporters had decided to sabotage Nehru's meeting and had conveyed their threat too. League members felt that Nehru would definitely oppose the demand for Pakistan. Therefore, they had decided not to allow his meeting. Local Congress leaders became restless when they got this information. Their two senior leaders, Chimandasji and Baba Kisanji, met city Sanghchaalak Hotchand ji and asked for Sangh's support and co-operation for a trouble-free meeting. Sanghchaalak agreed with an open heart. Many swayamsevaks attended this meeting, accordingly. Finding the R.S.S. swayamsevaks at the Congress meeting, the League members' condition was like mice that had seen cats amongst them. The meeting got over peacefully without any trouble.[8]

In short, the common Hindu populace was not in favour of Partition even after Jinnah's 'Direct Action'. Wherever the Sangh reached, the Hindu youth power began gearing up for self-defence. Communist Party was also in favour of Partition, apart from the Muslim League. It had also passed a resolution in favour of Partition. In this matter too, they behaved in their typical way, conditioned by their philosophy. At the same time, British rulers and other leaders were stealthily planning for Partition of the country in the background. Under a political settlement, a coalition government of Congress and Muslim League formed a government in Delhi in September 1946. The Central Assembly (called Parliament now) went into session with this arrangement. The League began throwing tantrums immediately. First day witnessed unruly scenes both inside and outside the assembly. *Goonda* power of the Muslim League showed its true colours. They decided to play this game with utter contempt even on the second day. But, leaders had decided not to allow the insulting behaviour to be repeated. To put this idea in place, top leader of Delhi state Congress, Lala Deshbandhu Gupta came to the Sangh office in Kamla Nagar and met state Prachaarak, Vasantrao Oke. As a result of these talks, hundreds of swayamsevaks got busy from early morning and surrounded the Assembly Hall to give a strong response to this unruly behaviour. Smelling the adverse conditions on the ground, they lost their nerves and the Assembly carried on with its session in a dignified manner.[9] In spite of all this, the Partition of our motherland was announced on 3rd June, 1947.

As a precursor to preparations for Partition, the British government had already divided the Army and Police on the basis of religion. As a result, areas falling under Sindh, West Pakistan and East Bengal were put under the command of Muslim Army-Police combine. Thus, the condition of the minorities there, namely Hindus and Sikhs had already become precarious. The vitriolic tongue of Jinnah, the militant Islamist nationalism, the volatile combination of Police and Army – the coming together of all these fiery elements led to a condition that is described by a Sanskrit proverb, as "a heavily drunk devil that has been stung by a scorpion and controlled by a ghost". The condition of the Hindus was like that of Draupadi caught in the evil grip of Duhshaasan. Eminent exponents of non-violence had turned silent witnesses like Bhishmacharya.

So, 'Madhav' reached out and set up the Punjab Relief Committee and Hindu Sahaayata Samiti. Lahore was the centre of activity for both of these. The Punjab state Sanghchaalak, Raibahadur Badridas was the Chairman and Dr. Gokulchand Narang was the Treasurer of these committees.

Around the same time, two Sangh Shiksha Vargas under Sangh's annual calendar of activities commenced on 16th July, in Phagwara and 20th July at Sangrur. The Phagwara camp had 1,400 student participants and Sangrur had 2,300. Both the camps had a sizable number of *'Keshdharis'* (Sikhs, who do not cut hair) among *'Sahajdharis'* (non-Sikh Hindus or those who cut hair). Sikh and non-Sikh brethren stood shoulder to shoulder, ready to defend vulnerable members of the society. As per his programmes, Guruji reached the Sangrur camp around July end. Sangrur stood on the borders of princely states of Patiala, Nabha and Malerkotla. Members of the Gurudwara Committee of the holy Mastuana Sahib Gurudwara visited the camp to invite Guruji to the *gurudwara*. Many *Jathedaars* (heads) of *gurudwaras* of PEPSU region had also been invited. One cannot enter *gurudwaras* without covering one's head as per tradition, while due to some undisclosed spiritual custom, Guruji never covered his head. Even while accepting salute as the Sarsanghchaalak in full Sangh uniform, he never wore the uniform cap. Understanding and accepting this self-imposed protocol of the head of Sangh, the chiefs of *gurudwaras* gave him a heart-warming welcome.

Bare-headed but with great humility, Guruji offered his humble tributes to the most sacred *Guru Granth Sahib*, lying prostrate before the Guru. He completed his circumambulation with bowed head, not raising his eyes even once. This was followed by a reception programme in his honour.

The chief of the *gurudwara* said, "It is our immense fortune that we have today amongst us a great soul who has tied the sacred thread of protection (akin to Sikh arm gear, *kadaa*) for defending *dharma*. He is raising a strong force with the power of his meditation that will surely defend *dharma*." He was offered *saropaa* (a sacred piece of cloth blessed by *Shri Guru Granth Sahib*) after his short speech. Expressing his gratitude, Guruji said, "As I witness this scene before me, I recall a page from three-hundred-year-old history, when the great Bharatiya power of North in the form of Guru Gobind Singh ji had tried to meet another similar power that had risen in the South, Chhatrapati Shivaji. But, it is a misfortune for this nation that they could not come together. The meeting that couldn't take place then is happening today. I firmly believe that we shall see the rise of an immense power in defence of *dharma* that will leave no doubt about any threat to our *dharma* in future."[10]

Observing the scenario carefully, Guruji had concluded that the Partition would soon take a demonic form and our swayamsevaks would have to take up the task of defending the society at the cost of their sweat and blood. Thus, after consulting the Sangh office-bearers of Punjab, he disbanded both the Sangrur and Phagwara camps. He directed the swayamsevaks to go back to their homes and prepare plans for defending the society. An additional direction given to them was that they should leave their posts only after the safe passage of Hindu brothers and sisters to Hindustan.

Guruji's judgement proved to be correct. The situation deteriorated so badly that even the Man of Steel, Home Minister, had to admit, "It won't be possible for the government to defend everybody. Each person will have to try to defend self." For the Hindu populace these were not the words of consolation but a helpless cry. In that dark night, swayamsevaks took up the job of securing the society at the risk of their lives. Sangh leaders like Guruji, Balasaheb Deoras, Madhavrao Muley, Vasantrao Oke and others descended on the battlefield to guide the self-defence teams. While listening to some heartrending stories from swayamsevaks, Guruji spoke to Chamanlalji standing next to him, "Even today, brave women like Padmini are alive in Hindu society. So, I am very confident that efforts put in by us will surely lead to progress of the society even in adverse conditions."[11] The security camps filled up fast and additional arrangements had to be made in this emergency. Middle-class swayamsevaks, in this situation, made arrangements for 50-60 displaced people in their homes. Nobody cared about caste, sect or profession of these people.

It is worth quoting the experience of Madhavrao Muley, who was spearheading the Sangh operations in those times, "This incident took place in September 1947. The Partition had just taken place. Hindus in Sindh and Punjab faced a horrible disaster. Displaced people were pouring in. Guruji was on a tour to fathom their plight. Rivers and *nullahs* were flowing relentlessly with rushing waters. Rains were lashing relentlessly. Guruji had reached Jalandhar during the tour. He had to reach Ludhiana after finishing this programme. But, roads had been washed away due to heavy rains. The highway from Jalandhar to Ludhiana was flooded, so it was not possible to reach there by car. Guruji was adamant that we must reach Ludhiana as per schedule. On enquiring with the Railways, we were told that they could arrange for a trolley. I sat on a trolley with Guruji and Shri Dharmavir. The trolley's energetic, alert pushers began running the trolley on the tracks with caution."

"We reached near Chahedu on the trolley. There was a huge *nullah* in Chahedu that was flowing fiercely with water overflowing its banks. Floods had washed away one pillar of the railway bridge. The structure over the bridge was standing erect, but, the railway track was swinging freely with rail sleepers as the land below it washed away. The trolley-pullers refused to take the trolley over this track."

"We tried to figure out what to do next. We couldn't think of any solution. Before we could think of anything, revered Guruji had already stepped energetically on to the swinging tracks and sleepers and begun moving ahead. Our hearts thumped with anxiety. Water was gushing with threatening speed just two-three feet below the loose railway tracks. It was a frightening scene, but Guruji still crossed the bridge. We also followed him from behind and crossed over. We reached Chahedu station and narrated our problem to railway people. An engine stood there. The engine was to go to Goraya. The driver, upon hearing revered Guruji's name, promptly agreed to take us with him. Guruji and all of us reached Goraya, sitting in that engine. Fortunately, for us, there was a goods train in Goraya that was ready to leave for Ludhiana. The guard gave Guruji and all of us some place in his cabin. We reached Ludhiana after three hours. This way, we reached Ludhiana at 5 in the evening after starting off from Jalandhar at 7 in the morning. And Ludhiana programme could be conducted properly."[12]

Thus, this servant of the people, like God Janardana ran to free distressed people, like the Gajendra elephant of Puranic story, from the evil grip of demon Narakaasur that had descended on them in the form of a horrible disaster of that time. Great poet Banabhatta has named such a brave person, *'kritpradnya dheer'*, that is, 'a brave balanced person who has taken pledge to act at any time', a person to whom huge earth is like a playground, oceans are like channels and deep recesses of earth are like levelled grounds and unconquerable mountain Meru is like an anthill.*

* *Anganvedee vasudhaa kulyaa jaladhih sthalau cha paataalam sumeruh kritpratigyasya dheerasya.*

He, then, reached Amritsar during the same tour. Justice Ramlal ji and highly respected Meharchand Mahajanji came to meet him. They began by saying, "Guruji, after all, we are refugees." On hearing these words, Guruji said immediately, "No, you are not refugees. This nation belongs to each and every individual. All of you have the same rights over her. How can somebody be a 'refugee' in one's own home?"[13]

This view of Guruji was the reflection of his unshakeable faith, "Bharat is one, unbreakable (*akhand*) and all her citizens are children of this unified nation." Even later, whenever he heard somebody use the word 'refugee' or '*sharanaarthi*' his face would twist into a pained expression as if somebody had uttered a foul language. If an unfortunate brother has to come into the loving fold of a fellow brother, how can he be a refugee? Is serving or supporting him an act of charity? Then, how can we talk of love and affection? What is the meaning of duty? We should look at the brethren of our society with a feeling of brotherhood and love. This was Guruji's viewpoint. He felt that only those people who did not have this sentiment about their unfortunate brethren could call them refugees. This word is an obscenity, an insult to those unfortunate fellow-beings. Such was his heartfelt and incisive analysis of the situation.

The public meeting in Amritsar was a mammoth affair. Guruji was given a 21-gun salute in this programme. A Brigadier came to attend this meeting. He made a special request to meet Guruji after the programme. On being asked about his purpose, he said he would tell it only to Guruji. The zonal Prachaarak, Thakur Ram Singh, brought him to Guruji. On seeing Guruji, he bent down immediately to touch his feet. Guruji promptly took his hand into his own and said, "Gentleman, what is this? You are a high-level army officer! Senior to me by age ....Please don't... don't..." The Brigadier turned emotional. In a choked voice, he said, "Guruji, I am not touching your feet. In fact, I am bowing my head to that power of the Sangh whose twelve-year and fourteen-year old young boys have done such feats of bravery in Lahore that even Jawans of my army couldn't do." He even described a hair-raising experience he had witnessed. After listening to his account with patience, Guruji said, "*Bhai saheb*, neither are these boys taught any magic nor any *tantra-mantra*. They come together everyday at one place and play *kabaddi*. This is how they have developed this courage. This is the importance of the daily Sangh Shakha."[14]

Defending the beautiful valley of Kashmir from deceiving aggressors, its merger with the nation, the role of swayamsevaks and Guruji in this historic chapter have been recorded with undeniable facts and proofs, with accurate dates by Manikchandra Vajpayee and Shridhar Paraadkar in their scholarly book *Jyoti Jalaa Nij Praan Ki* (meaning to lit a lamp out of one's own life). This book is the story of extreme courage exhibited by swayamsevaks who worked directly or indirectly, without any expectation or without waiting for orders; motivated by nothing but pure alloyed love for the country. Taking a detour from this story, we are presenting only the contribution of Guruji in our effort.

The British had left Hindustan, giving rights to princely states to have independent, autonomous rule or merge with Bharat or Pakistan, as they willed. Based on this policy, Kashmir became an independent state that didn't merge either with Bharat or with Pakistan.

The Muslim majority in Kashmir, Prime Minister Ramchandra Kak's intrigues who was married to a white lady and acted like an agent of the British, the secret wish of Lord Mountbatten to get it merged with Pakistan and his games to further this design, Sheikh Abdullah's agitation to throw out the king, personal grudge of Nehru with the king, and Nehru's support for Sheikh Abdullah – the political whirlpool generated by such conditions had left the king dazed. Deep in his heart, he wished to merge with Bharat. Guruji was aware of this situation in the alert tradition of Chanakya. He took steps to fulfil his duty to the nation in this scenario.

Raibahadur Badridas was Punjab state's Sanghchaalak and also the Chairman of Punjab Relief Committee. He was a well-known lawyer in the north-west region. He used to represent Maharaj in important cases in courts. Badridas went to Srinagar in September to meet the Maharaja and advised him to merge with India. As an icing on the cake, one of the senior ministers (Diwan) of the Maharaja was the father-in-law of Uttar Pradesh Sanghchaalak Narendrajeet Singh. This family also used its influence on the Maharaja. The Sangh Prachaarak of Jammu & Kashmir, Professor Balraj Madhok had good relations with Raja Saheb. He used to meet the Maharaja often for his social programmes. Now, they made contact regarding this matter also. As a result of these multi-dimensional efforts, the Maharaja decided to send a special envoy, Harnaam Singh Pathania, to Delhi with a proposal for merger with Bharat. But, due to the uncompromising approach of Pandit Nehru, this effort failed. Still, the Maharaja made a final effort again between 10th and 13th October. Singh was sent to Delhi again, but the result was negative. Guruji kept receiving all this information from time to time. He was sad with these ups and downs, but, as noted above, he was a *kritpradnya dheer*. He decided to go to Srinagar himself. Guruji reached Delhi by air on 17th October, 1947, with Delhi state Prachaarak, Vasantrao Oke and Barrister Narendrajeet Singh. The regional Prachaarak of that area, Madhavrao Muley and four to five state-level workers of Jammu & Kashmir waited for them. Under Sangh's arrangement, Guruji and his colleagues stayed in barrister's in-law's home in Divaniyat Bhavan. Next day, on 18th October, Guruji went in a private car to Karan Mahal to meet the Maharaja. The Maharaja and Maharani had great reverence for Guruji. So, both of them were there at the palace gates to receive and welcome him. Just as the Maharaja bent down to touch Guruji's feet, Guruji caught hold of his hands. After an initial informal chat, formal discussions began at 10.30 a.m. Nobody was present from either side during these discussions. So, nobody knows what transpired during the discussion, what kind of subjects or suggestions came up. When the Maharaja came out to bid farewell to Guruji after the discussions, he went near Guruji's car and said, "I will definitely weigh your suggestions carefully." At the moment of seeing him off, the royal couple presented two highly valuable shawls to Guruji. Before leaving, Guruji urged the Maharaja, "It may be a good idea to send the Prince to Jammu and you should remain in Srinagar so that the people's morale does not dip." Guruji and his colleagues reached their lodging before lunch.

That same evening a pre-planned get-together (*saanghik*) of senior swayamsevaks was held at DAV College in Mangal Bagh near Lal Chowk. It was attended by more than 500 volunteers. Guruji delivered his *Bouddhik* or discourse. He did not speak anything about his meeting with the Maharaja. He returned to Delhi on 19th October.[15]

Guruji met Home Minister Sardar Patel in Delhi and apprised him of the favourable attitude of Maharaja. Fortunately, Meharchand Mahajan had become the 'Prime Minister' by that time in place of Ramchandra Kak. The next step was taken by the strategist, Sardar. As a result, Jammu & Kashmir merged with the rest of the country.

One thing stands out in this entire episode and that is his nature that was totally egoless and not enamoured by any interest in promoting himself. Even later in life, when he was made to suffer gross injustice due to political vested interests, he did not sacrifice his natural behaviour nor did he broadcast his noble deeds to claim any credit or score points. He also used to caution Sangh swayamsevaks to avoid their petty urge for self-promotion.

The western part of Punjab, the eastern part of Bengal and entire Sindh were taken away from Bharat as a result of the Partition of the country. This, perhaps, may be the reason that Sindh has disappeared from the conscience of the current generation. The contribution of Sindh to Bharatiya culture, literature, music and excellent human liberal arts has lost its pre-eminent place in this partitioned Bharat. We have even forgotten the role played by Sindhis in the war of Independence against the British. The current dispensation doesn't even mention it. For example, who knows about the martyrdom of aforementioned Hemu Kalani? 'The martyr is a Hindu and the battle was waged by anti-Partition people' – for these two reasons Pakistanis also neglected him deliberately. Martyr Hemu's condition turned out to be that of mythical Trishanku, that is, neither here nor there. Our independent Bharat also seems to be ungrateful.

Guruji's tours took place annually, continuously from 1943 to 1947. His final tour took place just one week before Partition on 7th August, 1947. That day, 35,000 of the 65,000 population of Hyderabad city came to National College Grounds and heard Guruji with rapt attention. Two days before this, Karachi had witnessed a massive public meeting. This meeting overflowing with people at Fire Brigade Ground was presided over by a great spiritual personality, Sadhu

T.L. Vaswani. The common man of Sindh had sensed the coming of Partition by then that this was the Guruji's last visit to Sindh. It is a memorable fact from historical perspective that the people's hero, Guruji, was the last leader to tour united Bharat's Sindh till the end, that is, seven days before the Partition. By then, the so-called other great leaders of Sindh had reached their safe destinations.

Exactly one month later, there was a bomb explosion in the Sangh office building at Shikarpur colony of Sangh on 9th September. Taking advantage of this, the Pakistani government arrested 19 swayamsevaks. After hearing of the case, Barrister Khanchand was handed life imprisonment and fined fifty thousand rupees. The other accused were handed 10-year imprisonment and rupees ten thousand fine each. Any intelligent person who knew Muslim history could understand that practically it meant death sentence for these prisoners in Pakistani prisons. The entire leadership of the Sangh was deeply worried about it. They faced a very complex issue on how to get them freed. There was only one option – that of exchange of prisoners between the two governments. Guruji took this job up with great skill. The Central Government and Sardar Patel were in a mood of co-operation in the atmosphere that prevailed at that time. As a result, both the sides agreed for exchange of prisoners. The date was also fixed up for the swap at the Ferozepur border, but, there was a hitch at the last moment – Pakistan's stand for one-to-one exchange. There was a knotty issue behind this plan. Barrister Jinnah's close friend Dr. Qureshi was under arrest for a murder in Bharat. Jinnah was trying hard to arrange for his release. Pakistan was willing to free only Barrister Khanchand in exchange for Dr. Qureshi. If it was agreed, it would mean a hell-like torture and destruction of other imprisoned swayamsevaks.

Guruji was apprised of the entire situation. He analysed the situation with an intellect of Chanakya. Punjab was under President's rule at that time. Guruji contacted a Union Minister N.V. (Kaka) Gadgil through a colleague of the Chief Secretary Bhide of that state and after giving him a complete picture of the situation, suggested that transfer should be based on 'case' and not on the basis of 'person'. The minister agreed to the suggestion and this proposal was passed on to the right officer of the other side. Therefore, exchange could not take place on the appointed day. All the friends who had come to welcome their brethren had to return empty handed and among them was also Lal Krishna Advani. But Guruji's plan succeeded after one month. We got back all our swayamsevaks and Jinnah got back his Dr. Qureshi.[16]

Among the people who were practically reborn was a young and intelligent Nand Badlani. He secured admission to the Pune Engineering College later. While talking of his experience in the Karachi prison, he astonished everybody when he showed a confidential letter of Guruji sent to him in the prison. This letter is available now in the eighth volume of *Shri Guruji Samagra*. The hidden meaning lay in the last paragraph, "I have full faith that whatever is possible legally is being done. As per the available information, everybody is doing their best so that you are freed from all accusations and get justice. May God make these efforts successful and bless me so that I can meet you again. For the time being, wait with an inner and outer smile for the blessings of God."[17]

The scenario in Hyderabad in South was diametrically opposite to that of Kashmir in the North. Nizam of Hyderabad's intention was to declare Independence, get recognition from U.N.O. and then become a part of Pakistan. The Maharaja had not provoked the minority Hindus to exploit the majority Muslims in Kashmir. But the Nizam of Hyderabad had organised minority Muslims as Razaakars to terrorise the majority Hindus day in and night out. Neighbouring state of Central Provinces had to worry about protecting the helpless population from these human devils. Both the Chief Minister Ravi Shankar Shukla and Home Minister Dwarika Prasad Mishra sought Guruji's co-operation. Guruji asked them to contact Vidarbha Sanghchaalak Bapusaheb Sohoni. Sohoni ji writes about that episode thus, "We had planned a major publicity drive in Washim, Mehkar, etc. areas when Razaakars were running riot. The purpose of our campaign was to generate confidence in the people, banish their terror and generate confidence in the people about the government's ability to protect their life and property. The government provided us with petrol and other facilities."[18]

In summary, during the tragic time of the heart-rending Partition of the country, countless swayamsevaks of the Sangh made thousands of efforts to save the general public from the grave danger under the faultless guidance and balanced approach of Guruji. Writing about those terrifying times, Professor A.N. Bali, in his book, *Now It Can Be Told*, says, "Who came to the rescue in those difficult times to protect the people, except those young men known as R.S.S.? They arranged for safe passage of women and children in each and every *mohalla*, in every city of the state. They arranged for their food, medical help and clothing and took their care in every possible way. They organised fire-fighting teams in different cities and towns. They arranged for lorries and buses to carry the escaping Hindus and Sikhs and posted defence teams in railway trains. They patrolled relentlessly in different Hindu and Sikh localities. They trained people in self-defence. They were the first ones to reach these terrified people, first to help them and were the last to come to secure places in east Punjab. I can recount the names of many well-known Congress leaders in different districts of Punjab who took help from the R.S.S. for their own security and security of their families. They never ignored any call for help. There were many cases where Sangh volunteers took Muslim women and children from Hindu *mohallas* to Muslim League refugee camps.

"When the entire Punjab was on fire and Congress leaders were sitting helplessly in Delhi, at that time volunteers of R.S.S. saved the people of Punjab with their discipline, and physical strength, risking their own lives. Now, if somebody from outside Punjab was to tell the Hindus and Sikhs to forget those Sikhs and the brave heroes of Rashtriya Swayamsevak Sangh who put their lives at risk to defend them, then their calls would go unheeded.

"Each and every person from amongst the refugees who came from West Pakistan is indebted to the Sangh. When everybody had abandoned them, only the Sangh stood by them."[19]

□

Endnotes

1. *Shri Guruji Samagra*, Vol. 5, pp. 167-168
2. Ibid, pp. 168
3. Ibid, pp. 169-170
4. *Maa. Sa. Golwalkar*, pp. 92
5. *Shri Guruji Punjab Mein*, pp. 7
6. Ibid, pp. 7
7. *Nine Years of R.S.S. in Sindh*, pp. 101
8. *Rashtray Namah*, pp. 106
9. Ibid, pp. 108
10. *Shri Guruji Punjab Mein*, pp. 8
11. Ibid, pp. 8
12. Ibid, pp. 25-26
13. Ibid, pp. 26
14. Ibid, pp. 31-32
15. *Jyoti Jalaa Nij Praan Ki*, pp. 229-232
16. *Shri Guruji: Pioneer of New Era*, pp. 66-67
17. *Shri Guruji Samagra*, Vol. 8, pp. 42
18. *Maa. Sa. Golwalkar*, pp. 114
19. *Rashtray Namah*, pp. 99-100

20

Blooming of Optimism and Thorns of Envy

In his book *Golwalkar and R.S.S.*, author Jagat S. Bright writes, "R.S.S. had worked like the Red Cross Society during those days. The Sangh's contribution in saving innocent people from the spread of Islam before and after Independence was outstanding. The service that R.S.S. rendered to the society in those hours of grave danger was highly appreciated by the Deputy Prime Minister, Sardar Patel. (P.16)." What the author of this book had said was, indeed, a fact, but the Sangh was not an organisation like the Red Cross Society confined to a limited objective. Its principal dimension was about uniting and organising people. Guruji was careful to remind people about this aspect in those times. In various get-togethers of swayamsevaks in different places, he spoke eloquently, "The service (*sewa*) that the Sangh is tendering in extraordinary circumstances in Punjab and Bengal is *apaat dharma* (*dharma* performed in emergency situation). Such work is relevant or necessary only at the time of a calamity. Naturally, this kind of work is temporary. Sangh has a long term, perennial *dharma* that is its essence of being. That is to unite the weakened Hindu society, make it strong and forceful. This goal is long-term work unaffected by any prevailing situation. It should keep functioning forever like the natural breathing of a living being."

Tireless efforts put in by the Sangh to resettle the refugees properly could not be overlooked by anyone even if one wished to. However, in political circles, this generated jealousy and fear. Responding to it pointedly, Guruji noted at the Vijayadashami festival of that year on 24th October, 1947, "Reacting to the acknowledgement that the Sangh has received for easing the pain of affected Hindu people of Punjab, an English daily has commented that it is 'Unfortunate, but true'. Various political parties also wish to confront the Sangh in a similar manner. They are worried that in case the Sangh enters the arena of electoral politics, what will be their fate? I wish to assure these parties which are trying to save their respective reputations with means fair or foul, that their fear is meaningless."[1]

In the same public meeting, in order that swayamsevaks and friends of the Sangh keep a right perspective, he clarified, “The swayamsevaks provided wholehearted support to the people in that horrifying situation. For this, the Sangh has never appreciated its swayamsevaks, because Sangh swayamsevaks have only done their natural duty. Just like a brother taking care of his sick brother, keeping awake by his bedside does not get details of his services published in newspapers; similarly, swayamsevaks have served their brethren and helped them. There we didn’t feel the need to sing paeans to them.”[2]

Guruji’s views were also very clear about Independence that we got after the Partition; it is true that he did not accept the Partition of the country till his last days. For example, in his lectures, he always used the term, “Part of our country that is called Pakistan today”. Still, he never spoke in a critical way like the Communists who used to say, “This ‘Independence’ is not Independence”, that “Independence Day is a day of fraud”. He accepted the unpalatable truth, even if with anguish. Waiting for the dawn of Independence on 9th August, he spoke in Ahmedabad, as if pouring his heart out, “Members of a family do not celebrate the birth of the first child if the mother dies during the birth of her son. A deep sense of grief envelopes the family. I recall such an incident when a son was born in a family, but the head of the family died within a short time after that. The child was in mother’s lap, but the mother’s heart did not experience any happiness. Lord of her life had left her alone. Her life was totally destroyed. The mother’s life became meaningless and joyless. My condition is like that of that mother. Our relationship with the Hindu society is like that of the Arya husband and wife. For me the pain of getting separated from my brethren is unbearable.”[3]

Overcoming those sentiments of introspection, he sought people’s attention about their national duty, “First step upon attaining the nation’s Independence is to take pride in our forefathers, and not in philosophies of other nations like Russia, America, England, etc. When every individual owns up the goal of national welfare, forgetting about self, only then can the nation arise... Independence will be founded only on selfless sacrifice.”[4]

Guruji began his regular nationwide tours after handing over relief work of Punjab and Bengal to capable people. He reached Pune on 30th October after attending the Vijayadashami festival in Nagpur. Over one lakh people had converged on the playground of Parashuram Bhau Mahavidyalaya for this mammoth public meeting. He reached Akola on 6th December for the state-level camp of Vidarbha. Ten thousand swayamsevaks took part in that camp; 10,000 swayamsevaks and 75,000 other citizens attended the rally in Shivaji Park in Mumbai. The experience in Raipur and Jabalpur, etc. in Madhya Pradesh was also similar. This state in Mahakoshal region had 600 Shakhas and 36,000 swayamsevaks at that time.

South India was not far behind. The organisation kept growing there too.

Guntur district in Andhra Pradesh had 31 Shakhas and 3,000 swayamsevaks when Sarsanghchaalak arrived there. Hyderabad was not a part of Andhra at that time because the Sangh was not allowed to carry out its activities in the areas that fell under the Nizam's rule. During those times, leading Congress members, like T.S. Prakasham, Acharya Ranga, Pattaabhi Sitharamaiyya were supporting the Sangh and used to provide help, if requested. Karnataka had been favourable to the Sangh since its inception there. More than 8,000 swayamsevaks in full uniform were present at the state-level winter camp held from 19th January to 21st in Bengaluru. In the coastal city of Mangalore, the Sangh well-wishers transformed the whole of Mangalore into a sea of saffron and the schools declared a holiday on the day Sarsanghchaalak visited it. The organisation was growing in Kerala too. Hundreds of swayamsevaks and thousands of citizens were present at the meetings there too. So-called progressives tried to disrupt a meeting held in the month of January 1948, but they failed miserably. The scenario in Tamil Nadu was no different. Many scholars and public dignitaries, like Justice Rajamannar, owner of All India Law Reporter, K.N. Annaji Rao, and leader of People's rights movement T.R. Venkataram Shastri met Guruji during that tour. Motivated by Guruji's call, many swayamsevaks had begun to take up Sangh work as Prachaaraks in the South. On the whole, the atmosphere and sentiments were of evolution and growth.

It is said that a human being swings between extremes of happiness and grief. The year of 1947 was one such year. Regarding the heralding of Independence on the one hand after centuries and the cruel massacre of countless brethren of our country on the other, what kind of guidance did Guruji give the Sangh and citizens in that dark period? There is an incident of those days with a deep meaning. A sentimental swayamsevak had written an emotional song at that time. Its opening lines were:

Vang Panjnad balivedi par asankhya ye balidan,
Unaki punya raakh mein uthate prashna anek mahaan.

(Countless martyrs have sacrificed their lives on the sacrificial altar of Bengal and Punjab. Their sacred ashes raise many a pertinent questions).

Young swayamsevaks loved this song very much in the prevailing atmosphere of the time. Guruji heard the song in a *baithak* (meeting). Without hurting the sentiments of the swayamsevaks, he spoke immediately after it, "It is not right to sing such excitable songs collectively. The emotions generated by this will be negative and momentary." These words of Guruji remind one of the words spoken by Lord Krishna in the *Gita* while he talked of '*vaangmay tapa*' (literary penance). '*Anudvegakaram vaakyam satyam priyahitam cha yat*', that is, penance of spoken word is that which does not excite; a true dialogue that pleases others and does good unto others. In one of his speeches in Lucknow, he had said, "Work done as a reaction is transitory in nature. It doesn't invoke a balanced emotion and when reactionary feeling passes away, such a work gets annihilated too."[5]

As the day of Independence drew near, he explained the meaning of this invaluable word to the swayamsevaks. To his mind, independence did not simply mean transfer of power. Getting rid of slavery and being independent – he looked at both the conditions differently. For him, Bharat's 'Independence', not being dependent, and Bharat's freedom – being free – were not the same. The former word symbolises lack of dependence while the latter symbolises the power of 'self'. Addressing senior citizens in the capital, Delhi, he said, "Liberating our intellect from the values (*samskaaras*) of other countries and evolving a system (*tantra*) of growth with our own feelings and will is '*swa-tantra*' (system by self). But, a system that is born by ignoring our history and being slaves of intellect of others inspired by other societies will not be *swa-tantra* but *para-tantra* (system of others, or slavery of others). A system based on Russia's directions will be a 'Russian-*tantra*', not *swa-tantra*; a system inspired by the politicians of England, under their guardianship or their support, will be England's system; a federal system created with inspiration of free America would be an American system, never *swa-tantra*."[6]

Going a step further during that year while speaking about nurturing freedom, he said, "We wish to envision the soul of our nation. We want to keep our sense of nationalism alive. We wish to make our nation powerful and prosperous. The philosophy of nationalism is not a philosophy about political rights."

"We do not wish to borrow talent from outsiders to build our lives. We have our own talent. We will create our own way of life from it. A system that will symbolise our sense of pride, that would be built around comprehensive '*Bharatiyataa*', that through which flows perennial Bharatiya tradition, that is the system of the national way of life."[7]

Guruji doesn't pause here. He leads the workers dedicated to the nation to the profound meaning of freedom. According to him, self-rule is only a via media for freedom to make life-systems successful. In his discourse in front of Pune workers, he said, "The system of self-rule is there to provide a stable foundation to Hindu philosophy, to our way of life, so that the sacredness of our national soul grows, our noble philosophy expands. Political power is only a medium, not an end in itself; and an instrument cannot be a goal."[8]

In that period, the ideas propagated by Sarsanghchaalak were of this kind and of such high thinking. Of these, the views propagated in Mumbai are of critical importance. One cannot forget about its practical relevance in relation to the horrible disaster during the period of the Partition. When an excited society was moving towards the horizon of a new-found freedom after centuries of slavery, at that time Guruji definitely presented an integral and inclusive view about freedom. On 15th January, 1948, in the transitional period of Independence of the country, speaking at a public meeting in Shivaji Park, Guruji said, "This period of transition (*sankraman*) has taken us through varied experiences. It is wrong to expect that we shall only experience joy. In the life of a nation, one confronts countless dangers, calamities and hundreds of problems. But this is the time to do something with intelligence and thoughtfulness with a lot of patience and skill."

"We should reflect calmly that in the life of a human being, different experiments take place. They will surely result in victory-defeat, happiness-grief, success-failure. Getting upset with a prevailing condition and inflicting pain on fellow-beings is not right. We must give some time to any experiment, otherwise it will be grave injustice to the people who are committed to these experiments."

"In this transitional period, the wave of anger (*dwesh*) rises in the heart when one witnesses the state of chaos and poor conditions that one feels. 'What is going on?' But, to be angry due to the influence of our weakness will not help. Inspite of whatever is happening, we must have the readiness in our conscience to forgive. The sense of oneness with our brethren should not weaken even by an iota."

"The founder of the Sangh has put before us the ideal of Yudhishthir. Yudhishthir had no place in his heart for negative feelings like anger, envy, animosity or frustration. Yudhishthir never even showed any anger towards Duryodhan who was the cause of all his difficulties, adversities and the reason for being made to live in the forest. When the five Pandavas were staying in the forest in the clothes made of leaves and grass, Duryodhan came there with other Kauravas to show off his wealth. Offended at their insolent behaviour, the Gandharvas waged a battle against them and imprisoned them. When the Pandavas received this news, all the other four Pandavas, except Yudhishthir said, 'Good that the thorns in our path have been cleared.' But Yudhishthir, said, 'When we fight with each other, we are five and they are a hundred. But, if an outsider confronts us, we are one hundred and five. *Vayam panchaadhikam shatam*'.* This Yudhishthir is our ideal."[9]

Mahatma Gandhi was staying in a Harijan *basti* during this period. The Harijan brethren had built a small but beautiful and clean temple for their ancestor and effulgent soul, Sage Valmiki in one corner of the colony. On the other side, there was a large settlement of Muslims. Therefore, the government had acknowledged within that the Mahatma's life was not safe in that Harijan settlement. Gandhiji, on the other hand, was against posting of military or police for his security there. In this state of dilemma, top Congress leader Krishnan Nair met the state Prachaarak Vasantrao Oke and requested him to arrange for security of revered Bapuji. Vasantrao implemented a proper plan for this.[10]

---

* *Paraihe paribhave praapte panchyottaram shatam,*
Parasparvirodhe tu vayampancham shatam tu te II – Vanaparva, Chapter 285, canto-4

Not even thirty days had passed since the proclamation of Independence when the Muslim League hatched a conspiracy to blow up the top leaders of Bharat. They had made plans for a massive explosion. Alert swayamsevaks working day and night had done their own investigation and passed on information to Sardar Patel. Based on this information, the armed forces raided many places in Paharganj and surrounding areas and confiscated large cache of arms and explosives, and took action against the rebels. Dr. Bhagwandas, recipient of the Bharat Ratna has lifted the lid off this conspiracy on pp. 19 of his book *Crises*, published from Allahabad. He notes, "I have reliable information that some Sangh swayamsevaks of Delhi had gone to the extent of making a show of accepting Islam to gain the trust of Muslim League members in order to get details of the conspiracy hatched by them. It is only because of this that they could find and provide advance information to Sardar Patel about the conspiracy of 10th September to kill all the ministers and civil officers and thousands of Hindu citizens, unfurl Pakistan's flag on Red Fort and grab control of the Indian government. If these young men, fired by ardour and patriotic feelings, had not provided information about this conspiracy in time, there would have been no Indian government today."[11]

Guruji was in Delhi at this time. He met the Home Minister at 7 in the morning on 7th September. He apprised him about his personal experiences in Sindh and Punjab and about the arrangements the Sangh had made about safety, security and well-being of the citizens there. He got ready to go to Kolkata by air after returning to his lodging. Just then, he received a message from Mahatma Gandhi, "Please meet me before leaving." "As you wish," he said, and saying so, went with Lala Hansraj ji to meet Mahatma in Birla Bhavan at 10.30 a.m.

The situation was grave. Delhi was burning that week. Mahatma Gandhi had reached Delhi only on 9th September after moving around in Kolkata. The situation in the capital had already turned for the worse before his arrival. Displaced refugees, moving into Ajmeri Gate and Kashmiri Gate of Delhi, were livid with searing anger. Mahatma Gandhi and Guruji were meeting in the background of such an atmosphere. Probably, influenced by rumour-mongers, truth-seeker Bapu asked him, "Even your hands are dirtied by blood, aren't they?" Guruji's answer was, "Not at all. They are not dirty; they are pure and clean." Grasping the meaning of what Babu was indicating, Guruji clarified, "I cannot claim to be aware about the conduct of each and every swayamsevak of the Sangh. However, the Sangh's objective is to serve Hindu society and Hindutva piously and the Sangh wishes to achieve this objective without inflicting injustice on anybody else. Though, the Sangh doesn't wish to attack anybody. Still it doesn't believe in excessive non-violence. It teaches self-defence. It has never taught the policy of revenge even by mistake. During the discussions, Gandhiji asked Guruji to give a written statement that he would ask the people to be peaceful. Responding to the suggestion, Guruji said, "Who will listen to me? Your words are respected everywhere; you are senior. So, it is ideal that you release the statement. If you wish so, you can mention my acceptance of your views." Finally, this is how the statement was released. At the evening prayer meeting, Gandhiji declared, "Golwalkar has assured his full co-operation in establishing peace." Newspapers also published this statement on the next day.[12]

The Rashtriya Swayamsevak Sangh and Guruji gained popularity very rapidly in such an atmosphere. Unfortunately, opposition to the Sangh was rising slowly in the Congress circles. Guruji had expressed his views on the reason behind this opposition in his Vijayadashami lecture at Nagpur already.

Guruji had met Sardar Patel and Gandhiji in September. He had not been able to meet the Prime Minister due to Prime Minister's busy schedule. When Guruji visited Delhi again during his tour in October, this meeting became possible. Talks lasted for nearly one hour. Guruji could gauge that Nehru's attitude about the Sangh was different and unfavourable. Clarifying the objectives of the Sangh, Guruji began by saying, "Lack of a fundamentally strong and capable organised power has resulted in our nation's inability to influence the world today." Diverting his target towards the Sangh in an accusing tone, Nehru said, "But such a power should not be evil." Guruji understood the import of these words immediately. Responding that his understanding of the Sangh power as evil was against the ground realities, he went on to present his analysis of the disturbances in northern states and added, "The sense of bitterness prevailing across the country is not because of the Sangh, it is because of the tragic Partition." After discussing other related subjects, he took leave and requested him that such an atmosphere by the government should be created that the feeling of co-operation would be encouraged.[13]

It was decided to hold a full-fledged camp of young swayamsevaks of western Maharashtra at Pune on 1st - 2nd November 1947. One lakh swayamsevaks were expected to attend this camp. Being trained and habituated to volunteer for Sangh work, the swayamsevaks took leave from their jobs and businesses to make arrangements for the camp in sufficient numbers. Guruji's presence from the beginning at the camp was assured. Sardar Patel had also agreed to come as the Chief Guest. Akashwani (All India Radio) had also arranged for broadcasting the news about the camp. Support from all quarters for the camp was available as expected. There was an atmosphere of enthusiasm all around, but there were evil souls, like Mantharaa, feeling uncomfortable and seething with jealousy in the Congress camp. Ultimately, the state Home Minister gave the excuse of a grave situation and rescinded on the permission for the camp. It was clear that the Sangh had become a victim of internal pulls and pressures within the Congress.

In reality, there was not a trace of disturbance in the environment. Therefore, the swayamsevaks were more angered than disappointed. Any programme for condemnation and protest would have been successful, but, the Sangh office-bearers decided to convert this curse into a boon. Guruji sent out a notification immediately that there would be get-together rallies (*saanghik*) in full Sangh uniform in each district of Maharashtra and Guruji would be present in each of these get-togethers and would be greeted with 'Sarsanghchaalak *pranaam*' – salutation to the Sarsanghchaalak. The anger of swayamsevaks was transformed into zeal and they began working with a strong will to be victorious. Guruji toured all the thirteen districts from 24th October to 5th November. When the final reports were prepared, it turned out that more than four lakh swayamsevaks from 1,300 villages and towns had attended these programmes. Like the story recounted in the *Mahabharata,* the curse of the beautiful danseuse Urvashi became a blessing for Arjuna.

The pre-emptive, meaningless aborting of the state-level camp indicated the direction in which the thinking of the Congress government's machinery was moving. Next month, in November, a meeting of the Chief Ministers was called in Delhi. The topic of discussion was the increasing popularity of the Sangh and the challenge arising out of it. The problem facing them was how to bridle the Sangh.[14]

Around this time, accusing the swayamsevaks of fomenting riots at Kandale in Uttar Pradesh, the Congress government put up cases against them. (These accusations were proven incorrect later on). Such evil designs were witnessed in other places also.

According to the daily *Dainik Kaal*, dated 13th October, 1947, Satara Congress Committee in Maharashtra passed a resolution and asked Chief Minister B.G. Kher to 'uproot Rashtriya Swayamsevak Sangh'. In a threatening tone, the committee claimed that 'otherwise we will destroy the Sangh ourselves, using 1942-type of terrorist methods'. Giving sagely advice to them, Chief Minister told them, "Don't take up any action in a mood of pessimism, or else you would be totally destroyed."[15]

Later on, there was a meeting of All India Congress Committee on 17th January, 1948 in Delhi that passed a strongly worded resolution against the Sangh. It demanded state governments also to take anti-Sangh steps. The lowest units of the Congress were also asked to follow this policy. During this time, Central Government released a circular, which said, "It was illegal for a government servant to be a member of R.S.S." Leader of this anti-Sangh front was Uttar Pradesh Home Minister Rafi Ahmed Kidwai.

Even as the newly independent nation was passing through a grave crisis, diverse pulls and pressures and tensions between Nehru and Patel came into open. The Sangh too had to suffer because of this. Speaking at a public meeting on 6th January, 1948, Sardar Patel said, "Congress people in power should behave in a different manner with the Sangh rather than laying stress on their own rights and powers. It is not possible to suppress an organisation with the power of penal action. Sangh people are not the type who will fight for selfish interests. They are patriots who love their motherland." Within a few days, Pandit Nehru, as if in response to this speech, spoke at Amritsar, "Sangh and Hindu Mahasabha people have insulted our national flag. They are traitors. I will crush them." Such varied *ragas* give happiness in music, but they generate disturbing voices of dissonance in governance. The situation at the time was like this.

As described in this chapter, one could talk of countless leaders who came to Sangh offices begging for help in very difficult and helpless situations. But, today all this has become stale food. How and when did this feeling of ingratitude arise? Historian of Kashmir, Kalhan, has already given an answer to this – *yaksha prashna* – seemingly unsolvable riddle in his book; *Raajtarangini* written in the eighth century. His conclusion is that just as a newborn baby completely forgets about the pain of living in the womb, similarly, a ruler forgets about all that happened previously he comes into power.*

On one side, there was a defeatist feeling about giving in to the Partition, guilt complex that we are the cause of unexpected miseries and pains of countless people and the sense of failure that we couldn't lift a small finger to stop these excesses. On the other hand, there was this sense of brotherhood of swayamsevaks who jumped into the defence of helpless, displaced brethren and their rehabilitation without worrying about risks; pious emotions with which they brought leaders of various political parties to safety, without thinking about narrow party politics, to well-appointed centres. There is a living example of Guruji who jumped fearlessly into the terrible whirlpool of calamities and delivered life-giving support for a hope-filled future to the sufferers, and as a result, affectionate feelings of the populace towards the Sangh. This was a factual, comparative scenario.

Guruji kept his calm in this chaos of conflict between favourable and unfavourable emotions. It was not in his nature to express his opinion through press statements or to journalists. He was alert that in such an environment swayamsevaks and other workers should not lose their balance of mind or draw their attention away from the work at hand. He gave right directions to senior Prachaaraks and workers, whom he knew personally, across the country through letters or personal meetings. For example, at the fag end of year 1947 on 27th December, he writes to Rajabhau Deshpande of Pune, "…I am aware of the entire situation. This is a period of test, not of loss. We shall come out of it stronger and in a bigger form. Do not fall into the evil trap of opposition or confrontation and avoid bitterness in speech or action. Keep focussed on duty; it will lead to success and a favourable environment."[16]

Approach and analysis of newspapers was objective. They did not agree

* *Garbhaavasavyathaam taajah shareeree vismared yathaa. Praaptaraajyastathaa raajaa poorvachintinim – 5/201.*

with the government blindly. The daily *Hitavada* wrote on 28th October, "The Sangh has limitless capacity to unite and organise the Hindu society and take it above narrow emotions of caste, sect and language…people, who see signs of Hitler's Nazi organisation in the Sangh, are making a grave mistake."[17]

Madhya Pradesh's Home Minister, Pandit Dwarika Prasad Mishra's statement seemed like a statement given in favour of the Sangh. Giving a statement, countering the allegations of the opposing camp, to *Nagpur Navbhaarat* (19th December, 1947), he said, "The very idea that the Sangh can overthrow the government on the strength of *lathis* is laughable. It is surprising that this allegation was not made against the local D.S.P. I cannot believe at all that the Sangh is a political organisation and that there is a possibility of it overthrowing Pandit Nehru's government."[18]

Vaartaa Vihar of North Karnataka and South Maharashtra published the public speech of *Karnataka Kesari,* Gangadhar Rao Deshpande after another six days on 25th December, 1947. In this speech, he said, "Congress has passed a resolution recently very cleverly against the Sangh….strange are the games of fate that as soon as they got hold of power, they are parroting the idea of 'do not organise' whenever they think of the Sangh…. But, looking back at my experience of past 50 years, I can state not once but again and again, that organising Hindus is very crucial for maintaining peace in our country….. I pray to the people in power not to shirk away from this organisation. This organisation will ultimately come to their rescue at a crucial time."[19]

The most strident editorial appeared in *Tribune* that was being published from Delhi itself. It wrote on 26th November, "Pandit Nehru has instructed the East Punjab government to ban the R.S.S. and Akali Dal and destroy them. This news is so dreadful that it should not be true at all. And if it is true, then it can only be termed as a misfortune for this country because it is necessary for us to remind Pandit Nehru that if these nationalist organisations had not faced the cruel and inhuman Pakistanis with their bravery, then thousands of Hindu and Sikh sisters would have been raped, thousands of Sikh and Hindu children butchered. We wish to say this with full force at our command that the Sangh and Akali Dal have made a place for themselves deep in the hearts of the people of this bordering state. The people there looks at them as the sentinels of their state. It is nothing but ingratitude to brand these organisations communal or private armies. In fact, they are nationalist powers out to help us who have discipline like the Army, but have no arms. The Indian government should be proud of them."[20]

The Congress leadership never expected reactions of this order. They kept quiet for some time, but they were looking for the right opportunity. The real reason for this was pointed out by Shri Banahatti, the moving spirit of Sarvoday movement, in his weekly, *Savdhaan*. He wrote openly, "In this period, Rashtriya Swayamsevak Sangh is the only organisation that can challenge the Congress.

Talented, dedicated young class of high character is getting attracted to the Sangh due to its organised strength. This is the reason that the Sangh has become an eyesore for the Congress leaders. Congress is taking the nationwide work of the Sangh, its impact on educated, intelligent youth and rare qualities like readiness of its swayamsevaks to work patiently in times of any disaster, as a challenge to itself. The spiritual qualities due to which Congress used to think of itself as a superior power; the growth of the same qualities in the Sangh is making the Congress uncomfortable."[21]

What more can one say! Afflicted by Lord Devendra's mentality, the Congress government was bent upon not letting any pious soul to grow. It was waiting with an evil intention for the right opportunity 'sooner or later' to disrupt the sustained, unbroken meditation of the Sangh. Just at that time, as the Indian proverb goes, to the luck of the cat the pot broke down. For them, the incident that gave them this opportunity was the unfortunate assassination of Mahatma Gandhi.

□

Endnotes

1. *Shri Guruji Samagra*, Vol. 5, pp. 170-171
2. Ibid, pp. 171
3. *Shri Guruji Samagra*, Vol. 3, pp. 173
4. Ibid, pp.176
5. Ibid, pp. 167
6. Ibid, pp. 153-154
7. Ibid, pp. 169-170
8. Ibid, pp. 28
9. *Shri Guruji Samagra*, Vol. 5, pp. 269-271
10. *Pehli Agnipariksha,* pp. 25-26
11. *Maa. Sa. Golwalkar*, pp. 108
12. Ibid, pp. 109
13. Ibid, pp. 109-110
14. Ibid, pp. 119
15. *Pehli Agnipariksha*, pp. 41
16. *Shri Guruji Samagra*, Vol. 8, pp. 44
17. *Pehli Agnipariksha,* pp. 42
18. Ibid, pp. 42
19. Ibid, pp. 43
20. Ibid, pp. 43-44
21. Ibid, pp. 32

21

Dissolution of an Outlawed Organisation

Mahatma Gandhi was killed on 30th January, 1948 in the evening by an unknown assailant. Guruji was participating in a felicitation programme at Chennai on the lawns of the Ramakrishna Lunch Home with some elite citizens. He reached Chennai on the 29th after touring district centres in Kerala and Tamil Nadu in the second half of January. He had addressed a huge meeting overflowing with people in the grounds of Muthaiah Chetti High School that evening. On the second day, the 30th, there was a meeting with Prachaaraks of Tamil Nadu and Kerala in the morning followed by a meeting of Shakha workers of Chennai. The main agenda of the meetings was to strengthen the Sangh activities. He sought attention of the workers to the fact that real triumph of an activity doesn't stem from a successful programme, but creation of workers through it. His instruction to the workers was that we should not forget our regular working methodology while feeling exhilarated at the success of our programmes. He responded to Pandit Nehru's threat in his speech at Amritsar indirectly in the public meeting he addressed. He said, "We shall face successfully, any disaster that befalls the Sangh. This work has not grown with somebody's courtesy nor will it shut down if somebody stares at it with anger. It was not created by a paper resolution. Therefore, nor can it be dissolved by paper resolution." The host Rajagopalachari had invited 10-12 lawyer friends for a luncheon on the 30th afternoon. There were two members of the judiciary in it. The fourth programme on that day was this felicitation on the lawns of Ramakrishna Lunch Home. While people were carrying on with informal discussions in a cheerful atmosphere that evening, news of the murder of Mahatma Gandhi hit it like a thunderbolt. It was a grievous blow for all the participants. Guruji sat down in a far corner. He kept aside his cup of tea. Perhaps he was deeply troubled by the possible repercussions in the near future. Sanghchaalak Rajagopalachari adjourned the felicitation programme.

Guruji had to leave for Vijayawada the same night by *G.T. Express*. He cancelled the plan immediately and got busy sending telegrams or letters to the concerned people. He sent separate condolence messages to Prime Minister, Deputy Prime Minister, Gandhiji's son Devdas Gandhi, "I am deeply shocked to hear about the tragic murder of a divine soul because of a cruel fatal attack. In these difficult times, this has caused an immeasurable loss to the nation. May God give you the strength to fill the vacuum caused by the passing away of an incomparable organiser."[1]

Rajagopalachari's advocate chamber was converted into an ad-hoc central office that night. Typewriters began typing out messages and instructions to the concerned centres. On the same day, Sarsanghchaalak passed instructions from Chennai to all the Shakhas, "To express our grief due to the sad demise of respected Mahatmaji, Shakhas will observe a condolence period for 13 days and all daily programmes will be put on hold."[2] Guruji left for Nagpur on Saturday, 31st January by air.

He was disturbed on reaching Hedgewar Bhavan with receipt of information from various quarters. On hearing of the disturbing news, Delhi state Sanghchaalak Lala Hansraj Gupta, city Sanghchaalak Harishchandra Gupta and state Prachaarak Vasantrao Oke – all the three went to Birla Bhavan to share their grief. They met many Congress leaders they had good contacts with. All the swayamsevaks had gathered in the Mohite Shakha Ground on Saturday morning in Nagpur. City Karyavaah (Secretary) Advocate Bachcharaj Vyas criticised the murder of Mahatma Gandhi sharply and described in a touching manner, the impact the departed soul had left on the people that could not be erased, and a collective homage was paid. The same evening a large condolence meeting was organised in Patwardhan Ground. Hundreds of swayamsevaks had taken part there too.[3] So far, there was calm all around.

But, by evening, as darkness descended, evil souls and demons of envy, antagonism and destruction were seen getting into their act. Nehru, unwittingly, had done the job of pouring oil over the simmering fire. Reacting in anger from Amritsar, he declared, "R.S.S. is responsible for the murder of the Father of the Nation." Sadly, the identity of the killer had not yet been established, still the person holding the most responsible post of the nation had spoken like this. The Sangh had to pay the tragic price for his indiscretion.

Immediately upon reaching Nagpur, on 31st January, the same day, Guruji wrote letters to 'Respected Pandit ji' in English and '*Manyavar Sardar ji*' in Hindi. Apart from the difference in language, the contents and import of both the letters were same. In the letter written in Hindi, he wrote, "I was in Chennai yesterday when I heard about the tragic news that has shaken the entire humanity. Such an evil and condemnable incident would never have taken place in history. The heart is distressed with unbearable pain."

It is difficult to find the right words to condemn the person who has carried out this despicable act. One cannot even think of such a senseless evil act. What can one say of a person who has stunned the whole world into silence?

But, let us all carry out the responsibilities that have come upon us due to the untimely demise of a great leader by remembering that noble soul who could weave together people of different nature into a unifying thread and take them along on a common path; and let us all arise with renewed strength in this terrible time of a catastrophe with reasoned emotions, compassionate behaviour, controlled speech and fill the nation with a perennial sense of unity.

This will be a true and pious remembrance of that great personality. I pray to the ever-benign Supreme Being on behalf of our organisation that treads the path of unity with reverence that he may guide them on to the path that may inspire all the people of this nation to generate pure sublime patriotism."[4]

These were the earliest letters that Guruji wrote to esteemed Pandit ji and Sardar Patel. It is worth paying attention to the closing words of both the letters. In the letter written to Nehru, they were, "Yours in the service of the Mother" and in Sardar Patel's letter in Hindi, they were "*Matri seva mein sahabhaagi*". Indeed, 'Service of the mother' is the relation that ties together all the fine sons of Bharat. He uses the same words in all his subsequent correspondence.

Hardly six months had passed since the dawn of Independence. At that moment, the media groups uncritically accepted whatever was spoken by people like Pandit Nehru and Sardar Patel, who were considered architects of the freedom. Thus, newspapers trusted the accusations thrown by Pandit Nehru and looked at all the subsequent incidents through such an angle. This was clear from the way Guruji's first statement was neglected or twisted. Guruji had sent his first statement on the first day of February for publication. He had prefaced his statement thus, "Assassination of a most revered and popular supreme personality of the modern world is a despicable and beastly act of the worst kind. At such a time, leaving aside our tradition of giving public lectures and statements, I feel it is my duty to express the feeling of extreme revulsion and grief that has engulfed my heart." Drawing his attention towards the extremely difficult situation that had arisen due to Gandhiji's murder, he noted, "Today, the situation of our country is precarious. At such a time, presence of that person of unity and peace was acutely required. Murder of such a great personality is an unpardonable anti-national act. Our heart is enraged when we think of the harm that our nation has suffered and we are worried about future." In such a severely tragic scenario, while requesting people to take the path of service, he told the swayamsevaks, "If somebody speaks with irresponsibility due to irritation or passion, or somebody exhibits unnecessary fury, even then the swayamsevak brothers should understand that this is an expression of love and respect of every citizen for the Mahatma who raised prestige of our nation in the eyes of the world."[5] This statement was sent out for publication to the news agency A.P.A. It didn't release it in full but released it in a twisted form. Many newspapers simply overlooked it. The *Organiser* of Delhi published it in full, but it was merely a weekly with limited circulation.

The body of the priest of non-violence had not even been properly cremated when devotees of non-violence turned violent. They waged violence on swayamsevaks. Homes and properties of thousands of swayamsevaks were turned to ash. Taking advantage of the situation, even the Communist and Socialist hyenas took part in this act of looting that went on for the whole night.

A group of unruly elements collected before Guruji's house within two to two-and-a-half hours of his statement reaching A.P.A. Swayamsevaks too came together and threatened them with dire consequences if they advanced further. Stone-throwing began from outside the house. One swayamsevak began piling up the stones that fell inside the compound. In the meanwhile, police arrived and tried to calm down the atmosphere. Police officer who came to Guruji's house saw the pile of stones in the compound. He surmised, "You people must have collected these stones." That very moment stone throwing commenced again and the swayamsevak began his exercise again. Guruji looked into the eyes of the officer. He had got his answer about his suspicion.[6] For the time being, the group of ruffians went back. Police sealed Nagoba Lane where Guruji's house was situated and put tight control on vehicular movement around it. During the same time, ruffians broke the plinth raised in the sacred memory of Sangh founder in Reshim Bagh.

The atmosphere seemed to be calm from outside, but there was a raging fire of hatred in anti-Sangh camps due to provocation of their leaders. Therefore, all wise people were quite sure that, because of such an atmosphere, the condolence meeting of Chitnis could get converted into a meeting for taking revenge and people taking part in it would transform from grief-stricken people into violent crowds. Experience of stone throwing on Guruji's house was still fresh in everybody's memory. So, a group of eight to ten swayamsevaks was posted as per the decision and directions of Balasaheb Deoras in Nagoba Lane. In that team were experts in physical training, such as Raja Paturkar, Ram Joshi, Madhukar Bhagwat and others. Eknath Ranade, an expert strategist like Tanaji, also joined them without any delay. He went to other areas after finalising the strategy. These courageous people had decided that they will not allow even a hair of Guruji to be harmed. Guruji understood about this movement. He called the leaders of this self-defense group and said in a calm voice, "It seems that you have got excited. Stop worrying about me. You are asking me to move out of here and go elsewhere. But where? Why? This is my society. I have been working for it. If it doesn't need me, then so be it. Where can I go by abandoning it? Whatever has to happen will happen; leave it to God. You people, please get away from here. I am going for my evening prayers." Speaking thus, he went inside the house.[7]

The police force filled up Nagoba Lane within 15 minutes. All the neighbours and swayamsevaks thought that the government officers had taken their job of security responsibly. But, the truth was something else. The state government had received orders at midnight of 2nd February from the Central Government to arrest Guruji. Deployment of police force was an advance preparation for this action.

Kashinath Pawar, a swayamsevak, had already received information about this 'highly confidential' order of the Centre through his sources. He brought it to the notice of Guruji immediately. As a result, Guruji sat wearing his *dhoti-kurta*, ready to 'get arrested' at the appointed time. Police officer Bobade came pompously with his paraphernalia. He was late by 30 minutes as per the scheduled time. On seeing him, Guruji told him promptly, "Gentleman, you are late by half-an-hour."[8]

When the arrest warrant was being read out, Guruji exclaimed, "Is that so?" because it was written in the warrant that arrest was under Sections 302, 307 and 120. "Let's go," and saying so, he proceeded towards the police van. Pausing between the silently standing swayamsevaks, most of whom were Sangh office-bearers, he said in a few measured words, "The cloud of suspicion will melt away and we shall come out of this unblemished. Till that time, there will be lots of atrocities, but we should bear them with fortitude. I firmly believe that Sangh swayamsevaks will pass this test successfully."[9]

Bobade took Guruji to the senior officer Bambawale's house as per orders and from there on to the Nagpur Central Jail. Sarkaryavaah (General Secretary) M.N. Kale sent a telegram all over the country, "Guruji arrested, maintain complete peace." The government had suppressed the news of the arrest. In the same vein, postal department also showed carelessness in sending out the telegrams. Still the swayamsevaks received the news and succeeding notifications through its organisational network.

Home Minister of Central Provinces at that time, Dwarika Prasad Mishra writes in his autobiography, *Living in An Era*, "That Mahatma Gandhi's assassination gave a handle to unscrupulous politicians to defame and, if possible, to pull down their rivals is difficult to deny." (P. 59 of the original English version.) Actions that were initiated later on prove the legitimacy of this statement. Following the arrest of Guruji, the Nehru government issued a notification on 2nd February to create the right atmosphere and prepare grounds for banning the Sangh. It issued another notification to clarify it further on 4th February. Ban on Rashtriya Swayamsevak Sangh was announced through this notification. Major points of this notification of nearly 500 words are as follows:

- It has been resolved to uproot and wipe out all violent and inimical forces that are putting the country's Independence at risk and blemishing its bright reputation. Under this policy, Government of India has decided to declare Rashtriya Swayamsevak Sangh an unlawful organisation.
- The declared objective of Rashtriya Swayamsevak Sangh is 'to

develop Hindus physically, intellectually and mentally and bring about a feeling of brotherhood and spirit of service in them'. But it is a matter of regret that members of Rashtriya Swayamsevak Sangh do not conduct themselves according to this declared objective.

- Sangh swayamsevaks have also been carrying out illegitimate activities. Its members are involved in violent activities like arson, looting, robbery, murders, piling up arms and explosives secretly. It has also been noted that they distribute pamphlets asking people to take to path of terrorism using guns and creating disaffection against the government and motivating Army and Police to rebel. Such actions are taken up in a secretive manner.
- Such objectionable and lethal activities of the Sangh have been going on and many people have fallen prey to this idea of violence supported by the Sangh, amongst whom Gandhiji himself is the latest victim.
- Government accepts it as its duty to take strict steps to crush this extreme expression of violence. As a first step in this direction, the Sangh is being declared an unlawful organisation.[10]

One can summarise the above as (a) the Sangh is not working as per its declared objectives, (b) the Sangh is taking up acts of violence in a secret manner, (c) Gandhiji is its latest victim, and (d) the Sangh is being declared unlawful to crush this expression of violence.

Readers will need to pay special attention to this notification of the Central Government, only then will they be able to understand objectively the efforts of Sarsanghchaalak to get this ban withdrawn and the government's wavering stance in this matter in the following days.

Guruji received the news about this ban on the Sangh in prison. He prepared a small statement in English after pondering over the future course of action. He was sure that some senior worker would come to meet him. This belief was not unfounded. His old lawyer-friend, Dattatreya Deshpande came to meet him on 5th February. After discussing the matter with him, Guruji handed over the statement to him. He distributed copies of this statement to newspapers and agencies.

In the first year of Independence, old systems were still prevalent. The all-India centre of Post and Telegraph Department in Nagpur was working on the same lines. It was possible for the Government to suppress any news from there and it took full advantage of this power. But, it was not totally successful in this. Bharat *Jyoti* from Mumbai published it in full. *Dawn* supported by Pakistan's ruling party published it fully that highlighted the ban on the Sangh with a remark that betrayed its sense of satisfaction, "Our old demand had been fulfilled today." Guruji's statement was, "It has been Rashtriya Swayamsevak Sangh's policy to conduct its activities within the rules and regulations of the government. The present government has declared Sangh illegal. Thus, I deem it fit to disband the Sangh till this ban is taken back. However, I completely refuse to accept the allegations leveled against the Sangh."[11]

Just as advocate Deshpande returned after meeting Guruji, the jailor sent a message that A.G.P. Hirachand Jain was coming down to interrogate the accused under Section 302. The jailor ordered that Golwalkar be presented as soon as he arrived. To insult the accused and put him in awe, he settled his bulky frame on a chair and put his feet with shoes on the table in his front. He also kept blowing up smoke from his cigarette. When Guruji was brought in his presence, he spoke in a taunting tone, "Oh, so you are that Guru Golwalkar? And you are the chief, Sarsanghchaalak of R.S.S.? But, you are so thin and frail!" Seeing his insolence, Guruji shot back, "The Sangh founder Dr. Hedgewar had not fixed up the shape and size of the person while choosing the Sarsanghchaalak, or else he would have put a buffalo or even yourself on that chair." The police officer was totally taken aback by this unexpected repartee. He immediately sat up properly and asked for a chair for Guruji. He began, "Guruji, I have come to take an oral statement from you in connection with this case." Just as he spoke these words, Guruji asked him, "How long have you been serving the police department?" The officer was stunned and sat up carefully and said, "*Arrey*, I have straightened up even the most dangerous criminals." In a calm and fearless voice, Guruji repeated, "That is why I am asking you, how long have you been serving this police department?" Hirachand softened a bit and said, "What do you mean?" Guruji responded, "Nothing. I understand that the oral statement of a person charged with murder is not taken in a prison but in front of a magistrate, in the presence of his lawyer. You are not even aware of this primary knowledge of criminal law. That is the reason, gentleman, why I am asking you, how long have you been in this service?"

The officer was now shaken up and when he came to know that the person in front of him had passed law with flying colours, he was totally shaken. He abandoned his interrogation and stood up to leave. Guruji, then, added, "Gentleman, tell your Home Minister that do put up the charge of murder against me with permission of the courts. Then I will tell the court who were the ministers who had attended the Sangh programmes at different places and times, and what were the words they had used to express their views about the Sangh. I can even produce evidence of your Home Minister Sardar Patel and Pandit Nehruji."[12]

A.G.P. Hirachand went back quietly. He must have given this information, reporting it with the same feeling, to his senior officers. Whatever may have been the case, Sections 302, 307 and 120 were rescinded and Guruji was put under arrest for six months under sections of the Defence Act.

In short, the nine-day period, from 30th January to 7th February, was like a complete period of life-cycle in the life of Guruji.

- First day, 30th January – Lunch with judicial officers and solicitors; and lightning assault of heart-rending news on the same evening
- Second day, 31st January – Condolence message, release of statement and directives etc.
- Third day, 1st February – Getting stuck amidst dangerous stone-throwing
- Fourth day, 2nd February – Arrest under criminal charges of murder, solitary confinement in prison
- Sixth day, 4th February – Ban on his organisation
- Seventh day, 5th February – Dissolution of his dearest organisation with his own hands
- Ninth day, 7th February – Absolved of the charges of murder, arrest under Defence Act

Such are the games that fate plays. And for how various dimensions are transformed, one can only say, "*Baleeyasee kevalam eeshwaramechcha*" – Ultimately, the will of God prevails. Guruji was a guest of Nagpur Central Prison from 7th February to 6th August.

□

Endnotes

1. *Shri Guruji Samagra*, Vol. 10, pp. 5
2. Ibid, pp. 5
3. *Pehli Agnipariksha,* pp. 21
4. *Shri Guruji Samagra*, Vol. 10, pp. 7
5. Ibid, pp. 8
6. *Maa. Sa. Golwalkar*, pp. 123-124
7. Ibid, pp. 125
8. *Pehli Agnipariksha*, pp. 18
9. *Maa. Sa. Golwalkar*, pp. 125-126
10. *Shri Guruji Samagra*, Vol. 10, pp. 10
11. *Maa. Sa. Golwalkar*, pp. 129
12. *Pehli Agnipariksha,* pp. 20
    and *Rashtray Namah*, pp. 134

22

Glimpses of Life in Prison

Guruji's life in prison commenced from 7th February under the Defence Act. Nearly 20,000 swayamsevaks were arrested all over Bharat under the pretext of ban on the Sangh. In the words of newspapers, "It was hounding of R.S.S. by the government." One of the preys caught in this hunt was Shivram Shankar Apte, who did the spade work for laying the foundation of Vishwa Hindu Parishad in later years. In those days, he was the district Prachaarak in Tiruchirappalli in Tamil Nadu. He submitted a 'habeas corpus' petition in the High Court for his release from Vellore Central Jail. He presented his own case and won it. Another prisoner was also released in a similar case in Uttar Pradesh. Guruji remained in jail as the head of an outlawed organisation.

In the initial days, Guruji did not have anything concrete to work upon in the hazy atmosphere of that time. So, the only option was to wait for dust to settle down. Therefore, following his inherent nature, he began studying root scriptures like Valmiki-written *Ramayana*, Vyasa-created *Mahabharata*, *Gyaneshwari* of Sant Gyaneshwar, etc. He also took up reading of newly published *Gospel of Ramakrishna,* released in 1944. Those scriptures authenticated by the jailer of Nagpur are still preserved in the library of Dr. Hedgewar Bhavan.

From a prisoner whose whole view about life was bereft of desires, demands were naturally close to zero. Apart from the rush of programmes outside, his other daily routines inside the jail were same as they were outside. He got more time for meditation and studies. He started teaching yoga and *Pranayam* to his colleagues, who joined him after a week. Experience of his colleagues was similar to their experience with him in the Sangh *karyalay*, same type of interactions, same informal discussions, same sense of happiness and laughter. One cannot know the details of the subjects that were discussed there. Everybody experienced the truth that "Stone walls do not a prison make, nor iron bars a cage".

Guruji was not handed over all the items that he was expected to get as per the jail manual. Actually, Guruji was not the only one to t suffer this fate.

Whatever the laws may say, the fact is that our jails are still in the similar poor conditions that prevailed in the Middle Ages. Our pride is misplaced. All the prisoners, officers, supervisors and contractors are in cahoots and are comrades in arms in acts of corruption, theft, depravity. Smuggling was like an integral way of life in a perverted sense. Highly acclaimed senior police officer Kiran Bedi has described this disgraceful scenario in her book, *It is All Possible*. Anyway, Guruji's attitude was of 'neither demand, nor complaint'. After all, he was trained since childhood to believe that "wherever you land up, it is the land of cows (*golok*), that is, the abode of gods".

By the middle of February, Sangh officials of Vidarbha state Pandit Bachcharaj Vyas, Appaji Joshi, Bapuji Sohoni, Babasaheb Ghatate, and others also ended up in prison under Defence Act. Guruji and Ghatate ji were in the same cell. Describing his experience of that time, Ghatate ji says, "When we were in jail, I used to take bath before him. On the first day, I left wet clothes behind. I had decided to wash them after *pooja*. When I went back to the bathroom after completing *pooja*, I was astonished. Shri Guruji had washed my clothes too. When I argued with him, his answer was, "What difference does it make? What other work do we have in this place?" While recalling this episode, Krishna, son of Ghatate ji, says, "After his release, our father never got his clothes washed from anybody in the family. This incident became a lesson for life for him."[1]

During the discussions in the afternoon rest hour, one of his colleagues asked him, "Inspite of working honestly and without any ego, why has this calamity befallen us?" Shri Guruji responded, "Calamity hit us because of our strength. It will also be overcome on the basis of the same strength. If the Sangh proves its mettle in this period of trial, it will progress much better."[2]

It may be around March that the experienced Prachaarak, Rajabhau Paturkar was arrested and brought to Nagpur jail. He could understand Guruji's needs with his acute observation. He arranged for utensils for *pooja* and a bedsheet. Guruji was irritated when he saw these new items and asked him, "Why did you get these things?" Rajabhau whispered in a low voice, "How could I answer Balasaheb Deoras after going outside if he asked me about these matters?" Guruji's expression changed immediately and he spoke out, "Okay, okay, so this is not for me, but to save yourself from Balasaheb," and everybody broke into laughter.[3]

As noted above, all other office-bearers were released after a few days, only Rajabhau Paturkar was left behind. He became the self-appointed attendant of Guruji. Guruji's study of scriptures continued. One day Paturkar wished to clear his doubts. He asked, "Guruji, it is said that Shri Krishna embraced Arjun and made him like himself. What is the meaning behind this story? Is it possible?" "It is possible. Beyond any doubt, it is possible," said Guruji and also quoted four lines from *Gyaneshwari*, "*Hriday hridayek jhaale, hey hridayeeche te hridayee ghatale, dwait na moditan kelen, apnaas aise Arjuna*." (One heart became one with the other, this heart poured itself unto the other, without giving up *dwait*, he made Arjun like himself.) Explaining these lines, he said, "After lighting one lamp with another, both burn separately, but there is no difference in their light – that is one. Similarly, inspite of being two separate personalities, Arjun and Krishna became *ekaatma* – unified soul. Such was the energy unleashed by that embrace. Bhagwan Ramakrishna had done something similar in case of Narendra."[4]

Guruji also taught yoga to many jail employees. He would help them sit or lie down, hold hands or press them to help them get the *asanas* right and practise them. Once he asked an officer who came to meet him, "Have you ever had an experience of a criminal coming inside the jail going out as a reformed person? Getting an answer in negative, he said, "A person doesn't change due to punishment. One needs an emotional and psychological understanding. A human being transforms with education and moral values (*samskaaras*). That is why, it is said that even every sinner has a virtuous life ahead."[5]

Festivals of *Varsh Pratipadaa* (Hindu new year), Hindu *Saamraajya Din* (the day Shivaji was anointed a Hindu king) and *Guru Purnima* also occurred during these six months of imprisonment. It was not possible to celebrate these festivals due to the ban. Beyond this, the visit to Sangh Grounds for prayer had also stopped. One cannot imagine how this seer of the Sangh, for whom these activities were like daily rituals, would have spent those days. Maharshi Valmiki has given an answer to this question that would satisfy many. The episode is about the arrival of ambassador of Lord Rama, Hanuman, in Ashok Vatika. He sees the crying goddess in extreme grief. His heart races to his Lord immediately. Thinking about both of them, he asks himself, "O Lord! Her lord is on the other side and this goddess is on this side. How can they live apart?" Answer arises from his heart, "Heart of this lady resides in her lord's heart and heart of that god resides in the inner core of this goddess's heart. That is how they can live from moment to moment." Relation between Guruji and the Sangh was of that type. Let us hear carefully about it in his own words:

"I had a feeling of oneness with many swayamsevaks after travelling all over Bharat many times, and I had to sit confined within the four walls of the prison. I was alone and I had 24 hours before me everyday. I would remember villages one by one, bring before me the faces of dear swayamsevaks as if I was getting introduced with them in a *baithak*. I used to imprint such an image in my mind. But, human beings always wish to see people in person. Cowherd boys and girls were not satisfied with the description of Lord Krishna as the Supreme Being. They wished to see God in only physical form. Even otherwise, thinking about unseen is painful. My soul too would brim with pain. But I kept doing my necessary duties even as I struggled with these emotions."[6]

Thus, Guruji kept up his 'meditation-in-motion' through his high-speed intellectual vector superfast vehicle on pleasant roads that had no potholes and no hurdles, with the velocity of winds. This is how six months passed by. He was released from prison on Friday, 6th August.

□

Endnotes

1. *Shri Guruji Jeevan Prasang*, Vol. 1, pp. 140
2. *Maa. Sa. Golwalkar*, pp. 132
3. *Shri Guruji Jeevan Prasang*, Vol. 1, pp. 82
4. Ibid, pp. 36-37
5. *Maa. Sa. Golwalkar*, pp. 131
6. *Shri Guruji Samagra*, Vol. 10, pp. 89

23
In Delhi to Demand Justice

Guruji was released on 6th August, but he was not really free. His release was linked to many conditions. These conditions were – to stay within the municipal limits of Nagpur, not to leave Nagpur municipal limits without written permission from the District Magistrate, not to make any public speech, nor write for newspapers or write letters in them without the District Magistrate's permission, not to act or write in a way that would create disaffection directly or indirectly against the state governments, not to keep in touch with people who acted in such a way. Guruji studied this government order carefully. He smiled as he read the last condition and asked the officer, "Who are these untouchable people whom I cannot see? Please let me have such a list so that I do not undertake an act that may be against the prohibition imposed by the government." The officer laughed as he had no answer to this query.

Conditions did not prohibit writing letters to people. He turned his attention to this condition and decided to move ahead on this narrow pathway. Without delay, he wrote to Home Minister and later Deputy Prime Minister Sardar Patel on 11th August, requesting him to rescind the ban on the Sangh and give back its democratic rights to function. It can be said that efforts to lift the ban commenced that very moment. Wheels of time were turning. The case of Gandhiji's murder was being conducted at Red Fort in Delhi for two-and-a-half months. All the accused except two fugitives of Gwalior had been arrested. Even the chargesheet of the case did not mention either the Sangh or Sangh swayamsevak. Therefore, people and rulers knew clearly that the Sangh had no involvement in this incident. This was but a matter of common knowledge. But, there was another truth beyond this that was not known at that time, but is well known today. That is the report submitted by a high-ranking police official Sanjeevi about Gandhi's assassination within one month of the incident. Sanjeevi was a capable officer trained under the administrative services of British. The Home Minister had handed over the investigation of Gandhi assassination to him. He completed his job in 17 days and handed over the complete report in writing to the Home Minister. With the same alacrity and sense of responsibility Home

Minister wrote a long letter to the Prime Minister on 27th February, 1948, that is, on twenty-ninth day of Gandhiji's death. Today, this letter is available in the sixth volume *Collection of Nehru-Gandhi Correspondence* on page nos. 56 and 57. But, this was an unpublished government document at the time. The letter also exposes another truth of history. Parts of that document are as follows:

- All the materials received through known-unknown, true-untrue, named and unnamed sources have been sifted thoroughly. Ninety per cent of these are baseless speculative reports. Most of the allegations are about activities of the R.S.S. – that they distributed sweets, held celebrations. All this was found to be false upon investigation.
- Strong opponents of Bapuji's policies and thoughts, many of whom were members of the Hindu Mahasabha and R.S.S. did welcome this murder. But, beyond this, there is no way one can drag the R.S.S. and Hindu Mahasabha members into this conspiracy on the basis of the available evidence. R.S.S. may be responsible for some other disturbances but not for this one (P. 57).
- Confessions of the conspirators prove that the R.S.S. was not a party, in any way, to this conspiracy. (P. 56)

Thus, if one were to weigh the truth consciously, it would, doubtlessly, be clear that when the Sarsanghchaalak was writing letters to the Prime Minister and Home Minister, they already knew the truth about the Sangh for more than five months.

This was the background when Guruji began his correspondence with the Government of Bharat. Now, this entire correspondence between the two sides has been published in English and all other major Indian languages. Any researcher can examine them without any bias or pre-conceived ideas. The bitter truth is that the political leaders of that time covered up the truth deliberately and did grave injustice to the Sangh. It was expected that the steps taken in the emergency that arose out of the dark atmosphere because of Gandhi murder should have been corrected after true facts came to light later on. But, unfortunately, it did not happen. There was no acknowledgment from Prime Minister's office. The Home Minister's reply was sent after one month on 11th September. One is reminded of Bhartrihari's observation that 'politics is like a whore', because forgetting about the letter he had written to Prime Minister in the light of investigation of the police officer or pushing it under the carpet, he wrote, "Happiness that Sangh people expressed and sweets they distributed at Gandhiji's death has resulted in more resistance from people."[1] There is another sentence in that letter that needs to be read carefully as its tone is of pious lecturing, "I have firm belief that Sangh people can do justice to their patriotism only by working together with the Congress and not by opposing it or being separate from it."[2] As an honest, reputed person pledged to the Congress, Patel had all the right to sermonise to anybody about party politics. But, the issue here was entirely different. Guruji's letter was addressed to the Home Minister demanding undoing of the injustice done to his organisation, based on irrefutable facts. The Home Minister's rightful administrative duty was to prove the allegations true or take them back in view of lack of proofs. But, one will have to say with all due respect to the Home Minister that party politics overrode his duty to rule of law.

Guruji did not express any reaction to Patel's sermon. He wrote to Pandit Jawaharlal Nehru again on 24th September, "Eight months have passed since the Sangh was banned and every possible investigation in this regard has been conducted by now. I believe you would have fully understood that the allegations levelled against the Sangh are baseless and false. Therefore, it is only a question of administering justice in this matter now. We have a right to expect justice from our own government."[3] Much against the earlier bitter experience, a reply from Prime Minister's office was received on the fourth day. It was a repetition of the earlier government notification. Only one point was different – "Prime Minister had been informed about a note that the United Province government had sent to you containing some evidence collected by the state government about Sangh's above-mentioned activities before the ban was imposed on Rashtriya Swayamsevak Sangh. Other states also have such proofs."[4]

Within two weeks of Guruji's release from jail, the sacred day of *Shravan Purnima* arrived on Thursday, 19th August. He stayed back at home after his bath, meditation and religious rituals. This was the Raksha Bandhan festival of the Sangh. Many swayamsevaks came to his house till late in the night, touched his feet and tied '*rakhi*' on his arms. He heard the tragic stories of torture they went through at the hands of so-called followers of Gandhiji.

During this period many well-known people who knew him used to visit him. During discussions he had to inform his friends about the conditions the government had imposed on him. His comment on these was, "Now, my walls of jail cell extend to the borders of Nagpur." To his friends like Sohoni and Ghatate, he would say, "You are free, but I am in 'open jail' of Nagpur." The news spread through word of mouth and newspapers criticised the government. A large number of letters kept arriving in the secretariat of the state government. It is said that Chief Minister Ravi Shankar Shukla wrote to the Home Minister on this matter. Whatever may be the cause, Guruji was set free from the above conditions on 13th October. This was a pious occasion as the next day was the day of Vijayadashami. As per the tradition in Maharashtra, it was the day when people paid obeisance to their elders and offered golden leaves after completing the ritual of stepping out of the borders (*seemolanghan*). There were long queues of happy faces at Guruji's residence on that day.

Sangh leadership took a decision on its strategy in the changed scenario. It was decided that Sarsanghchaalak should go to Delhi to put forth his demand for justice and make Delhi his battlefield for these efforts.

Guruji left for Delhi on 16th October accordingly. However, newspapers suppressed the news of 'departure of the head of an outlawed organisation' under government's pressure. Inspite of this, young people started arriving at the railway station in Delhi in large numbers from 2:30 a.m. itself for the train that was expected to arrive at 4:30 a.m. When the train arrived at 5:15 a.m., after a delay of 45 minutes, nearly ten thousand people had collected at the station campus. The Delhi government had already banned raising of slogans at the station. As a counter to this policy, all the guests had arrived with roses and jasmine flowers. As soon as the apple of their eyes alighted from the coach, he was showered with flowers without any slogans. All the faces were happily aglow like the flowers. Arrival of the saintly personality for justice was greeted with the sweet fragrance of flowers. Writing about it, Home Minister informed Prime Minister, "Their discipline is still strong. I had made it clear that when he (Golwalkar) arrives in Delhi, there should be no display, etc. There were three to four thousand people to welcome him at the station. They greeted him in full silence. Not a word came out of their lips. There was no display of any kind. Everybody obeyed the orders of Guru Golwalkar."[5] This welcome in the capital was a proof of the reality that Sangh work had survived well despite a ban of nearly eight months. Guruji went to the house of Lala Hansraj Gupta from the station. This was the place of his stay till he was put under arrest again on 12th November. The weekly *Organiser* took out a special issue on the occasion of the arrival of Guruji.

All the senior workers of the northern area extending up to Jammu & Kashmir knew about Lala Hansraj's house very well. Everybody remembered its address 20, Barakhamba Road by heart. They were well aware of Guruji's nature too. So, they started dropping in alone or in groups without any hesitation to meet him whenever they could find time. The number of student visitors was also quite large due to Dussera holidays. One must say that actually informal meetings were taking place one after another. On receiving this information, displaced Sindhi brethren too came to meet him. During those days, Barrister Khanchand Gopaldas and Nand Badlani, who were freed from Shikarpur bomb case due to swapping of prisoners, also came to meet him. (Readers would remember about their escape to freedom from their dire situation.) On seeing them, Guruji got up and came forward to welcome them in a tight embrace. Words burst forth from his mouth, "God is great, God is great." (*Prabhu mahaan, Prabhumahaan*). It was indeed true. Their escape to Bharat was like a leap out of the cruel jaws of death.

Topic of ban always used to come up during informal discussions. Wasn't it but natural? But, he used to take care that swayamsevaks would not get agitated, "The ban on the Sangh is totally unjustified, but, it is our government. Therefore, efforts to get the ban lifted should be peaceful and within rule of law. It is possible that it may result in some delays. Still, it is not right to take law into our hands. It doesn't mean that we should squat down in a corner. We have developed and nurtured qualities of affection, brotherhood, dedication and selflessness since more than a quarter century. We shall have to find an area of action to put these qualities into practice. We should strengthen the social life, taking recourse to just a path. As far as the Sangh is concerned, victory is assured, because its foundation is based on truth." This was the direction given by Guruji.

The day Guruji reached Delhi, he met the Home Minister the same evening. Because the dialogue couldn't be completed that day, he met him again on 23rd October. But, discussions didn't move in the desired direction. "Because the allegations against the Sangh have proven to be so patently untrue and baseless, the government must lift the ban immediately. If the government still believes that these accusations have any basis, then it is its bounden democratic duty to prove them in the courts." This was Guruji's appeal. But, Sardar's pet theme was the sermon he had delivered in his earlier letter. "Only practical solution is to become part of the Congress." Sarsanghchaalak Guruji was totally against this suggestion. He was not ready to let die the freedom to organise. The dialogue failed.

Guruji had understood the mentality of the government in the very first meeting. Therefore, he invited journalists to the residence of Lalaji on 19th October at 9 in the morning. Journalists asked him about eight to ten questions. Of these, two were about the ban. The first question was, "Do you have any hope of the ban being lifted in the near future?" Answer was, "I am always optimistic, but it is the job of the government to lift it." Second question was, "If the ban is not lifted, what would be your first step?" Response was, "Then, the government will have to prove that the Sangh is guilty. Current democratic government has a major responsibility in this regard. It is not possible to prove an innocent guilty. Therefore, I believe completely that the government will lift the ban. Till this belief is firm, why should I have any other thought?"

Guruji met many leaders during his stay in Delhi. Of these people, worth mentioning are Dr. Baba Saheb Ambedkar, Shyama Prasad Mukherjee, N.V. Gadgil and Purushottam Das Tandon. After the ban was rescinded, Guruji wrote letters of thanks to all of them.[6]

The administration decided to take a more rigid stance about the Sangh after a close observation of the contacts Guruji made in the capital, the movement in Sangh circles in Delhi-Punjab-Uttar Pradesh states, attitude of the media etc. It thought that it would be dangerous to allow Guruji to stay in the capital any longer. Therefore, Guruji received a message from Patel ji, "The job for which you had come to Delhi is over. Therefore, leave Delhi now." This order, passed on 28th October, was handed over by the government representative on 2nd November at his place of residence. Guruji read it and expressed his disagreement with it and wrote on the same page in English, "I believe that this order is unnecessary and it takes away the civil rights of a law-abiding citizen. I also believe that I would be a party to this unjustified act and injustice if I accept it. By accepting this order, I would be failing to do my duty as a citizen of an independent state. Thus, I have to submit that I cannot accept this extraordinary order."[7]

Realising that this government was following the footsteps of foreign rulers blindly and would use similar tactics, the Sangh team awaited the arrest of Guruji that same night. Guruji prepared two statements to present the Sangh's side to the common people before this could happen, and got it distributed to the newspaper world one after the other. The first statement was refutation of the government's action and second was clarification about Sangh's position on various issues.

Main points of the first statement were:

a. We were aware even at the time when allegations were hurled against the Sangh that they were false and baseless. Still we had disbanded the Sangh, while not accepting those allegations.
b. During this period, all the charges have proven to be untrue.
c. Nine months have passed, still this injustice waged against us has not been set right.
d. Orders were received that the Sangh should merge with a political party. This will mean that there is no freedom or right for anybody to organise non-political activity in this country.

After clarifying these points further, Guruji appealed to the society, "It is my appeal to the Hindu society not to fall prey to misleading, false propaganda. We have already suffered a lot during last 1,000 years due to our disunity. At least, now we should have unity and we should build a healthier, strong and enlightened life based on mutual affection, dedication and trust that would result in we, the ancient Hindu society constituting our sacred motherland, Bharatvarsh happy and prosperous in our own home."[8]

Second statement was about Sangh's stand on symbols of national honour. Poisonous arrows of false propaganda were also being unleashed by various leaders on these issues. Clarifying about them, Guruji stated:

1. *Flag* – Confusion is being created deliberately about Rashtriya Swayamsevak Sangh's views about the flag. Rashtriya Swayamsevak Sangh has its own flag that symbolises its urge to create cultural unity among the Hindu race. Being a part of the nation, Rashtriya Swayamsevak Sangh has complete faith and respect for the national flag. And I can say without hesitation that each member of Rashtriya Swayamsevak Sangh will readily sacrifice his life to defend our national flag against any aggressor.
2. *Faith in democratic system of governance* – Time has proved that the democratic state is the best and longest lasting and successful in

comparison to all other systems of governance.

3. *State is a secular institution* – For a Hindu, state has always been a secular institution and so is it even now... Truly, it is unnecessary to give an adjective of 'secular' (*asampradaayik* – non-communal) for a state that is already 'secular'.
4. *Hindu state* – Rashtriya Swayamsevak Sangh does not propagate a Hindu state which has zero non-Hindu citizens.
5. We believe that no progressive organisation can stay alive long and grow if it works in a secretive manner. Question of Rashtriya Swayamsevak Sangh working in a secret manner also cannot arise as its work is cultural and it has no political ambitions.
6. It is state's duty to raise an Army, not that of any non-government organisation.... Therefore, it is not right to compare Rashtriya Swayamsevak Sangh's discipline with Army's discipline and its rules of work.
7. Idea of overthrowing the current government and capturing power taking recourse to violence is purely a figment of imagination. Keeping in view Rashtriya Swayamsevak Sangh's cultural form of work and its efforts to keep itself aloof from political ambitions, this question too doesn't arise.
8. I feel that after this, my brethren of this nation will completely believe that allegations against Rashtriya Swayamsevak Sangh are unjustified and propaganda against it is misleading. They will appreciate my efforts made to revive this organisation with lawful means.[9]

Guruji prepared both these statements in English and distributed them to the newspapers. Most of the newspapers published only a summary of these statements, but *Organiser* published it in full. The false and misleading propaganda against the Sangh and its limited dissemination by mainstream newspapers was seen as a curse turned out to be a blessing in disguise. Swayamsevaks took it up as a challenge. Both of Guruji's statements were translated in different languages and distributed in large numbers in different places all over Bharat. Many persistent college students preferred to make handwritten copies. They made hundreds of copies and distributed them. This proved to be a preparatory exercise for the upcoming struggle of *satyagraha*.

The Government did not arrest Guruji on 2nd November as expected by the Sangh team. Instead of this, Guruji received an intimation from the Delhi magistrate that if he wished to meet Prime Minister, then he could stay back in Delhi only for that work. But, this stay will be allowed only on the conditions that were imposed earlier on him by the Madhya Pradesh government. Guruji may have disregarded them, but he did not break them. He could understand easily that this re-imposition of conditions was due to his statement, press conference and allowing access to swayamsevaks. He also realised that the government had not shut its doors completely. Therefore, he restarted his correspondence with the Central leaders. He wrote a letter to the Prime Minister on 3rd November.

He stated four major points in this letter: 1. "I request to you that as our Prime Minister you should give us an opportunity in an impartial, justified and positive manner to negate the allegations and prove our innocence." 2. "Finding that the allegations are baseless, ban on Rashtriya Swayamsevak Sangh should be lifted immediately." 3. "Adding new points to this issue should be avoided." 4. "I will be highly obliged if I am given an opportunity to meet you."[10] But, Prime Minister's response was not to the issues raised in the letter. Revealing his pre-conceived bias, he wrote, "There is no relation between the declared objectives of the Sangh and the real objectives and activities of its members. These real objectives are completely contrary to the resolutions of the Indian Parliament and the rules and regulations of the proposed Constitution. As per our information, these activities are anti-national and generally destructive and violent. Therefore, you will agree that just an adamant stand will not be of much use."[11]

Guruji's suspicion proved correct. Now a new accusation had come up, which was not there in the government notification. Maintaining his expression of respect, Guruji wrote back with clarity, "It seems that on the basis of said information, you have concluded that our activities are anti-national. This is a grave accusation and it is not proper to raise it against anybody lightly. One needs solid and factual evidence for such an allegation. It is meaningless to keep saying repeatedly that the government has information without giving permission to the people against whom they have been raised to examine such allegations. Both of us should agree that 'just an adamant stand will not be of much use'."

"As far as the talk about being contrary to the regulations of the proposed Constitution is concerned, it would have been better if our Prime Minister had not written it. It is like punishing somebody for attempting to kill a person who is going to be born after a year or more than that."

"Another point is that we do not know what actions of ours make you say that our declared objectives and activities are different from our real objectives and activities. We are just simple servants of the society involved in developing character and unifying in the cultural field, keeping away from politics. There is no place in our work for the art that conceals real objectives from the declared objectives."[12]

Guruji had also written to Home Minister in the same period. The situation at that end was no different. At the end, the Madhav's Delhi mission was a failure. He received the final directive from Secretary of Home Ministry, H.B.R. Iyengar, to leave Delhi within 24 hours and return to Nagpur. Guruji and his colleagues realised where the future was heading. They decided to utilise every minute of these 24 hours well. First of all, he wrote to Prime Minister about this last directive in a forthright manner, "We claim to be a cultured State. Such unconstitutional, uncivilised approach can suit only a dictatorial government or to some extent a one-party foreign rule. But in my opinion it does not behoove a modern, cultured, democratic government that claims to protect civil rights impartially.

"Therefore, I have decided to stay in the capital till this injustice to us is set right."[13]

For 11 days, from 3rd to 13th November, handcuffs of the State hanged in front of Guruji, begging for justice. He had worked on two fronts during those days – one, meeting top people in power and demanding justice through letters; two, clarifying his stand in the newspaper world through dialogue with journalists and statements. Now only one action was left – present his analysis of the situation and views in front of the swayamsevaks, for whom he had come to Delhi as their representative. He prepared a letter in Hindi and English containing 10 paragraphs. In this he described in complete details what had been done from his side so far and stated at the end, "Thus, I am taking back the directive that I had given on 6th February, 1948 to dissolve the Sangh after giving it full thought and I request you to begin your activities regularly. Along with this, we should try our best that peace is maintained and feeling of enmity is kept under check. I have asked our Sarkaryavaah Shri Bhaiyyaji Dani to inform all swayamsevaks about this decision and decide on the day and date to restart our work as it was running earlier."[14]

Police officers came to the bungalow at 20, Barakhamba Road at midnight of 12th November, 1948, and arrested M.S. Golwalkar under the Bengal State Criminal Procedure Act of 1818. This 130-year-old Act gave unbridled power to arrest anybody anywhere without any proof or reason. In the words of Pandit ji, spoken just three days prior to this, was it not "against the rules and regulations of the proposed Constitution of Bharat?" Guruji was brought secretively to Nagpur on 15th November. The tag put on his luggage by the police officers accompanying him in the flight was 'accompanying person'. He was taken to Nagpur Central Jail from the airport, from where he was shifted to Sivni sub-jail after two-three days. Second imprisonment of Guruji commenced thus.

□

Endnotes

1. *Shri Guruji Samagra*, Vol. 10, pp. 14
2. Ibid, pp. 14
3. Ibid, pp. 15
4. Ibid, pp. 20-21

5. *Sardar Patel Patrachar*, Vol. 7, pp. 261
6. *Shri Guruji Samagra*, Vol. 10, pp. 77-80
7. Ibid, pp. 24
8. Ibid, pp. 28-29
9. Ibid, pp. 30-32
10. Ibid, pp. 34-35
11. Ibid, pp. 39-40
12. Ibid, pp. 41-42
13. Ibid, pp. 43-44
14. Ibid, pp. 49

24
Successful Satyagraha

End result of efforts to get the ban removed was bitter. Therefore, the Sangh did not let the ammunition of the struggle to dry even as it kept the doors of dialogue open. Shakhas had been disbanded as per directives of the Sarsanghchaalak. Working style seen through orders like *daksh, aaram, dhwaj pranaam* of Shakha had been put on hold but the habit of regularly coming together to impart values (*samskaaras*) was kept alive. Activities like games, social service committees were being conducted within the laws of the land. Mutual contacts, discussions, warm relations with each other – all this was also going on. Weekly magazine, *Organiser* was being published regularly. Even otherwise, the system of passing information to swayamsevaks across Bharat was also working without any hurdle. Thus, all the swayamsevaks were aware of Guruji's activities in the capital and the government's harsh stance against him. Without talking about it or suggesting it, everybody believed a clash with government was inevitable. When they read Guruji's letter, dated 13th November, that took back his directive for dissolution of the Sangh, their doubt turned into belief. When they had read the closing lines of the letter, "I request you to commence your activities regularly", their belief turned into a strong sense of duty. More so when they read the lines that followed, "I have asked our Sarkaryavaah Shri Bhaiyyaji Dani to inform all swayamsevaks about this decision and decide on the day and date to restart our work like earlier times." This sense of duty took the form of a pledge. In short, this letter from Guruji was like blowing of the conch shell *Panchjanya* for the coming struggle. When Sarsanghchaalak was in solitary confinement in Sivni jail, it was a period of preparation for action for the swayamsevaks to restart the Sangh work.

Inspite of the government ban, starting the Sangh Shakhas was now the action plan of the Sangh, that is, it marked the beginning of the clash with the government. This is what people called the *satyagraha* of Sangh. It was a *satyagraha* that was different from the *satyagrahas* that had taken place during the freedom struggle. There was no disturbance like *rasta roko* nor did it involve sitting in *dharna* in front of the government offices. Common people would not face any disorder in their daily lives. Sangh *satyagraha* was not against anybody – neither the government nor the police, but it was definitely against injustice. The form of this protest was very simple. A designated swayamsevak would send written information to the office of local administration that "we are starting a daily Sangh Shakha at xyz place at abc time". A pre-decided team of swayamsevaks would reach that place at preplanned time and begin Shakha activities, shouting slogans like *Bharatmata ki jai*, *Sangh se pratibandh hatao*. This was the format of *satyagraha*. To strengthen this plan, all the Prachaaraks, who had been moved to different, small and big places, came back to their areas. *Satyagrahis* were prepared through personal contacts by working over ground, without going underground, without depending on motivating speeches and without support from newspapers. Whatever the reaction of police against conducting the Shakhas – whether lawful or unlawful – they bore it peacefully. There was not even a small counter-reaction anywhere. Credit for this goes to the way the *satyagrahis* were prepared. It would not have been possible simply by broadcasting the directions. The leadership took common swayamsevak into confidence and informed them about the actual conditions on the field transparently. Office-bearers informed them openly that the government could act in a devilish way, students' studies may be stopped, members' jobs could be at risk, government servants would surely be removed from jobs, farmers' properties may be confiscated, businesses might be shut down, some close brethren could lose lives due to unfortunate accidental attacks, families may force their members to seek pardon, imprisonment may be for longer periods than expected, etc. A factual picture of the scenario was presented to the swayamsevaks. They were not given assurances like 'ban will be lifted in four weeks' as was done by leaders in earlier times when they had assured that 'Independence will be achieved in one year'. Members were reminded how they had suffered all the atrocities with bounden hands in the first week of February, holding Guruji's telegram with high respect, due to values imbibed in the Sangh. It may be said that the Sangh leadership had prepared the *satyagrahis* through fire so they would not wilt under the heat of a relentless Sun. After making all these preparations only did Sarkaryavaah Bhaiyyaji Dani declare that Sangh Shakhas would re-commence from 9th December.

Another information may be shared here. After writing the detailed letters to all the swayamsevaks on 19th November from Lala Hansraj's bungalow, Guruji wrote another special letter for the swayamsevaks who were to offer *satyagraha*. It was handed over to each *satyagrahi*. It was found later on that many swayamsevaks in jail had learnt this letter by heart. It would be ideal and inspiring to present that historic document:

Message

20, Barakhamba Road, New Delhi
13th November, 1948

Dear Swayamsevak brothers,

Today, ten months have passed since our sacred work stopped. Our Rashtriya Swayamsevak Sangh has been working in a sustained manner to create a pure Bharat*iya* national way of life by serving our sacred *dharma*, culture (*Sanskriti*), society and uniting entire society in an unbreakable bond of love; sacrificing our lives at the feet of our most sacred *Bharatmata* with these divine sentiments. Suddenly, this sacred flow has been interrupted. Many despicable allegations were made against it. It had to suffer many kinds of torture. But, we bore all this with our inherent fortitude. It was hoped that after a time, when falsehood of all these allegations were proven, ban on our organisation would be lifted. We would see victory for justice. With this view, I had put in my efforts to get justice through peaceful means.

But, I found that the gentlemen sitting at the top in this government are not interested in justice. Party politics and blind hunger for power is dominating the discourse; un-*Bhaaratiya* tendencies are on the rise. Therefore, there is hatred for any cultural work that supports Bharat*iya* ethos. Intolerance has cast dark shadows over the hearts. Then, where is the chance for justice and thoughts that seek truth?

Vested interests of parties and growth of intolerant hunger for power will give rise to differences, animosity and absence of affection that is bound to hurt and weaken our national life force and destroy it. It is the prime and most sacred duty of every individual who calls himself a son of *Bharatmata*, to eliminate these evil sentiments. We, the swayamsevaks of Rashtriya Swayamsevak Sangh, have taken a pledge of uninterrupted and sustained worship of *Bharatmata*. We have to confront this nation-damaging tendency. For the sake of this noble goal, we have to put in efforts for its renaissance and work for its great mission to take it to its absolute success. Ahead and ahead, we must always move ahead. We are not to stop for any reason on this path. We have to endure difficulties, hurdles, unfortunate rebellion by our own dear ones. We have to prove the purity, righteousness, greatness and undisputed necessity of our work.

There is no time for thoughts like 'me and mine' in this terrible time of calamity for *Bharatmata*. Whatever happens to us as individuals, we have to set *Bharatmata* free from the impact of un-*Bharatiyataa*. We have to rescue all the children of this Mother from seizure of their natural rights by parties in power that are blinded by selfishness. We have to see that everybody benefits from a free, happy and honourable life. Only we have to do this.

Our work is undoubtedly the finest; it is exalted, it is divine work of God and in its fulfilment is the highest achievement for mankind. It is like envisioning the Supreme Being.

Therefore, arise and make up for the loss of 10 months of inaction. Truth is with us. It is a sin to sleep at times of injustice, and live as its victim. Let us set right this injustice. Establishing firm belief in the Supreme Being that personifies true justice, focussing your whole life force unto Bharatmata, inspired by the love of her children, take forward this work and march forward till you have achieved success.

This is a clash between *dharma* and *adharma,* justice and injustice, greatness versus pettiness, love and evil. Victory is assured because with *dharma* is Supreme God and with Supreme God is victory.

So, arise with a victorious roar for *Bharatmata's* glory that would reverberate from the horizons of the heart to the horizons of the universe and rest not till the work is accomplished.

Bharatmata ki jai.

Yours

Maa.Sa. Golwalkar[1]

Absence of frustration in swayamsevaks despite arrest of Guruji and increasing movement seen within their ranks prompted the newspapers in Nagpur that the Sangh was going to initiate an agitation to oppose the ban. Intelligence department also expected something like this. So, the government side began its verbal assault from the beginning of December. Speaking in Gwalior on 5th December, Sardar Patel cautioned in a threatening tone, "Hearts of Sangh members are filled with venom of hatred, therefore they can never run a *satyagraha* agitation successfully. Government is armed fully to accept their challenge."[2] While addressing the annual conference of Congress in Jaipur, Pandit Nehru said, "This is not *satyagraha*. It is an ill-conceived insistence of Sangh urchins. We shall use all our power to suppress this agitation. We shall never allow these people to raise their heads."[3]

On the other side, newspapers opposed this dictatorial and unjust step of the government unhesitatingly. Editorial of 21st October in English daily, *Hitavaad*, from Nagpur noted, "Prove the allegations or remove the ban – This demand of Shri Golwalkar is logical and one cannot disregard it. People from Congress should definitely not ignore it because they were in the same situation in 1942 that the Sangh is in today. Congress had been outlawed and the British government in its charge-sheet had claimed that Congress is responsible for the disturbances of year 1942. So, Gandhiji had made a humble demand that allegations against the Congress should be presented to a court of law and they should be proven."[4]

Talking of *satyagraha*, one can say that it began quite satisfactorily as per plan. Sarkaryavaah Bhaiyyaji Dani offered himself for arrest on 8th December as he got down at the Delhi station and declared that Shakhas will begin functioning from the next day, that is, from 9th December. As per directives of Guruji, Kashmirthat was facing an attack, and the disturbed Hyderabad were kept out of the agitation. Swayamsevaks from these areas were asked to take part in agitation from neighbouring states. As expected, even before the bugle for commencement of *satyagraha* was officially blown, leaders of Delhi, like Lala Hansraj, Vasantrao Oke, and others were arrested. Senior leaders like Balasaheb Deoras were arrested in Nagpur. But, Sarkaryavaha Dani reached Delhi nevertheless, throwing dust in the eyes of the government and blew the conch-shell, *Panchjanya*, to declare the *satyagraha*.

Blowing away all the estimates of government and political circles to the winds, the Sangh agitation surged ahead. Presenting the facts as they were, the daily *Hindu* reported about *satyagraha* in Chennai, thus: "There were three *satyaagrahas,* one after another. Police resorted to severe *laathi* charge, raining *lathis* even on the spectators. Thirteen *satyagrahis* were wounded so badly that they had to be taken to hospital instead of the police station. Some police personnel were also hurt due to stone throwing by people. Finally, police crammed 76 *satyagrahis* forcefully into police vans who had stuck to their positions inspite of tear gas smoke and took them away."[5] Still the *satyagraha* continued. Most of the *satyagrahis* were children as Pandit Nehru had said, but they were not 'urchins' as described by him, in any way. They were like friends of Prahlad in the kingdom of Hiranyakashyapu. They were unconquerable in that period of oppression. They remained non-violent even against violent atrocities. A member of Madras Presidency, Swami Venkatachalam Chetti gave a statement against the insufferable *laathi* charge in the 26th December edition of daily *Hindu*, "What an irony of fate that members of Congress are in power today and they are justifying the *laathi*-charge on youth of the Sangh on the basis that they belong to an organisation that has been banned, that the power used against them is being reported in an exaggerated manner. And that the government doesn't wish to make them into heroes by putting them in jails. This indeed is strange that those gentlemen, who were beaten black and blue by police under British in 1930, one amongst whom is Chief Minister today, are justifying a similar behaviour against members of the Sangh. At that time also, the government of the day had not felt that excessive force was used."[6]

Strong reaction expressed by an ex-Advocate General and renowned liberal leader, T.R. Venkataram Shastri two days later was also published in the same daily, "It is not a crime to express an opinion that Sangh swayamsevaks are innocent and it is not right to run this campaign of oppression against them. I have been told that the infamous Moplah police has been brought to Madras to teach a lesson to these agitators of the Sangh. Some years back, the British government had brought this same police to crush Congress agitators. I had agitated against this cruel oppression of the British government. This agitation of mine was not taken as a crime, though there was a foreign government at that time."[7]

This criticism of newspapers was not a cry in the wilderness. The government policy of oppression softened to some extent. But, in those days of winter, *satyagrahi* prisoners were harassed by not being given necessary facilities. Still the *satyagraha* outside ran with full vigour. *Satyagraha* by women in Mumbai and Nagpur drew admiring attention of the masses. The Mumbai agitation on 2nd January, 1949 saw presence of Marathi, Gujarati, Rajasthani, Sindhi and Punjabi women. This was an example, by itself, of dignity, discipline, broad-based participation, fearlessness and enthusiasm, etc. An agitation six days later, on 8th, in Nagpur was held comparatively on a smaller scale. But, its highlight was the participation of 70-year-old mother of Guruji. A delegation of that group presented a memorandum to Chief Minister of the state to lift the ban on the Sangh.[8]

Even in this short period of two weeks, the *satyagraha* left a strong impression on the people. Government's idea that this kids' game would lose steam in four to five days proved to be totally wrong. Highlighting this, *Navbharat* daily from Delhi wrote, "Government cannot neglect the powerful ideology behind the Sangh. Organisational quality of the Sangh is quite outstanding. Swayamsevaks' steadfastness to ideology and discipline is worth appreciating. Honouring the oath of non-violence literally, they set an unexceptionable example to other people conducting agitations. They have begun this agitation and run it without creating hurdles in the country's productivity, without erecting barricades in free movement of traffic and not inflicting any problems on people in general; with a spirit of forbearance and sacrificing all self-interests."[9]

Highly respected *Kesari,* founded by Lokamanya Tilak in Pune, roared, "This *satyagraha* has literally followed Gandhiji's technique. While informing government officials about the *satyagraha* in advance, they also provide the names of *satyagrahis.* Nobody creates any unruly scenes with the police. They do not give any speeches that could hurt anybody's feelings, nor do they raise such slogans. In their speeches, they clarify that the purpose of their agitation is not to give any kind of challenge to the government, rather they are demanding justice by inflicting pain on self. Even in the times of '*jail bharo*' agitation, one cannot find an example of filling up of jails in such large numbers even if one searches hard."[10]

Satyagraha was running with same vigour even in the third week of January. Official propaganda channels of the government were reporting very low numbers of *satyagrahis*. The truth was that all the major prisons of the country had not only been filled up by the second week of *satyagraha*. In fact, they were packed to more than twice or thrice their capacity with *satyagrahis*. Most of the jailers had intimated the rulers of this situation through telegrams. But, how could *satyagraha* stop? So, the government began another experiment. Police began picking up *satyagrahis* and pushing them into jungles that were 60-70 miles away from their homes. But, those people would come back again to take part in the *satyagraha* as additional teams, after moving around from village to village in small groups like the pilgrims of earlier times, partaking food in different homes and spreading the word about the Sangh too.

Within a month, the threatening tone of rulers mellowed down. The Government thought of opening a dialogue with the Sangh again. For that they had to stop the *satyagraha* first. To this end, Sardar Patel asked for co-operation of Moulichandra Sharma, who was well known to both the sides. He was running a democratic informative movement under the aegis of Janaadhikaar Samiti in major cities of the country for restoration of democratic rights. He was the all-India President of this organisation. Moulichandra Sharma contacted the editor of *Kesari*, G.V. Ketkar in Pune to make Sardar Patel's idea a success. As a result, Ketkar met Guruji in Sivni jail on 12th January. The topic of stopping the agitation was raised. Initiating the conversation, Ketkar said, "I had sent you a telegram that said, 'Do not start *satyagraha*' before you had begun the *satyagraha*. I had also sent a letter following that telegram. I hope you didn't find it odd." Guruji replied, "There is no question about it because I received the telegram 10 days after the *satyagraha* had already begun." Ketkar said, "So late? Then why would one send the telegram?" Guruji said, "This is an example of the administration's efficiency."

Discussion went along the expected line. Ketkar met Sardar Patel and reached Sivni again on 16th. Writing about it, Ketkar says, "I went to Sivni again, met Guruji. Discussions went on for four hours. Guruji would read each and every word of the directive that I needed from Guruji to suspend the agitation very seriously and kept correcting it time and again. Four drafts were made one after another, but each was rejected due to incorrect construct of words. Fifth draft was satisfactory. Guruji would examine each word in depth so that the prestige of the Sangh would not be compromised in any way. Of the two copies of the fifth draft, Guruji kept one with him while I got ready to take the second copy to leave the jail. When I was about to leave, Guruji said with a laugh, 'You know well that I cannot come to the door to bid you farewell.'

"I took his leave, carrying with me the agreed draft with a view to suspending the *satyagraha*."[11]

Coordinator of the entire *satyagraha* movement was Doctor Bhai Mahavir. After getting Guruji's directive through G.V. Ketkar, he gave a statement on 21st January about suspending the *satyagraha*. The statement said, "The Sangh had not begun the *satyagraha* to put government in difficulty. Its objective was to raise a strong voice against injustice being perpetrated against the Sangh and seek attention of the government and enlightened people. It seems that our voice has attained expected success. Therefore, experiencing a friendly atmosphere and to make next level of action a success, the agitation is being suspended."[12] It is beyond doubt that these were the words of Guruji.

Thus, *satyagraha* of Rashtriya Swayamsevak Sangh ran for 45 days from

9th December, 1948 to 22nd January, 1949. As per the last count, the number of *satyagrahis* was 77,090.[13] This figure was bigger than the number of prisoners held during 1942 agitation that was recognised as the biggest movement for Independence.*

When Guruji suspended the *satyagraha* on advice of well-wishers, many newspapers supported Guruji's move through their editorials and also reminded the government that the ball was in its court now. Nagpur's *Hitavaad* noted that Sangh's *satyagraha* to raise public opinion against suppression of democratic rights had succeeded. On 8th February, 1948, *Kesari* wrote, "Taking an overall view, we must admit that *Sarsanghchaalak* of the Sangh has chosen the right time to stop the *satyagraha*. Strength of *satyaagrahas* can be gauged from the discipline of *satyagrahis* and their capacity to bear pain. As per Gandhiji's theory, first victory of a *satyagraha* is entirely moral. And, based on this moral victory, practical benefit can be derived by initiating talks with the government for an agreement. We must say that the Sangh has achieved that moral victory today."[14]

Statesman of 22nd January carried both the editorial and statement about withdrawal of *satyagraha* together. It said, "For this, not only the government, but the Sangh leadership also deserves compliments and thanks. Credit goes to them for the way they conducted the *satyagraha*. Though people had doubts, *satyagraha* ran as per directives of the leadership from the beginning till the end. It remained completely non-violent… many people amongst those who took part in the *satyagraha* are good people and they can make good contribution in the service of the nation. They are disciplined, rich in idealistic values, physically capable, self-sacrificing and highly cherished human values have taken physical form in their lives. Some of them can be placed on the fragrant pedestal of ideal Hindu youth."[15]

Reaction of media was even more favourable than the Sangh had expected. Be as it may, the atmosphere of struggle mellowed down and apositive environment for dialogue got built. But one has to note with regret that yet again the Congress government's stance was not straightforward. Leaving aside the points there were present in the notification about the ban, they began throwing up unrelated issues like, "Sangh doesn't have a Constitution, so in its absence, it is difficult to lift the ban." Instead of sitting across and discussing issues in an atmosphere of friendly co-operation, their behaviour smacked of feudalism. T.R. Venkataram Shastri and G.V. Ketkar had taken on the role of mediators between the government and Guruji. Guruji looked upon Shastriji like his father. He was senior to Guruji's father by one year. Guruji listened to sagacious advice of this wise elderly person, and also clearly put before him, wicked political games being played

* 1. United Province-113210, 2. Bihar-465, 3. Madhya Pradesh & Berar-8822, 4. Mumbai & Gujarat-13500, 5. Madras (including Karnataka, Andhra, Kerala)-15583, 6. Punjab-6400, 7. Bengal-2910, 8. Assam-732, 9. Utkal-568, 10. Rajasthan-3641, 11. Madhya Bharat-5113, 12. Delhi-1960. Total = 77,090.

by the government. Guruji told Shastriji, "Sangh work has gone along well from 1925 with good systems till the ban. It has well-defined office-bearers like Chairman, secretaries, chief of a Shakha, etc. There is an in-charge who keeps accounts accurately. There is already a well-defined system of rules and regulations for its working. Only thing is that it is not in written form. Why is there so much insistence on it? If obstinacy is about constitution then I would like to ask, did the Congress, which was established in 1885, have a written constitution for 14 years till 1899?" Shastriji, who was well aware about history, listened to him attentively.

It would be instructive to take a break from this time-frame at this moment. Shri Venkataram Shastri, who was very well known in South, had seen Guruji for the first time in 1946. It was a Sangh programme held on the grounds of Shri Ramakrishna School at Thyagaraja Nagar in Chennai. Guruji was there as Sarsanghchaalak and venerable Shastriji was present as the Chairman. He had come on the condition that, "I will speak plainly from my heart." As per Sangh customs, Guruji's lecture was before that of Shastriji. When Shastriji's turn came, Shastriji did 'speak from the heart', "I had come prepared to say a lot of things. But, I have heard a lecture which has shaken the beliefs from their roots on which I had lived all my life and made me rethink. Now I am left with nothing worth speaking about. I only wish to say to you that ponder seriously over the lecture given by Shri Swamiji."[16] Looking at the external appearance of Guruji, Shastriji had taken him to be a '*Swami*' (that is, a *sadhu*).

Now after three years, on 13th February, Shastriji was sitting in the company of that same 'Swamiji' in Sivni jail. Actually, Shastriji's role of intermediary was not accidental. There was human endeavour behind this. The statement given by Shastriji against the severe inhuman *lathi*-charge on *satyagrahis* of Chennai had been noted by S.S. Apte (who became the General Secretary of Vishwa Hindu Parishad later) who was underground those days. Eknath Ranade and he met Shastriji immediately. Both requested him humbly, "May we also receive the blessings of your commitment to human rights that is beyond doubt." Shastriji had not run away from such problematic issues in his life. Apart from this, he was also motivated from another side. He had gone to seek blessings of Paramacharya of Kamakoti one day during this period. That divine soul had also motivated him to set right the injustice being perpetrated. The wish of Paramacharya was like a religious edict for Shastriji.[17]

As he came out of Sivni jail after meeting Guruji, he told Eknath Ranade, "To make your Guruji agree to anything is like moving a mountain. Still, due to his respect for me, he agreed to my views with an open heart. Now, provide me with the necessary material to help me prepare the Constitution." Eknath ji and Pandit Deendayal Upadhyay sat together to chalk out the working methodology of the Sangh. Then, this was discussed in the *baithak* (meeting) of principal workers in Delhi and a primary draft was handed over to Shastriji. Shastriji, an authority, shaped it into a proper constitution and sent it to Barrister M.R. Jaikar in Pune for the final finishing touches. He gave it the required finishing touches and sent it back quickly. Finally, the constitution of the Sangh took form. Shastriji reached Sivni again on 10th March with this draft. Explaining the whole story behind drafting of this document, he handed it over to Guruji. Guruji flipped through each page and signed at the required place. He read it again on the insistence of Shastriji. About this simple act of Guruji, Shastriji told his friend Rajagopalachari, "What a trust on his colleagues! He read it attentively only when I told him."

Now, the only thing left was to send this Sangh constitution that had taken shape on the insistence of the Central Government. On the advice of Shastriji, Guruji gave this authority to Shastriji through his signed power of attorney. The letter said, "I have read the constitution prepared by Shri T.R. Venkataram Shastri. I accept it. With a view to saving time and as a matter of convenience I am requesting Shri Shastriji to submit it to the Central Government and accept him as my authorised representative." Shastriji came to Nagpur with these documents and met the state Home Minister Dwarika Prasad Mishra and after handing over the entire material to him for the purpose of submission to the Central Home Minister, he proceeded to Chennai with a deep sense of satisfaction and relief. This ex-Advocate General had believed that the next steps would take place without any hurdle. But, as a Bharatiya saying goes, the smell of garlic doesn't go away from utensils even after thorough cleaning. Home Minister of independent India found one fault with the whole exercise. He sent all the documents back to Chennai with a letter stating, "Though you have prepared this Constitution, it is the Constitution of the Sangh. Therefore, following the right procedure, Golwalkar should himself send it to the Central home department through the Madhya Pradesh Home Ministry. The permission given to you for meeting Golwalkar was not given to you as a mediator." This behaviour of the Home Minister was found distasteful by the elderly gentleman, but he was sincere about making the job successful that he had taken up. But, in his age, that too at the height of the summer, it was exhausting for him to travel to Nagpur again via Sivni. Therefore, he handed over all this material with another letter from his side through Shivram Shankar Apte, with whom he had been in constant touch, to deliver it to Guruji. Apte ji accomplished his job by going to Sivni in April 1949.

Important parts of the accompanying letter that Shastriji had written to Guruji are given here. He noted, "The process through which I have dispatched the Sangh Constitution has not been found proper by the Home Ministry. The Home ministry feels that this might create a confusing impression in the minds of the people that I am acting as a mediator between you and the government. The outcome of this objection is that you will have to send copies of this Constitution with your own covering letter, asking the government to lift the ban on the Sangh....About what should be written in the covering letter, I only have a suggestion that without raising old points, you may simply write that written Constitution of the Sangh is attached with the letter. Now onwards, the Sangh will work as per these provisions. Even otherwise, the Sangh has been functioning more or less as per the same provisions. I believe that no clause of this constitution will be found objectionable. If after studying the Constitution, the Bharatiya government doesn't find anything objectionable in it, I hope the Bharatiya government will lift the ban on the Sangh by releasing a notification very soon."[18]

Accepting various opinions and discussions, Guruji submitted the Constitution of the Sangh to the Central Government through the Madhya Pradesh government from Sivni jail on 11th April. The attached letter carried the following lines: "I am sending the written Constitution of the Sangh alongwith. Now onwards, the organisation will work as per its provisions. It contains mainly those provisions the Sangh had been working on for years.

"I hope the Constitution prepared now will be acceptable and will fulfil a sharply felt weakness. With a hope that the administration will approve the Constitution, I also hope you show the courtesy of releasing a notification to lift the ban on the Sangh and let it work as per its Constitution (which has been prepared and sent to you). When this possibility is created, I will get this Constitution printed. The required notifications that are to be released may be released fast so that the Sangh work can be conducted with ease.

"It pains me a lot that the Bharatiya government looks at my words and general conduct with suspicion. But, time will prove my work, that weaves together a scattered and highly divided people into a cultural tie built with a common goal and common discipline and generates unity, will prove to be useful for overall good of the nation. The future alone will tell that my nature is of co-operation, maintaining a positive feeling for all and not tuned to fighting with some group. I expect a positive response very soon."[19]

In fact, the demand of the government had been met fully. Now, all that was left was to lift the ban with a liberal and open heart. Expecting this, generous-hearted Venkataram Shastri had written special letters to Madhya Pradesh Home Minister Mishra ji on 16th April and Home Minister Patel on 29th April from Chennai. But the government was thinking in a contrary manner. It had a different regrettable objective. There was a meeting of Chief Ministers on 8th-9th April, in which it was decided to continue with the ban. Because of this, the government decided to play some complex political game of its own. Instead of Home Minister, Home Secretary took over the correspondence in this matter. After that, the humane contacts established so far, began to melt away. Dry bureaucratic processes took reins then on. This group is known for its quality of always being more loyal than the king. The result was splitting of hair. Home Secretary raised objections over sub-sections of the constitution.

Guruji sent his reply to the letter sent by the state Home Ministry in Sivni jail directly to the Central Home Minister. This time he wrote in a more terse manner, "Even my demand for producing evidence against the allegations against us is more than six-month old, but no proof has come up during this period...In such a scenario, it doesn't behoove a supposedly cultured government to keep repeating the so-called allegations even after such a long lapse of time and showing disrespect to truth, justice and judicial system." And finally, drawing attention of the Home Minister, he clarified, "Before closing this letter, I would like to bring to your notice another fact that there is no Constitution in which you cannot pick holes in some way. All Constitutions can be amended suitably over time. Therefore, I think if somebody criticises a Constitution right upon its introduction and expects it to be perfectly complete like the final words of God, it is not right to have such a view. I have been told that the government wants the Sangh's Constitution in writing. I have submitted it. I feel the right way is to implement the Constitution in practice and change and improve it as the situation arises. This is, in fact, a constructive and useful way of doing it."[20] The response that Iyengar sent after a week exposed the true intent of the government. He had written in conclusion, "The government's approach about Rashtriya Swayamsevak Sangh is completely transparent and without any confusion. It is the custodian of people's interest and this is how it should be. It is its duty to protect them from undesirable and foul elements. Till it is not fully assured that Rashtriya Swayamsevak Sangh will not be in a position to repeat such incidents and it will be able to stop negative fallout of such actions that are a result of its activities in the past, it cannot take a lenient view about the organisation."[21]

Guruji sent his response to this letter, too, to Home Minister. Upon scrutinising the letter, one finds that it throws light on more than one aspect of Guruji's personality. Attacking the intoxication of power, he wrote in his last letter, "In a matter like this, a suggestion of an independent enquiry committee can come only from people who do not understand even the basics of governance – I am obliged for being told about this. I accept my ignorance on this subject. Not just an ordinary human being, but even Mahatma Gandhi himself had a right to this ignorance. So, I consider this a matter of pride for me. If this is how your government basically thinks, then it is dangerous."

Not sparing the people in power, he wrote bluntly, "Letter dated 3rd May, 1949 gave me a sense of satisfaction. That is, that the assessment of the mentality I had done about the people who have the right to rule, was not wrong."[22]

Guruji also apologises once in this letter. That is about lack of etiquette while objecting to the first paragraph of the Home Secretary. It was written thus, "The Government of India regrets that in your letter, you have used sentences in it like 'meaningless steps' and accused the government that it is behaving in an unjust manner, and has scant regard for justice and judicial processes.

Such a language goes totally against the simple rules of humility and etiquette. One should use a language similar to what I have used, while corresponding with the government, so that it reflects complete responsibility desirable in correspondence with the government."[23] His reply reflected irony of a deeply hurt soul that had been denied the human rights conferred by freedom of a democracy. Actually, it was a piercing statement. Guruji wrote, "It seems from the first para of the present letter that the government has been upset with my language. I deeply regret this. I am a simple man. Therefore, I did not have an opportunity to learn and practise the art of using the right language while talking to administrators and rulers. Therefore, I wrote directly and clearly whatever I deemed correct and true. Still, if expressing a truth frankly has unwittingly hurt the government, I apologise for it."[24]

He seeks apology once more. The basis for this is his truthfulness. His words are, "I once again apologise because though I have respect for the person who is holding the reins of power, I could not persuade my heart to accept the allegations that I knew are false to please him."[25]

Thus, dialogue between the two sides stopped, but atmosphere outside was against the government and in favour of the Sangh. Neutral, independent intellectuals were feeling uneasy about the unjust role of the government. In the meanwhile, many newspapers published the Sangh's constitution that had been submitted to the government. *Navbharat* of Delhi wrote in its editorial, dated, 24th May, "The Sangh has submitted a written constitution due to the adamant stand of Congress government. Why is government silent now? After studying the constitution of the Sangh, we have come to the conclusion that the Congress rulers should not object to any part of it."[26]

Readers also began writing letters on this subject. One reader wrote, "Government is playing the drama of the fox and the lamb. Seven prominent lawyers of Nagpur, like K.A. Shrinivas, Thakur Ramcharan Singh Pawar and C.K. Naidu said in their joint statement, Sangh people have broken all records of Congress people in going to jail within a short period of one-and-a-half months. Sangh leadership stopped the *satyagraha* on insistence of mediators. Government's noise about constitution should also stop now. We have read Sangh's constitution. We have not found any shortcoming in it. Therefore, the ban imposed on the Sangh should be lifted at the earliest."[27]

Professor K.R. Malkani, writing in the counter-offensive manner in Organiser, dated 22nd May, noted, "Work of cultural and voluntary organisations is entirely different from political parties. They don't need a constitution. Sarvoday Samaj is also such an organisation. It has no written constitution." *Yugdharma* from Nagpur went to the extent of writing an editorial with the title, Declare 'Sarvoday Samaaj Illegal' and attacked the government's policy strongly. Inspite of all this, no movement was visible in ruling camps. Main reason for this was the previously mentioned resolution of the Chief Ministers' meeting to continue the ban on the Sangh. Opposing this policy of the government strongly, *Kesari* of Pune wrote a sharp editorial, "Hitler ruled like a dictator, but he did so openly and with full sense of ownership. Therefore, we find our own government's behind-the-curtains dictatorship in case of the Sangh more brutal. There was a method in Hitler's eccentric ways. But, this ban based on the false accusation that Sangh is responsible for Gandhiji's murder that is taking cover under new objections everyday is now stuck finally on the clause in the Sangh's constitution about giving admission to children below 18 years and giving post of Sarsanghchaalak to an individual for his entire life. We see no reason at all for sustaining the ban on such a rotten basis. The government is misusing its unjust right to impose a particular type of Constitution on organisations that wish to conduct only cultural work."[28]

Having understood the thinking of the government, the Sangh began preparing a new strategy. Actually, the Sangh had kept its working structure intact during the period of ban. The daily get-together was taking place in different forms. The sense of trust between senior workers and swayamsevaks was strong. Contacts and interactions outside jail were even better than inside the jails. The talk those days about Officers Training Camp (O.T.C.) –training camps of the Sangh – was, "We are running J.T.C. (O.T.C. in jail)."

For those who have experienced life in jail, it is known world over that there is no secret that cannot escape in or out of jails. Those who wish to talk confidentially are cautioned that 'even walls have ears'. This is, indeed, true. But, the truth extends further. Walls not only have ears but they also have lips. It doesn't matter whether Guruji is inside or Eknath ji is outside. Actually, taking Krishna across Kalindi from Kansa's prison is an illustration of this truth. Leaders and organisers had kept the message broadcasting systems very fast, based on this truism. Because of this, the morale of the swayamsevaks was very high inspite of being in prison for four-five months. In fact, the Congress leadership's estimates about the scenario slipped off the tracks here. They had assumed that the policy of procrastination will weaken the opposition. That is why they had dragged the matter for five months after suspension of *satyagraha*.

Sangh leadership's thinking was quite opposite to this. It decided to get back in the battle grounds again with the co-operation of a favourable society. Noticing the last sentence of Home Secretary's letter, "Government cannot take a lenient view about the organisation", Guruji decided to face the challenge head-on. He handed over a letter on his letterhead carrying his name, containing his plan for struggle to the jail warden, to be handed over to Balasaheb Deoras who was to be released after a week. The jailer intercepted it and sent it directly to Dwarika Prasad Mishra, who sent it to Home Minister Patel.[29]

Who knows whether even this was some kind of drama? The story of this letter was strange. It gave an idea about the intentions of the Sangh leader. He had written to his closest colleague, "I had told Shri Venkataram Shastri from the beginning that this is what the government will do. He assured me, 'leave it to me'. From his confidence, I felt that he may have talked to a couple of very senior members of the government. Because of this and even otherwise, with a feeling that I should not become a hurdle in this gentleman's efforts, I accepted his offer. But, my view is that it is not possible to resolve this issue without informing members all over and launching a powerful agitation again. Thus, without rushing into it, this agitation will run for many days with faultless preparations. With this understanding, there is no alternative but to relaunch this agitation by June end or at a suitable time. This is my opinion. It would be better to include and add other types of strikes, etc. to this. A good resolution should be documented that we had agreed to mediation of Shri Shastriji, etc. Based on their advice, we had sent our Constitution to the government. But, the government keeps repeating its old arguments and keeps up its adamant stand. Copies of this statement should be distributed all over the country. The statement should also declare that as a result of the government putting hurdles against the right of the people to assemble, we are launching this peaceful agitation because we have been left with no other alternative. This statement should be sent from an unmarked place by post to the Central and the State governments and agitation should be launched in a peaceful manner.

"This is but my opinion. However, you people, who are outside, should sit together and take the right decision. My effort is only that this sense of indecisiveness must end. This situation of being 'neither here nor there' with washing away of mediator's efforts must come to an end."[30]

As expected, Sarkaryavaah Bhaiyyaji Dani and Balasaheb Deoras reached Nagpur after being released from jail on 5th June. None of them received the above-mentioned letter suppressed by the jailer, but they had received complete information from other 'information highways'. Eknath Ranade also met them later. The opinion of all the three was similar to that of Guruji. Their assessment was that discussions about some agreement with the government were like a cry in the wilderness and that the government was playing a game of stretching and delaying the issue. They also assessed the situation on the ground. They could notice that the atmosphere prevailing at the time of imposition of ban had changed radically. Now, people had understood the truth. Newspapers had also not opposed the Sangh's *satyagraha* blindly. Many newspapers had protested strongly against the unrestrained cycle of oppression and also supported Sangh's demand for justice. In the meanwhile, the case of Gandhi murder had also got over. In that case, prosecuting lawyers had not even mentioned the name of any swayamsevak. In the judegment that Justice H. Atmacharan gave, the Sangh's name didn't appear anywhere. During the hearing, the accused had kept aloof of the Sangh in the long statement that he read out in front of the judge. Thus, the case, the accused and the judge – all three had left out the Sangh. In short, the triumvirate came to the conclusion that hearts of the swayamsevaks in jail were still ready for the struggle and ready to bear with more pain, but there was serious shortage of funds; when they looked at their side. They got ready for the policy of not bowing down. All the underground volunteers were sent out this directive all over the country. Series of contacts, discussions and broadcasting of instructions were used to prepare the souls of swayamsevaks to be ready for hard work.

An episode comes to mind at this stage. Dadaji Paramarth was moving around South India with an assumed name of 'Govindan'. He told select workers in a secret meeting, "We have to keep our sacred Shivalinga as our presiding deity. If a big black scorpion sits on it and doesn't leave it, kill it with your sandals. We shall cleanse and purify the Shivalinga with sacred water later."

The government must have received information about the movement in Sangh camps through its intelligence department. Student organisations had started functioning in different states of country. Experienced and polished workers of the Sangh, like Balraj Madhok, Dattopant Thengadiji, Dattaji Didolkar and Nagaraj Reddy were leading this activity. Large numbers of students from amongst displaced citizens had joined the organisation in North. Simultaneously, discussions and workshops began on desirability of a new political party to make real democracy more effective in the new post-Independence period. Professor Malkani wrote a series of articles in the weekly, *Organiser*, about the possible shape of a new political party. The Sangh had begun its moves, but the Sangh leadership was aware that the government run by *Sardar Patel* would not give way so easily. The government was hatching a conspiracy to create fissures among Guruji and his followers. After receiving the letter written from Sivni jail by Guruji, Sardar Patel wrote to Dwarika Prasad Mishra, "If this letter reaches the desired destination, it will have the authentic stamp of the chief of the organisation. In its absence, there will be pulls within the organisation about the problem. As a result, we shall face groups rather than a well-united organisation. Therefore, as a policy and strategy, it would be ideal to not let this letter reach the desired destination."[31] A manifestation of this move was shifting of Guruji under the orders of Dwarika Prasad on 7th June from Sivni jail to Baitul jail, which was 200 kms away.

It was clearly a vengeful step of the government. Even the imperialist British used to put political prisoners in jails like Yerwada, Naini, etc. with normal facilities. Dangerous prisoners used to be sent to Cellular Jail of Andaman or Mandalay Jail in Burma. Baitul was a younger sibling of these two jails. Guruji was put in this oven in those hot days of summer. His physical condition was not good even in Sivni. It got worse in Baitul. But there too he stuck to his policy of 'no demands, no complaints'. Bhauji and Taiji went to Baitul Jail on 18th June to see their son. They could meet their son only on the second day and could talk to him with affection. But, they came out with moist eyes. On being asked, the mother, a reservoir of affection, said, "Even when he put up mountainous efforts without pausing for a moment in day or night, or without eating, his condition had not gone this bad." The mother could not speak anything beyond this.

News about falling health of Guruji spread all round. Newspapers like *Hitavaad* criticised the government strongly. Central Home Department was flooded with letters and telegrams full of anger, fear and suspicion. Finally, Home Minister of the state set up a one-man commission to examine and present a medical report about the health of prisoner Golwalkar. Accordingly, Mangalmurti went to Baitul with a doctor and met Guruji. After preliminary pleasantries, when he asked about his health, Guruji told the law officer smilingly, "I have deposited it in a bank. It will never be destroyed."

The atmosphere outside was becoming favourable to the Sangh. The Dani-Deoras duo took an aggressive stance. When a government-appointed anonymous person met Bhaiyyaji Dani to get Sangh's opinion, Bhaiyyaji showed him the typewritten copy of the document about the formation of the proposed political party. Vasantrao Oke also followed the same strategy. When these details reached various ministries, many Chief Ministers started saying, "We shall have to reconsider the proposal of April about ban on the Sangh." Many ministers expressed the opinion that if the Sangh entered politics, it would be transformed from a 'brahmin' to a '*brahmraakshas*' (from a peaceful pious person to a demon). It seems Nehruji's thoughts were also moving in the same direction. We can conclude so because the title of the chapter covering this issue in the words of Nehru is 'the less of these bans the better'.[32] The government seemed to have made up its mind to somehow find a solution to this problem. To achieve this, the dialogue that had broken down had to be reopened. There was an intractable hurdle here. Guruji had stopped his correspondence with the government and so had the government. Now, the dilemma was how to move ahead? Sardar Patel found a way out. Thus, Dwarika Prasad ji reached Delhi and stayed with the Food Minister, Babu Rajendra Prasad. He called Moulichandra Sharma, who was known and acceptable to both the sides and apprised him of the problem. And, he also told him that this was a 'directive from Sardar Patel taking rest in Dehradun'. Moulichandra ji accepted the brief immediately. He reached Nagpur on 7th July. Home Minister made arrangement of a car for him. He met Dani and Deoras without delay. They informed him of their experience from the beginning to date and told him that their faith in the government had broken. It was fruitless to talk with those people and requested him to leave them alone on their path. They talked bluntly. Moulichandra ji returned after meeting told Mishra ji, "Patel ji really wants to lift the ban. If Golwalkar were to write a letter to Patel on the same issues that he had talked about in his statement last November on 2nd, that is, about the national flag, the system of governance, secular state, etc. then it would be possible." Dani and Deoras did not soften their stance even this time. Both said very clearly, "Whether they lift ban or not, there is no possibility of anybody from among us, including Guruji, of writing a word to the centre of power." Again, another round. Moulichandra ji came back after meeting Mishra ji and offered a new idea for a solution. According to it, Moulichandra Sharma ji would be the person who would ask for clarification and Guruji would give him clarification in writing. The ban would be lifted on the basis of that clarification. The Sangh leadership was agreeable to this, but only on one condition. They told Moulichandra ji, "You will first give us the list of those questions; after expressing our opinion only will we pass it on to Guruji." According to this, Moulichandra ji presented the list with eight issues given to him by Dwarika Prasad. They were about Sangh's faith in Indian constitution and flag, Sangh's view about working secretly, the process of election in the Sangh, meaning of lifelong oath of the Sangh, admission of children in the Sangh, process of appointment of Sarsanghchaalak, balanced representation of members and the system of income and expense.

Deoras-Dani duo didn't find anything unacceptable in this list. Actually, Guruji had given answer to most of these issues already. Still this hypocrisy! But, if this could lead to a solution, why would there be any objection? Therefore, they wrote together a detailed letter to Guruji, sealed it in an envelope and while handing it over to the mediator, they said, "Sharma ji, please do not read this, nor allow anybody else to read it. Give it directly in Guruji's hands. Show Guruji's clarification directly to us, only then hand it over to Mishra ji." He accepted the condition and while leaving, said, "*Shubham bhavatu*" (may good things happen). He kept his word. He did not hand over the sealed envelope to Mishra ji, taking refuge under his promise. Activities went ahead smoothly after this.

Moulichandra ji reached Baitul by car on 10th July. There was no time limit to the meeting that day. He touched Guruji's feet as soon as he met him. When he told him about the purpose of visit, Guruji said, in the words of Moulichandra ji, "We will talk about these things later. My first duty is to welcome you."

"He took out a stove out of a gunny bag lying there, lit it and made tea quickly.He made me drink two cups and took one cup himself. His carefree countenance, generous heart and sense of affection was creating an impact on me with every passing moment. I could feel in my heart that I was sitting with an extraordinary divine personality. I kept the letters in front of him after this. He said, 'Give these to me, I will sign them.' Opposing this, I told him, 'First read these letters properly, think over them. It is possible that some words in them may not be to your liking.' He wrote that letter on a letter pad with his name, signed it and gave the letter to me."[33] Moulichandra ji showed it to Dani-Deoras first and then gave it to Dwarika Prasad Mishra. He read it out to Sardar Patel in Dehradun on telephone, where he was taking rest after a heart attack. Sardar gave it his acceptance and directed that the letter be sent directly to Delhi office. Dehradun-Nagpur-Delhi hotline did its work on the midnight of 11th and before sunrise on 12th July, the Sangh ban became a page in history.

But, there is still a riddle here. Guruji's authorised letter sent along with

Sangh documents sent by Venkataram Shastri was returned to the sender with the reason, "You are not the official mediator."

And today, Moulichandra Sharma sends a clarification given to him to the government and that is accepted, though he has not been declared a mediator. Not only this, acceptance is done on telephone and with the brave spirit of a Napoleon, the complex problem is resolved at a lightning speed. This is the mystical way of politics. But, what was the game behind this game?

Venkataram Shastri had met Guruji in Sivni prison with B.G. Khaparde of Amravati in the third week after suspension of *satyagraha* on 13th February. After this, Guruji had presented the Sangh constitution on 11th April. Then, sensing no movement from the government's side, countless letters started coming from all over Bharat to Shastriji in Chennai, enquiring about the situation. Most of the senders were respected members of Janaadhikaar Samiti (Human Rights Committee). It became a moral duty for Shastriji to calm them down. He prepared a long statement describing his bitter-sweet experience in a matter of fact way. The first sentence of this statement was, "I had been receiving many letters for the last two months to find the current status and my efforts in the matter of Sangh problem. I feel it is the right time to present all the facts before the people…." Further ahead, there was response to the questions raised by Home Secretary Iyengar when the constitution was presented to him. In the last paragraph, he wrote, "Now I would have to end this letter on an optimistic note that the government will find a way to lift the ban and give permission to the Sangh to carry on its activities like earlier times. To my mind, continuing with the ban and imprisoning Sangh leaders is not justified, nor intelligent or profitable for anybody."[34]

He had handed over this statement to *Hindu* newspaper with the stipulation to publish it only after 12th July. The government had received the complete statement through its intelligence officers. But, it could not do anything about it. The government realised that it would be exposed now. Not allowing such a thing to happen was a matter of prestige for the government. There was time till 12th July to somehow do something in the matter. That is why, when a member of the commission reached Baitul to get information about Guruji's health, Moulichandra Sharma reached Nagpur from Delhi the same day.

Finally, when the ban was lifted on the midnight of 11th July that news was broadcast on 12th July from Akashwani and was published in all newspapers on 13th July. Shastri ji's statement also got published the same day as per his directions. Thus, the government 'had to receive lashes and also had to eat onions' – as an Indian proverb goes. Guruji was freed from Baitul prison on the morning of 13th July and he left for Nagpur in the afternoon by Grant Trunk Express.

□

Endnotes

1. *Shri Guruji Samagra*, Vol. 10, pp. 50-51
2. *Pehli Agnipariksha*, pp. 101
3. *Maa. Sa. Golwalkar*, pp. 148
4. *Pehli Agnipariksha*, pp. 97
5. Ibid, pp. 111
6. Ibid, pp. 111
7. Ibid, pp. 111
8. Ibid, pp. 210-211
9. Ibid, pp. 163
10. Ibid, pp. 163-164
11. *Jeevan Prasang*, Vol. 1, pp. 215-216
12. *Pehli Agnipariksha*, pp. 215
13. Ibid, pp. 166
14. Ibid, pp. 216
15. Ibid, pp. 215
16. *Maa. Sa. Golwalkar*, pp. 1-2
17. *Chennai ka Hindu Neta Ramagopal* – interview (15.1.2005)
18. *Pehli Agnipariksha*, pp. 221
19. *Shri Guruji Samagra*, Vol. 10, pp. 56-57
20. Ibid, pp. 61-64
21. Ibid, pp. 66
22. Ibid, pp. 67
23. Ibid, pp. 64-65
24. Ibid, pp. 67
25. Ibid, pp. 67
26. *Pehli Agnipariksha*, pp. 222
27. Ibid, pp. 223
28. Ibid, pp. 224
29. *Living an Era*, Vol. 2, pp. 78
30. Ibid, pp. 78
31. Ibid, pp. 80
32. Ibid, pp. 56
33. *Jeevan Prasang*, Vol. 1, pp. 218
34. *Justice on Trial*, pp. 92-98

25

All is Well that Ends Well

Baitul had a Sangh Shakha. This Shakha used to be run as a sports club (*kreeda sangh*) during the ban. On 12th July, 1949, when games were being played, the head of that Shakha informed everybody, "Our revered Sarsanghchaalak Guruji will be released from jail tomorrow." Upon hearing this, a school student, S.K. Patrikar and his friends stood a little away from the prison gates since early morning to catch a glimpse of their dear Sarsanghchaalak. The gates opened on time and these children saw their Guruji as he came out. They ran towards him without a second thought, touched his feet and greeted him with folded hands, following the value system they had learnt at home as a part of growing-up. After asking about their well-being lovingly and patting their backs, Guruji moved ahead.[1]

Thus, these innocent children had the first sacred glimpse of Guruji as he walked out from prison into the radiance of freedom. This was a sweet revenge of fate. The government had raised objection to a section of the Constitution that talked about the admission of children of this age into the Sangh. Today, these were the same children who were giving the first welcome to the top leader of the Sangh!

At this moment, senior swayamsevak of Baitul, Babasaheb Deshpande stood there with his wife waiting to take Guruji home. As soon as he reached home, the housewives who had collected there welcomed him with *aarti* with lighted lamps.[2] Everybody went together to the railway station as the time for the train drew near. Guruji had to go to Nagpur on Grant Trunk Express.

Guruji left for Nagpur in first class per his entitlement of a released prisoner. News of the arrival of Guruji had already spread everywhere in Nagpur. As a result, the whole complex around the station was crowded to the brim with people from the Sangh. There was a smile on every lip and glow in every eye. Guruji's parents, Babasaheb Apte, Bhaiyyaji Dani, Balasaheb and other leaders stood at a designated place on the station, waiting for him. Finally, the wait was over. The train bogey stopped right in front of Bhauji and Taiji. Their son alighted and bent down to touch his father's feet and just then, the father garlanded his son. Only after this, could he pay his salutations to his father. Tai lifted her Madhu, lying at her feet, with loving hands. And finally, the whole family hugged together. Bhaiyyaji put a garland on behalf of the Sangh in Guruji's hands immediately and also handed over a telegram of T.R. Venkataram Shastri. It said, "All is well that ends well." Thus, he received the blessings of a father-figure just as he met his respected father.

There was an outburst of joy everywhere. The date was 13th July. The words written exactly eight months back to the swayamsevaks, "Arise with a victorious roar for *Bharatmata's* glory that would reverberate from the horizons of the heart to the horizons of the universe" proved to be literally true. Slogans like 'Sangh *amar rahe*' (May Sangh be immortal), '*Guruji ki jai* (Victory to Guruji) reverberated in the air. Colourful, fragrant flowers rained from everywhere. It took 90 minutes to come out of the station from the platform. Guruji went straight to his Nagoba Lane home. He had stayed there for five days till he left for Chennai. These days saw a continuous flow of Sangh well-wishers, close friends and relatives and saintly people. There was a flood of letters and piles of telegrams. Only the telephone bell did not ring as there was no telephone instrument in his home.

Written good wishes received from Shyama Prasad Mukherjee said, "I am sure that now an atmosphere can be created to bring together all positive spiritual forces of the nation." We have noted earlier that Venkataram Shastri had sent the Sangh constitution to M.R. Jaikar to give it the finishing touches. This specialist's compliments contained an expectation and also a guiding advice, "I believe that the Sangh will adopt a working system that would not result in displeasure of the government. The Sangh has set a lofty goal for itself that can be achieved without a confrontation with the government."[3]

Guruji did not have time to get buried in the piles of telegrams and letters. He got busy with his colleagues in making plans for the future. First priority was circumambulation of the nation to express his gratitude, and also obtaining a sacred glimpse of the swayamsevaks all over the country. In that atmosphere even Tai did not have the heart to advise him to let his health improve. He made a reservation in a train for Chennai on 19th July. He was eager to meet Shastriji, who was not keeping well. A telegram was sent with the message, "Coming to meet you."

It was not a tough job to get back Dr. Hedgewar Bhavan confiscated by the government. It was given back on 17th July falling on Sunday. It was cleaned and set up properly in no time and made serviceable for general use. Sangh Shakha was restarted on the second day in the presence of highly revered Sarsanghchaalak. As per plan, all the members of Nagpur Shakha came together at Mohite Sangh Ground. In an atmosphere that was surfeit with joy, enthusiasm and devotion, revered Sarsanghchaalak said in his *bouddhik* (discourse), "Our work is beginning again today. A person waking up from sleep feels refreshed and energetic. We too have to get down to work with the same enthusiasm. We have to make this work magnificent by developing it. Purity of the work depends on the purity of heart. The heart cannot be pure without the pure emotion of love. Whether one is a friend or an enemy, our approach should always be '*maa vidvishaav hai*' (animosity towards none). Immersing ourselves with utmost pure emotions, that Bharatvarsh represents the colossal form of our nation and we are all arms, limbs and parts of this body, we have to develop this gigantic magnificent work, winning over everybody with allegiance to the goal and our affectionate behaviour."[4]

During all this busy time, 10-12 old lawyer-friends like Dattatreya Deshpande, Manohar Oke and others arranged a homely get-together with their lawyer friend Golwalkar. Some people out of these recalled later that the atmosphere that day was sparkling with joy and humour. There were jokes galore all around that followed one after another. Talking about the incident of the visit of the judicial officer appointed by Home Minister, Guruji said in a satirical vein, "In view of our brave ministers, judicial officers even have the special ability to check the health of a person."

Guruji was to leave for Chennai on 19th. He found time for two to three days before this to respond to the messages of goodwill received by him. As was his habit, he wrote letters in Hindi, Marathi, English himself as it suited the sender. He wrote more than 20 letters on 18th. Of these, there were letters to Gopalswamy Iyengar and Shyama Prasad Mukherjee in English, to Sardar Patel and Purushottamdas Tandon in Hindi and to Ambedkar and Khaparde in Marathi. Apart from these, he also wrote his replies later in the month of August. He met Pandit Nehru and Sardar Patel in the first week of August. Both of them gave time for these meetings. The only thought behind these efforts was to put an end to the mindset of conflict that had erupted in the interregnum and create an environment of mutual co-operation, affection and friendliness once again in the country. In a letter to Pandit Nehru, he wrote, "I am trying hard as it requires uncommon efforts to wipe away bitter memories from the hearts of my co-workers. There is no sense in remaining lost in memories of the past. I am doubtlessly sure about receiving co-operation from the government that will help generate a healthy atmosphere based on mutual affection, respect and co-operation, which would result in a helpful environment of goodwill."[5]

Calling this view desirable, Sardar wrote back within three days on 21st July, "As you have said in your public address, situation in the country is such and things are happening in such a manner that we should all look at the present and the future rather than into the past."[6]

One can see an interesting fact in all the letters of thanks that Guruji wrote. His inability in not meeting anybody personally is not due to weak health, but due to his being busy in re-establishing Sangh work. He writes to Babasaheb Ambedkar, "The duty of meeting well-wishers like you is getting postponed due to my busy schedule to set up Sangh work properly again."[7] He writes to Kakasaheb Gadgil, "Work will slowly become systematic, but I will have to keep involved with this work to accomplish this."[8] To Purushottamdas Tandon, he writes, "I have got down to put the work back in order."[9] He writes to Babasaheb Khaparde, "My busy schedule will continue till I put this train back on tracks."[10] He wrote like this to each person. Wherever he went according to the organisation's plans, he made it a point to meet all the gentlemen involved in this effort. Getting to have a divine view (*darshan*) and worshipping gods, knowers of *Vedas*, teachers (*gurus*), scholars is called a penance of the body. This physical penance of Guruji went on without a break.*

Guruji reached Chennai by G.T. Express with Bhaiyyaji Dani on 20th July. Close colleagues like Dadarao Paramarth, Dada Apte and V. Rajagopalachari were there at the station. All of them went to Rajagopalachari's home. His old mother was standing in the central courtyard for Guruji's. He touched her feet immediately on entering the home and told her smilingly, "There is not a scratch on this robust body." "All this is grace of God," the mother said with folded hands. Her face was calm and blissful. People standing around could not fathom this to-and-fro dialogue. When Guruji went for a bath, Rajagopalachari disclosed the secret behind this exchange. There was story behind it. Guruji was ready to leave for Nagpur on 31st January, 1948, in the dark shadows resulting from Gandhiji's tragic end, abandoning all his programmes. He went ahead to touch the feet of the old mother as was his custom. Highly upset with the complexity of the scenario, Rajagopalachari requested his mother, "Amma, give him pious blessings of a robust (*vajra*) body." At that sacred moment, this saintly angel stood silently with folded hands and shut eyes. Guruji was expressing his gratitude to that silent saintly blessing of that day. It would not be out of place to note that when this mother died after five years, Guruji remembered this incident and wrote to Rajagopalachari, "I remembered 31.1.1948. During those grave times, when I was about to leave for Nagpur from Chennai, you asked respected Mother to bless me at that time with '*vajradeh*' (robust body) and that I may be bestowed with that, which would be for the best. I have talked about it even publicly. I have also accepted with gratitude that I could come out stronger out of the terrible test by fire (*agnipariksha*) without even a scratch only because of her blessings."[11]

After lunch and some rest, Guruji and Bhaiyyaji Dani went with Rajagopalachari to meet and seek blessings of Venkataram Shastri. Since both Guruji and Shastriji were good conversationalists, their experience-sharing was an interesting learning experience for those who were sitting with them. Shastriji explained the essence of the sentence he had written in the telegram. This elderly gentleman heartily supported the sentence '*ma vidvishava hai*' that Guruji had

* *Dev-dwija-guru-praagyapoojanam. Shaariram tap uchyate (Gita, 17-14)*

spoken in his Nagpur discourse. Without any formal words, Guruji presented his emotional gratitude at the feet of the great personality, saying, "I pray to ever merciful God for a long healthy life for you." He, then, took his leave.

Guruji proceeded to the felicitation programme from Shastri ji's home. This was the first felicitation outside Nagpur. Hundreds of swayamsevaks and well-wishers of the Sangh had gathered there. He appealed to them in English to 'forget and forgive'. It was this same Chennai city that had witnessed the naked dance of demonic atrocities by infamous police battalion on *satyagrahis*! From Chennai, Guruji's next destination was Pune. He was to meet editor of *Kesari*, Gajananrao Ketkar and his assistants. He also had to bring the Sangh work back on tracks there.

Enroute to Pune, Sangh supporters had gathered together at stations like Renuguntha, Cudappah, Guntkal, Gulbarga, Solapur, etc. to have a look at his divine personality without any concern about the time of the day or night. These simple selfless souls thought of only their bliss and it never occurred to them that it could inconvenience Guruji. When Sanghchaalak, Dr. Muley requested him to speak a couple of words at Solapur station's platform, Guruji said humorously, "That capacity has weakened in prison. But, are you sure these are only two words?" and then went on to speak two highly meaningful sentences, "From now onwards, we have to get down to work with open hearts. One needs a nectar-filled heart for the Sangh work."[12]

Guruji reached Pune on 24th July. Fortunately, it was a Sunday. Pune people had also got sufficient time to make preparations. But, it was the monsoon season and that proved the only inconvenience. But, Mother Nature played along on Sunday and there was no rain that day. A human ocean of nearly 25,000 was spilling over in and around Pune station. The main road was decorated with buntings and flags. As Guruji's motorcade proceeded slowly, nearly all the spectators showered flower petals on him, as if it was a different type of rain that day! Full-throated cries of victory rent the air.

The felicitation meeting was to begin at 6:15 p.m. in the huge ground of Parashuram Mahavidyalay. Aware of Sangh discipline, Pune citizens reached the ground about 15 minutes earlier. In the vast sea of black caps, nowhere could one trace a single police cap. Guests took their seats under a capable, well-planned arrangement. Guruji reached the venue at exact time. He was welcomed in traditional Marathi style with the blowing of *tutari-shring* – a type of local trumpet. Two hundred forty-three organisations greeted and garlanded Guruji, who had been liberated from major difficulties that had eclipsed his life. Accepting the felicitations, he spoke from his heart, "Since ages, all the great people had to bear pain. They never enjoyed the smallest worldly pleasures. The only satisfaction they had was that of fulfilling their duty. Did the highest of all manifestations, Bhagwan Ram and Krishna face any less difficulties? I believe that the all-powerful God gets all such acts done deliberately. A human being comes out much stronger and luminescent from such difficulties. The Supreme Lord made us go through such a test. The result is for all of us to see. I don't have to spell it out for you. What had to happen has happened, but there is no need to swell with pride. In the *satyagraha* that Sangh swayamsevaks conducted, they did not break any rules and regulations of the government, nor did they confront the government. And, there was no reason for conflict. This is our government, why should we oppose it? Why should we have animosity towards it?"

"It is true that there are differences between the government and us, but is there any place where there are no differences? There are differences even within families. Nurturing unity in diversity is the real test of democracy. We have proven true to this test, but the government's view was quite contrary. It perceived something different in Sangh's agitation. So, it tried to suppress it. Hearing about the games the government played to suppress the agitation, we felt that we were not living in the twentieth century but had moved back a century or two; the age of Sultanate has returned."

"Our own desire is that this nation, like the sacred Ganga, should flow uninterrupted with fulfilment of all the desired traits. For this, responsibility is upon on each of us. Let us reinitiate our work with renewed energy, but while doing this, let us not harbour the mentality of jealousy or animosity. While doing this work, we should keep our hearts pure and pious. It is but natural to feel angry, but in not letting it overpower us is our greatness. Attaining the highest stage is humanity. It has been well said, '*Beeti taahi bisaar de, aage ki sudhi ley*' (Forget the past, take care of the future)."[13]

All the newspapers appearing on Monday appreciated Guruji's views. He went to *Kesari's* office that day and met gentlemen Gajanan Ketkar, G.S. Karandikar, L.B. Bhopate and others, and expressed his gratitude with all humility. There was an informal get-together of swayamsevaks in the evening. It was planned that Guruji would only be present there. But he had to speak there in deference to affectionate insistence of old dedicated swayamsevaks and Sangh office-bearers. His subject on this day was totally different. On this day, he presented an invaluable way of looking at things. In fact, this different view is always a guiding principle for any dedicated and unselfish worker taking up social work. His words are, "Sangh's agitation had gone on around December for nearly one to two months. Many had to suffer hardships at that time. People had to suffer different kinds of pain. This agitation is an unparalleled event in history. People who suffer some pain for somebody expect to receive some rewards for this suffering. This is a natural and normal response. However, the Sangh workers do not expect any kind of reward.

"There is no such tradition to reward or give positions of power to those who are prepared to bear pain, nor do we wish to start any such new tradition. One who works for a cause is only doing his duty; we have no tradition of giving any prize to such a person.

"Actually, respect for those sacrificing people, who serve, does not decline in the hearts of people ever. It only rises continuously. It should be understood that when one develops an ego that I have shown people how I have done something, then his fall begins. When people with such thinking have to go to prison, they feel, 'We have accomplished a great task.' It is not right to expect fruit for any work that one undertakes."[14]

Guruji went from Pune to Mumbai by train. Chinchwad falls on this route. The train Guruji was travelling in did not halt there, but 4,000 displaced Sindhi brethren had settled down in that locality. These people managed to get it to halt by requesting railway officials (but, not forcing them with a '*rail roko*'). When Guruji alighted amongst them, he could not control his emotions. He had stood in Hyderabad and Karachi just eight days before dawn of Independence. These people were rich, well-to-do people enjoying self-sufficient lives there. But, today, whose crime was this? Who was the culprit? Definitely, not these people. Guruji did not give any speech at Chinchwad. He called by name the people he knew personally, put his arms around their shoulders and enquired about their well-being. Eyes filled with tears were looking upon him. When an elder among them said, "None of them is a beggar," Guruji said, "A human being's hidden virile strength awakens in times of calamity." Encouraging them to awaken their inner virile strength, he got back into the train. All the stations on way saw huge crowds, because of which the train reached Mumbai very late. Mumbai saw a repeat of the scenes witnessed in Pune.

Guruji was a guest at Sanghchaalak Bhai Sethdayal's home. While talking to the local office-bearers, perhaps based on his experiences during the day, he expressed his view, "Due to some confusion in their mind, people think anarchy means democracy. During the last two years, your sense of discipline may have been forgotten. But, now this work will have to be restarted. Please remember that we are not a crowd."[15] Guruji met Barrister Jamnadas Mehta, the labour leader N.M. Joshi with Sethdayalji to convey his thanks.

Guruji returned to Nagpur from Mumbai. This week-long tour was truly a tour about expressing his gratitude. He was in Nagpur till August for the next three weeks after this tour. He was extremely busy in those days. He also had to face some unforeseen issues during this time.

Two or three phrases used in the government circular about rescinding the ban had created some confusion. It had a deviant statement that the Sangh leadership had agreed to government conditions and given assurance to it. Newspapers picked on those words and started passing adverse comments about it. The responsibility of clarifying his position fell upon Sarsanghchaalak.

Guruji received complete information about the prevailing conditions from his colleagues after returning to Nagpur. Saying, "We shall see," he went on to Bhaiyyaji Dani's village, Umred, on 27th for a felicitation programme. Guruji's lecture in Umred was quite different from his earlier lectures. The underlying theme there was about the Sangh's power and patience. He said, "If the attacks during the last one-and-a-half years were mounted on the Sangh by people of foreign culture, they would have got a good idea about Sangh's strength that it has built over the last twenty-four years. They would have been stunned with our response (*chhatee ka doodh yad aa jaataa*). When the tongue gets caught between our teeth, we don't pull out teeth. Since people who attacked us are our own countrymen, our brethren, it would be desirable to forget the old painful incidents and not let differences in opinion widen in future.

"Clouds appear in the skies and then move on. Nobody becomes unhappy when they come, nor does one clap with glee when they go away. We shall have to say exactly the same thing about incidents that happened during the last one-and-a-half years."

"Sangh swayamsevaks showed appropriate fortitude, understanding the difficult times that our country was facing and followed a moral path in these conditions. I am very happy about it."[16] He returned to Nagpur after this programme.

There was a felicitation on 28th by Nagpur University and a public felicitation on 29th July. Editor of newspaper *Hitavaad*, A.D. Mani wished to know during his felicitation speech about the so-called conditions of the government and assurance by the Sangh. Guruji expressed his views accordingly in his acceptance speech, "I had wished to keep silent on this issue of me giving a written assurance to the government. I can definitely say this to you that at that time, I was not speaking as Golwalkar, as an individual, but as a representative of a nationally spread-out massive organisation. For the organisation on whose behalf I was speaking, I would have given up my life before it was insulted, but would never have allowed it to be insulted. I wish to assure you that I have not given any acceptance or assurance of any type. I can just clarify that reaching an agreement means that both sides take a step back. With this view, on advice of respected T.V.R. Shastri, I gave my permission to put in writing the way the Sangh work had been conducted for years. Shri Shastriji is older by a year to my father. I had given this permission in deference to his prestige and knowledge... That the Sangh to whom you look up with such love and sense of hope, for that Sangh I have not spoken or written even a word that could result in an insult to it."[17]

Still this matter raised a lot of smoke for nearly two-and-a-half months. After this, a legislator from Surat, Shri Lallubhai Makanji Patel submitted a list of questions in Maharashtra Assembly. Following is the detailed questionnaire:

"Will Hon'ble Home and Revenue Minister please let us know:

a. Is it true that ban on Rashtriya Swayamsevak Sangh has been lifted?
b. Is it so, what are the reasons for removing this ban?

c. Has the ban been removed with some conditions or without any condition?
d. If it has been removed conditionally, what are those conditions?
e. Has the government been given any assurances by the leader of Rashtriya Swayamsevak Sangh?
f. If so, what are these assurances?

Shri Morarji Desai's answer on behalf of Shri Dinkar Rao N. Desai:

a. Yes.
b. Ban has been lifted because it was not found necessary to continue it in future.
c. It was removed without any conditions.
d. Such a question doesn't arise.
e. No.
f. Question doesn't arise."[18]

Our vastly experienced forefathers have stated that where six qualities of industriousness, courage, fortitude, intellect, strength and bravery are present, God himself becomes a helping hand. This is what happened in the case of Sangh. Among six festivals that the Sangh celebrates, *Guru Pooja* festival was due on 10th July, just two days prior to lifting of the ban. Normally, *Guru Poojan* and *Guru Dakshina* take place in different *Shakhas* till the Raksha Bandhan festival. Coincidentally, the ban was removed around the same time. Thus, re-commencement of *Shakhas* all over Bharat took place more or less with the worship of highly sacred saffron flag (*bhagwa dhwaj*) and offering of *dakshina*. Even in Nagpur, after the public felicitation programme, Shakha-wise *Guru Poojan* festivals were held. Guruji visited *Shakhas* as per his planned programme till *Raksha Bandhan*, but the speech would always be delivered by another office-bearer. In words of Guruji, all this helped 'bring the train back on track'.

Immediately upon lifting of the ban, Guruji wrote to Sardar Patel, asking for an appointment to meet him. After receiving confirmation, Guruji, Bhaiyyaji Dani and Balasaheb Deoras went to Mumbai on 15th August. They met Patel on 16th August in Birla House, situated on Mount Pleasant Road at 11:35 a.m. Patel's secretary and daughter were present at that time. It was a pleasant heart to heart talk. There was not an iota of animosity in it. Over time, this pleasant relationship lasted till Patel's death.

On 21st August on a Sunday, Delhi was to hold a programme. Bhauji, Taiji, Babasaheb Ghatate, Balasaheb Deoras, Bhaiyyaji Dani and others had come from Nagpur to take part in it. For the swayamsevaks of Delhi this felicitation programme in Delhi was a question of Sangh's and Guruji's prestige. Therefore, they literally brought the sky down to make this programme an unprecedented, incomparable and memorable event in every respect. The result was a magnificent celebration of victory. *Amrita Bazar Patrika* wrote on 28th August, "When Shri M.S. Golwalkar reached Delhi station and the way he conducted himself when he was greeted by huge crowds, one could see that he had all the qualities of a winner. Such a huge sea of humanity had gathered to listen to him in the public meeting organised in the capital of our nation that it could only be called unprecedented. It seemed that his standing was in no way less than that of Pandit Nehru and Sardar Patel. Management of the crowd that had collected there was better than in any meeting organised by the Congress. When there was need for silence, such would be silence that you could hear a pin drop and when there was an occasion to exhibit enthusiasm, then claps and cheers rose from thousands of throats in unison. People seemed to have as much faith in the swayamsevak wearing black caps as they had in members of Army and Police managing the programme…. All these things have certain significance. It was a brilliant living example that can anything be impossible with discipline, hard work and strong belief?"[19]

B.B.C., perched on top of the world for its credibility those days, noted, "Who after Nehru and Sardar Patel? Answer to this question is not the Leftist leaders but Sangh chief, Golwalkar. When he came to Delhi, 2.5 lakh people were present to hear him. Only Nehru can attract such a big crowd. Such a grand welcome of the chief of an organisation banned for 19 months and such a mammoth meeting is an example by itself. Propaganda has been unleashed showing the Sangh as a Nazi organisation and the Sangh chief as a dictator. But, one could not discern anything in Shri Golwalkar that could be compared to European dictator Hitler or Mussolini."[20]

Guruji's speech in Delhi lasted 55 minutes. There was no show of anger in it, nor was there a feeling of revenge against any party. This lecture was an excellent example of self-control and balance. Well-established intellectuals praised his speech. People in governance also took it to be very positive. Experts in the political field called it a presentation of skillful moral strategy. A brief summary of that famed lecture is given herewith:

"With grace of God, I have been blessed with this great fortune to have a divine view (*darshan*) of all of you. This period of one-and-a-half months is full of many diverse experiences. Some of them give one great joy while some are painful. Obstacles come up on the path of renaissance of Bharatiyataa, and that too from our own people. But, against whom should we show our anger? People who desire to destroy this national life force may express anger any number of times, but one who has envisioned this grand national personality, he cannot be angry."

"A gentleman had told me many years back, 'If you wish to work, then collect money because every work requires three Ms, that is, Man, Money, Munition.' I had replied, 'There is no place for munition in Sangh's spiritual and cultural work. If somebody thinks it is necessary, then he is bereft of intelligence. Now, what is left are man and money. Of these, we have paid attention to the first one, because money is a lifeless entity. If there is man, money will follow him on its own."

"A human being does not mean a two-legged animal who is only worried about his selfish ends and pleasures. He is but a living image of Lord Shiva who represents the spiritual power of the Supreme Being and one who has achieved the high ideal of envisioning Brahma in this material world. Only when there are such people, will work be accomplished."

"Understanding this foundation for national work, Rashtriya Swayamsevak Sangh is working towards building national spirit and national character in crores of brethren of Bharat. The meaning of 'national character' is that I should carry this emotion in my consciousness that I will not let prestige of Bharat be lowered even at the cost of my life. There is no place in it for party politics. Party is not bigger than the nation. There is no place for an individual's honour or ego because the individual is only a small organ of the nation. There is place only for one humble emotion – that I shall serve the nation."

"The programme today is also a result of both love and opposition of the society. Opponents have also served our cause. By expressing their criticism, they have given an opportunity to our swayamsevaks to ponder over them. By opposing us, they have not let people forget the Sangh. Therefore, they deserve our thanks."

"What words should I use to express my gratitude to our various supporters spread in different corners of the country for empathising with us? When they saw the calamity striking the Sangh and saw that there was nobody else to build the national character, nobody to awaken the soul of Bharat, they came forward to help in the Sangh work. It is with their help, love and efforts that a situation has arisen today when the Sangh is ready to serve the nation again from purely the cultural viewpoint. Their obligation is not on the Sangh but on the entire Bharatvarsh. They have saved the sinking ship of this nation."

"We shall move ahead in this job of human-building and move ahead towards progress of Bharatvarsh, looking at various problems from cultural perspectives in accordance with their wishes and feelings, and build a well-organised power-house for the nation. My request to other people is that, please take a purely nationalist viewpoint and convert your love into an action-oriented form."[21]

22nd August was a day meant for Sangh workers. Revered Sarsanghchaalak was to conduct meetings with them for the whole day. Workers from Delhi to Srinagar were present to take part in this meeting. After introductions, general enquiries and presentation of reports, Guruji stood in front of the mike to provide his guidance. The speech here was totally different from his public speech of the previous day. Now, there sat before him highly attentive, committed, duty-bound groups of workers. He plunged directly into their hearts. Drawing out from his exemplary experiences from all over Bharat that could provide lessons to all, he said, "Discipline and faith of swayamsevaks is so outstanding and worth appreciating that in this period of one-and-a-half years there has not been any deterioration in our strength. All the instructions received from the Centre were followed properly. When they were asked to shut down Shakhas, Shakhas all over Bharat were shut down without exception. When they were asked to be active again, they commenced activities. When they were asked to begin the agitation, the agitation took place with unstoppable momentum from the Himalayas to oceans. When they were asked to stop it, it was stopped. When they were instructed to restart the work, work started all over Bharat the very next day, as if they had slept only the last night and now they are back to work after waking up from sleep. It seems that a network of bulbs has been built across Bharat that has a single button. All the bulbs lighted up upon pressing it and extinguished when it was released. During all this, there is no anger, no animosity."[22]

Giving his analysis of the real purpose behind the ban on the Sangh, he explained to the workers, "Sustained growth of Sangh work day-by-day, like the expanding phases of the Moon, its programmes involving lakhs of people, gigantic organisation of disciplined swayamsevaks, who jumped into disastrous situations to help the exploited and battered brethren of our society without any regards for our lives – all these examples had terrified petty and selfish people very much. They felt that if this positive spiritual power kept growing like this, then they may not be able to enjoy encashing their cheques of sacrifice. They were trying to find excuses to put hurdles in this pious work and they got this opportunity by grace of God, which they exploited fully."[23]

At the same time, he warned against falling into the trap of quantifying the quality of workers on the basis of the experiences gained during *satyagraha*. This incomparable organiser of people suggested, "We should look at these things with broader vision and enlightened, an open heart so that capable brothers who had worked to their full capacity, with their best qualities during times of peace but who fell behind during the agitation, should not drift away from us."[24] This *baithak* of Delhi workers was, indeed, a great learning and guiding experience. For workers, it was a well-proven guiding light. Efforts of this successful action-oriented organiser of people were focussed towards seeing that workers should not be blown away into the skies that had no base with the enthusiasm generated by the successful public meeting.

On the third day, there was a programme of senior citizens to felicitate Guruji. Around 1,500 senior brethren came together on the evening of Tuesday at the Ramlila Ground. The programme commenced on time. Guruji noticed from the programme sheet that the last part of the programme was to be recitation of *Vande Maataram*. After the initial formalities, he called the proposed singer and asked him, "Can you sing the whole song?" "Yes, I can, but I don't remember it fully," was his response. "Don't worry about it. I will write it for you." Saying so, Guruji wrote down the whole song in his beautiful handwriting and gave it to him. The programme that day ended with singing of the complete national song.[25]

Guruji went to Jaipur from Delhi. A grand felicitation programme was conducted at the huge ground next to the Statue Circle. After this, Shri Sohanlal Duggal wished to present a cheque of ₹ 5,000/- to Guruji for the organisation. Even as he tried to do this, Guruji promptly refused it and said, "Whatever small or big contribution is made for Sangh work, it is submitted in front of *bhagwa dhwaj* as *guru dakshina* (offering to Guru) on the Sangh ground. You may please do it similarly." Following the lessons he learnt from the Gita, Guruji raised the status of a generous donor to that of a spiritual donor.[26]

Guruji entered Punjab from Jaipur. He went to 17 places on a single day. Most of the people present in these programmes were displaced brethren. During the train journey, slogans of '*Guruji ki jai*' were heard as it passed through Jalalabad. When Guruji came out of the train, he saw nearly 1,000 people collected there. He alighted from the train and asked an elderly gentleman, "Why did you take pains at such an odd hour?" His answer was, "To have your *darshan*." Guruji promptly caught hold of both his hands and spoke out emotionally, "*Arrey bhai*, one can have only *darshan* of God. I too am travelling around having *darshan* of God in the form of this society." He returned to Delhi after finishing his Punjab tour and met the Prime Minister on 30th. After expressing his gratitude in this meeting, he turned east. After touring cities like Lucknow, Patna, he reached Kolkata on 7th September. There were repeat scenes of Nagpur-Pune. But, there was an incident while he was touring Uttar Pradesh that gave a hint about the possible opposition that he would face in Maharashtra. After a huge meeting in Lucknow, the touring party was moving towards Varanasi. This group had people like Atal Behari Vajpayee, Bhaurao Deoras, Barrister Narendrajeet Singh, Dr. Abaji Thatte and Anantrao Gokhale. There was a grand welcome at all the stations on the way. His train reached Gusaiganj. Respecting the sentiments of the people who had collected at the station, Guruji began speaking. Suddenly, a group of 10-15 people started throwing stones. One stone hit Guruji near his eye and blood spilled out. Guruji asked others not to react in any way. He only said, "We should make such confused Hindus our own with affection." His wound was cleaned after the train moved. He kept a wet towel on the wound to stop the flow of blood till he reached the next station. On reaching the station, he came out with the same smiling countenance at the crowd that had collected there to see him. Nobody had even a small inkling about the incident that had taken place in Gusaiganj. When the journalists at Varanasi asked him about this incident, he waved away the question with a laugh.[27]

Guruji reached Nagpur after finishing his tour of Madhya Pradesh in the third week of September and stayed there for one month. The festival of Vijayadashami fell on October 1 during this period and after that followed the queen of festival, Diwali. In this short period, he met all the family members of

Sangh workers in goodwill meetings (*sneh milan*) of Nagpur-Vidarbha *prant*. During this time, senior Sangh officials of Nagpur arranged a lecture series for five days, from 18th to 22nd October, in view of the changed scenario. All the swayamsevaks would gather at the Mohite Sangh Ground in Nagpur from 6:15 to 7:30 p.m. for this programme. The views Guruji propounded during these five days have become an unforgettable roadmap for the Sangh work for all the swayamsevaks. Taking all swayamsevaks into confidence, he began his series of lectures with these words, "There passed by an intervening period when many of us got an opportunity to take up fundamental study of various philosophies and thoughts in a carefree manner. I think they would also have pondered about the position of our work in the background of these streams of philosophies or whether with presence of these various streams of thoughts, is there a need for our work or not?"[28] He then went ahead and made a scholarly presentation of his thoughts about identity of our nation, building-up of national tradition, pious awakening, self-observation and surrender of self, eternal form of work that is absolute, i.e., independent of any situation, true work that stands the test of time, successful method of work, etc. Then, in the end, he spoke with the force of his deep reverence, "This path must lead to success. It is not at all possible that the situation outside can create any hurdle for work being carried out with high momentum this way. This sense of reverence is present deep in my soul. All of you should awaken the same reverence in your soul. This work has to succeed. It will succeed. It will become strong. This work will be hailed all over and the picture of Bharat would emerge just the way we wish to create it."[29]

Guruji's South tour began on 26th October. There was a grand programme in Vijaywada, from where he went to Madurai in Tamil Nadu. He entered Kerala from Tamil Nadu and reached Mangalore in Karnataka on 31st. From there he reached Kolhapur in Maharashtra on 4th November via Mysore, Bengaluru, Hubli and Belgaum. Local opponents of the Sangh in Kolhapur and Sangli had resolved that they would not allow the welcome of Guruji there. They collected some crowd with this objective. But, Guruji had to perform a religious ritual apart from the Sangh work in Kolhapur. When he was leaving for his South tour, his respected mother told him, "*Arrey* Madhu, I had made a vow that I would take you for *darshan* of Goddess Amba after you are released from prison. When you go there, do honour that vow." Goddess Ambabai is the presiding deity of the Golwalkar clan. With intelligent handling by Sangh officials, this job was accomplished successfully with joyful participation. Other programmes also went off successfully with some good planning by Sangh officials and the police inspite of strong opposition. But, it is true that this programme was not as grand as the ones in Pune and Mumbai. Guruji's tour across the country that began from Baitul, went on without any hurdle due to his strong willpower within, or with backing of the Supreme force. His health too remained satisfactory.

However, according to his personal secretary Dr. Abaji Thatte, he lost 5 kgs. during this period.

The main objective of this incessant travel of Sarsanghchaalak of Rashtriya Swayamsevak Sangh was, in fact, the reinstatement of Sangh's credibility. It was for re-establishment of the soul of people that had been misled by false propaganda, for rehabilitation of souls of innocent swayamsevaks who had to bear avoidable difficulties as victims of justice and washing their hearts of animosity, for rehabilitation of patient workers who had worked hard to unite the society with the required large heart and affection, for re-establishment of faith about the vibrancy and superiority of working methodology of the Sangh that had created selfless dedicated workers. All this was achieved by this roaming seer of the nation.

His exhortation in Lucknow was, "I pray to you persistently to give up any feeling of animosity that may have been built up during the period of pain and difficulties and let your soul be filled with pure love. It does not reflect well on us to carry petty sentiments in our souls and store hatred in our mind for people, as is said, *shwaanvat gurgurayate* (grow like a dog). Dignity of heart is true humanity. We should cleanse our souls of all such incidents that generate anger in us and inflict pain, so that our heart overflows with pious feelings. Our soul should have love, goodwill and spirit of co-operation for all. This spirit is the only answer to all our questions. This is a marvelous medicine like penicillin."[30]

His guidance in Patna was, "There was violence in the last one-and-a-half years. Misleading propaganda was carried out against the Sangh. False news were printed in newspapers. Books with baseless allegations were also published. Violent acts were perpetrated in the name of the high priest of non-violence. Still, we should forget their wicked deeds with an understanding that they all are ours. Let us pray to God, 'O God, please forgive them, they are ignorant.' Sangh swayamsevaks have the good fortune of expressing themselves like this."[31]

Welcome to Guruji from the Himalayas to the oceans was grand everywhere. This created an impact in both the favourable and unfavourable camps. Nobody could ignore it. A reporter quoted what had been said by a British historian about Julius Ceaser, "Golwalkar came, he saw and he conquered." Unknowingly, perhaps, Guruji was measured on the scales of a political leader. But, what was the innermost feeling of this dedicated swayamsevak? We get an inkling of his feelings in his Madurai speech. Like an uninvolved seeker, he said, "It crossed my mind, why should I take it personally? I should work like a letter-box. Letters are dropped in it. Some of them are very important too. But, what has it got to do with the letter-box? It is just a medium, through which a letter reaches its desired destination. In the same way, the respect I have received, I dedicate to that work which I represent and have been fortunate to perform."[32]

He did not stop here. Indicating the fatal effect of praise, that sage with steady intellect said, "Lord Shiva drank fatal poison to save this world. He digested it. It did not affect him at all. Nature was saved, but that same Lord could not digest his praise. Listening to Bhasmaasur's praise, he was so happy that he gifted him a boon. If God is affected this way, what can one say of a normal human being? It means that showering of praise is a very serious hurdle in a human being's progress on the path of evolution. It is my prayer to God that he may please save me from these songs of praise."[33]

While touring all over the country, Guruji asked workers with lot of persistence not to evaluate their colleagues with any prejudice. The yardstick should not be whether one was a *satyagrahi* or not. Guruji had to practise this advice on himself too. He had personal relations with all the Sanghchaalaks across Bharat. Many of the Sanghchaalaks had not taken part in the *satyagraha*. Therefore, many of them, out of self-embarrassment, had written to him requesting him to relieve them of their responsibilities. Guruji sent handwritten letters to all of them or talked to them personally. For example, he writes to Sanghchaalak of Mangalore district in Karnataka state, Karkala Sadashivrao, "While talking to swayamsevak brothers, I have tried to tell them that we are going to present a new, right example that will illustrate that it is not necessary that only a person who has gone to jail will be the recipient of a post or honour."

"Those who had to suffer during the agitation fulfilled their duties in a specific situation. It is not necessary for such people to swell with pride nor is it necessary to show those workers in poor light who did not participate in it."

"After all, people face specific situations according to their qualities and capabilities at that time. Therefore, I have requested our earlier respected Sanghchaalaks that they should let go of this feeling of failure and, keeping in mind the demands of the current situation, they should put in their efforts to enhance the strength of the organisation again."

"I am writing this to you because being highly sensitive, you might think that since you have not taken part in the agitation, you have no right to be in this post. Please do not let such a feeling enter your heart."[34] Guruji wrote a similar letter to V. Rajagopalachari of Chennai too. It is needless to say that both these gentlemen remained Sanghchaalaks till the end of their lives. Same would have been the experience elsewhere too.

In short, after resolving this debilitating phase, Guruji brought the Sangh back to a normal situation after eight months. It was not in his nature to attend big festivals with garlands hanging around his neck, nor was this the way of Sangh founder, Dr. Hedgewar. In that period, the following lines of the Sangh song echoed in the heart of each swayamsevak, "Give up this petty thought, O' saviour of Hindu nation, that my name will appear in newspapers, that I will wear garlands. We have to fill up the foundation of this nation by being stones and gravels; we have to become immortal worshippers of an effulgent brave spirit."

But, to improve health one has to take a bitter medicine after recovering from severe sickness. The Sangh faced a similar situation, when opposing forces hatched a conspiracy to somehow uproot the Sangh with means, fair or foul, it was duty of the Sangh to come out of this successfully. It became necessary in that environment to present the Sangh in a courageous manner in front of the common man. It seemed a necessity to arouse the brave nature of swayamsevaks again. Efforts had to be put in to make the wilted support base of the Sangh to bloom again. Thinking over it, the Sangh leadership had to take up demonstrative programmes after lifting of the ban as an action taken in an exceptional situation. There was a clear understanding about taking this medicine and its temporary nature. As a result, the meaning of the telegram 'All is well that ends well' that Bhaiyyaji Dani had handed over to Guruji at the Nagpur railway platform on July 13 was given an extended meaning. Standing in front of the refurbished memorial of Dr. Hedgewar in full Sangh uniform, Sarsanghchaalak Guruji clarified, "This work is not that of a party or an organisation. This work is, in fact, about bringing together all the Bharatiyas bereft of any competitive spirit and working with coordinated efforts. So well should this work develop and grow that the Sangh and society should become one and there would be no need to work in different names. If we receive co-operation from all in this work, then the moment of all-round growth and revolution is not far off."[35]

□

Endnotes

1. *Madhyabharat ki Sangh Gatha*, pp. 281
2. *Chitraanjali,* photo 17
3. *Maa. Sa. Golwalkar*, pp. 162
4. *Shri Guruji Samagra*, Vol. 10, pp. 89-90
5. Ibid, pp. 75-76
6. *Pehli Agniparikshaa*, pp. 250
7. *Shri Guruji Samagra*, Vol. 10, pp. 78
8. Ibid, pp. 79
9. Ibid, pp. 80
10. Ibid, pp. 81
11. *Shri Guruji Samagra*, Vol. 8, pp. 78
12. *Maa. Sa. Golwalkar*, pp. 164
13. *Shri Guruji Samagra*, Vol. 10, pp. 91-93
14. Ibid, pp. 94
15. *Maa. Sa. Golwalkar*, pp. 166
16. *Shri Guruji Samagra*, Vol. 10, pp. 96-97
17. Ibid, pp. 104
18. Ibid, pp. 86
19. *Pehli Agniparikshaa,* pp. 242-243
20. Ibid, pp. 242
21. *Shri Guruji Samagra*, Vol. 10, pp. 105-108
22. Ibid, pp. 113

23. Ibid, pp. 112
24. Ibid, pp. 111
25. *Maa. Sa. Golwalkar*, pp. 170
26. *Shri Guruji Rajasthan Mein*, pp. 17
27. *Jeevan Prasang*, Vol. 2, pp. 300-301
28. *Shri Guruji Samagra*, Vol. 2, pp. 3
29. Ibid, pp. 49
30. *Shri Guruji Samagra*, Vol. 10, pp. 122-123
31. Ibid, pp. 125-126
32. Ibid, pp. 143
33. Ibid, pp. 143-144
34. *Shri Guruji Samagra*, Vol. 8, pp. 45
35. *Shri Guruji Samagra*, Vol. 5, pp. 177

26

Back to Sangh Grounds

It is true that Guruji returned to the Sangh headquarters after rehabilitating Sangh work, but wartime obligations (*yuddha shisht*) were carried out as an immediate plan of action. What is a wartime obligation? War ends with victory for one side and defeat of the other. But, it does not mean end of the questions arising out of it. Some of these questions are such that one has to come up with immediate answers, while there are some questions that need solutions over a longer period of time. Let us look at the Mahabharata war as an example. The 18-day war ended with the killing of Duryodhan, but who would perform the last rites of soldiers from 18 *aukshouhini* (an ancient nomenclature of military unit, like a regiment) who had died in the war? Would bodies of killed horses be left rotting in the fields? Thousands of injured soldiers like Bhishma Pitamah would also be thirsting for water. Which Gandeev carrying archer like Arjun would offer them water? There is also the question of nursing others who were left behind. Such are the countless questions left behind in the battle-ground. Long term questions left behind by this war would be: responsibility of pregnant Uttaraa and the large number of such 'Uttaraas'. Who would protect their wombs? Question of taking care of innocent children of young fighters who died on the battle field. Such are the questions that raise their heads beyond the battle ground. All these fall under this wartime obligation. Everybody has to suffer equally at its hands. Victor and the vanquished are on the same ground here. If the problem of wartime obligation is not faced as a challenge, nature would come back with a vengeance like a famished ogre and create havoc.

Something similar to this wartime obligation confronted the Sangh. The condition of the Sangh after an eight-month-long ban, the *satyagraha* conducted during this time, more than 77,000 swayamsevaks who suffered imprisonment for five to six months, the silent sufferings of their family members, poisonous environment created by Sangh opponents – these were the wartime obligations that confronted the Sangh even after being triumphant in the battle for justice. Immediate and long-term solutions were expected and were unavoidable.

Guruji's tours after the felicitation programmes were focused on this issue.

All the travels during this period were aimed at organisation building. There were three-day camps of active swayamsevaks from 23rd December to 3rd January, 1949 in east, central and west Uttar Pradesh. The spring camp of Delhi state was from 3rd to 6th March. From state-to-state, there were either state-level or division-level camps. There was no public programme. There were no showers of flowers, sloganeering, street decorations, handing over of pious memorabilia, press conferences, interviews, photo sessions, etc. and specific instructions were given to this effect. Regular Sangh style of working and old customs were followed and efforts were made to resolve the war obligations.

Camps had sessions for Guruji's intellectual discourses and meetings. The theme at all these places was generally that of the October lecture series held in Nagpur. There were some minor changes based on regional variations. In workers' meetings, he drew their attention to the necessity of removing weaknesses in the organisation's structure. If the subject of ban and *satyagraha* came up, it was only to remind people of the excellent working methodology of the Sangh. His stress was on this subject. Guruji got maximum time to interact formally and informally with the workers in Uttar Pradesh. Therefore, his presentation there was more analytical and educative. The way of thinking and doubts of the people who had been inactive behind prison walls due to *satyagraha* were of a particular nature. Naturally, their views were different from people who had struggled outside against the venomous environment created by opponents. Guruji satisfied both with his piercing, farsighted vision.

Immediately after lifting of ban, Guruji had written to Purushottamdas Tandon, "Presently, I am busy getting our work back in order." Underlining the same thought, he spoke right in the beginning of the lecture, "At that time, structure of programmes was like public programmes. The enthusiasm of all the swayamsevaks was like any other mass organisation. Therefore, it was but natural that our programmes, being for everybody, ended up being nobody's programme. I cannot say how much happiness and enthusiasm you may have received from those programmes. I did not get any (happiness or enthusiasm) because our working methodology is such that these so-called felicitations, etc. are unknown to us in our lives."[1]

Stressing the natural forte of the working methodology of the Sangh, he said in simple words, "There are only two secrets of our work: first is that there is no secret, and second is *kabaddi.* This programme, even today, has the same character. Our motherland below, God created skies above, and Hindu society all around us – based on these elements, *kabaddi* has been successful. So much power was generated by this *kabaddi* – power that saved lives, honour and wealth of lakhs of people during Partition of Punjab."[2] "From where did this power come? Did we have manifestos at that time? Did we have rosy pictures of the future? Or did we organise conference or publicised our views? We only played *kabaddi*. This is absolutely true. The foundation of our unified soul in *kabaddi* came to signify 'organisation'. We need to understand this well."[3]

Finally, invoking a positive emotion in workers, inspired by a fierce sense of dedication to the mission sans animosity, sans feeling of revenge, he said, "We must exert ourselves to make this nation eternal and build up a very strong power for this. This whole nation, from the Himalayas to the ocean, should stand up and be able to look at the entire world with pride. With this vision, we should think of spending our action-oriented lives without being distracted in any way. This is the only job, this is the path to get liberated from every type of problems; there is no other path."[4]

Just as the alert, dedicated swayamsevaks were deeply engrossed in the Sangh work, Bengal saw a repetition of Punjab. A heavy flow of persecuted and oppressed refugees began pouring in from Pakistani Bengal to Bharatiya Bengal. Hindu organisations, like Shri Ramakrishna Ashram, Pranavananda Ashram, and others also fell prey to such Islamic attacks. Guruji rushed there as soon as he got the news and met Hindu leaders personally. The Sangh work here was not as strong as it was in Punjab. In comparison, the number of Shakhas was also low. Still, Vastuhara Sahaayata Samiti (Displaced People's Relief Committee) was constituted under the chairmanship of Barrister Ranadev Chaudhary on 8th February, 1950. Additional Prachaaraks were deputed from the nearby states to help it out. Responsibility of the whole exercise was put on the able and strong shoulders of Eknath Ranade. After reaching Delhi from Kolkata, Guruji appealed to the people to send relief material to Bengal. He gave a detailed statement informing people of the tragic situation in Bengal. He stated, "I have recently come back from Bengal and after getting information from various sources about the conditions in East Bengal, I believe it is of utmost importance to help Hindus there. It is not possible to describe the horrible condition of the people there. Piercing the steel wall put over East Bengal, we are getting news regularly about inhuman killings, robbery, arson, rapes and religious conversions."

"It would not serve any purpose if we forget that the atrocious condition of these people is a result of our leaders' acceptance of religion based division of our country. It is paramount that our leaders should free themselves and the people of this delusion that Partition is not based on religion but on geography. The reality is clear and we should face it. It will not do any good if people who control the reins of power do not accept this truth."

"This confused thinking about Partition along with distorted ideas about secular (*vidharmee*) state being presented before the nation on and off are proving to be a major hurdle in resolving the problems faced by the nation. What will you call these one-and-a-half crore unfortunate brethren – foreigners or locals? The rehabilitation Minister has concluded that they are foreigners and they have become an unnecessary burden on us. But, is this view right? Using the softest possible words, one can only say that this view is absolutely inhuman. Not only is this view condemnable, but also an insult because of which they are being deprived of their right of Bharatiya nationality and being sacrificed at the altar of Pakistani cruelty."

Appealing to the rulers in his statement, he said, "It is my request to the government and especially to the Prime Minister that he should find a solution to stop these bestial atrocities of Pakistan and rescue our brothers and sisters on the other side of the border. If our policy is going to be vague, confused and weak, then the government will be accused of sin of complete devastation of one-and-a-half crore innocent Bharatiyas and its esteem will be reduced to dust. This may take police action or mean sending Muslims to Pakistan and getting Hindus back to Bharat in exchange. Any stern action must be initiated immediately, so that our one-and-a-half crore brethren of our own flesh and blood should be able to lead a secure life."

While he reminded the government of its duty, Shri Guruji appealed to the people, "They should not exhibit their anger in a way that would create hurdles in the government's working. Everyone should come forward to serve with body, soul and funds and open their hearts to give place to their miserable brothers and sisters."[5]

All the newspapers published this humanitarian statement. The other reason for this was that Guruji's prestige had risen high in the in the aftermath of the Sangh ban. Response to the statement was very good. More than 5,000 swayamsevaks joined the relief work. Guruji wrote a letter that was like a report on the current scenario and the state of relief work to Sardar Patel on 5th April. He also met him on 12th April and informed him about his efforts. Patel expressed the hope that the Sangh work would also expand in the north-east region of Bharat.

When the capital city had given a grand welcome to Guruji last August, Bharat had not been declared a Republic yet. Babu Rajendra Prasad was also not the President of Bharat yet. Both these events took place on 26th January, 1950. Guruji sent Sangh's congratulations and wishes to His Excellency, Rajendra Babu at an opportune time. On 25th January, he wrote to him, "I greet you with great pleasure on the occasion of your election as the President of the republic of independent Bharat... May the merciful God bestow you with strong health and long life to help you succeed in this immense job."[6]

The environment in socio-political circles in Delhi was clear with no visible dark clouds. Elite citizens of Delhi organised a felicitation programme in honour of Shri Guruji in this background. A massive well-wishers' convention was held on 30th April in Anand Park. Thirty thousand people were present in this programme. A goodwill amount of ₹ 1,01,101 was presented to him in his honour. Accepting this honour, Guruji requested, "This respect should not be restricted to contribution in terms of money, but all the brothers should also get involved in the Sangh work."

Sangh Shiksha Vargas, which had been stopped since last two years, were also restarted in the months of May-June. As a rule, Guruji went to all the camps. The same old tradition was followed again – detailed introduction of the participants, guidance about Sangh work during *baithaks* or meetings, directions about Sangh's mission during intellectual discourses. The majority of discourses were on three words of the Sangh, viz., *Rashtriya* (national), *swayamsevak* (volunteer), *Sangh* (corps or organisation). As an exception, Sangh prayer was also the subject in such discourses in two or three states. He did not mention, the 'ban' in any of these camps.

There is another interesting piece of information that can be shared here. These camps were the first ones in free Bharat. The last camps were held in May-June 1947, prior to Independence. Swayamsevaks used to say in their pledge at that time, "To gain independence for Hindu nation." There was a change of time now. These words were out of context in the changed scenario. 'New songs for the new age' was the Sangh song's opening lines echoing in the air. The pledge was also modified with the same spirit. The modified words were, "For all-round growth of Hindu nation."

Republic of Bharat was getting ready to celebrate its first Independence Day in August 1950. Unfortunately, there was a disastrous earthquake in Assam the same day, resulting in immeasurable losses. Waters of Brahmaputra changed course and began flowing unabated. The Sangh swayamsevaks rushed to help the affected people. Sarsanghchaalak Guruji also reached there. A Relief Committee with its centre at Dibrugarh was set up under the chairmanship of retired Justice Kamakhya Ram Baruah. Guruji had alighted at the airport in Kumbeer village to go to Dibrugarh. People lined up on both sides of the road from there to the city to have his divine view. He was so disturbed when he saw the pall of gloomy pain over their faces that he stopped on way at one village. He came closer to those desolate brethren and said, "This disaster has struck due to Nature's fury. There is no way but to face it. For this we require discipline and organisation. With these two, one can overcome any disaster, howsoever severe it may be. It would not be proper to put blame on anybody." One can clearly see the difference between a social worker and a political leader with this incident. Roads were not suitable for transportation. He saw the cruel play of fate in this massive destruction with his own eyes. He could not utter a word there. After reaching Kolkata, he sent out an appeal to all the countrymen to help the unfortunate victims of the earthquake. Response to this appeal was also good.

Guruji had begun his organisation-related tour to strengthen the Sangh work. However, it was disturbed in between with the man-made disaster in Bengal and nature-made disaster of Assam. As Guruji had reminded, one needed organisation and discipline to overcome such disasters. The Sangh could face these challenges because it had both and could succeed as a non-government organisation. One saw the conception of a new dimension. A sage has said that every bend in the branch of a tree signifies an earlier challenge and the way it was faced. Something similar happened in the case of the Sangh. Multi-faceted experiences of Punjab, Bengal, Assam gained in the relief services done by the Sangh opened a new path, a new direction for it that resulted in the creation of a '*Seva Vibhag* (Section for Social Services). Here the people who showed Guruji this path were Dr. Hedgewar, who had served people during the floods in Damodar river and Swami Akhandananda who had tried to bring relief to the sufferers of draught in Sargachhi.

Sardar Patel left this world on 15th December in Mumbai. Guruji was in Nagpur that day. Relations between the two had improved and warmed up during the last two years. Therefore, it was natural to have a strong urge to go for the last rites of his senior friend. It was impossible to reach in time by train. He immediately called his friend, Chief Minister Ravi Shankar, "Is anybody from your group going to Mumbai? If you are, will you have a free seat in the air-plane?" Shukla ji gave his assent to the idea and went with his father's friend to Mumbai and took part in the funeral procession. Saddened at the passing away of the great son of Bharat, Guruji said, "News of passing away of Sardar Vallabh bhai Patel has torn asunder my heart. His death is an enormous blow to the nation. It our duty, for whom Sardar Patel lived and for whom he had abiding love, to save the nation from internal conflicts and external aggressions by making it powerful, and, thus, complete his job. It will be the best last respects that we can pay to this great son of Bharatmata."[7]

Thus, the rise of the republic of Bharat in that year saw the departure of the great organiser, who had imparted great administrative strength to the political state of Bharat with merger of more than 500 princely states.

It was 5th January and dawn of the year 1951. That day was the day of coming together of the Golwalkar kin in Pune. Bhauji Golwalkar had reached Pune with his spouse to take part in the marriage ceremony of the only son of his brother Ramchandra Golwalkar. Celibate (*brahmachari*) Golwalkar had also come to be a witness to the marriage of his paternal cousin. Golwalkar couple had to complete one of the important family rites. Golwalkars had to hand over the ancestral idol of their presiding deity to the newly married couple, who had taken up familial responsibilities. Characteristically, they undertook this task in the presence of their celibate younger member of the family.[8]

Nine days after this event was the festival of Makar Sankranti on 14th January, a Sunday. Guruji was present in Pune for the festival according to his preplanned programme and celebrations were in the form of a state-level convention. Like Delhi brethren, Pune people had decided to present Guruji some funds as a mark of respect to him. But, they did not forget to give as much importance to collecting people as given to collection of funds. Guruji put a condition for the workers as he set a target for the collection. Target was one lakh and condition was that they would accept only one rupee from each donor. This met three objectives of getting people together, invoking faith and strengthening the Sangh work. Huge convention for Makar Sankranti took place in the Deccan Gymkhana ground. Celebrations began with a grand salute to Guruji as the Sarsanghchaalakin the presence of state Sanghchaalak Kashinath Pant Limaye as the chairman of that function. After performance of a solo the song, '*madhupark amchaa sweekaaraa*' (please accept a drop of sweetness from us), a purse of one lakh one rupee was dedicated to Guruji as a mark of respect to him. The speech that day began with a simile. The sentence was, "I do not long for this goal, I long for our collective goal. Creating enmity between people on the basis of language and extending this logic and creating linguistic states is fatal for national unity. There is no problem in accepting that language is an important part of administrative facilities." This was the opinion expressed by him on the problems of that time. The impact of this programme was felt all over the state. This programme proved to be a great help in correcting the weaknesses resulting from wartime compulsions.

Now, attention of this organiser of people was drawn towards the region of Hyderabad that had been liberated with the help of police action. The Sangh was not allowed to carry out its activities during the rule of Nizam in his state. Therefore, its supporters used to work in the form of Bhajan *mandlis* (hymn-singing groups), *seva samitis* (social service committees), *vyayamshalas* (gymkhanas), etc. After liberation of the state, an atmosphere was created to work openly, but by that time the Sangh work was stuck by the eclipse of ban. Now, the atmosphere was favourable for it to be set free from this situation. The first thing that Guruji did was to divide the state from organisational point of view. For the purpose of easy operations, he divided the region into three parts and merged it into Maharashtra, Andhra and Karnataka states, respectively. The centre of the state was shifted from Vijayawada to Hyderabad without delay. As a result, the Sangh work began growing there and tours and guidance of Sangh leaders increased accordingly.

According to the new Constitution of independent Bharat, 1952 saw the advent of the first elections in the country. Political circles had started preparing for it right from 1951. Congress party had fallen completely under the grip of Jawaharlal Nehru after the demise of Sardar Patel. In this situation, nationalists started forming their new political parties in their areas of influence. A large group of youth influenced by the Sangh began thinking about utilising the right to vote given by the Constitution. During those days, there were three principal claimants of people's favours in this political *swayamvar* – the Congress, Socialists and Communists. None of these three were acceptable to the Sangh. In the eyes of swayamsevaks, these three were killers of the undivided motherland, crab-like querulous day-dreaming critics of our culture and traitors of the nation, fifth columnist lapdogs of Russians, respectively. They were in a state of moral dilemma in deciding whom to vote for. Shyama Prasad Mookerjee was also in a similar dilemma. He had resigned from Pandit Nehru's cabinet in protest against his impractical policy that was against our own people but favourable to outsiders. He was thinking about forming a new political party. He met Guruji, Balasaheb Deoras and Bhaurao Deoras in early 1951 at the home of Nagpur Sanghchaalak Babasaheb Ghatate. It was decided to launch Bharatiya Jansangh after the discussions. Guruji expressed his views in very strong terms about the non-political background of the Sangh work during these discussions. He had, thus, destroyed the seed of any possible confusion there itself. However, as a sign of his acceptance of this idea of a new political party, he deputed highly experienced Prachaaraks such as Deendayal Upadhyay, Atal Behari Vajpayee, Nanaji Deshmukh to work for this important national cause.

Election fever touched new highs in the latter part of the year. In keeping with his nature, he walked out of the political stage of electoral drama with his colleagues like Bhaiyyaji Dani, Balasaheb Deoras, with the words, '*yathechhasi tathaa kuru*'. They went to the famed Simhagarh Fort famous for its history of self-learning and introspection. He stayed there from 25th December, 1951 to 18th January, 1952 in Lokmanya Tilak's bungalow. It was the winter seaon and the hills were very cold. He may probably have experienced and enjoyed the cool peace of the high altitudes coming from the hot, stifling atmosphere of worldly affairs at ground level. According to his personal assistant, Dr. Abaji Thatte, his daily routine after morning ablutions used to be *Yogasana*, *Surya Namaskar*, taking long walks around the hilly slopes after sunrise, meditation after a bath, studying scriptures, meeting and chatting with residents of the Fort after post-lunch rest, Sangh prayer, reading and discussions. His food intake comprised of two cups of tea before afternoon, lunch in the afternoon and two cups of tea in the evening. He celebrated Makar Sankranti in the Simhagarh Fort that year. Descendants of Shivaji's famous soldiers, the Mavlas, took part in this festival. Guruji fed them *tilgul* sweets personally. If Guruji's last Makar Sankranti celebration was in the capital of Shivaji's empire, then this year it was amongst descendants of the brave soldiers responsible for establishment of that empire. He had stayed for four days with them. He came down from the Fort on 18th January and went back to the people who were excited about the change-over experience of democracy.

□

Endnotes

1. *Shri Guruji Samagra*, Vol. 2, pp. 48
2. Ibid, pp. 105
3. Ibid, pp. 108
4. Ibid, pp. 110
5. *Maa. Sa. Golwalkar*, pp. 182-183
6. *Shri Guruji Samagra*, Vol. 7, pp. 94
7. *Maa. Sa. Golwalkar*, pp. 187
8. *Vivekananda Patrika*, pp. 99, 2006-2007, Vol. 2

27

Reaching Out to the Masses

Many respected Sanghchaalaks had entered the electoral arena either on Bharatiya Jansangh ticket or independently, with energy and a new optimism at the right to vote offered by the first General Election in the free republic of Bharat. As per the Sangh Constitution, they were free to do so. It is possible that lack of enough experience and understanding of politics had raised their expectations very high. Their optimism may have been fueled by the way they had served the displaced people of Punjab and Sindh, or the Sarsanghchaalak's nationwide tour that seemed something like a victory march or the comments by news media like B.B.C., etc. But, Guruji, himself, was not at all moved by such expectations. He had clearly told the people who met him that such expectations would prove to be a mirage and it would only result in disenchantment. There were those overenthusiastic people who believed they were good at crystal gazing and had taunted Guruji about his non-political wisdom or lack of it. Guruji's analysis turned out to be closer to the truth. All the candidates lost the elections, many of them losing their deposits. A sense of despondency prevailed all over. Despondency reached the depths in the same way as the expectations had touched the skies.

It was in Guruji's nature to rush where there was pain, grief or inequity. The same scenario got repeated this time too. He reached out to frustrated swayamsevaks and stayed with them. He held get-togethers, intellectual discourses, discussions, question-answer sessions and dialogues with people in many places. He was able to revitalise the hearts of many with these moves. Here is an example. A famous lawyer of Punjab, who had lost his deposit, spoke out with an aggrieved heart, "These people are ungrateful." Guruji showed his angry disapproval of such a thought. Looking directly at him, he asked, "Dear friend, do you consider your insistence on the fruits of your services, and its failure to the ungratefulness of others? Is this what, Sangh has taught you?" There was total silence and the atmosphere turned serious. Guruji added, "It is unjustified to blame your countrymen if your expectations are wrecked; it is wrong."[1]

During this period, there was a get-together and the subject of his speech was 'National Construction Versus Political Animosity'. Stating his views, Guruji said, "As long as the germs of national disintegration that nibble away at our national strength are present, it is a misplaced thought that copying the political and other institutions of other countries will solve our problems and we shall see a complete transformation of our nation. Our disease has much deeper roots and it is necessary to treat it from the roots. To uproot this fundamental disease, the Sangh has developed the system of daily training, instilling qualities of sacrifice, discipline and patriotism in a sustained way every day so that it leads to creation of an organised, unified and progressive nation."[2] In fact, in that post-election period, Guruji took care that politics would not encroach upon Rashtriya Swayamsevak Sangh. Common swayamsevaks and workers received his guidance accordingly.

The annual training camps of the Sangh in southern states began in May 1952. Guruji's tours commenced in line with these programmes. He arrived in National College in Tiruchirappalli in the first week of May for a training camp. From there, he went to the Pune camp. Another excellent historic programme awaited him in Pune during the same period. Preparations were afoot for official dissolution of Abhinav Bharat, the organisation that was set up by the great revolutionary, Vinayak Savarkar to fight for freedom of the country. It was a clear opinion of the founder of this organisation that it was ideal to dissolve an organisation whose goal had been achieved by whatever means. It would be proper to recall here that Mahatma Gandhi's views about Congress were also the same but were not accepted by his followers. As the heir of national seer Dr. Hedgewar, Guruji received a special invitation for this massive conference that had excited the whole of Maharashtra. Large masses of people had gathered on 9th May, Friday, on the large ground near Parvati Pond on Tilak Road. Hearts of young and old alike were lit up with thrilling memories of the long-drawn war for freedom. Veer Savarkar, Senapati Bapat, G.S. Karandikar and many other revolutionaries were present on the well-decorated dais. A little before the programme, the master of ceremonies declared, "Golwalkar Guruji has arrived." The atmosphere was filled with cheers all around. The master of ceremonies seated Guruji next to Savarkar ji. Speeches of great worthies followed one after another. The master of ceremonies kept pleading with them with humility to follow the limitations of time. It was a task like forcing a bitter medicine down the throat of a person. Guruji's turn came too. Bapat ji gestured to Guruji silently, signaling 'only ten minutes'. Guruji removed his wrist-watch and handed it over to Bapat with a smile. Coming on the mike, he began in a balanced tone, "People give proof of their wisdom by calling revolutionaries either lunatics or hotheaded. But, the truth is that such people cannot stand the brilliant heat of patriotism of revolutionaries. But, because I have been fortunate to follow in the footsteps of Dr. Hedgewar, who sacrificed his life to light up the young hearts with fire of revolution, I greet the revolutionaries with respect and consider it my duty to pay my respects to them. It is necessary to take pains each day of our lives and keep trying for an everlasting revolution through the peaceful path. It is also important that we keep this flame of revolution alight in our hearts. To attack anti-national thoughts and create a happy and prosperous nation in the real sense by putting an end to the pain of miserable lives of poor people, that is to make the life of Hindu *rashtra* truly fulfilling, we shall have to resolve in our hearts on the occasion of these celebrations that the saffron flag of this nation shall keep fluttering eternally with the emerging of Sun to setting of the Moon."[3] As soon as he finished his speech, Bapat came on the mike and said, "Special thanks to Golwalkar Guruji for finishing his speech within the given time limit." He returned the watch with a smile. Guruji touched Savarkar ji's feet after four to five minutes and sought leave from him to return to the camp.

Generally, the Sangh's working year and schools' academic years coincide. Every state prepared its annual plan in June-July of 1952. Uttar Pradesh decided to step into another field of activity. The Sangh work in the form of Shakhas had grown very well. Most of the senior workers were highly educated, but, their state was quite backward in education. This fact disturbed them. Talk of *swadeshi* education, prevalent at that time, caught their attention. They also recalled the series of *swadeshi* schools that existed during the young years of Dr. Hedgewar's life. After all, Doctorji was a product of two such schools in Yavatmal and Kolkata. They also decided to experiment in this direction. Prachaaraks who had retired from their regular Sangh work and had returned to normal family lives were to be the torch-bearers of this new exercise. When leading lights like Professor Rajendra Singh, Nanaji Deshmukh, Pandit Deendayal Upadhyay, Bhaurao Deoras discussed this project with Guruji, he gave his go ahead very happily. As a result, the first Saraswati Shishu Mandir came into existence under the leadership of Nanaji Deshmukh at Gorakhpur. All its teachers were graduates, who had retired from their Prachaarak life. Guruji laid the foundation stone of the building. Our experience over years tells us that this beginning proved to be the sowing of seeds of the movement for *swadeshi* culturebased education. This movement has struck deep roots and is blossoming well in a sustained manner in Bharat.

Immediately, following the sacred work of serving Goddess Saraswati, Guruji had the good fortune of attending a convention of *sadhus*. Bharat Sadhu Samaj had organised a '*Saarvabhoum Sadhu Sammelan*' (Autonomous Saints' Convention) on 12th-13th October in Kanpur. Its objective was to prepare *sadhus* to develop a high character, the spirit of service, morality, humanity, etc. in people. Swami Naradanand was the president of this convention and His Excellency, President Babu Rajendra Prasad inaugurated the convention. The final call during the closing session was to be made by Guruji. Essentially, Guruji's speech did not limit itself to the subject of reformation of society.

He laid stress on the ultimate goal of our highly sacred Sanaatan Dharma, that is, welfare of the world. He requested everybody to take responsibility of accomplishing this divine task. In effect, he reawakened the spirit and ultimate objective of *'krinvanto vishwam aaryam'* (civilising the whole world) in the religious masters there. Summary of his lecture is given below:

"Today, there are two ideologies in the world apart from Bharatiya philosophy. One is the democratic system of the West, represented by America and West European nations; second group has countries like Russia, Eastern Europe and Pacific Ocean countries who call themselves 'Communists'. Both the groups organise 'peace conferences' and proclaim 'universal brotherhood', but, behind these pronouncements one can see their ambition of establishing their hegemony. Both are out to destroy humanity with atomic power.

"It is the need of the hour to understand the philosophy that can establish true brotherhood between human beings. Only those people who have had the realisation that 'the whole world is my home' can establish peace in this world. This truth has been proven by practice and experience, and it can be established even now. Defending the pride and structure of the society, liberating it and taking it to heights of excellence – this is our job.

"When the British conspired to enslave Bharat intellectually, a tradition of *sadhus* was also born at that time to spread the flame of brilliance. Swami Vivekananda, Swami Ramteerth, Maharshi Raman and Maharshi Aurobindo awakened the nation. Vivekananda went overseas and astonished people by telling them about Bharatiya philosophy. They honoured him and this resulted in generation of self-confidence in the common people. Bharat came face-to-face with its greatness that resulted in an awakening among people, making it impossible for the British to stay in Bharat for long. However, the credit for this goes to those great *sadhus* who were working selflessly, inspired only with noble thoughts of making the people's lives better.

"This saffron flag that symbolises the flame of sacrificial *yagna* of our culture is our living ideal that speaks to us. This group of *sadhus* is the one that can take its message to every home. We need to build a nature of non-accumulation, giving up what is beyond our basic needs (*aparigrah vritti*). We shall have to construct our social life with a deep sense of affection so that the weakened society of ours would again experience the pride of being supreme; a valiant society against whom no enemy would stand a chance. We expect the right guidance to our national life from our *sadhus* and saints."[4]

The assembly reverberated with the sound of '*Aum*' on completion of Guruji's speech. Guruji met many of his previous acquaintances after the adjournment of the assembly. The atmosphere was family like. He was able to accomplish another important task during these discussions. The Akhil Bharatiya Pratinidhi Sabha (National Committee of Sangh) had passed a resolution in Nagpur a month earlier in September about banning cow slaughter across

Bharat. This resolution had asked for co-operation from every one – individuals, organisations and institutions. Guruji raised this subject in his discussions. There was all-round acceptance of this idea and offer of full co-operation. Many respected dignitaries said, "Only you can give it a pan-Bharat shape."

It would be a mistake to imagine that passing of a resolution and its publication, on its own, could generate support and people would come out to implement it. For this the leaders of the organisation required to make proper plans and programmes. The Sangh went through a similar exercise regarding this resolution. First of all, it was decided to collect signatures of adult citizens of the country right from the Himalayas to the oceans. It was also decided that all swayamsevaks and well-wishers would visit people door-to-door and explain to them the importance of the subject, take their signatures without disturbing the daily Shakhas in any way. However, it was also decided that signatures were not to be collected in places like markets, offices, stations, etc. where people crowd together for their routine work. Every state decided to have pamphlets in their own languages and an illustrative sample was sent from the central office. Title of this campaign was to be printed on all the pamphlets. The period for collecting signatures was from 26th October to 22nd November. 26th October was the day of Gopashtami. A large number of booklets, handbills, a stamp of mother cow suckling her calf were printed as publicity material. Apart from this, Guruji's statement was printed, to be distributed in every home. His statement stated, "The main objective of this signature collection is to submit a gigantic request containing crores of signatures to the President. This is an act of fiery patriotism. It is my request that each citizen of this country should rise above the differences of religion, sect, caste, party, etc. and participate in this sacred work."

Guruji also wrote letters to political leaders, editors and religious heads individually. Though the subject was cow protection, the content of the letter differed, depending on whom it was addressed. He wrote to Rajarshi Tandon, "It is my desire that the activity I have initiated against slaughter of cows should not seem to be the work of a particular organisation. This is a question of the whole country and its entire populace. Therefore, my wish is that people should get credit for all this work and it should be carried out by people as their own work." The letter sent to Sadhu T.L. Vaswani noted, "I am aware that this pure spiritual thought is close to your heart. Therefore, we would receive your blessings for the success of this job. And you should educate people about it; this is my humble request." His request to the well-known, highly respected Venkataram Shastri was, "My only request to you is to get your articles on this important subject published in English and Tamil in *Hindu* and other prestigious publications."[5]

Thus, with this skilled and careful planning, the campaign was launched on the pious day of Gopashtami. Signature campaign was launched in Delhi by

Sarkaryavaah Bhaiyyaji Dani and by Guruji in Mumbai. In the largely attended public meeting organised in Shivaji Park, Guruji described the close relationship between mother cow and Mother Bharat (*Gomata* and *Bharatmata*). There was a wave of enthusiasm everywhere. Teams of swayamsevaks went house-to-house for the welfare of mother cow. They were welcomed everywhere. There was no opposition; nowhere did caste, clan, politics, wealth or poverty become a hurdle. If there was a shortcoming, it was only in the shortage of workers. Still, 54,000 workers came out in the field. Travelling by foot and by cycles, they collected signatures from 94,459 villages and towns. Complete accounts reached the Centre on 5th December. Total count of signatures was one crore seventy-nine lakh eighty-nine thousand three hundred thirty-two (1,79,89,332)! This whole collection, packed in state-wise bundles, was transported on vehicles from Narayan Sabji Mandi at 9 a.m. on 7th December, about 20 kms away to Ramlila Grounds and the caravan reached there at 12 noon. The meeting commenced at 2 p.m. Apart from Guruji, other respected gentlemen on the well-decorated stage were Dr. Shyama Prasad Mookerjee, Lala Hardev Sahayji, Moulichandra Sharma ji, Mahashay Krishna ji, Nirmalchandra Chatterjee, Sadguru Pratap Singh ji and others. Each of them gave speeches that matched the spirit of the programme. At the end, Guruji presented a complete account of the campaign. However, he did not forget to mention "The central point and foundation of our work is the daily programme of the Sangh. I cannot neglect it. I do not know the art of keeping a tree green after cutting the roots. A tree can survive only if there is root. Knowing this, we only believe in watering the roots. This is the reason why we have collected these signatures without neglecting the daily Sangh work."[6]

When this campaign was running across the country with no opposition, Pandit Nehru tried to disrupt it by calling it a 'political stunt', but, Guruji did not pay heed to it at that time. He did not wish to spoil the pious atmosphere of strong focus by getting entangled in pointless debate. But, now he accounted for this point too on the concluding evening of the campaign. His response was, "Acharya Vinoba says, '*Sarva Bhoomi Gopal Ki*' (All this land belongs to the Lord who protects cows). But, I want to ask, is this the land of *gopaalaks* (protectors of cows) or *gohatyaare* (killers of cows)? Our work is not new. Maharshi Dayanand also took it in his hands. Did he take it up as a political stunt?" He did not pause here, but went on a counter-offensive, saying, "There was a ceremony for consecration of sacred ashes of two great disciples of Lord Buddha recently. Our Prime Minister also took part in that programme with enthusiasm. But after going six miles away to Bhelsaa, he announced the continuation of cow slaughter. Pronouncement of this policy of cow slaughter was done after giving sermon about Lord Buddha's non-violence!"[7] Thus, he exposed the inconsistency in Nehru's policy.

Next day, on 8th December, Guruji met the President along with Lala Hansraj in the afternoon. He presented the signature collection to him formally. This collection of more than 1.75 crore signatures was a world record. Collecting so many signatures from such a large number of villages in such a short time was nothing less than a miracle; one that was never witnessed earlier in history. Giving his assurance, President of the largest democracy said, "I will see to it that the government looks at this memorandum sympathetically." Humming the *mantra*, '*Karmanye vadhikaraste*', Guruji returned from there.

This was the cow protection campaign of 1952. It resulted in the transformation of the Sangh internally. The despondency that gripped swayamsevaks ten months earlier due to electoral debacle was totally dispelled. The faith of swayamsevaks strengthened further with experience that even in so-called progressive age, people's reverence for the national symbols of pride is rock solid. The enthusiasm of swayamsevaks for sustained people's contact grew again inspite of four years of baseless negative propaganda against the Sangh. In short, the nationwide campaign conducted for mother cow resulted in furthering the path of progress for organisations working for the cause of Hindutva.

□

Endnotes

1. *Memoirs of Chamanlalji of Delhi*
2. *Shri Guruji Samagra*, Vol. 11, pp. 380
3. *Maa. Sa. Golwalkar*, pp. 193
4. *Shri Guruji Samagra*, Vol. 5, pp. 94-97
5. *Shri Guruji Samagra*, Vol. 7, pp. 100, 99
6. *Maa. Sa. Golwalkar*, pp. 205
7. Ibid, pp. 206

28

On the Path of All-round Growth

The compulsions of finishing the immediate job at hand led to neglect of the main work many a time. Such a situation is faced by all of us in our life. Organisations also face such situations in their lives. Rashtriya Swayamsevak Sangh too faced this scenario during the period 1947 to 1952. Declaration of 'Quit India', acceptance of Partition of Bharat by leaders of the country, massive inflow of displaced Hindus from Pakistan into Hindustan, emergency situation of relief and resettlement, the bolt of lightning in the form of declaration of ban even before one could pause for a little rest, the struggle to get the ban lifted, exhausting efforts to re-establish the atmosphere of positivity meant organising programmes with this objective. It was not possible to get away from any of these issues. As a result, the critical work of the organisation suffered.

Swayamsevaks would still discuss the problems arising from time to time. Such was the environment in the Sangh. Most of the swayamsevaks were below forty. They were young, educated and habituated to meeting every day even without an invitation. It was an atmosphere where people were not enslaved by time; rather time was enslaved by them. There was an implicitly understood sense of equality with not a thought about low or high status. Senior workers and office-bearers never tried to curb independent thinking in swayamsevaks. If there was any indication of control, it was over criticising others or negative gossip. Swayamsevaks had full liberty to talk freely and ask any questions from Sarsanghchaalak. There is an interesting anecdote. During one such chat, a swayamsevak asked Sarsanghchaalak, "Guruji, why do we yawn?" Guruji replied, "We cannot take deep breath during our routine movements in the day. We do this work only during deep sleep. We get the required oxygen due to it. When we do not get good sleep, deep breathing is also reduced. Thus, we do not get the right amount of oxygen. But, the body does require that much oxygen. Nature has created an alternative system for this. That is this yawn. We open our mouth wide during yawning, so we get more air through it and our body gets more oxygen. Therefore, yawn is an alternative to our imperfect and flawed breathing that gives the right amount of oxygen to our body." The swayamsevak was very happy. Where is any topic of organisation in this entire conversation? Where is any philosophical analysis here? The Sangh is that place, where a common swayamsevak can ask any type of question to his most senior leader.

During the ban, Guruji had written letters to swayamsevaks, telling them that they should do something for the society as their conscience dictated them. Many swayamsevaks promptly moved in that direction.

For Communists, there is 'intellectual gymnastics' (*mastishka prakshaalan*) but for the *karmayogis*, men of action of this country, there is 'intellectual training'. The great *mantra* here is igniting '*ghee*' not just agitating *ghee*. Reiterating this truth, Guruji had said in the winter camp at Uttar Pradesh on 23rd December, 1949, "If there are differing views and different ideologies, then it is not a matter of worry, but of joy. Outsiders say, we don't have freedom of thought. The answer to their allegation is that we too have differing views and every person tries to find a way out of the environment that surrounds us. Still, such people are still united and will remain united."[1]

Many views came up during that period, like, what is the relevance of an organisation that worked with the pledge to free the motherland after it has been achieved? The direction of the Sangh work should change in independent Bharat. The Shakha style of working is outdated and it should be changed. The Sangh should become a political party in democratic Bharat and the Sangh should become a major movement of non-political social service. The Sangh should develop an alternative education system at national level. The Sangh should become a religio-cultural organisation, and there is no need for the Prachaarak system. There is a need to redefine our goals and path, etc. These views did not arise out of a prevalent problem. They needed to be pondered over in a peaceful environment.

Infact, a major meeting had been organised in 1947 even before the above-mentioned emergency activities came up before the Sangh. Let us hear about it from Guruji himself, "I just recalled a similar programme organised at Anand Parbat in Delhi about two years back. I had presented very clear views about our policies and working methodology. A few well-wishers of the Sangh had proposed that policies of the Sangh be altered to some extent. My speech was meant to give a detailed answer to their questions, I still remember clearly. Our work came to a standstill within two months of this programme and many of us had to enjoy life in prison."[2] That is, these thoughts could not be taken forward.

Guruji felt that it was necessary to have such a workshop in the prevailing atmosphere. Therefore, it was decided to have an all-Bharat workshop of workers during a suitable period. It was finally planned to hold this workshop in March 1954 at Sindi, where the Sangh founder Dr. Hedgewar had held the first brainstorming workshop 15 years back. The workshop was organised from 8th to 16th March. Expected participants were all the Prachaaraks till district level and workers above this position.

Guruji had to face an unexpected disaster in the beginning of the new working year of 1953-54. The founder of Bharatiya Jan Sangh died on 23rd June in a prison of Kashmir under suspicious circumstances. According to Guruji, his heart had a foreboding and indicated that Shyambabu should not go to Kashmir. He had conveyed this feeling to senior workers of Jan Sangh too, but, Shyambabu's decision to enter Kashmir had been announced all over the country. He was the biggest non-Congress leader, president of a rising Jan Sangh and the roaring lion of Lok Sabha. It was not possible in any way to rescind his declared programme. Guruji also realised the dilemma that the workers faced. So, he did not insist upon forcing on others what his heart feared. Ultimately, the thunderbolt hit the ground. The expectations that Guruji had with the birth of Jan Sangh were reduced to dust. He was in Secunderabad when the news reached. His face turned ashen on hearing this news. He went inside a room and shut the door.[3] In the words of state Prachaarak Bapurao Moghe, who witnessed this entire scene, "It was a disaster that shook the Himalaya."

Guruji sent his condolences to Ashutosh Mukherjee, son of Shyam babu, after reaching Nagpur. He wrote, "We had been in touch for the last 10-12 years and our affection and relations were becoming stronger over time. I am very distressed to note that nobody would be able to fill the void left by his death."[4]

In the statement issued in Nagpur, he said, "Shyama Prasad Mukherjee has sacrificed his life on the battlefield of the struggle waged to press for complete merger of Kashmir in Bharat, that Kashmir should remain an indivisible part of Bharat. The news about the demise of Shri Shyambabu in Srinagar has hurt me grievously. I could not even have his last *darshan*. The wound left by this incident in my heart will never heal. A scholar of the highest order, skilled organiser, an impressive speaker, incomparable parliamentarian, a servant of the people who dedicated his life to the sacred motherland, a fearless crusader for pure nationalism and civil rights, and most importantly, a rare idealistic, cultured individual in today's times with unblemished character has gone from amongst us. Imprisonment of Dr. Mukherjee, his death in prison – it is difficult to forget all these things. If nothing else, responsibility of leaders of so-called government for the people for the fatal lack of care definitely lies at their doorsteps."[5]

Many a time, misfortune does not visit alone. Something similar happened here. 1st July brought the inauspicious news of the demise of Venkataram Shastri from Chennai. If untimely death of Shyambabu was a blow to Guruji's dreams for the future, Shastriji's death was a blow to the obligation-filled memories of the past. He wrote his message to Shastriji's dear son Ramamurthy: "Because of his love for truth and justice, hate for injustice and atrocity, and his love for the mission of the Sangh, its working methodology, the Sangh work, Shri T.R.V. Shastriji helped us on his own without even our asking for it. Neither I nor any member of the Sangh can ever forget this debt."[6]

Guruji stayed from 6th to 9th August in Kurukshetra camp after providing his guidance to various camps till July and came to Delhi from Kurukshetra for two days. During his speech on the occasion of Gopashtami, he presented the economic aspect of cow protection and showed that one gets five times more than what one spends on a cow. He strongly opposed killing of cow-wealth in the land of Gopal.[7]

He reached Chittor in Mewar region on 19th September during his routine tour. Bowing to the wishes of local Sanghchaalak he agreed to visit the famous historical fort there. After seeing various parts of the fort, he reached the castle of Maharani Padmavati. Describing the place, the government guide said, "This is the place where Maharana Ratan Singh showed Maharani Padmavati's face to Allauddin Khilji in a mirror." Just as he heard these words, Guruji shot back immediately, "This is utterly false! How could Rajputs, who would make any minor matter into their prestige issue, show Padmini to a person of opposing faith? This is a falsehood."[8] The local Sanghchaalak added, "All the people here call these only as a rumour." Guruji criticised this distorted mentality in that evening discourse.

January 1954 was the occasion of Kumbh Mela in Prayag. Taking advantage of the occasion, a *Gosamvardhan Sammelan* (Convention for Nurturing Cow) was held on the expansive banks of '*Triveni Sangam*', sacred confluence of three rivers. Under the directions of Prabhudatta Brahmachari and Guruji, signatures collected from the constituency of Pandit Nehru were displayed. They numbered 2,47,580. These were more than the votes polled by Pandit ji. There was another point worth noting in this matter. Each form for collecting signatures had a line, "We demand through democratic means that you should support the Bill presented in this regards in Parliament. A person supporting cow slaughter can never be our representative."[9] But, what can we do? There is no provision in our Constitution to recall an elected representative as available in many other countries. Therefore, even this signature campaign faced the same fate as faced by earlier signature-collection drive.

Now was the time for the proposed all-Bharat workshop of workers. Guruji had met all the expected participants of this workshop personally during his year-long tour of Bharat. He could call nearly all of them by name. There were many amongst them who used to write to him regularly. At that time, there was no state-level Prachaarak for Kerala-Tamil Nadu states. Dadarao Paramarth, who was the state Prachaarak at that time, had left for Shri Aurobindo Ashram in Puducherry owing to his growing inclination towards spiritualism. Therefore, Guruji himself sent the list of expected participants to the state Karyavaah Dakshinmurthy. All the expected participants reached Sindi on the evening of 8th March. The workshop commenced next morning. The daily programme included the daily Shakha, discourse by Guruji, discussion on it and Q & A session. They stayed in tents. Everybody used to collect under the shadow of a great banyan tree in the centre of the ground for intellectual sessions.

There is a tradition of reciting '*Aum sahanaavavatu*', the *Upanishad mantra*, before taking food. A new custom of reciting the *adveshtadi*, eight *shlokas* from XII chapter of the *Bhagavad Gita*, was started in the Sindi workshop. The aim of this addition was inner development of workers. A lot of thinking had gone behind it. Many days before the workshop, Acharya Vishwabandhu of Hoshiarpur Sadhu Ashram had presented a book written by him, and titled '*Manavata ka Maan*' (Honouring Humanity) to Guruji. It was an elucidation of *adveshtadi,* eight *shlokas* done over 160 pages. The forte of this exposition is the dimension of collectivism in these *shlokas*. Guruji felt that recitation of the *shlokas* would be very useful for the workers. Therefore, he added them ahead of '*sahanaavavatu*'. After the completion of the workshop, Guruji wrote to Acharya Vishwabandhu, "You had blessed me with a copy of '*Manavta ka Maan*' sometime back. I read it very attentively. The twelfth chapter describes qualities required to live one's life successfully while maintaining the highest spiritual level. These have all been described briefly but comprehensively in *adveshtadi* eight *shlokas* and have been a part of my regular daily reading. Their exposition in this book is done in such simple, easy and touching manner that I felt it entirely fitting that I should motivate all the leading workers who have come together from all over Bharat to study it and I have asked them to read this book. I have also begun a new custom of reciting these eight *shlokas* collectively, and completing them with *shlokas* '*brahmaarpanam….*', etc. and concluding with '*Aum sahanaavavatu*' before taking food."[10] Guruji's view was that great thoughts are acceptable and good for the organisation, from wherever they come.

For the participants of Sindi workshop, it was a life-changing experience. The essence of Guruji's exhortation was, "The idea about Independence during freedom struggle had incomplete meaning. Its meaning was limited only to the extent of liberating self from the grip of foreigners. The Sangh understood its meaning more deeply. In view of the Sangh, Independence is about reaching a stage that leads to expression of the essence or pride in one's nation. It becomes an unavoidable duty of that nation to be prepared for and achieve the power that will help it realise that essence. This assumes within itself the duty of expressing that speciality of the nation in the world community. Responsibility of accomplishing it does not lie with the leaders but each and every organ of the society. For this, we shall have to remove the visible shortcomings in the society and raise it higher. To achieve this, a system to nurture the required *samskaaras* will have to be developed. It is unfortunate that the current education system has not paid attention to this lacuna. The Sangh has taken upon itself to fill this gap. For this, the responsibility lies with the worker, specially the Prachaarak. With a view to making this ancient society capable and strong for fulfilling this national and global objective, we shall have to expand the Sangh's influence in all areas of work. No field is untouchable for us. Our worker is the commander or ambassador for entering every field. He has to acquire the required qualities for this to happen. We wish all-round progress of our dearest nation."

Finally, Guruji reminded, "I just wish to say one thing – that we are conducting this programme at a place where highly revered Doctor Saheb had finalised different aspects of our protocols, our prayer and orders, etc. It is an occasion to remember and revise our thoughts about our work once again at the place where we had sat together for a week to plan out our work. If we ever get some doubts in our heart due to any situation around us, we should resolve that we shall not let any weakness develop within us, and working day and night with all our energy, we shall spread our work in all fields to such an extent that nobody would remain untouched in that environment."[11]

At the conclusion of the workshop, Guruji declared Dattaji Didolkar, who was well-known in Kerala-Tamil Nadu already, as the state Prachaarak. Guruji returned to Nagpur after the workshop on 22nd March. He spoke about foreign policy of Bharat in the Sunday meeting of Rotary Club on 23rd. His view was, "That we should be a recipient of somebody's charity, shake hands with somebody with a mentality of inferiority – this mentality is even worse than slavery and should be thrown off. We have to develop such strength that the people should look towards us for favour... Our nation can reach such a stage only on the foundation of fiery patriotism."[12]

Sangh Shiksha Vargas (training camps) commenced as per schedules after Sindi workshop. Guruji went to Bengaluru where joint camp of Karnataka, Tamil Nadu and Kerala was being conducted. He stayed for three days from 11th to 13th May in Acharya School with the participant students. It was Guruji's habit of listening to the solo song with closed eyes and bowed head that was sung before the intellectual discourse. He sat in the same posture in Bengaluru in that period. The singer of the song that day was a Pracharaak who loved to show off. He used to boast that he had learnt over hundred songs by heart. With that confidence, he began singing a long song '*Badh rahe hain hum nirantar*' that had 30 lines. The beginning was very beautiful, but he probably forgot one line in the second paragraph. At that moment, Guruji raised his head and prompted him with that line. The champion singer probably got nervous. He kept forgetting lines and Guruji continued prompting him each time. Finally, just as he managed to complete the song somehow and, reassured thus, proceeded towards his seat, Guruji hummed '*Badh rahe hain hum nirantar*'. The other participants managed to suppress their laughter somehow. Guruji told that Prachaarak during the meeting of trainers: "Overconfidence creates problems sometimes." This lesson seemed to have influenced the Prachaarak in later days. It is truly said that defeat is a stepping stone to victory.

Linguistic and regional feelings were running high during the latter half of the sixth decade. Guruji was the chief guest at a conference against regionalism on 23rd May, Sunday in Mumbai in such a surcharged atmosphere. The chairman of the reception committee was Barrister Jamunadas Mehta. Chief of Mumbai city Sangh, Dayabhai Patel inaugurated the conference. The lecture delivered by Guruji in front of the august gathering of elite citizens was highly logical that could force the agitators pushing for linguistic states to rethink. His words were, "Due to the wicked strategy of British, we have begun to believe that difference in language leads to difference in culture, but this assumption is wrong. This thinking has even forced its way into the Bharatiya Constitution. We have called our country a 'Union' in our Constitution, which is incorrect. 'Union' actually means sticking together some fragmented pieces to make them stand together. Ours is a nation with a unified soul, and it is not fragmented. Some people call themselves supporters of 'united India'. But, from where has this term 'united India' come? This idea itself contains an unconscious thought of differences, which is spreading like an epidemic across the nation."

In his lecture, he asked the supporters of linguistic states a question, "Why should those people, who talk of the whole world being one single state, be afraid in their hearts about making Bharat into one state?"[13]

Guruji reached Nagpur after two-three months of continuous travel. As usual, he used to visit his home every morning, afternoon and evening. While returning to the RSS office on 16th July, he told his mother that he had a fresh tour programme from the next day. Bhauji immediately asked him, "Which places are you going to?" Guruji told him about his entire tour calendar. Next morning, he began his tour of Mahakoshal after completing his morning rituals and touching his parent's feet, seeking their blessings. His programme on 20th July was in Khandwa and the place of meeting was the house of a trader. Bhauji's family used to stay in Khandwa in 1915. This is where the sacred thread ceremony (*yagyopaveet samskaar*) of teenage Madhu had taken place. During a conversation, the trader told him with pride that Bhauji used to be his teacher. As he got immersed in old memories, he asked about Bhauji's health. The son answered, "I have seen his sacred face just before leaving for the tour. I must say that considering his age he is in good health. He goes for a walk every day. He has no disease like diabetes. Yes, he does have a little problem of blood pressure."

After concluding the evening programme and a meeting with workers, Guruji left for Sagar along with Dr. Thatte and the state Prachaarak. When the train reached Bhopal in the morning after traversing 280 kms, station master gave him sad news that his respected father had expired the previous night. Everybody got down and arrangements were made to reach Nagpur immediately. But, they had to cover a distance of 400 kms to reach Nagpur. Therefore, message was sent to his maternal nephew, Dinkar Tikekar to complete the funeral rites at the earliest after seeking advice of the family priests. On 20th, Bhauji had chatted till 10-10:30 in the night as was his habit and gone upstairs to sleep after taking milk. Nobody had an idea about when he laid down in the large middle room and breathed his last. When Guruji's nephew went upstairs to offer tea to grandfather in the morning, he witnessed the situation there. This was a death that was '*vinadainyam, anaayasen maranam*' (sudden death without any pain).

Madhav went from station to the Sangh office to change his clothes, reached home and sat down next to his dear mother. Clasping her hand between two hands of her son, she looked at her son with tearful eyes. The son too saw into her eyes. A saintly mother with an enriched soul that had matured through various worships, rituals and meditations and a son, who had earned high intellect with his inborn urge since his childhood coupled with various rituals and practices – both remained silent. But, that silence was much more vocal than any spoken words. Both felt reassured with each other. Madhu stayed with his mother for five days. His *guru-bhai, disciple from same guru,* Swami Amoortanand had also reached Nagpur upon hearing this news. Guruji held a personal discussion with him. The problem was small but peculiar. The initiation into sannyas that 'Gowalkar' had received from Swami Akhandananda was '*mantra diksha*'. He had let his hair grow only on the affectionate command of his guru. Now, should he shave off his head as per social customs or not? There was a dilemma. *Guru-bhai* had no doubts. He advised that Guru's directive cannot be overturned – *agya gurunam hyaviharaneeya*. Thus, without any change in his outer appearance, this son carried out the last rites of his father on the banks of the holy River Godavari in Nasik and went back to Nagpur on 3rd August.

Guruji had reached Nagpur from Bhopal on 22nd. He wrote a letter to the station master of Bhopal that throws more light on his personality.

"Dearest Station Master,

"The pure sympathetic emotions, with which you conveyed to me the unhappy news you had received from Nagpur, has resulted in deep faith and respect for you in my heart. News being unexpected, I forgot to convey my gratitude to you while I was trying to recover from this grief. You obliged me by conveying this news to me promptly in a gentlemanly manner. I am sending mine and my colleagues' heartfelt thanks to you through this letter. I hope I would get a chance in future to know you better by meeting you personally and offering my respects to you in person."[14]

Nearly everybody in Bharat accepts the importance of Sanskrit language. But, very few actually encourage it in the manner Rashtriya Swayamsevak Sangh has been encouraging the use of Sanskrit since the beginning. The Sangh converted its physical drill orders in Sanskrit in 1939; prayer was also written in Sanskrit. A rule was made that Sanskrit *amrit vachan* (immortal words) should be read out in all training camps. Under the same thought process, Sanskrit magazines *Bhavitavyam* from Nagpur and *Bharati* from Jaipur began their publications. Guruji and specially Dadasaheb Apte encouraged this move and prodded Shri B. Varnekar and Dadabhai Sharma to help this cause. *Bharati* completed its five years in 1954. At that time, Guruji expressed his views about this magazine being published in Sanskrit – "This language is so easy and simple that apart from one or two states of Bharat, all others, specially litterateurs can understand it. For example here are words – '*Sanskrit bhashayah sarvatrik prachararth*', '*kritam karyam nitaram abhinandaneeyam*', *adhunik sushikshiteshu akarameva bhramah*', '*hindi-prabhritayah sarvah bhashah sanskritodbhotah*', '*swaswabhasha durabhimanen paraspar parthakyam*', '*vivekvidhuraih sanskrtibhasha mrita itijalpitam*', '*sanskrit bhashayah sarvabhashavyapitvam sarvabhashaantaryasmitvam*', '*raashtrakalyaankaamaih Sanskrit bhashadhyayanamavashyameva kartavyam*'.[15]

In 1955, all the political parties except Congress initiated an agitation for freedom of 450-year-old Portuguese colonies. Bharatiya Jan Sangh also took a leading part in it. The previous state Prachaarak of Delhi, Vasantrao Oke, was also the leader of one team. Before leaving for *satyagraha*, he wrote a letter asking for Guruji's blessings. There was not much time in hand. Therefore, Guruji sent his letter to Vasantrao personally through a swayamsevak rather than depending on the Post & Telegraph Department. The letter was brief but carried deep meaning, "All my good wishes are with you for this great task. I pray to the Supreme Lord from the bottom of my heart that He may bless this programme with success. Whatever pious deeds I may have accumulated with God's blessings in my life, I offer them to you for your success and protection."[16] The letter was in Marathi, mother tongue of both of them!

Vasantrao entered Goa as per plan. He was injured with a police bullet, which hit him in the upper part of his leg and he was rushed to hospital for treatment. To the swayamsevaks, who reached there to take care of his nursing, he said with folded hands, "Guruji's pious deeds saved me."

A part of this episode is yet incomplete. The then state Prachaarak, Chamanlal ji noted in his diary, "10th August, 1955 – Shri Guruji was staying in Shri Lalaji's bungalow. Shri Vasantrao Oke came their and woke people up at 12 in the night. He expressed his desire to see Shri Guruji. He told others that he had sent a letter to Guruji in Nagpur, seeking his permission to go for the *satyagraha*. He had a little dialogue with Shri Guruji and then he left."[17]

The Congress government's attitude about people's agitation for Goa's liberation was that of disinterest and non-cooperation. Guruji expressed his strong displeasure at this attitude.

Immediately after Independence, leading dignitaries like Guruji, Bhaiyyaji Dani and Balasaheb Deoras had done a detailed study and analysis of the organisations working in different fields of the society. The ban led to an interruption in this activity. After removal of this ban, their attention was drawn again to this activity. Coincidentally, Sangh Prachaarak, Dattopant Thengadiji received an invitation from the president of INTUC, P.Y. Deshpande, in 1950 to work for that organisation. Deoras asked him to accept it immediately. Guruji added, "Follow the discipline of the organisation you are going to work for.

When its discipline and your ethical intellect lead to any conflict, it would be ideal to resign at that time. But, as long as you are in that organisation, you should always consider its discipline your yardstick."[18] Thus, Thengdi ji was sent to a labour organisation. So far none of the leader of Hindu renaissance movement had taken any step toward entering this field. To enter that strong fortress of conflicting ideologies, it was critical to have qualities like reasoned thinking, study, research, moral conduct, strategy, outgoing nature, etc. Dattopant had all these qualities and the Sangh appointed him for this bold act. Finally, on 23rd July, 1955, Bharatiya Mazdoor Sangh was born in Bhopal. Its flag was saffron. The entry of saffron in the field of labour was a major historic event. Bharatiya Mazdoor Sangh declared Vishwakarma Jayanti the Bharatiya Shramik Din (Indian Labour Day). Guruji's thoughts were surely behind this declaration. Thengadiji had gone to Nasik once to discuss various issues with Guruji. Thengadiji asked him, "Do we have an honoured labour day in our tradition that would be acceptable to all, could inspire everybody and also weave them together in a common thread of unity?" Guruji told him, "Yes, there is such a day and that is Vishwakarma Day." Guruji imparted enough information in its support and told him that all material about it was available in various books available in *Kesari* library."[19] There is no doubt that Dattopant succeeded in this research.

Guruji had talked about all-enveloping work that would spread in all the fields during the brainstorming workshop held in 1954. Swayamsevaks had already entered the fields of education, students, magazines, politics, sustaining of culture and many others. Now labour field also got included in this list. The saffron family was evolving and progressing gradually. In this period of transformation, the Central Working Committee of Sangh took a decision to observe respected Guruji's 51st birthday from 18th January, 1956 to 8th May 1956, i.e., for a period of 51 days.

□

Endnotes

1. *Shri Guruji Samagra*, Vol. 2, pp. 49
2. Ibid, pp. 49-50
3. *Smriti Paarijaat*, pp. 7
4. *Maa. Sa. Golwalkar*, pp. 211
5. *Shri Guruji Samagra*, Vol. 1, pp. 114-115
6. *Shri Guruji Samagra*, Vol. 7, pp. 198
7. *Shri Guruji Dilli Mein*, pp. 44
8. *Shri Guruji Rajasthan Mein*, pp. 48
9. *Maa. Sa. Golwalkar*, pp. 213
10. *Shri Guruji Samagra*, Vol. 7, pp. 10
11. *Shri Guruji Samagra*, Vol. 2, pp. 200-201

12. *Shri Guruji Samagra*, Vol. 5, pp. 24
13. *Maa. Sa. Golwalkar*, pp. 215
14. *Shri Guruji Samagra*, Vol. 7, pp. 200-201
15. *Shri Guruji Samagra*, Vol. 6, pp. 105-106
16. *Shri Guruji Samagra*, Vol. 8, pp. 102
17. *Smriti Parijat*, pp. 16-17
18. *Avismaraneey Guruji*, pp. 107
19. *Jeevan Prasang*, Vol. 2, pp. 128-129

29

Birthday Celebrations and Ayurveda Oil Treatment

Rashtriya Swayamsevak Sangh does not celebrate the birthday of its Prachaarak in its programme. The birthday of the Sangh founder was never celebrated in his life-time. Not a single of the six *utsavas* (festivals) of the Sangh include celebration of a birthday. *Guru Pooja utsav* celebrated in the Sangh is the occasion to worship the saffron flag that is considered to be Guru; it is not a celebration of *Vyas Jayanti* (birthday of Sage Vyasa). In the same way, *Varsh Pratipada utsav* is the first day of Hindu new year and is not a celebration of Sangh founder's birthday, who was incidentally born on this sacred day. After the death of Doctorji, this day became an important day as his memory inspires people. We shall have to understand the celebration of Guruji's 51st birthday in this background or else it might give people a wrong idea.

The experience of mass contact programme of the Sangh during the agitation for banning cow slaughter in 1952 had been highly encouraging. The Sangh decided to expand and strengthen its work on the basis of that experience. It was decided to take another step ahead to expand and strengthen the Sangh work. An average common Hindu does not like the slaughter of mother cow and his heart considers it an unbearable act. All the Hindus consider it a sin and against *dharma*. Therefore, people collecting signatures for the cause held the firm belief that there would not be any opposition to it. In fact, it would be welcomed everywhere and their belief turned out to be true. Next thought that came up was that one should go a step further and address the society and enlighten it about the critical necessity of Hindu unity and organisation. For this, Guruji's 51st birthday seemed to be the most suitable occasion. Because of Guruji's life and his thoughts, Hindutva and Hindu consolidation had become identified with each other, it was impossible to separate them. In short, the birthday celebration of Guruji in 1956 was a follow-up exercise to the 1952 Cow Protection Movement.

This idea of the members of Central Committee was good but who would speak to Guruji about it? All of them knew about Sangh's tradition and Guruji's own nature. Still senior Sanghchaalaks like Lala Hansraj, Barrister Narendra Singh, Bholanath Jha and Dharmavir met Guruji and presented the proposal of this programme to Guruji. A Sanghchaalak at that time told Guruji, "This programme is for the growth of Sangh work, please accept it." On hearing this, Guruji replied, "Is that so? So, this is for Sangh's progress? Then do sacrifice me, I shall present myself." Actually, it was not just a logical response to the question but only an echo of his lifelong pledge. Guruji observed the whole programme from an impersonal perspective. Planning for the programme was in the expert hands of people like Eknath Ranade, Dattopant Thengadiji, Professor Bapurao Varhadpande, and others. The target for people contact programme (called *sampark yagna*) was kept at 2 per cent of adult population, that is, 3.6 million adult citizens. It was also decided to present a purse to Guruji as a respectful offering to him. This programme was to contact people and bring them up from an affectionate relationship towards commitment to the mission. For the first time, the Sangh published two booklets in large numbers in all Indian languages. One was *Vyakti Darshan* about Guruji's life and the other was *Vichaar Darshan,* which contained his thoughts. It was also translated in Myanmar language of Burma that is called Myanmar now. The price of booklet about Guruji's life was two anna (12 paise) and booklet about his thoughts was priced at eight annas (50 paise). Apart from it, there was a handbill to be distributed to households. The handbill contained a beautiful *shloka* from the famous scripture '*subhashitratnabhandagar*'. Some anonymous seer may have created it, perhaps inspired by the second *shloka* of the philosophical work *Vivekchudamani*, written by Jagadguru Adi Shankaracharya.

The *Shloka* is:

Manushye sati durlabha purushata pustve punarviprata|
Vipratve bahuvidyatatigunata vidyavatohrthigyata||
Arthagyasya vichitravakpatuta tatrapi lokagyata|
Lokagyasya samastashastravidusho dharma matidurlabha ||

Meaning: "Taking birth as a human being after passing through countless other forms of life; that too taking birth in a family that is keen to seek knowledge about Brahma (Supreme Being), then educating oneself with vast knowledge, understanding the meaning of that knowledge, after understanding its meaning, spreading with skill the right kind of speech, along with this also being expert on all the sciences and scriptures; while doing all this, being enriched with a spiritual consciousness – this is a rarity." The handbill indicated that such was Guruji's life.

In this people contact effort, there was no other type of publicity. There were no modern-day exercises of image building. Wall paintings, posters, cut-outs – there was none of it. Yes, articles by well-known personalities, who knew Guruji, were published in newspapers. The methodology was to spread the message through contact and have dialogue through contact. There was no exemption from the regular Shakha.

Guruji's birthday was on 8th March. The mass contact programme began 51 days ahead of this day. From Sanghchaalaks to common swayamsevaks, the entire strength of the Sangh was put behind this penance. They went from home-to-home, introduced people to the Sangh and Guruji. The experience was of warm welcome everywhere and the target of mass contact exceeded by five lakh, purse of reverent offering crossed the target by 21 lakh rupees.

S. No.	State	People Contacted (numbers)	Contributions to Purse		
			Rupee	Anna	Paise
1.	Andhra Pradesh	1,33,722	1,03,230	5	9
2.	Assam, Manipur, Tripura	80,713	45,107	11	0
3.	Bengal	63,581	60,001	0	0
4.	Bihar	1,72,025	55,248	0	0
5.	Gujarat	55,117	60,001	0	0
6.	Karnataka	2,65,000	83,051	0	0
7.	Madhya Bharat	2,18,600	1,00,151	0	0
8.	Maharashtra	6,50,585	2,80,151	0	0
9.	Mahakaushal	2,55,783	84,022	11	3
10.	Nagpur City	1,10,347	1,25,674	11	6
11.	Utkal	23,000	9,417	14	0
12.	Punjab, Delhi, J & K	4,80,000	3,20,000	0	0
13.	Rajasthan	1,05,000	83,847	9	9
14.	Tamil Nadu, Kerala	1,02,000	54,050	0	0
15.	Uttar Pradesh	8,43,125	3,51,000	0	0
16.	Vidarbha	5,43,813	2,50,151	0	0
17.	Burma (Myanmar)	1,000	10,000	0	0
Total number of people contacted		**41,03,411**	**Purse – 20,75,105**	**5**	**6**

The second phase of mass contact programme was of 32 days, from 8th March to 8th April. The first phase was the phase of action and second was the phase of felicitations. In this phase, one or two major cities of each state hosted a felicitation programme for Guruji. Each state organised a reception committee for the purpose. Chairmen of these committees were highly reputed personalities of that state. For example, Chairman of Nagpur committee was the famous historian Radhakumud Mukherjee; Delhi had ex-Ambassador to Pakistan, Dr. Sitaram; legal luminary Dundiraj Shastri Vinod was the chairman in Mumbai; retired Justice of Supreme Court Patanjali Shastri in Chennai; compatriot of Netaji Subhas Chandra Bose. Mutturamlinga Thevar in Madurai headed these committees. Symbols of sacredness (*mangal patra*) and purse of respectful offering was presented to Guruji at all the places.

There was a difference in the emotions and levels of the felicitation that took place six-seven years back after his release from prison and this time on the occasion of his birthday. The first occasion carried an overwhelming wave of enthusiasm and excitement, while the second simmered with a sense of purpose of taking the Sangh to the forefront under the leadership of Guruji. On that day, people had seen Guruji as a sacrificing personality freed from the prison; today, he was being seen as the protector of Mother Cow and a seer dedicated to organising the Hindu society. The call of those days was 'Forget, forget, work without conflict'; the theme now was, 'March ahead, march ahead, keep marching ahead without pause.'

Guruji made a special appeal to Christian and Muslim societies of our nation during the felicitation meetings this time. He expressed the same views publicly in those meetings that he had expressed in the article he wrote on 25th October, 1955 in the weekly, *Rashtra Shakti*. "We have a large number of people who have become Christians and Muslims in our country. A large majority of them are progenies of the people who have been living in this very country for many generations. They did not convert to the religions of the rulers out of any devotion to their rulers, but they converted to their faith out of fear from the attacks of aggressor, rape and greed when there was no other way left. If they wish to make use of the freedom, then all Muslims and Christians, who were Hindus earlier, should give up the religions and sects that symbolise foreign pillage and rape and return to the original faith of their forefathers. Only then the freedom of this nation will attain its completeness."[1] He appealed to traditional Hindu members of the society, who represented the other side, "We should accept all our own people into our families with our hearts very happily. Their return is coming back to their self-faith and is not a conversion."

It would not be out of place to recall a dialogue Guruji had with Kerala state secretary of RSS, advocate T.V. Anantan 13 years later on the same subject. Anantan had asked, "Didn't the noble people who founded the Vijayanagar Empire accept their original faith after giving up Islam?"

Shri Guruji said, "Yes, this is true. Before Vidyaranya Swami became the head of Shringeri Peeth, he was known as Madhavacharya. He was the person who motivated Shri Harihar and Bukka Islam to give up Islam and return to their own faith. Shri Madhavacharya had inspired them to accept their self-faith and establish the Vijayanagar Empire. Famous commentator of *Vedas,* Shri Sayanacharya was brother of Madhavacharya."

"There have been such incidents of returning to faith later on too in our history. Shivaji Maharaj accepted the famous Maratha commander, Netaji Palkar back from Islam into his original faith. He also accepted Shri Bhalji Nimbalkar back into self-religion and got his own daughter married to him to reinstate his prestige in the society. These were the people who became protectors of Hindu society later on. If we had not given them our respect and status after bringing them back to self-religion, history would have taken a different shape altogether."[2]

But, even a great personality like Guruji had to wait for 10 years, till the 1966 Kumbh Mela in Prayag to get his revolutionary ideas accepted by religious leaders at that time.

While Guruji expressed his gratitude for the felicitations, the philosopher in him would come out once in a while. In one of his meetings, he said, "I have been felicitated today on crossing 50 years. What is it that is being celebrated in all this? This body is made up of seven elements. Its growth, deterioration and merging back with elements is pre-ordained. Then, how can we celebrate this body, for what purpose? Eternal is that which resides in this body. There is no growth or weakening of that. It is unaffected in this growing and decaying body. Then, why do we celebrate even that too? Only one thing that comes out of it is that these kinds of programmes have no meaning."

As he moves on, he gives credit to destiny with humility, "I never started off to do something big in this life. But, there is something inside that pushes one and a person works accordingly. I do not know what transpired in my life. I came in touch with this great organisation only because of my good fate. I had to take up its responsibility. I am carrying out the responsibility. Whether I was successful or failed, it is the Supreme God's decision."

Further, he talks about the Sangh. At that time what he said reflects the feeling of *saha-yagya* (collective yagna) that Lord Shri Krishna talked about. He says, "I am being given entire credit for the Sangh work. I do not understand this. No work depends on one person. Any effort results in success only with sacrifice, penance, enthusiasm and dedication of many people to the mission. The Sangh is growing today. Credit for this goes to the painfully hard work of countless workers. These gentlemen have felicitated me today as a representative of all those people."

Analysing the role of an individual in the organisation, he explains, "Nobody should be arrogant that the work being accomplished is because of me. This thinking is incorrect. Individuals will come and go, but work will carry on. Many people wonder what will happen after me? Actually, when a great personality leaves this world, then his people come together and accomplish his work. Same thing happened after the demise of the founder of the Sangh, Dr. Hedgewar. All of us worked together and work is growing."

We have mentioned the booklet *Vichaar Darshan* in an earlier part of this chapter. Clarifying his views on it, he said, "Swayamsevaks would contact you, saying that these are 'my views'. I wish to say that there is nothing like 'my views'. Views are that of the Sangh, I am just a gramophone record that broadcasts those views."

He expressed his views thus, during the grand rally organised in Madurai on 26th March, "I know very well what my status in this organisation is. During one of these noisy days, I went into a reflective mood. I witnessed a scene in my mind. A group of traders is travelling on camels. The reins of the camel of the leader of the group is hanging on to the sands of desert. A rat comes running out from his rat hole and starts walking with the rope clamped in his mouth. He hums, 'I am the leader of this group. Yes, I got the message. I understood my place. You, too, should recognise it, please.'

This *karmayogi* urged people, "The Sangh needs your full co-operation. The mission of the Sangh is unalloyed well-being of the nation. Its goal is to see the country on the pinnacle of growth, and prosperity – *paramvaibhav*." The last programme in this series of felicitations was to be held on April 8. Thus, a novel festive programme in Guruji's life came to a close with festivity and joy.

A special mention needs to be made about Guruji's birthday celebrations. The story of these celebrations would be incomplete without this information. Where was Guruji when every swayamsevak was going from home to home, contacting people in his name? What was his yoga of action in that period? After taking part in Makar Sankranti festival in 1956, he stayed in Nagpur till the end of January. On 31st January, he went to west Pattaambi that is 12 kms from Shonannur junction in central Kerala for Ayurveda treatment. Dr. Y.K. Warrier, who had been declared *tehsil* secretary by Guruji himself exactly a month back in 1955, had made arrangements for his treatment in his clinic Kamalalayam. But, Guruji's treatment was in the hands of one of the eight traditionally recognised top *vaidyas* of Kerala, respected Vaidyaraj Pulamantol Moos.

Respected Vaidya came on 31st January to Kamalalayam and started asking questions. Only then did the near ones sitting with Guruji could get the true picture of his health. Guruji informed Vaidya that he hardly had any sleep since the last 10-12 years, took no breakfast in the morning, only one sweet tea, lunch in the afternoon, evening in the team, no snacks and had to take one or two cups of tea additionally out of social compulsions. He had good digestion, had no diabetes, food cooked in any oil from coconut to mustard oil was fine, including *ghee*, but even a drop of Dalda could create a lot of problems; both the throat and stomach suffered. He could digest any kind of food – sweet-bitter, salty-spicy completely that was offered. He added laughingly, "Vegetarian only and I do not take milk or fruits." Response to the question about daily routine was, "*Surya Namaskar* in the morning, *Yog Asana*, bath with lightly warm water, no problem in walking and thin pillow. I cannot lift left hand above the shoulders, there is continuous pain there." Treatment began from 1st February. Treatment consisted of putting *tel-lepan*, *tel-dhara*, *vasti* and *nasya*. Sleeping in the afternoon after a treatment like this is prohibited. With this issue in mind, Dr. Warrier asked Vaidya, "Can one sleep in the afternoon?" The question was indicative. Vaidya found out from Guruji before responding to the question that he had a habit of taking rest in the afternoon. He responded after this clarification, "It is best not to sleep. But, if it is a habit, then suppressing it could result in irritation, which is not good. Therefore, it would be better to reduce it as far as possible." The patient got the message. He stopped taking afternoon rest till the treatment was complete. He used to close his room, sit down and read the special issue of *Kalyan* from Gita Press, Gorakhpur. Writing about his experience on reading it, he told the proprietor and writer of Gita Press, Hanuman Prasad Poddar, "I had received '*Satyakathaa ank*' of *Kalyan* last month. I brought it along when I came to Pattaambi on 31-01-1956 for some treatment. Having received orders to take complete rest and live in isolation, I got enough time to read this volume and felt peaceful. Because of this edition with me, even my mind and intellect got wonderful treatment with these stories along with physical treatment. It is your blessing."[3]

Scholars of traditional Ayurveda treat the patient in proportion to the sickness. As a treatment for insomnia, Vaidya told him, "I will send you a special oil. You can apply it on the sole of your feet while lying down. You will get sleep." Guruji told him promptly, "Vaidyaraj, I do not think it is possible for me. If any such thing is applied to my body, I feel unclean and I would not be able to sleep." "Oh, is that so?" Vaidya asked and suggested, "Then we shall try *tel-dhara* on the forehead, you will be cured with it." The patient accepted this treatment.

Oil is applied and rubbed on to the patient with massage in a long wooden tub called *droni* in which he has to lie down. *Droni* was brought from Vaidya's clinic. *Droni* treatment began on 1st February. Two attendants soaked his body from both sides in thick sticky oil for 45 minutes. When Guruji got up from the *droni* and proceeded towards the bathroom to bathe, Dr. Warrier cautioned him. Prompt came the response with a smile, "Yes, I put forward each step very carefully." Oil treatment was repeated the next day too. When he was told that it was over, he asked affectionately, "Why did you take five to six minutes more than yesterday?" The attendants had no answer, they stood quietly. Dr. Warrier asked a counter-question, "Why did you feel like that?" The answer was unexpected, "I had started reciting *Bhagwad Gita* after lying down in *droni*. I remembered where I had stopped when the treatment was completed. Today, I finished that part and went even into the next chapter. This is my watch." Vaidya Moos and Dr. Warrier looked at each other silently with astonishment. Truly, time for mere mortals passes by but extraordinary souls live each moment!

The turn for '*nasya*' treatment came after one week. This is the process of sucking in oil through the nostril. Oil is decided on the basis of the patient and sickness. To take a decision, Vaidya and his students sat together in the evening. Discussions were being done in Malayalam language. Guruji, Dr. Abaji Thatte and Dr. Warrier were listening to it. A student suggested, "How would

Mahamashtailam work?" "Oh, that's non-vegetarian," Guruji said immediately in Hindi and his face turned sour. Guru told his disciple, "See, his body has rejected it, now that is useless. Change the oil." And it was changed.

The period of treatment took four weeks and lasted till 28th February. This was the period of mass-contact programme all over the country. Kerala was no exception to this. State Prachaarak Dattaji Didolkar had also come only once to Pattaambi in the beginning, to check out the arrangements. But, well-wishers of the Sangh and families known to him, who were not involved in day-to-day Sangh activities, used to come occasionally. Three senior workers from Karnataka came one day in a group to Pattaambi. Coincidentally, two-three workers also came from Tamil Nadu. One amongst them was a district Prachaarak. It was a non-working easy day, so the two workers from North Calicut and South Thrissur had also come with coconut, rice, etc. All the workers were well known to Guruji. There was lunch and rest. After that, all of them met Guruji and had good chat with him. The evening Shakha also took place. Dr. Warrier and Dr. Abaji Thatte, who had gone for the mass-contact programme, hadn't come back yet. The whole group sat around Guruji, chatting informally, Guruji spoke out from his heart, "It would have been better if I had not come here during this period. Workers all over are busy with the given programme. The owner of this house, Dr. Warrier is also moving around with Dr. Abaji Thatte. I am the only person shut alone here for taking rest! A thought crosses my mind often, is it not a sin?" Everybody understood the subject and got the message. All of them were intelligent. Everybody went back to his field of work that night itself!

However, another interesting incident, of an entirely different kind took place in Kamalalayam during this time. Wandering around like a spiritual seeker since 1953 in various places of meditation of noble souls, like Shri Aurobindo's place in Puducherry, then to Thiruvanmallai of Raman Maharshi, Kanchangarh of Swami Ramdas, past state Prachaarak Dadarao Paramarth dropped in at Kamalalayam like a bolt from the blue. Fortunately for him, district Prachaarak and local Prachaarak, who knew him, were around when he reached there. Guruji was busy with rituals after his bath and treatment at that time. They met each other at lunch-time. The faces of both the souls were lit up with happiness. After lunch, Guruji, who was not allowed to sleep in the afternoon and Dadarao who did not need sleep in the afternoon, sat together and started chatting. Dadarao raised a question to Guruji to resolve a complex puzzle about spiritual exercise, "Form of *Atman* is full of purity and sacredness. Why should the normal activities of our body, made of flesh and bone, seem to raise doubts about harming its purity and cleanliness? Sentiments about ethical behaviour are linked to this physical body. So, why should one follow the social constraints in spiritual practices that are based on such morality? Why should a person immersed in realisation of self be bound by these rules?"

Shri Guruji was quiet for nearly a minute. Then he said, "Your thinking is logically correct. But, it would not be possible that people living in this society around us would have such a high intellectual level. They can only understand simple practices followed in a human being's lives. Therefore, it is not possible for a seeker to avoid the bonds of social behaviour. He cannot show disrespect to these social bonds. Thus, a person who wishes to take up spiritual practice should follow these rules of social customs born out of average intellectual level of society. If one wishes to meditate and free self from all these bonds, then he should do so in isolation, go to distant jungles where there are no people. Otherwise, society will force such a seeker to go to jungles."

The pleasure of getting his doubts cleared completely with Guruji's answer could be seen clearly on Dadarao's face.[4]

The subject of discussion moved away to the ongoing mass contact programme. Since Dadaji Paramarth had not been in touch with day-to-day work for many months, he was not aware of the thinking behind this programme. He expressed his opposition to this programme based on the policies set by Dr. Hedgewar and wished to know its relevance from Guruji. On hearing his question, Guruji felt reassured and he gave his clarification for nearly 10-15 minutes in Marathi. Dadaji seemed to be well satisfied. Expressing his satisfaction, he went away quietly just as he had arrived.

Guruji went to Kalladi on the second day of completing his treatment on 29th February. Swami Agamananda, who had founded Shri Ramakrishna Ashram in the birthplace of Shri Shankaracharya, was a close friend of Guruji. Swamiji had come down to meet Guruji in Pattaambi just as he had arrived there. Both of them had decided that he would have a view of divineKalladi. Guruji reached Kalladi that was about 100 kms away from Pattaambi at 4 in the evening. Dr. Abaji Thatte, Dr. Warrier and divisional Prachaarak Shankar Shastri accompanied him. Bhaskar Rao Kalambi had also come there with seven-eight swayamsevaks.

When Guruji reached Ashram, Swamiji was busy during those days in constructing a college in the birthplace of Shri Shankaracharya in the name of that divine soul. Guruji heard the problems of material world he faced in this construction from Swamiji. Saying, "Everything depends on Thakur's kindness," Guruji got up from his seat and offered an envelope with humility in Swamiji's hands. It contained a cheque of ₹ 25,000. Swamiji was speechless with overwhelming emotion. A spiritual gentleman had handed over that cheque to Guruji in Nagpur to be given to some right project. On reaching Nagpur, Guruji gave complete information to that anonymous donor and wrote to Swami Agamananda, "Please utilise the funds handed over by me the way you deem it fit. I have already told you that the gentleman who has given me this money would be entirely satisfied with the way you use the funds and that gentleman would be obliged when you inform him how you have utilised the money."[5]

Guruji performed Shakha prayers in the compound of the Ashram and returned to Pattaambi the same day. On reaching Kamalalayam at 9 in the night, he saw a group of swayamsevaks collected there. On enquiring, he was told that some Muslim ruffians had attacked *tehsil* Prachaarak Krishna Sharma in a village 7 kms away from Pattaambi and had been admitted in a serious condition to a local clinic. More information than this was not available yet. Guruji went in the morning at around 7-7:15 a.m. to the clinic that was 23 kms away and called out loudly to Sharma,"Sharma, Sharma", who was lying unconscious, to which there was a weak murmuring response. After returning home, Guruji said, "Sharma will not go, he will not go, he will stay with us to work." The eyes of people who heard this were moist with emotions. Incidentally, this is what happened at the end of this episode. Krishna Sharma remained active for nearly 40 years after gaining back his health.

That same evening, Guruji went to Chennai from Shonannur and then returned to Nagpur by G.T. Express on 2nd March. His birthday was on March 8. In deference to the loving request of his mother, Taiji, pious Vedic ritual of '*sampoorna mangalartham*' was conducted under the priesthood of Vedmurti Jhadgaonkar Shastri. After the concluding *poornahuti*, Guruji paid his respects to the elders present there and received their blessings. His felicitation programmes commenced from that evening. As a sacred beginning he went to Reshim Bagh, paid his respects to revered Doctorji and went to Patwardhan Ground from there. Then on, as described earlier, it was a non-stop march – *chalanam, chalanamavirata chalanam* – till 8th April.

□

Endnotes

1. *Shri Guruji Samagra*, Vol. 6, pp. 32
2. *Shri Guruji Samagra*, Vol. 9, pp. 289-290
3. *Shri Guruji Samagra*, Vol. 7, pp. 211
4. *Shri Guruji Samagra*, Vol. 9, pp. 267
5. *Shri Guruji Samagra*, Vol. 7, pp. 11

30

Saffron in Brahmadesh/Myanmar

In the last chapter, it was noted that the short biography of Guruji *Vyakti Darshan* was translated into Burmese language and the figures about the mass, contact programme (*sampark yagna*) indicated that number of people contacted in that country was 1,000 and contributions amounted to ₹ 10,000. It is possible that alert readers would have wondered what relations did Guruji share with this neighbouring country. Was there some Sangh work, what was its form? etc. It seems it would be opportune and relevant to give information about it now.

Brahmadesh (now called Myanmar) was a part of greater Bharat before 1935. The Dhir family had gone and settled there to earn its living. Ram Prakash was born there in 1927. He came to Jalandhar in 1942 for studying and became a Sangh swayamsevak. Later, he became a Prachaarak and was appointed in Punjab. During this time, Dr. Mangalsein, who was a swayamsevak from Punjab, had founded an organisation named Bharatiyaswayamsevak Sangh with a few of his friends in Rangoon in 1950. But, during this period, countless Bharatiyas had to leave Brahmadesh and come to Bharat due to political upheaval there. In that storm, Sangh activities stopped. After a lapse of five years, when the idea of Guruji's birthday celebrations was mooted, Shri Ram Prakash Dhir, who was a Burmese citizen, was sent there to re-organise the Sangh work.

Ram Prakash restarted the work based on his experience in Punjab. He began contacting eminent citizens of that country with literature, like *Personality and Works of Guruji*. One of them was president of World Fellowship of Buddhists, writer of Burmese Constitution, Chief Justice of its Supreme Court and highly respected U. Chhan Thun. As its Secretary General, the responsibility of organising the Sixth Boudh Mahasangyan on the occasion of 2500th birth anniversary of Bhagwan Buddha in May was also upon his shoulders. Ram Prakash gifted him English copies of the booklet, *Shri Guruji – The Man and His Mission* and another book about him. He was highly impressed with both the books. U. Chhan Thun expressed his wish to meet Guruji whenever an opportunity arose. Ram Prakash created a Boudh Pradarshani (exhibition on Buddha and Buddhism) for the Mahasangyan with support and co-operation of U. Chhan Thun for the international community. The objective of this exhibition was to provide historic and geographical information about Bhagwan Buddha to devotees, specially those coming from Buddhist countries for this Mahasangayan.

A very large map with 3D-relief was constructed on the ground with cement. It was marked with auspicious signs for four sacred places, Lumbini – birthplace of Buddha, Sarnath – the place of realisation and Kushasthali – place of his *mahanirvana*. Every Buddhist has abiding faith that a person who completes pilgrimage of these four sacred places will be liberated from the cycle of rebirth. The map indicated all the sites where Bhagwan Tathagat had traversed and stayed during his *Dharmachakrapravartanay* march. The map also showed the paths that the groups of missionaries (*bhikshus*) had taken after taking the *mantra* from Trisharan. Names of the *bhikshus* were also listed. Their small idols were placed in the identified spots. A commentary in Burmese or English was also given from time to time during the exhibition. Hundreds of thousands of people saw the exhibition. It created a powerful impact on everybody who visited the exhibition. Reverence for Bhagwan Buddha and place of his birth increased manifold. This historic exhibition had such an effect on U. Chhan Thun that he presided over the Makar Sankraman festival organised by Bharatiya Swayamsevak Sangh that year (January 1957) and was present on the stage. He laid stress on Buddhist-Hindu unity in this meeting that took place in the city hall of Rangoon.

U. Chhan Thun visited Bharat with his wife in 1959 to take part in the World Jurist Conference. He took part in the Mumbai Makar Sankraman festival of the Sangh according to his planned itinerary. He was also on the stage with Guruji for some time. He witnessed the formal welcome and salutation to Sarsanghchaalak by 13,000 swayamsevaks in full uniform, standing in rows in the huge tree-lined grounds of Shivaji Park and heard Guruji's speech. He may not have understood the lecture in Hindi but this wise jurist with his incisive observation and intellect would surely have understood the unity of minds between the audience and the speaker through their focused attitude. After conclusion of the programme, this celebrity couple of Burma went to Guruji's residence along with Ram Prakash. According to Maharashtra's tradition for that day, they gifted sweets made of cumin seeds and jaggery (*til-gur*) and pronounced Maharashtra's traditional greeting for this occasion, "Let our relations be as sweet and strong as this sweet." All those present burst into happy laughter. Such was the pleasant beginning of the dialogue.

During this trip, U. Chhan Thun met many worthies like jurists, lawyers, journalists, neo-Buddhist and Sangh leaders. He discussed Hindu-Buddhist relations with them. Based on these discussions and his experience here, he presented Guruji his views and plans for the future:

- Universal brotherhood and global peace can be achieved only through oriental religions

- Bharat and the Sangh should take the initiative in this direction
- Ways should be found to connect Buddhists with Sangh work
- Name of Bharatiya Swayamsevak Sangh should be changed to a more appropriate name so that the Burmese Buddhists could also get involved with the Sangh.

Guruji appreciated U. Chhan Thun's views and sentiments and assured him that he would take appropriate action after discussing these ideas with his colleagues. From Mumbai, the distinguished guests reached Nagpur after visiting Pune, Nasik, Aurangabad, etc. Eknath Ranade and Dattopant Thengadiji were present there to welcome them. Their boarding and lodging was made in a Burmese home instead of a hotel. After visiting the Central office of the Sangh, Dr. Hedgewar Bhavan, the Memorial of Dr. Hedgewar (old plinth), office of *Tarun* Bharat newspaper, etc. during the day, Thun reached the bungalow of Nagpur Sanghchaalak Babasaheb Ghatate where a meeting of *mukhya shikshaks* (chief physical trainers) of *Shakhas* had been called. Thun presented his views. The central theme of his speech was 'Equality and similarity of Hindu and Buddhist cultures and inescapable essential unity of both societies'. A few elders who had attended that meeting talked of that uncommon meeting thus, "There was gentleness, affection, sweetness in the words of the highly spiritual Buddhist brother." Then, he proceeded to Chennai and went back to his country from there. While leaving the country, he sent the following message to Nagpur, "When I had started out on the tour of Bharat, I carried an opinion that Bharat does not have the capability or strength of leading the world now that she had during the times of Emperor Ashok. But, during my journey through Bharat, I got opportunities to meet many scholars, self-sacrificing, selfless people, devoted to service of society and to hold discussions with them. Based on these experiences, now I have a firm belief that even today Bharat has the power to send out spiritual ambassadors to the world and Bharat should shoulder this responsibility." Correspondence between Guruji and Chhan Thun went on even later, till the end. He used to insist upon Guruji to visit his golden land. He made many efforts for this, but political myopia of our political leadership did not allow these efforts to succeed.

Guruji called a meeting with Ram Prakash Dhir, Madhavrao Muley and Deendayal Upadhyay in March end in 1960 at Nagpur to ponder over suggestions made by U. Chhan Thun. All agreed about the change in Sangh's name in Burma. When Guruji informed others that U. Chhan had suggested the word 'Sanaatan Dharma' in place of 'Bharatiya', everybody agreed with the idea and it was decided to change the name of Bharatiya Swayamsevak Sangh to Sanaatan Dharm Swayamsevak Sangh. Then came the subject of prayers. Guruji's suggestion was that prayer should be in Sanskrit, its form should be similar to the prayer in Bharat, but backdrop should be that of Burmese history, culture and traditions. Deendayal ji was given the responsibility of preparing such a prayer in prose form. After the content was agreed upon, Sanskrit poet Shri Shridhar Varnekar was given the responsibility of transforming it into a structured poetic form and set it to music. Thus, Sanaatan Dharm Swayamsevak Sangh also got its new prayer. Ram Prakash was of the opinion that Burmese Swayamsevaks should also imbibe the value system of the Sangh pledge. Who could not but agree with such a positive suggestion? But, preparing its content was not an easy task. Looking at the silent eyes of Ram Prakash requesting for his help, Guruji started writing the proposed pledge on paper:

"The pronouncement of Trisharan with which we greet that Supreme Being, remembering the Supreme Being and my venerated ancestors, I pledge that I have become a part of Sanaatan Dharm Swayamsevak Sangh to protect my sacred Sanaatandharma, culture and nurture the whole society, and to work for its unified all-round progress. I will perform the Sangh work with honesty, selfless mind and with my body, soul and wealth and I will fulfil this pledge throughout my life – *jayatu sarvamangalam*."

Guruji handed over the paper to Ramprakash, an inherently emotional person. Taking the paper like sacred *prasadam,* received from a temple, he started reading it carefully and began sobbing with a heart overflowing with emotions even before he could finish reading it. Thus, he returned to his land of action in due course, carrying the newfound wealth of a new name, new prayer and a new pledge. U. Chhan Thun also received detailed information immediately. He wrote a letter of thanks to Guruji with happiness. Ramprakash and other workers kept receiving guidance from Guruji from time-to-time through his letters. On 4th April, 1964, he wrote to Ramprakash on his Rangoon address, "Camp must have begun on 2nd April, 1961. You are making a fresh beginning with a new name, new prayer, etc. from this camp. This indeed is a matter of joy. May you be successful. You will surely pay attention towards keeping the memories of the original source of way of life alive in your heart even as the organisation takes on a new form. Please remember well to convey my respectful greetings to respected Shri U. Chhan Thun."[1]

It may be in response to this message that a young 25-26-year-old Buddha *bhikshu*, U. Mahendra came to Benaras to study Sanskrit language. He came to meet Guruji during his holidays as per instructions he had received from back home. He saw Guruji on Mohite Grounds during Sangh Shakha. Guruji took him home after Shakha. Other senior workers also accompanied them. Before entering home, he stopped everybody outside the home, went inside to bring a sacred pot filled with water, washed *bhikshu's* feet and welcomed him inside. He offered him milk after introducing him to his respected mother. During discussions later on, it came to Guruji's notice that he was receiving only 30 rupees grant per month from Birla Trust, which was insufficient. Guruji arranged for more funds from Halwasiya Trust of Kolkata to cover the shortfall. Study period of U. Mahendra was of three years. He became a swayamsevak of Kashi Shakha and went on to do two years of one-month-long Sangh training camps. He went on to become a scholar of Hindi and Sanskrit languages. He became a capable helping hand in translating the Sangh literature in his native language on his return to Burma.

Today, Sanaatan Dharma Swayamsevak Sangh's work is going on independently on its own strength and they have their own Prachaaraks too. The first part of their prayer is Panchasheel prayer of Buddhist religion. One of the Sangh songs is:

'Dharma Sanaatan ki santaan,
Nitya karenge isaka dhyan,
Neel gagan mein leharayenge
Bhagwa amar nishaan.'

Meaning: We, the children of Sanaatan Dharm, will always meditate upon thee; we shall wave the saffron flag in the blue skies.

□

Endnotes

1. *Shri Guruji Samagra*, Vol. 7, pp. 73

* This whole chapter is based on an interview with Shri Ram Prakash Dhir and on his written documents.

31

Actuator of a Dynamic Society

Mass contact programme on the occasion of Guruji's 51st birthday concluded with a felicitation programme on 8th April in Delhi. Swayamsevaks put in massive efforts to strengthen the organisation and make it powerful, taking advantage of the conducive atmosphere created by this programme. Sangh Shiksha Vargas that take place in May-June followed this programme. South India used to have the first of these training camps due to weather conditions. This year it was held at Vivekananda College in Chennai where students from all the four states had assembled. One of the subjects of the three lectures that Guruji delivered that year was 'Swayamsevak'. To highlight the mindset required for connecting with people, he gave an example, "One swayamsevak became a Prachaarak to work for the Sangh. He had lived in a city all his life so far. He had experienced only that life. After becoming a Prachaarak, he was assigned a region that had large rural areas. He did not like his stay there. He used to feel fed up the way rural folk spoke, lived, dressed and followed their customs. He used to feel, 'What kind of life is this?' Due to this sense of boredom, he found staying there uncomfortable. He talked to a friend of his about his state of mind. That friend told me about this Prachaarak's state of mind. I called him and told him that a Hindu can be of any type. I have to improve his lot – if you are unable to work with this sentiment, you can happily go home. What happened to that Prachaarak is a different matter, but why do such thoughts even cross our minds? If somebody has become backward or is not civil, what is his mistake in this? The problem lies with us because we did not care about the brethren of our society so far."[1]

Moving northward gradually from South, he reached Kaithal in Haryana on 10th August. On 12th, he told another story that rounded off his earlier narration, "Last year, I was touring Nagpur. Some swayamsevaks had come together at one place to meet me and asked me to have tea before leaving at the gentleman's house where my stay had been arranged for this short duration. Five to seven of our colleagues sat down in the porch, waiting for tea. Actually, the kitchen and eating arrangements were in the same room. Water for making tea was kept on a stove in one corner and tea leaves were being boiled in it. Jaggery was added after a while and milk was added finally. People sitting around were a little surprised to see that tea and jaggery had been boiling for long enough a time when they saw the gentleman struggling to find cloth to filter the tea. When he couldn't find anything, he used his *dhoti* to filter the tea and presented it to us in big glasses. My colleagues kept making faces but I drank the whole tea and took his leave.

"When discussion veered around tea that evening, I said, 'How hard would his emotions have been hurt if I had not drunk his tea?' I would never insult his affection even if drinking or eating something created problems for me. An individual is most important, he is paramount."[2]

He awakened the spirit of serving the society by presenting such personal examples in front of the student participants. Not dry education born out of only intellect, but awakening emotion –enriched values born through the heart – such was Guruji's style of working.

Political environment of 1956-57 in the country was troubled and rife with a feeling of animosity. Regionalism and linguistic fanaticism ruled the roost. Nationalist feelings had vanished. Every party was eager to fish in troubled waters on the subject of Partition of Mumbai province. Congress had hatched a plan to take advantage of Maharashtra's common man's devotion to Shivaji by unveiling a statue of Chhatrapati Shivaji at Pratapgarh at the hands of Nehru. Opposition parties decided to oppose this move in every possible way. Nehru had said many years back that Shivaji was a misguided patriot. They decided to give life to this dead story all over again as a part of strategy to halt this programme. In all this, emotions of nationalism were being crushed by both the sides. Guruji was faced with the problem about how to strengthen the nationalist emotions. Guruji prepared a statement both in Hindi and Marathi to present a correct view about unalloyed nationalism before the people. All the members of the Sangh, Jan Sangh, Vidyarthi Parishad, Mazdoor Sangh, Rashtra Sevika Samiti distributed this statement moving from house to house. They never bothered whether the media biased by the propaganda motivated by prevailing circumstances co-operated or not. Millions of copies of this statement were distributed. The statement read, "I was not just surprised, but pained to read the resolution of Samyukta Maharashtra Samiti against the forthcoming programme of unveiling of Chhatrapati Shivaji Maharaj's sculpture in Pratapgarh. This Samiti is a tie-up of many parties opposed to the Congress and have come together on populist slogans of Samyukta Maharashtra (United Maharashtra) and is full of contradictions. This Samiti does not realise that it is insulting Shivaji with its decision to demonstrate against this programme and it is also destroying the respect for this great, brave personality of Bharat."

"Congress party's political agenda behind getting Pandit Nehru to unveil this sculpture is to restrengthen the roots of the Congress that have been badly shaken because of the anti-Maharashtra feelings of the Congress High Command."

"Instead of expressing their respect for Chhatrapati Shivaji, both the sides are cooking their own political recipes. I am of a clear opinion that we should allow this programme to take place in a grand way and avoid being part of any kind of protest. This programme will establish the fact that so liberal and grand was Shivaji's character that Pandit Nehru, who used to be pleased so far in insulting Shivaji Maharaj, was forced to pay respect to his sacred life by unveiling his sculpture, as if Pandit Nehru, who is the fountainhead of this government, has accepted this great national hero to be the icon of this nation even if a little later in the day."

"I appeal to all the brothers, sisters and mothers of the nation and specially of Maharashtra that they should awaken their conscience. They should give whole-hearted support to make this programme a success so that it leaves behind an indelible mark on the people's hearts forever."[3]

The outcome of these efforts was encouraging. Brothers and sisters of Maharashtra kept their conscience awake as Guruji had appealed. The programme was held without any disturbance. It was a victory of nationalism over regionalism.

Guruji had imbibed the teachings of Dr. Hedgewar that building of individuals leads to building of the nation and reformation of society leads to reformation of the nation. Therefore, he had to provide right guidance about social equality, social equity and esteem of individuals. He had to take upon orthodoxy within Hindu society. He had to face such a situation in 1958. Swami Chinmayananda was conducting *Gita GyanYagna* in Palghat city. About 3,000 well-educated and well-established gentlemen and ladies used to attend it regularly. Guruji reached Palghat during this time in his tour. He went to Swamiji's place of residence the same day and met him. On his return, district Sanghchaalak saw that a group of four to five Brahmins was waiting there to meet Guruji. Among them was a brilliant scholar, Anantkrishna Shastri, who had published a book called *Shatabhushani* that contradicted a book *Shatadushani,* written by a Vedantic scholar, Venkatanath. After initial formalities of introductions, Shastriji spoke to Guruji in fluent Sanskrit, "Guruji, you are a religious scholar. You also know the religious protocols. Can a non-Brahmin present a critique about *Shruti* scriptures and teach them?"

Shri Guruji understood where the question was leading to. He responded with humility, "Gentleman, I am not a religious scholar, nor do I have authoritative knowledge of religious protocols. I will not even dare to say that I know Sanskrit, but, I do know a little about Sanskrit. (Scholars had smiles on their faces upon hearing this.)

"But, some doubts do rear their heads in my mind too about this subject once in a while – 'Was the visionary of great *Gayatri mantra* a Brahmin? Valmiki, who gave us *Ramayana*, was he a Brahmin? One who rendered *Gita* and the one who heard it, were they both Brahmins?' I have similar doubts about the dialogues in *Upanishads*. The problem is a little complex. So, what do I do? You are the right people to search for an answer." Naturally, this dialogue came to a halt there itself.[4] The team went back after presenting a copy of *Shatabhushani* to Guruji.

Around the same time, theists of Maharashtra had a difference of opinion. Many ritualistic people wished to sacrifice animals as a part of Vedic rituals for a *Vajpeya yagna*. This led to a chaotic situation in Maharashtra that had been a leader in social reforms.

Revered 'Gojeevan' Shri Chaunde Maharaj was highly worried. He discussed this matter with Guruji through correspondence. Guruji wrote to him, "It is the job of scholars to find the right meaning of *mantras* that appear in *Vedas*. I do not have that authority. But, whatever be the opinion of Vedic *mantras* in opposition or support of animal sacrifice, *yagyas* with such animal sacrifice have been taking place in the intervening period. Poet Jaidev says that Gautam Buddha had opposed this custom of sacrifice. Later, the entire society changed the way *yagyas* were conducted or simply stopped conducting *yagyas*. In place of this, it took in a wider meaning of *yagna* and took refuge in different ways of worship, selfless work for the others, etc. This is the generally held public opinion since many centuries. Therefore, there is no reason to believe that it is necessary or mandatory to conduct *yagna* with animal sacrifice."[5]

In Guruji's view, it was undesirable to use *Shastras* as a shield to resurrect stale systems and rituals that were outdated. He was in favour of what great poet Kalidas had said, *"Purnamityev na sadhu sarva, na chapikavyamnavamityavadyam"*. At the same time, he also did not feel that setting time-honoured and timeless values of the oldest civilisation in tune with immature value systems of the latest civilisations was scientific. Guruji's views talked of refashioning ancient value systems and not uprooting them, which was contrary to the intellectual confusion created by orthodox or progressive elements.

Guruji received a long letter from Swami Agamananda of Kalladi during this period. The letter was, in fact, an 'S.O.S.'. The Swamiji had taken a huge amount of loan from a landlord for building Shri Shankaracharya College. He failed to repay the loan as per the terms and conditions of the loan. It was a fight between a social individual and a spiritual individual who had no practical knowledge about social systems. There was a suggestion to repay the loan and hand over the college to Belur Math for running it. Efforts were also made to raise funds in Tamil Nadu and Kerala on Guruji's suggestion.. Unfortunately, they were not successful. In such a scenario, Belur Math showed its inability to run this college. Chairman Swami Madhavananda sent this news to Guruji through a telegram. Naturally, Guruji was unhappy, but he looked at this failure in an objective manner. He wrote about his heart's feelings to his dear friend and *gurubhai*, Amitabh Maharaj in a letter, "I had received a telegram from Swami Madhavananda Swami (Belur Math) about Shankar College (Kalladi). I talked to him on the phone in Chennai. People there were not successful in raising the funds. I am feeling very sad and embarrassed. I have just written a letter to Swami Madhavananda about it. Supreme Lord did not wish me to be successful this time. It is possible that the kind Lord had planned my failure to save me from the problem of getting egoistic. I believe this and saluting him with a sense of obligation, I am trying to free myself of these worries by handing all this over unto his strong hands."[6]

Still, Guruji made another effort. He wrote to honourable Shrimad Shankaracharya Swamiji of Shringeri Math immediately after getting free from the Sangh Shiksha Vargas on 20th July, 1959. Swamiji was in Ayloor village of Musiri *tehsil* of Tiruchirappalli district of Tamil Nadu at that time. That letter of Guruji was a humble submission, a request, a call of a spiritually disturbed heart of a believing Hindu. The letter read, "Kalladi has one Shri Shankar College. Swami Agamananda of Shri Ramakrishna Ashram must have presented his report about the situation there at your respected feet. It seems that Swami Agamananda would not be able to carry the onerous responsibility of the college due to its financial crisis; and his unpopularity because of these problems. Even Belur Math's chief is unable to take over from Shri Ramakrishna Ashram because of lack of funds. News is that he will be able to take up the responsibility once the loans are repaid. However, if Shri Shringeri Math were to carry out the right kind of reforms and changes in the college and create a place for study of Sanskrit, *Vedas*, Vedang, philosophy, Hindu scriptures and introduce it as a branch of regular studies in the present college, then it would not be against the traditions of Shri Shringeri Math. It could allow the present-day college to run and save the college established in the birthplace of Shrimadacharya in his name from the danger of shutting down. This is the view of many knowledgeable people and I am just presenting these views humbly at your divine feet.

"Please save the college after due consultations and give your directions for rescuing it. I feel that the current workers associated with the college would accept this order as your divine blessing. They are also well aware of thyself."[7]

When he was writing this letter to Shringeri Acharya, he was well aware of the limitations of the Math in this matter. Shringeri Math does not run any materialistic educational institutions apart from institutions for religio-philosophical subjects. This is Math's tradition. This is why Guruji wrote, "It would not be against the traditions of Shri Shringeri Math," and suggested a way out of this problem. Finally, Guruji's wish was fulfilled. Shrimad Shankaracharya saved the college after calling the people associated with this problem and holding consultations with them. Thus, a symbol of Hindu self-respect was rescued.

□

Endnotes

1. *Shri Guruji Samagra*, Vol. 4, pp. 114
2. *Smriti Parijat*, pp. 46-47
3. *Shri Guruji Samagra*, Vol. 10, pp. 254-256
4. *Shri Guruji Samagra*, Vol. 9, pp. 268-269
5. *Shri Guruji Samagra*, Vol. 7, pp. 18
6. Ibid, pp. 20
7. Central office – Collection of Correspondence, 1959 – letter – 811

32

Construction of Smriti Mandir

The period from brainstorming workshop of 1954 up to 1960, was a period of progressive growth and evolution of the Sangh work. General Secretary (*Sarkaryavaah*) Eknath Ranade provided a very strong infrastructural framework to the Sangh work after the mass-contact programme of 1956. He implemented the *mandal* system by dividing *tehsils* into *mandals* during his tours, from state to state. Similarly, he also created a structure of *vibhag* as an apex body of four to five districts. Thus, he structured the work scientifically at geographical level. A workshop, similar to the one earlier in Sindi, was organised in 1960. Keeping in mind the growth of work, it was decided to invite workers from *vibhag* to higher levels. All the expected workers, apart from a couple of exceptions, were present in this nine-day workshop from 5th to 13th March. It was held at Sukhnivas Complex in Indore in Madhya Pradesh. There was also a beautiful clean lake with a huge garden adjacent to the complex. Guruji, Bhaiyyaji Dani and Babasaheb Apte's staying arrangements were made in a small bungalow next to this lake. All others stayed in the buildings around it or in tents. The place of intellectual discussions was under an eye-pleasing porch of a garden covered from all sides with tall green trees. The stage for intellectual discourses was set under a huge banyan tree, standing tall like Sage Ved Vyas. Arrangements for the workshop were with Shri Kushabhau Thakrey. Moropant Pingley was the chief physical instructor (*mukhya shikshak*). The responsibility of intellectual department was given to Deendayal Upadhyay and Bapurao Moghe. This workshop of Indore was made with the view to make it come up with a specific plan. It was a workshop about self-introspection, self-study, intellectual exchange and discussions under Guruji's guidance.

Guruji would present his views about a pre-decided topic everyday. Then, there would be a question-answer session and in-depth discussions. This was an arrangement in which both the speaker and the audience had a share.

Topic of the first day was, 'Our Responsibilities in the Present Scenario'. Summary of the lecture and discussions on this were as follows: "This Hindusthan is our nation. We have to organise our land and our society.

Independence or slavery was not only about British leaving or not leaving this country. Establishing our life in tune with our nature and our dignity – this is true independence. We talk about this freedom in our pledge. We need to live a purposeful, action-oriented life to bring this about in reality. To lead such a life is Sangh's work. It is our responsibility not to let it weaken. If necessary, we can jump high even to touch the skies, but when order of *daksha* (attention) is given, we shall only stand in *daksha*. This is what people expect from us today."

Subject on the second day was Shakha. Shakha is not just a get together of friends. More people should join it in a sustained manner. They should imbibe the *samskaaras* of self-sacrifice for the nation. Such should be the atmosphere there. Speaking incisively on the subject, he said, "In earlier times, a system, *upaasana* (regular worship) had been created for strengthening '*samskaaras*'. Similarly, to make these *samskaaras* pure, strong and pervasive throughout the society, this methodology of daily Shakha has been evolved. With self-introspection, having firm faith in this system, taking everybody along, try to expand this work properly, not with verbose sermons but with personal guidance, then our work shall grow."

Discipline (*anushaasan*), a word that seems to be easy and a common word, was the topic on the third day. Listening to Guruji's calm, in-depth and serious analysis, workers realised how deep and meaningful this word was. Guruji began the subject from the periphery. He said, "There are two aspects of discipline – anushaasan; one, following an order literally – word by word; second carrying the responsibility of a work together. We witness both in the Shakha. But, this is not the end of discipline. Discipline is a *samskaara* of our heart. It develops a capacity to carry out large responsibilities that come from doing small jobs properly. Managing our wisdom, developing focused intellect – this is discipline." Quoting '*Etat anushaasan*' from *Taittareeya Upanishad,* he said, "In our culture, both individual freedom and systematic living that finally merges into the universe are conceptualised in this. Only a person who can balance the two can work for the organisation over a long period of time and achieve success."

On other days he took up subjects like the unique features of our nation, pledge of the Sangh, inner and outer life of swayamsevak and Sangh work is God's work. He gave directions to workers involved in different social fields to evaluate their work and their own working. "Scriptures have talked of two types of work – one regular and the other occasional. If somebody says that he can perform occasional work like *yagna*, *Satya Narayanpooja*, etc. and there is no need to do regular work, then this thinking is harmful. Even if one performs occasional action, he will have to perform regular worship too. Only then can one take up occasional activities. Occasional activities performed while giving a go by to regular worship will not only be useless, but also prove to be harmful."[1]

Concluding the workshop, this seer appealed, "Let us resolve now that there is no time for running businesses or industries, etc. at this juncture. There is no pause for enjoyment or grief in life. We will think of accumulating wealth some other time. Do not be under the impression that there is no place for wealth or pleasure in our culture. All our gods are wealthy. Even Lord Shankar, who hardly wears anything, sits atop Himalayas that is home to all kinds of precious stones. But, because of the times we face, we have to keep ourselves away from these things. We need not be afraid of opposing forces that are trying to create problems for our nation. I have said so many a time that all such ideologies all over the world face their graves in Bharat. The Sangh, like the incarnation of God, has taken birth to finish off *adharma*. This is my belief, my conviction... As organs of this divine force, we have to take a firm pledge to complete this work in our field of action while taking care of its sanctity, purity, strength, fortitude, meditative powers, etc. While working in our respective areas of work, we must think that it is written in our fate to destroy the danger lurking ahead of us. We alone have to humanise the entire world. This is the message of the Supreme Being and this is his command for us."[2]

The valedictory programme of the workshop fell on the festival day of Holi. Festivities began in right earnest when state Sanghchaalak Pandit Ramnarayan Shastri sprayed coloured powder (*gulaal*) on Guruji's *kurta* followed with *gulaal* joyously being sprinkled all over by all the participants. With this ran the feeling of brotherhood, happiness, joy and enthusiasm. This was a practical and right kind of valedictory programme for an organisation built on the sentiments of a large family.

It is said that human life is full of expected and unexpected events. An unexpected event also took place in Guruji's life in the form of a wish. The head of Govardhan Peeth of Jagannathpuri, Shrimad Bharati Krishnateerth left for his heavenly abode before he could ordain his successor. However, he had left behind a list of possible successors in a document. It also had the name of Madhav Sadashiv Golwalkar. He had handed over the responsibility of setting up a proper system to the head of Dwarkadheesh Peeth. Guruji received this information. He had to go to Sangh Shiksha Vargas that used to take place from May beginning. Therefore, without wasting time, he wrote to Dwarkapeeth head who was in Mumbai during the time. The letter was in Sanskrit. Its meaning was "I saw my name too in the list of possible successors published as the last wish of divine, highly-revered Shri Bharatikrishna Teerth. I have never felt any urge to occupy that seat, nor is there any urge even now. I lack critical qualities of scholarship, asceticism, penance, etc. required to occupy the high seat of Jagadguru. Only a rare great person with such highest qualities can occupy the seat of revered Jagadguru Peeth."[3]

Guruji did send the letter but he did not keep quiet with this. Inspite of his forthrightness, one could not rule out the possibility of pressure being exerted on him. Therefore, he took the initiative to meet the head of Dwarkapeeth in

Gujarat and urged him, "Honoured divine sir, before giving your directive please listen to my side too. Please save me from the sin of disobeying your order." Respected Acharya listened to him carefully. "I have dedicated my life for the Sangh work. I am tied down with the pledge I made to Doctor Hedgewar accordingly. Thy divine self is also aware about this. Thy divine self also knows of the importance of this work. So, please excuse me. Please give your blessing to me for continuing this very work." Respected Acharya acquiesced to his request. Later, he gave him the responsibility of talking to the principal, Shri Chandrashekhar Shastri of Jaipur Sanskrit College about this matter. Guruji knew him as well. Guruji called the Rajasthan state Prachaarak Brahmadevji from there itself and asked him to arrange for a meeting with the principal. Guruji went to Jaipur and met the principal at Dr. Harikrishna Javaay's home and had a dialogue with him for nearly one hour. Guruji told the principal, "I have come here with only one-point agenda. It is a matter of great pleasure that Dwarka Peethadheesh Jagadguru Shankaracharya has nominated you to be the Shankaracharya of Govardhan Peeth at Jagannathpuri. Your brilliant scholarly knowledge, sharp intellect, great spotless character are beyond compare. I have only a small request – in my humble opinion, you need to undergo the exercise of some more meditation. If you could go to the Himalayas or some other place for two to two-and-a-half months, it would be wonderful." Thus, this problem was resolved to the satisfaction of all.[4]

Another golden opportunity arose during this time to meet another great saint. Dattopant Thengadiji has given detailed account about it in his Hindi book *Dr. Ambedkar aur Samaajik Kranti* (Dr. Ambedkar and Social Revolution). It would be ideal to quote it verbatim:

"This incident took place around 1960-61. Shri Guruji had gone to meet Swami Karapatriji at his residence near Nigambodh Ghat in Delhi. Shri Guruji had a very high regard for scholarship and meditation of Swamiji. He was the president of Ram Rajya Parishad at that time. He was a strong supporter of *chaturvarna* (basic fourfold jati system). During discussions, he asked Guruji, 'How many Shakhas do you have? How many swayamsevaks do you have?' On getting the desired information, he said, 'Golwalkar ji, do one thing. You have so many swayamsevaks all over the country, ask them to work according to their *varna* (caste). They will listen to you.' Guruji said, 'I am chief of the Sangh, but all these people are not my disciples. They are my brothers. I don't give them orders. Still, since you are directing me, I will ask them. If they like it, they will surely follow this idea. But, there is total disorder in our society today. Therefore, if they were to be shown an example, then we can tell them that this is the type of society that we wish to build. You can do this job very well since you have thousands of disciples. You are their Guru. They should surely listen to you. You ask your disciples that they should set an example by working according to their *varna* (caste). I will see what I can do.' Hearing this,

Swamiji was upset and said, 'You are trying to push things on me. If you do not wish to do this, tell me frankly'. Guruji said, 'Please don't be displeased. Please tell me what is left of *varnashram*? Is there anything left of the caste system? It is waste of energy to try to resurrect this highly decayed system. Time has come to demolish all this completely and create a new *varna*. Only that will lead to creation and development of a new social order and that would be apt too. This is what the Sangh is doing. It is the Sangh's view that everyone should be brought together on the eternal foundation of society and nation to build an orderly society. There should be no other differences.'

"It is difficult to fathom whether Karapatri ji agreed with this thinking or not, Guruji did try to explain his views on this matter."[5]

Actually, Guruji had inherited the essence of social equity and harmony, and *samskaar* (imbibing right value systems) from Swami Akhandananda and Dr. Hedgewar respectively. This became the lode star for him throughout his life and his life's work.

The Central Committee had decided to build Dr. Hedgewar Smriti Mandir at Reshim Bagh, Nagpur, immediately after conclusion the of 51st birthday celebrations of Guruji. At that time, there was only a simple platform at that place. To implement this decision, Dr. Hedgewar Smarak Samiti had been constituted and registered in 1957. Guruji was chairman of this Samiti. Funds required to build the memorial could have been collected easily from Nagpur and Vidarbha alone, but, to enable swayamsevaks to contribute to this effort, fund collection was made a nationwide programme. 'One swayamsevak – One Rupee' – this is how the fund was to be raised. For this purpose, a picture of the proposed memorial was printed. Prior to this, Guruji also released a statement regarding this programme on 21st October, 1959.[6]

The fund-raising programme was completed. Construction work also began in 1959. Architectural drawings showed the decorative arches in Moghul architectural style. Guruji asked it to be changed to the shape of bows, and the designer agreed to it. It was decided to inaugurate the memorial on 5th April, 1962, on *Varsh Pratipada* (Hindu new year) day. It also happened to be the birthday of Sangh founder. Everything related to it was, thus, completed before this date. It was as if Smriti Mandir came up on its own, in keeping with the heartfelt wishes of countless swayamsevaks.

Guruji and other senior leaders felt strongly that the memorial should be inaugurated from the sacred hands of Paramacharya Jagadguru Shankaracharya of Kanchi Kamakoti. However, it was not possible for this monk, who had pledged to move on feet throughout his life, to reach Nagpur in a short time. Therefore, upon receiving Guruji's ardent request, he had replied, "Not physically, but we shall be there in spirit." Reminding him of this promise, Guruji wrote to him and requested him to "send your blessings in the form of your words and oblige us". He sent his blessings as promised. Along with this, he also sent '*vibhooti-kumkum-mantraakshat*' (sacred ashes, vermillion and blessed rice). Guruji personally read out the words of blessings sent by Kanchi Kamakoti in Sanskrit at the massive meeting that evening. Nearly everybody could understand it. The last sentence of this letter was, "May this Smriti Mandir (memorial temple) inspire all Bharatiyas to remember Shri Hedgewar's loyalty to own *dharma*, his self-sacrificing life dedicated to development of this country, and move on that same path."[7]

Inauguration of Dr. Hedgewar Smriti Mandir had a far-reaching impact. The programme that day was proof of this. Dr. Hedgewar's idea of the Sangh being a family was right. Thousands of guests and district-level Prachaaraks had converged on Nagpur from all over the country. Nearly 2,000 families took the guests to their homes in a systematic pre-planned manner. It was the festive day of *Varsh Pratipada*, an ideal day for entertaining the guests. Both the guest and host were unknown to each other. So, guests were asked about their native places, but not about their castes. Enquiries were made about their professions and businesses, but not about their incomes. The goddess of the home had a guest whom she fed with affection, a guest who took food as if it were nectar. Both hosts and guests came to Reshim Bagh together in the evening.

'Uchch neech lavalesh nahin, chhua chhoot avashesh nahin,
Ek lahoo sabaki nas nas mein, apane pan kee reet gahi.'

Sentences of this Sangh song could be seen in practice (Meaning: There is no feeling of high or low, no sign of untouchability; same blood flows through the veins of all. There is a feeling of brotherhood.) As a silent witness to these feelings stood the full-size statue of Dr. Hedgewar inside the Smriti Mandir. In front of this statue was not just 'a miniature form of the nation' but it was a grand view of the 'Ocean meeting the mighty Himalayas'. At the end of his speech, Guruji said, "There is not an iota of doubt that this Smriti Mandir will become an eternal source of inspiration that will empower us to get rid of all threats to the nation and build an everlasting, very happy, prosperous, honoured and paramount national life."[8]

However, next morning on 6th April, Guruji's guidance during the get-together of swayamsevaks was of a different kind. This address was directed towards courageous, dedicated hard-working swayamsevaks. Clarifying the subject of 'We and the Smriti Mandir', he said, "This Smriti Mandir has not been built with the idea that we should become high priests of a place of worship. I have no taste for mud and brick structures. Even then I want this Smriti Mandir because this is a highly sacred place. This is the land the founder of the Sangh walked on, the place where he shed his sweat and blood to expand this work and finally gave up his physical body to rest in eternal peace – we have to look upon this Smriti Mandir with such a deep reverence that this sacred place should provide us inspiration to make our lives like his."[9]

Upon conclusion of this programme without any hurdle in a pleasant atmosphere, Guruji sent his acknowledgement letters to the well-wishers in the same week.

While various religious rituals and *yagyas* were taking place on the pious occasion of *Varsh Pratipada* at Reshim Bagh, Guruji's mother, Taiji, expressed her wish, "I too wish to see the Smriti Mandir." Her body had been in a very poor condition for many days. So, Dr. Abaji Thatte arranged for her visit to Reshim Bagh in the morning to avoid crowds in the evening. Taiji was very happy to get the divine look of Smriti Mandir. Her health began to deteriorate after a week. Guruji's heart was quite upset those days. One can experience it through various letters of his during that time, "I could not get have the last view of my father's dead body. Will I face a similar misfortune this time too? How practical is it to abandon pre-planned programmes and wait for the God of death? On the other hand, is not the only son's touch itself healing for the mother? After all, am I not in debt of my mother and father?" This chain of thoughts kept grief of Madhu under control. Once in a while, he would go somewhere and come back after seeking mother's permission. At that time, his condition in words of Kalidas was, "Body walked ahead, but heart raced backwards." During this period, he would open his heart and express his sentiments to his colleagues without discriminating between old or young. But, what else could the poor soul do? All he could do was to hear about his mother and pray silently to God. Finally, with grace of God, he could visit all the training camps that year and return back. He kept himself free from any programmes, stayed in Nagpur and was by his mother's sick-bed.

One day, mother expressed her wish to see her Guru. Son Madhu went on foot immediately to Vedantkesari Babaji Maharaj Pandit's house that was situated on Pataleshwar Road and told him about his mother's wish. He too came walking to his disciple's home immediately. The disciple felt fulfilled after looking at his sacred face and getting his blessings. She tried to touch his feet even as she could not get up from her sick-bed.

Taiji used to offer daily worship. Only after making a small sacred symbol made of a mix of garden soil and cow dung and offering her worship to it would she take her food. Even in her weakened health, she would insist on carrying out her practice. Guruji took help of Shri Bachcharaj Vyas in this regard as he too was a member of the same sect. He would come home, complete the rituals of worship and offer food to Taiji after this. Her condition worsened further and she could not speak, nor could she take food. Her son took both her hands in his hands and told his mother, "Stop worrying, forget everything, recite only '*Shri Krishna Govind Hare Murare*'." He got to hear a weak '*hoom*' in response. Her lips started moving. Son too began the same recitation in a low voice. This pious blessed lady's journey of this material world ended the same night in *brahmamahurta* (pious early morning time), that is early morning of 11th August.[10]

After performing his mother's last rites Guruji made Dr. Hedgewar Bhavan as his centre of daily activities. He stopped visiting his house in Nagoba Lane like he used to do earlier. Over time, even relatives left that house. As time passed by, the demon of town planning swallowed that house too. As a result, 'Guruji's house in Nagoba Lane' just became a sign post. Destiny had, perhaps, understood his wish in the last Will he had written, that there should be no memorial in his name.

Countless letters of condolences arrived in Dr. Hedgewar Bhavan. All the letters were replied. One can understand the agony of Guruji's heart while reading those letters. For example, he writes to Pandit Parameshwaraanand of Kapurthala, "It is true that I feel a sense of loneliness in life. Someone who had totally given up all natural wishes of a mother's heart so that my path would be without hurdles, this vacuum is being felt because I am missing that soul. There is only one way of curing that pain, that is to put all the strength in my life to complete that work for which she had let go off all her desires, so that this heart would not have any time to think about anything else."[11]

Of all the messages of condolences, the most enlightening, elevating and extraordinary was the one sent by Kamakoti Paramacharya. Actually, it was not a condolence but a solution to grief. That angelic saint had sent three *shlokas* of *Anushtup* Chhand.*

Their meaning is, "Our mother is Bharatmata. Even as the mother who gave birth has left this planet, this mother is always close to us to offer her boundless affection and indulgence. One who is only devoted to her, loves her and loses oneself while offering service to her experiences this divine feeling – that this mother, full of undying affection, is standing there with her blessed hand to give her support. This is totally true in your case."[12]

This letter was like *Sanjeevani* – life-giving plant – for Guruji. With tearing away of that thin thread that had bound him with this world, he got totally absorbed in the service of motherland.

□

Endnotes

1. *Shri Guruji Samagra*, Vol. 2, pp. 240
2. Ibid, pp. 275, 279

* *Shloka:*

Matrimaanitshrutyuktmaatrishikshabalaadih|
Rashtraswayamsevakasya dhruvam Bharatmataram ||
Matrivat sevamaanam syasvamaatriviraho na te
jananeejanmabhoomashyoshcha na hi gopaal te bhidaa|
Mahaatripurasundaryaah chandramaulishwarasya cha karunaa
tway inityaast umaatrideve shubhaashraye ||

3. *Shri Guruji Samagra*, Vol. 7, pp. 21
4. *Jeevan Prasang*, Vol. 1, pp. 241-242
5. *Dr. Ambedkar aur Samaajik Kranti ki Yatra*, pp. 256-257
6. *Shri Guruji Samagra*, Vol. 10, pp. 260-261
7. *Shri Guruji Samagra*, Vol. 7, pp. 29
8. *Shri Guruji Samagra*, Vol. 1, pp. 40
9. Ibid, pp. 44
10. *Shri Guruji Samagra*, Vol. 6, pp. 252
11. Ibid, pp. 253
12. *Shri Guruji Samagra*, Vol. 8, pp. 344

33

Kushtha Nivaarak Sangh & Vanvasi Kalyan Ashram

Guruji got an opportunity of visiting a deprived region during the subsequent period. There is a purpose behind calling it an 'opportunity or coincidence' or *sanyog*. A person involved in working for the good of society unselfishly may not be able to work in a calculated manner by taking into account all possible aspects. He also faces the same uncertainty that a normal human being faces. His path will also be crossed by unexpected problems and challenges. How he overcomes them successfully is the measure of the strength of his personality. Supreme Lord Shri Krishna has called this *Yogah karmasu kaushalam*.

Bharatiya Kushtha Nivaarak Sangh was registered at Champa in Madhya Pradesh on 5th May, 1962. Leading this organisation was a team comprising a lawyer from Bilaspur, Jamunaprasad Verma as its president, Sadashiv Govind Katre as its general secretary and six other members. There were eight members in all. This organisation has born out of a whirlpool of emotions created due to a social under-current of revulsion, insult, scorn, non-acceptance, neglect, life ignored by society and indefatigable urge to live, unyielding capacity for struggle, deep faith in society, and readiness to surrender self for the good of others. There was a good deal of support from respected Guruji in helping this idea evolve. To grasp its significance, we shall have to go back a little in time.

Sadashiv Govind Katre was a railway employee. He carried the responsibility of marrying his three sisters off to cultured families. He had two children. Of these, the boy died in childhood. He was left with his only daughter, Prabhavati. Unfortunately, his wife died of severe leprosy. Jealous neighbours alleged that it was not a natural death but a murder. Katre had to face prosecution and he was sent to prison. Misfortune assaulted unfortunate Katre further and poor Katre too caught leprosy. When he came out of prison, he saw that his daughter had reached marriageable age. She was lucky. She got married to Madhukar Sarvate in Gwalior just as she passed out of standard tenth. Katre was left to live his life cocooned in the Christian Leprosy Centre of Bilaspur. He told Dr. Esic one day, "Doctor Saheb, you offer best services. My thanks to you. But, you use this as an excuse for conversion, which is not right." Doctor said frankly, "Mr Katre, even I am not in favour of conversions, but how can I stop missionary priests?" Katre did not give up and he complained to the Governor, Haribhau Paataskar. Governor advised him, "What you say is right, but can you see that they are coming all the way from across oceans to work here? You should also do your duty." But, Katre did not retreat. He carried out protests in Bilaspur two to three times, but since it was a matter related to leprosy victims, people simply ignored it. Guruji visited Bilaspur during this time. Katre met Guruji and complained to him about the matter. Guruji also gave the same advice as given by Governor. In fact, he went a step further and said, "Such protests are meaningless. They will only result in discord. A person, whose heart is agonised, will have to get involved in this kind of work. You are a swayamsevak who has been a victim of this disease. Why don't you think that God may have planned to make you work for this neglected field?" Thus, Katre got his direction. He founded Kushtha Nivaarak Sangh with the help of state Prachaarak Yadavrao Kelkar. Based on written instructions sent by Guruji, the Sangh brethren helped him in every possible way. Guruji converted a challenge into an enduring service project through Katre, transforming a soldier into a social servant.

Guruji had a special attachment to Katre's work till his last days. He arranged help from time to time through his contacts. The following episode took place two-and-a-half years later. The King of Nepal was to arrive for Makar Sankraman celebrations of the Sangh in 1965. On receiving information, Shri Jugal Kishore Birla had sent 1,000 rupees on behalf of Akhil Bharat Arya Hindu Dharma Seva Sangh. The King's programme was cancelled due to political cussedness. He could not come for the programme. In this background, Guruji wrote to Birla, "It has been brought to our notice that the King of Nepal's tour has been abandoned. We still do not know the reasons for this. The programme, for which the funds were received, will not take place now. Therefore, it is necessary to receive your instructions about where to use this amount. I do not find it proper to spend it anywhere without your directive."

"I have a humble suggestion. Bilaspur district in Madhya Pradesh is widely affected by leprosy. Only Christian missionaries are putting in efforts for medical care.But for them it is a powerful tool for spread of Christianity. Therefore, some friends have established an organisation named 'Bharatiya Kushtha Nivaarak Sangh at Champa to cure and serve people affected by leprosy. They have a huge shortage of funds for primary medicines of regular use. Still some friends move enthusiastically from village to-village to provide medical aid selflessly. If you permit and Akhil Bharatiya Arya Hindu Dharma Seva Sangh gives its assent, I will make arrangements to send this amount to Bharatiya Kushtha Nivaarak Sangh at Champa. Please arrange to send permission letter at the earliest."[1] Needless to say that the letter came and the funds reached Champa.

Actually, Sadashiv Katre was not a committed or missionary social worker like Thakker Bappa or Father Damien. He was a simple railway employee and an ordinary swayamsevak. Guruji gifted him the vision or *divyam dadaami te chakshuh*. Katre became 'Baba' for the village-folk. Once again, the saying that 'no person is useless in the eyes of an able organiser' was literally illustrated. Guruji was providing sick people a social vision using Katre as the medium. And today, swayamsevaks of Uttaranchal, Karnataka, Maharashtra and Punjab are working in this neglected field with compassion. Saints and good people are supporting them in this endeavour.

Vanvasi Kalyan Ashram's story is also quite similar. The objective of both was welfare of the society. The battlefield of both was Madhya Pradesh. Inspiration behind both was to stop conversions activities of Christian missionaries. Central characters of both the organisations were from Madhya Pradesh. Both were swayamsevaks. Both were born in the same decade. Both had received guidance from Shri Guruji Golwalkar who had spent his childhood there. Only difference was that Kushtha Nivaarak Sangh was an association like an institution while Vanvasi Kalyan Ashram was a full-fledged organisation.

Pandit Ravi Shankar Shukla was the Chief Minister of Madhya Pradesh in the first decade after Independence. When he went to Jashpur region in his new persona, he experienced black flag protests from the local tribals and slogans like 'Shukla go back', 'Jharkhand *Zindabad*'. For Shukla ji, who had led a spotless life so far, it was a big blow. Foreign missionaries were behind these protests. Education and social welfare departments were under his ministry. Government servants were also under his command. At that time, Father Vernier had written to the Bishop of Kolkata, "The ministers are always coming but never arriving."

Chief Minister decided to alter this serious scenario. Ramakant Keshav (Balasaheb) Deshpande, who had fought the British fiercely during the Independence struggle, was appointed the regional officer. Observing his capability, honesty, dedication, courage, strong will power and grip over administration, missionaries took him as their biggest enemy. Using their clout with bureaucracy, they began harassing Ramakant. He became a victim of baseless accusations and senseless transfers. Balasaheb Deshpande came to the capital city Nagpur once for some official work. Incidentally, Guruji was in Nagpur at that time. Ramakant met Guruji and apprised him about dishonest bureaucracy and cunning missionaries. Guruji expressed his opinion, "If you think that you can serve the society by being a government servant, you will never get rid of this problem. You are a lawyer by training. Why don't you remove this weight of government off your shoulders? You can work as a lawyer without any help from anybody. You will get sufficient time for this work and it will also give you respect and power in the society. 'One's own hand is hand of God' (*apna hath Jagannath*)." Saying so, Guruji added, "I remember clearly that I had met you in Dhantoli Shakha in 1938." This one sentence stuck up a relationship and also provided guidance. Balasaheb threw away the government job like a rotten fish. He began his law practice in Jashpur in 1951. In 1952, Guruji sent a 37-year, old Prachaarak of Khandwa region, Moreshwar Ketkar, to assist him. Both of them strengthened and took forward the work like the brother duo, Ram-Laxman. Maharaja of Jashpur, Shri Vijay Bhushan Singh Judeo was their strong pillar of strength. The confluence of this triumvirate resulted in the birth of Vanvasi Kalyan Ashram, joined in by nine more local people in 26th December, 1952.

Around the same time, Pandit Jawaharlal Nehru and Babu Rajendra Prasad had a similar experience in northeastern hill areas that Pandit Ravi Shankar Shukla had earlier in Madhya Pradesh. There too, foreign missionaries like Fizo, Michael Scott were behind tribal protests. Noticing all these facts, the Madhya Pradesh government appointed a Commission in 1954 under Justice Bhawani Shankar Niyogi, called the Christian Missionary Enquiry Commission. Two other members were Ghanshyam Singh and S.K. George. Guruji welcomed this initiative of the government. He was also aware of his own responsibility. He knew well that though the case legally justified if it was not presented properly to the Commission, it would be lost. He was also aware that lack of interest in disorganised Hindu society, and the silence of illiterate, unaware tribal brethren would be a hurdle in presenting true facts in front of the Commission. For this purpose he sent an intelligent, hardworking Prachaarak to help Balasaheb Deshpande. He was 23-year-old Krishnarao Damodar Sapre. Arrival of Sapre was a great help to the Hindu cause. He presented many anti-national documents of the missionaries to the Commission with a lot of efforts and skill. Finally, the report, very important from the point of view of national security and unity, was presented in 1956 to the government. This document about dastardly activities of missionaries, who worked like aunt Pootana who fed poison in the name of milk to Lord Krishna must be read by patriotic individuals who wish to serve the society. Chairman of the Commission, Justice Niyogi, later, specially thanked Shri Krishnarao Sapre for his work. Later on, Guruji used to call Sapre, 'Reverend Sapre' jokingly.

Two years after this, in 1958, the Bharatiya government set up a Commission under the chairmanship of Dhebarbhai. The purpose of this Commission was to formulate policies for the development of tribal people spread across the country in hilly and forest areas. Dhebarbhai came to Jashpur with other members of the team and saw Kalyan Ashram's work with his own eyes. He also talked at length with Balasaheb. Later, a letter and a telegram were received by them informing them that it had been decided to provide government grant for Kalyan Ashram School. Balasaheb went to Bhopal to receive the grant with the required documents. When he met the concerned officers, he came to know that the grant had been rejected due to interference of the Education Department. Balasaheb was a born fighter. He met the Education Minister. Upon enquiry, the minister tried to close the matter with some pre-emptory answers, but Balasaheb was a lawyer and a former government servant too. He demanded a clear answer. The minister blurted out, "You are Jan Sangh people." Some Jan Sangh people had burnt his effigy to protest against some political matter. The minister was angry with that action! Balasaheb had no clue about it. There is a saying in Malayalam, "Outpouring one's anger on mother on being beaten up in the market." The minister was in that state of mind, but Balasaheb was not to be cowed down. He responded in a hard-hitting way and taunted, "I am not a beggar who has come wearing a white cap instead of a black cap," and walked out. The Education Minister was left gaping. The gentleman was Pandit Shankar Dayal Sharma who went on to become the President of our country later.

But, did Balasaheb return empty-handed to Jashpur from Bhopal? No. While returning from Bhopal, he got down at Nagpur and met Guruji in the Sangh office. Hearing about the aborted matter of grant, Guruji laughed heartily, raising his hand and said, "It is very good, it is really good. We should be self-reliant in our work, whether it is a matter of workers or resources. We should stand on our own feet. We will have to do all the work with people's co-operation. Any work that runs with the help of government's support and grant becomes dependent on government and gets ruined if it is not received."[2]

For Balasaheb, Guruji's words were not just words of consolation, but of guidance. This was the invaluable grant he received from Dr. Hedgewar Bhavan – a grant that could never be rejected by anybody. A grant that would always be received in full even after one distributed it!

There is an episode in this story of penance that took place 20 years later on 19th October, 1977, when Prime Minister of Bharat, Shri Morarji bhai Desai came to Jashpur and stayed for 20 minutes in Kalyan Ashram. Balasaheb met the Prime Minister four months later in February 1978 in his office. Prime Minister asked him, "How can I help you? What is the policy of Kalyan Ashram about government grant?" Balasaheb responded, "Policy of Kalyan Ashram is not to accept any government grant. When you visited Kalyan Ashram, I could not express my gratitude to you due to my busy schedule. Therefore, when I came to Delhi this time for some work, I thought I should meet you personally to express my gratitude." Morarji bhai expressed his pleasure and said, "Your policy is highly admirable." He told Shri Kantbhai of Aadim Jati Sevak Sangh, who was sitting there, "Look Shrikant, you were asking the secret behind the success of Kalyan Ashram. This is the secret; it is completely self-reliant."[3]

'Self-reliance' – this is the very word Balasaheb had heard from revered Guruji and today the Prime Minister of the country was repeating the same words.

The new building of Kalyan Ashram was to be inaugurated in 1963 by Guruji Madhavrao Golwalkar on 2nd April, Thursday, the pious day of Shri Ram Navami – birthday of Lord Ram. The atmosphere in the Ashram was alight with enthusiasm a day ahead of the programme. Students of the Ashram recited *Ramayana* non-stop (*akhand*) for 24 hours. Noble souls like Rambhikshuk Maharaj and Sant Gahira Guru who came that day were very happy. Inaugurating the building and stressing the necessity of Kalyan Ashram's work, Guruji said, "Since our tribal brethren stay in distant mountains and forests, they are cut off from the rest of Hindu society. Their livesface scarcity of every kind. They live in penury. They have no facilities in education and health care. They live a life of severe hardships and hunger. Still they are innocent, straightforward and simple-hearted. We too have neglected our brethren. Taking advantage of this, foreign missionaries run schools, hostels and medical centres and in the guise of service make them anti-national and rebels by converting them and put our country in danger."

"The tribal people do not wish to give up the belief system inherited from their ancestors ininspitespite of living in utter poverty. Because of their uncorrupted character their hearts are pure. God lives in these pure hearts. It is as if they were a living image of Lord Shiva. Therefore, we shall have to come forward with our full energy without further delay to serve them with the highest form of devotion. It is with this objective that our work in Kalyan Ashram is being carried out. We expect co-operation from everybody in this. Some primary needs have been fulfilled with construction of this Kalyan Ashram building. Actual work will need to be done now. My prayer at the divine feet of Supreme Lord is that we can move ahead with devotion for this work on the sacred festival of Ram Navami."[4]

The objective the building was constructed for was very successful. Krishnarao Sapre has written about it, "So far, Hindu tribals had been feeling helpless for the last the 50-60 years in Jashpur area, suffering from Christian dominance and atrocities. But, success of this programme generated self-confidence in the Hindu tribals and they began feeling that times had changed and they could move ahead in every possible way on the path of development and progress."

On the wishes of Guruji, a small Ayurveda clinic was opened in Jashpur in 1964. Guruji sent Narayan Puranik to run it. One day, Guruji arrived in Jashpur without prior information. The most respected Ayurveda practitioner Pandit Ramnarayan Shastriji was accompanying him. He was also Sanghchaalak of Madhya Pradesh state. In the informal atmosphere after lunch-time, Guruji announced, "The clinic will be officially inaugurated tomorrow morning from the hands of Pandit Ramnarayan Shastriji." That is how it happened next day. No lectures, no photographs, no welcome, no thanks-giving. The only people present there were the king of Ayurveda, Shastriji, patients, their friends and Guruji with workers' team of Ashram."[5]

Guidance received by Sadashiv Katre regarding Kushtha Nivaarak Sangh and by Balasaheb Deshpande regarding the Kalyan Ashram was in line with the guidance received by Guruji from Swami Akhandananda and Dr. Hedgewar about their philosophy of life. Both *karmayogins* believed that family of birth is gift of God, but ability to put in effort is one's own. With this thought, Guruji told both swayamsevaks to work on the basis of one's own efforts, telling them that victory would be assured. Both Katre and Deshpande had similar experiences and based on their hard work, the two towering trees on the path of human service came up in the form of Kushtha Nivaarak Sangh and Vanvasi Kalyan Ashram. □

Endnotes

1. *Shri Guruji Samagra*, Vol. 7, pp. 251
2. *Shri Balasaheb Deshpande*, pp. 45
3. Ibid, 69-70
4. Ibid, pp. 51-52
5. Ibid, pp. 53

34

Aggressive China and Affectionate Nepal

It has been said that eternal vigilance is the price of Freedom. This is true about Freedom, but when we talk of a nation, we shall have to say that life force of a nation is fiery dedication. The system of absorbing this eternal truth in daily life is called daily Shakha of the Sangh. For this reason, each moment of Sarsanghchaalak, who has immersed in this duty in his life each and everyday, is critical. However, circumstances change sometimes and there are ups and downs. There are new demands and expectations of the prevailing times. At such moments, one is forced to pay attention to those situations and be ready for them immediately. Four to five years from 1962 were of this nature.

On 20th October, 1962, the national leadership openly accepted that Bharat had been attacked by Communist China. During that time Guruji had been on a tour of Rajasthan for 10 days from 10th to 23rd October. On 16th, there was a programme in Chittor. Guruji said in clear words at a public meeting that evening, "I have definite information that China is going to attack Bharat. Our country's leaders are shouting slogans of 'Hindi-Chini *bhai bhai*' and welcoming Chinese Prime Minister at Red Fort in Delhi. But China will attack us." He was in Alwar after two days on 18th. Guruji repeated this statement there too. There was a strong reaction in newspapers to these statements. Progressive columnists commented, "What kind of irresponsible leader is he?" One columnist declared, "Golwalkar's statement is nothing but his imagination runs wild." However, when All India Radio announced this imagination as actual news, everybody was astonished. Now, newspapers had a new question, "How did Golwalkar get this information?" Simple citizens wondered, "Is Guruji Golwalkar a futurist or an astrologer?" Guruji finished his Rajasthan tour on 24th and stayed at Lala Hansraj Gupta's house upon reaching Delhi. Seven to eight leaders of the ruling party gathered there. All of them had the same question on their lips, "From where did you get the information that China will attack us?" Keeping his anguish in his heart, he responded calmly, "Anyone who wishes to see honestly, can see everything. My eyes are not covered with any glasses of politics or power. Therefore, I can see everything. Even political leaders can see all this, but they do not speak out due to political compulsions. They are worried about what will happen to the high-sounding principles they had been talking about?" Everybody listened to him silently.[1] Guruji met President Radhakrishnan that afternoon.

Actually, China's encroachment was much older than the above-mentioned attack. When journalists had asked about it 33 months back on 2nd February, 1960, in Mumbai, he countered them with his own query, "I cannot understand why you got this information about China's aggression so late, while I had received this news nearly four to five years back? I had mentioned it in a public meeting also... In that period, Shri Mirajkar had written in the monthly *Kalyan*, published from Gorakhpur, that there were Army posts on way to Kailash and Mansarovar pilgrimage route where belongings of the pilgrims were thoroughly checked before they are allowed to proceed further."[2]

The last question in this meeting was, "Will you co-operate with the government if it decides to counter Chinese attack?" Guruji's answer was, "Definitely. We have made announcement to this effect. Other parties will also co-operate. Only one party will oppose it, that is the Communist Party."[3]

Sarsanghchaalak gave a statement on 29th October in which he requested all the citizens, especially swayamsevaks to give unquestioned support. Guruji stated in it, "Most important job is to protect common populace from fear, panic and sense of terror. If someone tries to carry out untoward activity, he should be stopped immediately. It is true that the threat is immense. Therefore, people should maintain a balanced mind, fortitude, mutual trust, co-operation and have a much bigger and firm resolve to be victorious over this threat and raise our national flag to its pinnacle in the world.[4]

"There is the possibility of many anti-national elements taking advantage of this sensitive situation and be involved in sabotage. It is necessary to be careful about them. The government should get full support from the people to be alert and scotch such possible incidents at their root. It is not correct to think that there is no possibility of such activities of sabotage. It is of utmost importance to be prepared that such activities don't take place. It is our duty to organise people in every village and every town with self-motivation and pay attention towards maintaining peace and order."[5]

Next day, on 30th October, he sent his written letter of support to the Prime Minister, "All of us brothers, will spare no effort to carry out our natural duty to free the nation from this danger with all our strength. I feel highly fulfilled in giving this unconditional assurance to you as the person heading the government."[6]

Guruji had expressed his pain or foreboding indirectly in this letter. He had written, "There is a lot that I wish to say. If some day you can give some time, I will surely present my views to you."[7]

The environment in the country at that time was not calm and peaceful. The behaviour of common populace, national leadership, political parties, especially of Communist party, social service organisations, elite citizens and intellectuals was coming into open as time passed. Keeping all this in mind, Guruji gave another statement on 5th November after a lot of thought. On reading it in full, it is doubtlessly clear that the target of this statement was the irresolute government. It is an open testimonial against a leadership that was totally bereft of self-confidence. It has suggestions about sensible changes in foreign policy. It has suggestions about keeping an alert watch on the activities of treacherous lobbies. Perhaps, Guruji wished to talk about these very things when he met Prime Minister, as he had noted in the letter that 'he would surely present his views'. Some of the lines of this celebrated historical document are, "Instead of fighting the enemy, the government is making pessimistic pronouncements. People in power are saying that the geographical situation is adverse for us. If the geographical situation is adverse, then our government is wholly responsible for it. The problem is that instead of talking of real power, we are giving more importance to protracted discussions. If the situation deteriorates, then the present Communist elements would try to take advantage. Still there is no need to ban the Communist Party. Yes, we should keep a close watch on its activities, so it cannot create any trouble... It is not right to knock at the doors of United Nations Organisation. We would have to have faith in our own capability. United Nations cannot give justice; it can only bargain... The government and its top leaders should generate self-confidence and courage in the hearts of common people... Today, the nation needs a strong and visionary leadership, leadership that can inspire the nation."[8]

In these times of mixed feelings, the Sangh planned a huge rally in the capital of the country to ignite self-confidence, dedication, will power, feeling of co-operation, etc. on the foundation of strong patriotism. The meeting took place on 23rd December at Ramlila Grounds. Guruji addressed the people in line with his two statements above.

The Sangh work does not run on the basis of public statements. Therefore, instructions were passed on at organisational level to co-operate with and help the government in a required manner as and when required. Teams of swayamsevaks gave full support to government officers in different places, as per their demands. In North Assam, even the morale of para-military forces was maintained by the Sangh swayamsevaks. When the myth of Chinese brigade reaching south after crossing Bondi valley spread and government servants began fleeing their posts, at that time, hundreds of swayamsevaks stopped them courageously putting their own lives at stake. The President and Prime Minister received such information from time to time from the armed forces. Finally, for reasons that only God knows, China declared one-sided ceasefire and drew back, thus giving our country respite. Republic Day came up on 26th January 1963, two weeks after this incident. To reinvigorate the national morale, the democratic government came up with plans to get people's participation in the Republic Day parade. Invitation for this parade was also received by Sangh office in Delhi. Not even one week was left for making the preparations. Still the Sangh being an ever ready and alert powerhouse, 3,000 swayamsevaks were ready in full uniform in that short time to take part in the grand Republic Day parade, coming up behind the formal armed forces. Actually, this was an acceptance of Sangh's service in the time of war.

Inspite of the Republic Day celebrations in the beginning of 1963, the heart of entire Bharat was smouldering with unhappy memories of Chinese attack. Guruji made preparations for going to Nepal at that time. The purpose was to have *darshan* of Pashupatinath in Kathmandu on the pious occasion of Mahashivaratri. Considering the situation in the country and nature of Guruji of not going to any pilgrimage after being appointed Sarsanghchaalak, many thinking people would surmise that the actual purpose may have been different when they put these two things together. In the statement mentioned above, Guruji noted, "It is important for the Bharatiya government to establish strong and affectionate relations with Nepal at the earliest. If slogan of *'bhai-bhai'* can be proclaimed inspite of Communist dictatorship in China, why should democratic system be mandatory to have pleasant relations with Nepal? How is this our responsibility? It is not difficult to have congenial relations with the Nepal King. After all, they are a part of our heritage. Their roots are same, as they are Hindus. If we are unsuccessful then our difficulties will only increase."[9]

24th February, 1963 was the Mahashivratri day. Guruji visited Pashupatinath temple on the day. He stayed in Nepal till 26th. He met the Prime Minister of Nepal Dr. Tulsi Giri during those days. He also met King Shri Mahendravir Vikramshah as per his plans. Prime Minister was present in the meeting. Discussions were held in a cordial atmosphere for nearly 60 minutes. The King of Nepal talked about his heartfelt feelings in the very meeting. Summary of the discussion was:

"Nepal's people are backward in economic and education fields. Extremist Leftists run back in Terai area of Bharat after their destructive activities. Because of religious and cultural unity, there is a natural sense of affection between Bharat and Nepal. Leftists are our bitter opponents due to our religious faith. Nepal's northern borders face China. Therefore, we have to conduct ourselves very carefully with China. Nepal had sought permission to import foreign goods through Kolkata harbour but it was not granted this permission. Therefore, we were forced to seek permission from Pakistan to import goods through Chittagong harbour in East Pakistan. Pakistan agreed to it without any fuss. It seems the very idea of Hindu nation is unbearable for Nehru. We suspect that somebody has poisoned his mind with wrong notions about Nepal. Bharat's views have become biased. If they can be changed, then it would be beneficial for both Nepal and Bharat."[10]

Guruji listened attentively to King of Nepal's feelings. Guruji's response was, "I suspect that feelings of your heart and your views do not reach Pandit

Nehru. There might be some confusing perspectives too. It seems Bharat will have to do some rethinking about Communists because of Chinese aggression. Home Minister of Bharat, Lal Bahadur Shastriji is arriving on 1st March, 1963, in Nepal. You may please talk to the Home Minister on the basis of religious and cultural unity of Nepal-Bharat. I feel that it will result in a strong and congenial relationship with Bharat. I will also definitely try to have dialogue about this with the top leaders of Bharat, whom I know."[11]

Shri Guruji himself was very happy to have meetings with the King of Nepal and Dr. Tulsi Giri and the Prime Minister bid him an emotional farewell. Guruji and his personal assistant Dr. Thatte returned to Varanasi on 27th February by air. There was very little time. The Home Minister was to leave for Nepal within the next 48 hours. Guruji immediately wrote letters to Pandit Nehru in English and to Home Minister Shastri in Hindi and sent them by hand through a responsible swayamsevak. Both of them received these letters on 28th February. The content of both the letters was nearly same. The letter concerns the nation and is important from the historical perspective. Therefore, it would be ideal to quote it here.

First letter

Varanasi
27-2-63

Hon'ble Pandit ji

I had gone to Kathmandu to pay obeisance to Lord Pashupatinath on the sacred occasion of Mahashivratri. I got an opportunity to personally meet and have discussions with King of Nepal and Dr. Tulsi Giri. Our discussions were held in a free, informal and congenial atmosphere. I realised that people of Nepal, at every level, feel a close relationship with the people of Bharat due to the tradition of common blood in our veins. And they also feel that destinies of both the nations are tied together in an eternal and unbreakable bond of unity. Both the nations share a common fate.

There are some small misconceptions between the two countries, but, I feel those can be easily cleared by adopting a holistic view. If we leave aside the academic stand and unreal practices then whatever difficulties and hurdles we see in this regard, can be easily overcome.

I feel our officials, that include our officials in the consulate, have failed to do their expected jobs properly. I cannot really comment about the present officials there. But, I feel it is essential to bring about positive changes in our policies and practices to improve our relations effectively with the people and the government of Nepal.

I can also see that there is very little affection for China within the Nepalese government and it is even lesser for the international imperialist communism. Due to this reason, Nepal is in a position to rise as a strong power in opposition to Chinese imperialism. But, we Bharatiyas will have to provide different kind of help to them. We should specially create confidence in them about our objectives and policies and assure this sovereign brotherly nation about its independent prestige so that it can be free to create its own governing system and utilise its inherent rights as a proclaimed sovereign nation.

There are some other aspects also that come to my attention. But, it would be ideal to talk about them in person. I would perhaps be unable to express my views and future possibilities in this kind of letter. Still I have written this letter with a view that it is my duty to inform my Prime Minister about my experiences gained during this visit to Nepal.

I am happy to know that our Home Minister is going to pay a goodwill visit to Nepal very soon. I have complete confidence that he will be able to generate the expected atmosphere of cordial relationship and friendship by resolving all the present feelings of suspicion between Bharat and Nepal with his amiable nature and intelligence.

I will reach Nagpur on 6-6-63 after completing my programme of Orissa tour. If I can get an acknowledgement of this letter, I would be obliged. With respect and reverence,

Yours

Maa. Sa. Golwalkar

Second Letter

Varanasi

27-2-63

Hon'ble Shri Lal Bahadur Shastriji

Respectful greetings

I had gone to Kathmandu to pay obeisance to Lord Pashupatinath on the sacred occasion of Mahashivratri. During my stay there for three days, I was fortunate to have met His Highness the King. I have noted, whatever I could understand, in my letter to Hon'ble Prime Minister. I am enclosing a copy of that letter alongwith.

With improvement in our conduct, extending due respect and establishing a cordial relationship with Nepal and understanding Nepal's economic, educational and other requirements, and adopting right policies about them, Nepal can come up very fast as a strong, close friend, a brother securing our borders. Interests of both Nepal and Bharat are tied to each other. Therefore, it is highly important to improve our relations and establish an honest friendship from the point of view of our own security.

You are going to Nepal very soon to create an atmosphere of goodwill. People there are waiting eagerly with hope for your arrival. I am sure that with your intelligence, affectionate behaviour, sweet speech you will be able to dispel all doubts in the hearts of their topmost leaders and remove bitterness arising out of heartless and dry behaviour of the Bharatiya officials till now. Whether these actions were done knowingly or due to carelessness; by planning to appoint liberal, congenial people in their place; you will be able to establish indestructible affection, mutually complementary relationship and fulfil the objectives of this tour.

If I get a chance to meet you again, I will present my information that I could gather about the situation there and the solutions that I have in mind. But, when will this happen, how it will happen – I leave all this on the will of God.

I will be going to Utkal state for four days after starting from here on 28-2-63 and going via Kolkata. After reaching Nagpur on 6.3.63, I plan to stay there for nearly three weeks. That is all for now.

Yours

Maa. Sa. Golwalkar[12]

Prime Minister sent his reply the very second day on 1st March, on receipt of the letter. Nepal tour of Home Minister was a success. When Atal Behari Vajpayee met Shastriji after two-and-a-half years in 1965, he noted with pleasure during the dialogue, "While talking to King of Nepal, I realised that three-fourth of my work has already been done by Shri Guruji by preparing a favourable background for strengthening Bharat-Nepal friendship."[13]

But, there is an epilogue to this whole episode. It would remain incomplete without talking about it.

During the dialogue Guruji had with King of Nepal, Guruji had given detailed information about the efforts at Hindu consolidation and organisation being done under the banner of Rashtriya Swayamsevak Sangh. He also showed his keenness about it. Guruji had presented an oral invitation to the King to come for a large-scale festival of the Sangh in future and he had agreed to it too. Later, King was slated to go for an overseas tour. It was understood that he would arrive in Mumbai in October. Why not organise a large Hindu *sangam* (assembly) at that time? This idea came up. But it was inconvenient for the Nepal King. Therefore, this plan was postponed. He agreed to attend Makar Sankraman festival programme of 1964. But, Pandit Nehru had plans to visit Nepal at that time, so this programme also had to be put on hold. In a way, it proved to be a good decision because Vishwa Hindu Parishad was to be established that year on Shri Krishna Janmashtami. If the King of a Hindu nation was to arrive after this, then his tour could have an added dimension. Therefore, many felt that the delay was for good.

Guruji sent a formal letter of invitation to Maharaja Mahendravir Vikramshah to grace the Nagpur Makar Sankraman festival of January 1965. Kathmandu sent his acceptance to Nagpur. A wave of happiness swept across the organisation. Sarsanghchaalak sent out formal letters to all the leaders, including President, Prime Minister, Home Minister, Chief Minister of Maharashtra, etc. as a matter of national, political and administrative protocol. He also met

Maharashtra Chief Minister, Vasantrao Naik, on 14th December, 1964, and showing him the confirmation letter from Nepal, asked him, "What should the government and we do together and separately on our own?" The answer was, "Centre will surely inform you."[14]

The Nagpur branch began preparing for the programme with brimming enthusiasm. Each *gatnaayak* (team leader) started visiting individual homes and contacting new and old, regular and irregular swayamsevaks. Colleges and hostels were contacted. It was resolved that Makar Sankraman festival of 1965 at Nagpur headquarters would be a historical milestone for Hindu consolidation. But, alas! All India Radio broadcast the message of Foreign Ministry spokesperson, "Nepal King's tour has been stalled." Even 24 hours after this announcement, there was no message from the palace of King to Nagpur office. Only after a telephonic call was this news confirmed.

It was clear that the Central Government had stopped Nepal King's tour to abort his plans of attending Makar Sankraman festival of the Sangh. Still the programme was conducted properly, the way Sangh festivals are celebrated, on 14th January, 1965.

Dr. Abaji Thatte read out the speech of Nepal King, sent through his consul. The King may have suspected that the letter could be intercepted by the government on the way. One cannot think of any other reason for the way the letter was sent. In that letter, the King said:

"Nepal has been a perennial source of inspiration for Hindus of Bharat for centuries. Not only this, Nepal feels proud that it has granted them protection whenever they have faced any calamity. Commanders of first war of Independence of Bharat like Nanasaheb Peshwa received asylum in Nepal. Nepal has always played the role of sentinel for Bharat. The culture of both the countries is nearly the same, both receive motivation from the same ideals of life. All this is a matter of joy for all of us Hindus. This is a matter of pride for the entire Hindu society the world over.

"Hindu dharma is the oldest *dharma* of the world. It has the best concept about the process of birth of universe. It has all the principles that can grant peace, welfare and happiness to all, at the same time, it is capable of removing all the signs of conflict from the face of the earth. Hindutva, for all of us, who are the followers of this ancient, pre-eminent and proud Hindu *dharma*, is a matter of pride.

"Unfortunately, humanity is rushing towards its own annihilation and absorbed by jealousy and wars. The highest principles of Hindu *dharma* alone can rescue us from this terrible situation. For this, it is necessary that Hindus should consolidate, organise and stand up as an indivisible power. It cannot be said that the Sangh is not playing any useful role in this movement.

"We are naturally happy to understand that this organisation is putting in efforts to give the citizens of Bharat an organised and disciplined form. We,

Nepalese, as the only independent and sovereign nation of the world, and in a way represent all the Hindus, are eager to co-operate with all the dynamic Hindu forces. We pray to Lord Pashupatinath and Goddess Gyaneshwari that they give us their divine blessings and help us create an ideal Hindu society and human life a reality."[15]

Guruji's lecture followed the speech of Maharaja. Guruji presented the facts about Nepal King's message in a scientific manner as a professor of science in front of the audience. He finally spoke about his heart's feeling, "If this get-together had taken place, how beneficial it would have been for both the countries!" And he added to it his hurt feelings, "But, politics has overpowered the people who are sitting at the Centre."

When people heard the King's speech, their Hindu self-pride was awakened. Everybody strongly criticised the pettiness of the rulers in not allowing the the King's visit. Most of the newspapers also criticised the Central Government. Reaction of Pune's *Kesari* newspaper was, "When Pope comes to Mumbai, the whole government machinery, right from President downwards, rushes forward to welcome him, but the same government stops Maharaja of Nepal from coming to Nagpur. Is our government bent upon avenging some kind of revenge on Hindu society for some reason?"

Hindustan, the daily from Delhi, wrote, "Does this government hope to have friendship with Nepal by taking a negative, dry and scornful view about Hindutva, when most of its citizens are strong Hindu believers? This is like striking at the roots and still expecting flowers from the tree."[16]

On one hand, Home Minister of Bharat had said, "Three-fourths of my work has already been done by Guruji," on the other hand, this was the reward Guruji received from Prime Minister of Bharat. But what can we say? In the words of character Mark Antony in the play *Julius Caesar*, "They are all honourable."

On the next day on 15th January, after celebration of Sankranti, Guruji wrote to Nepalese Prime Minister, Dr. Tulsi Giri, "Citizens of Nagpur were deeply saddened that His Excellency could not come to Nagpur. Everybody was waiting for this moment very eagerly. Preparations for a grand reception had been nearly complete, but, all this had to be stopped half way. Things happen as the Lord wills. Therefore, it is ideal and necessary for us to get back to our duties with firm resolve and calm mind."

"It is natural that whatever has happened would have deeply pained your heart. All of us had tried to strengthen the ancient ties of common blood and affection, culture and religion as a necessary duty that would result in mutual prosperity and security. Your contribution to these efforts has been invaluable, but mental agony is expected when a planned programme that had the capability to give positive results. His Excellency's heart has also faced this agony. It comes out loud and clear from each of his words. Still all of us should keep working for consolidation of the entire Hindu society with wisdom and strong will power, strengthen the indestructible bonds of love between Nepal and Bharat – places of pride for Hindu society and keep ourselves busy with enthusiasm in our duties with the hope that we shall definitely be able to welcome and be host to His Excellency."[17]

Does the agony not in the heart of this son of the nation who dedicated day and night to Mother Nation, emerge crying out of this letter?

□

Endnotes

1. *Jeevan Prasang*, Vol. 1, pp. 248-249
2. *Shri Guruji Samagra*, Vol. 10, pp. 147-148
3. Ibid, pp. 153
4. Ibid, pp. 155-156
5. Ibid, pp. 155
6. *Shri Guruji Samagra*, Vol. 7, pp. 125
7. Ibid, pp. 125
8. *Shri Guruji Samagra*, Vol. 10, pp. 156-158
9. Ibid, pp. 158
10. *Smriti Paarijaat*, pp. 296
11. Ibid, pp. 297
12. Ibid, pp. 297-301
13. Ibid, pp. 303
14. *Shri Guruji Samagra*, Vol. 10, pp. 268-269
15. *Navyug Pravartak Shri Guruji*, pp. 197-198
16. Ibid, pp. 198
17. *Shri Guruji Samagra*, Vol. 7, pp. 131-132

35

Following the Path of Swami Vivekananda

In the Central Working Committee meeting held in Nagpur after Sangh Shiksha Varg of 1962, it was resolved to celebrate the forthcoming birthday centenary of Swami Vivekananda in an appropriate manner, both inside and outside Bharat. It was also decided that rather than getting involved in building large halls, setting up institutions, etc. it would be more productive to make efforts to carry revered Swamiji's philosophy to the people, especially to younger generation. Based on this thought, the period, from Makar Sankraman of 1963 to Makar Sankraman 1964, was celebrated as the centenary year. Two to three months after this Sangh resolution, the Bharatiya government also announced its intentions to celebrate Swami Vivekananda Birth Centenary.

It was necessary to have a proper compilation of Swamiji's thoughts in a fitting manner to make the centenary year celebrations as successful as possible. Guruji gave responsibility for this activity to Eknath Ranade. He handed over the charge of Sarkaryavaah to Bhaiyyaji Dani at the 1962 Akhil Bharatiya Pratinidhi Sabha, who had the responsibility of intellectual training at that time. He was very hardworking and incomparable planner by nature. Just before the centenary year, he had compiled a 200-page book named *Swami Vivekananda's Rousing Call to Hindu Nation.* It was translated in all the Bharatiya languages. 21,000 copies of the English edition were sold off in the first month itself. Meetings in schools, colleges, small and big organisations and meetings of youth, men and women were held at different places. There were also programmes for children about narrating life stories of Swamiji.

Guruji himself went to one or two programmes in each state. He took part in a grand programme in Delhi, the capital of Bharat, on 13th January, 1963, the very day he had received *diksha* from the brother disciple of Swamiji 26 years back. "Bharat is our sacred land, this nation is a Hindu nation, our heritage is ancient and sacred.We should respect our forefathers; a student studying Sanskrit becomes a cultured individual. Let us re-establish our *dharma*, let us be devotees of triumphant thinking. Power is life, weakness is death. There are many paths of different sects but destination is one, not just welfare but service and only service. Let us take birth again and again only for service." Guruji presented views of Swamiji to the audience with great reverence.

The Chennai meeting was held on 3rd February, 1963, on Triplicane beach. Kerala's Mannat Padmanabhan presided over that huge meeting and words or blessing were delivered by Swami Chinmayananda. Lecture of Guruji that day was truly historic because Guruji presented a new dimension in that speech. His subject was Bharat's global contribution in the unprecedented progress of human beings. His view was, "Swamiji used to say that every nation has a purpose for its existence. It has a message and it is its life's mission to spread it throughout the world. When it fails to perform its life's mission, it gets destroyed. If it has completed its life's mission, then there remains no reason for its existence. Therefore, it gradually becomes extinct."

"It is, perhaps, life mission of England to bring together East and West. Even if she did this due to its own thirst for conquering lands or subjugating others or expand its commerce by any means, or did this with a self-serving objective of benefitting the nation, but the two-half circles did meet to complete the circle unknowingly or without expectations. Now, the rationale for its existence is fulfilled."

"Presently, there are two very important countries leading two power blocs – Russia and America. America is in favour of individual freedom, dignity and glory, and is in favour of independence for other countries. She is working in that direction. It seems 'levelling down' for economic equality is the mission of Russia. Now, its life's mission is also accomplished because the world has accepted that there should be no economic inequality. Even then, they are trying to eliminate class differences. Thus, it seems that either they will change or they will stick to their views stubbornly, the way they have done so far. This will lead to its conflict with democratic nations. This would be harmful to both the sides. It is possible that they would understand and accept their mistakes or it may simply cease to exist; and may not even get a chance to realise its mistake."

We can see that these egoist societies are becoming extinct one after the other. Old Egypt, Greece, Rome, Babylon and many other nations are extinct. Then, why we, Hindus, are still alive? In the words of Swamiji, "Mild-natured Hindu, Hindu bound in slavery, is alive because the mission before it is that each individual of each society should realise his/her soul, know the ultimate truth and build this universe for the well-being of the world on this strong foundation."

"This is a mission that will continue forever; a work that will never be completed. Therefore, our nation is immortal, our existence can never cease. This is the real truth."[1]

Actually, this lecture was an exposition of visionary Swamiji's analysis of the present scenario. In this, he indicated the possibility of the collapse of

Communist Russia. Surprisingly, this forecast proved to be true.

During this period, Guruji also paid back another of his debts. Bengali book *Yugacharya Vivekananda*, written by the head of Shri Ramakrishna Ashram Swami Apoorvananda, was released on the occasion of centenary celebrations. It was also translated in Hindi. Shri Guruji arranged for this book to be distributed free of cost through Vivekananda Janmashataabdi Samiti on instructions from Swami Apoorvananda. He also got the book translated in Marathi through one of his friends.[2]

In short, Guruji took the message of architect of modern Bharat, Swami Vivekananda, to distant villages on the strength of his organisation that was spread across Bharat.

Guruji was in Belgaum in Karnataka on November 24, 1963. On that day, parliamentarian ShambhunathKapildeo from Trinidad in Caribbean Islands came to meet him. His arrival in Belgaum has an interesting story of chase behind it.

In 18th century, when European imperialists established their different colonies in Caribbean Island nations, they got many poor Bharatiya people exported there as bonded labour. When all these colonies became free, independent nations, Trinidad was one of them. It also became a modern democratic republic. Majority of citizens of Trinidad are followers of Hinduism. Inspite of the wicked efforts of Christian missionaries, they have remained Hindus to date. They also have a strong influence in the political field. But, Hindu systems still worked in religious rituals in marriage, birth and death, while their customs were more close to Christianity. In all this, Tulsidas's *Ramcharitmanas* played the role of guiding scripture for these people. It is their all-in-all for them for every kind of ritual. With this background, what kind of systems could be set up for their religious understanding, training and growth? What support could they get from Hindustan? Shambhunath Kapildeo Tiwari was the person who had brought a delegation of select parliamentarians in search of an answer to these questions.

They knocked at the doors of many rulers with great expectations and met many ministers, who disappointed them by telling that 'this is a secular country'. Local Hindu leaders also showed their helplessness. But, there was one considerate leader who told Shambhunath, "You should meet Guruji Golwalkar for this objective; only can he help you in this mission." He also gave some brief information about Golwalkar. Based on this, Shambhunath Kapildeo came to Sangh office in Jhandewalan. He then proceeded to Mumbai as per information he received there. He got the information that Guruji was on a tour of Karnataka state. So, a telephone call was made immediately to Bangalore. Information from there was, "Guruji will reach Belgaum tomorrow from Guledagudda as it is a district-wise tour. Shambhunath Kapildeo reached Belgaum at the lightning speed of a telegram and met Guruji, finally. He told Guruji, "I have come to meet you, not as an individual, but as a representative of Hindus of my country." He explained the reason behind his visit and also mentioned his disappointing experience in Delhi. Shambhunath was emotionally thrilled on meeting Guruji and experiencing his affectionate care for his guest. He took part in the programme that evening. After the programme, he came back again to the place where Guruji stayed, seeking special permission. He mixed well with all other people who were present during the discussions. His objective was accomplished by the afternoon, but he did not want to leave the company of Guruji. There were more discussions after dinner. At that time, this Parliamentarian, familiar with American system, raised his doubts, "I am afraid that your security system is very weak. Only one swayamsevak with a wooden stick on each side of the stage, that is all? Is there no need for more caution?" Guruji responded, "We are part of this society and working for this society, then why should society oppose us? It is better to leave everything else at the feet of God. Look at the Kennedy episode; was there any shortcoming in security? Security forces all round, wife and governor on both sides, bullet-proof car, intelligence agents in the crowd, still what happened? There is a limit to what we can do. Beyond that is all His '*leela*'." Shambhunathji sat back quietly.

Shambhunath Kapildeo came again next morning before leaving. He prostrated himself in salutation before Guruji. He presented two pictures of Guruji to him with a request, "When I tell the people in Trinidad about my meeting and discussions with you, they will ask me, 'How do you look?' Please give your autograph on these pictures for their satisfaction." Guruji gave his autographs on the two pictures happily, one in Devanagari and the other in English.[3]

Look at this play of destiny. Guruji's attention was drawn towards hopes of Parliamentarians of Trinidad. After this, Laxmanrao Bhide, who used to travel around the world as a Prachaarak to organise Hindus, and Deendayal Upadhyay, who had toured the world, informed Guruji about the expectations and necessities of overseas Hindus. During this same period, Swami Chinmayananda had expressed his views in this regard in his Ashram's monthly magazine *Tapovanprasaad*, "A vague idea is taking seed in my heart – that a global Hindu conference should be organised. An appeal should be made to Hindu brethren spread all over the world to send their delegates to this. There should be discussions in this conference about development and spread of Hindu culture. Problems that may come up should be discussed. There is need to ponder over how the spiritual base of Hinduism can be strengthened and stabilised. A plan should be made to give a practical shape to the conclusions drawn from these discussions. This global conference should be held in Delhi or Kolkata."

Swamiji's views, expressed in short notes, were like small fragrant flowers of jasmine. Guruji read this monthly in Hedgewar Bhavan where it had come through post. He contacted Swamiji immediately. Both had close relations from earlier days. Both of them decided to move in the above-mentioned direction. To accomplish this work successfully, skilled activist S.S. (Dada) Apte was given its responsibility. He was also well aware of these problems. He had written some articles in Pune daily *Kesari* on this subject, based on his experiences during his world tour. He had been well known to Guruji since 1940, the year had been he attended the Nagpur training camp as a student and Guruji was its Sarvadhikari (overall in-charge). Apte ji had been a Sangh Prachaarak since 1945.

Dada Apte took up this job wholeheartedly. He met over 200 religious preachers and 40-50 religious institutions. His contacts were quite widespread among religious sects. Finally, Vishwa Hindu Parishad was established on 29th August, 1964, in Sandipani Ashram of Swami Chinmayananda. This act saw the rise of a global movement for resolving religious, social and community problems of Hindus.

Upon the insistence of Swami Chinmayananda as the president of this meeting, Guruji offered his concluding remarks. In these concluding notes, Guruji said, "We all know that for different reasons, many members of our society are settled in various countries. If one were to take a view of ancient times and present times, there is no doubt that one would feel unhappy. In the ancient times, our forefathers had gone overseas as triumphant propagators of our *dharma*, culture and prosperity. But, in the last one-and-a-half century, our brethren, who have gone overseas, have gone there for serving has been labour. This is a paradox that pains our hearts. It would not serve any purpose if we were to be immersed in reminiscing about our past. We shall have to think about our brethren, who are presently there. We shall have to make them capable enough so that they can wave the banner of our *dharma* and culture. We have come together with this thought today. Bharat is the fountain-head of Hindu *dharma*; our brethren should come here from all directions, experience its pious atmosphere, have a divine view of its pilgrim centres, great noble souls and saints, strengthen their religious faith by listening to their invaluable discourses, expand their spiritual wealth and make our elevating Hindu tradition commonly acceptable in their residing countries. We are meeting today with this objective. We should get down to work for this objective."

Major decisions of this first meeting were: 1) There should be a global Hindu conference (*Vishwa Hindu Sammelan*) on the occasion of Kumbh Fair in Prayag from 22nd to 24th January, 1966. 2) It should have a religious parliament with participation of all religions and sects. 3) There should be programmes in that conference that would propagate 'Unity in Diversity'. 4) An exhibition should be organised showing the continuity of Hindu *dharma* from Vedic times to present times. Elite scholars present there were looking upto Guruji for making these programmes successful. Guruji's response was, "This can be achieved with every kind of support and co-operation from all of you."

While Dada Apte was busy with his programme of contacting people and holding discussions with them for founding of the Vishwa Hindu Parishad,

Guruji carried on with his regular organisational tours during these nine months. Based on the programme chalked out at the beginning of the year, Guruji was slated to tour Bihar from 16th to 24th March, 1964. He reached Hazaribagh on 22nd night at 11.30 after finishing his programmes in Sasaram, Patna, Chhapra, Sitamarhi, Narayanpur, Munger and Nawada. The programmes there were slated for 23rd and in Ranchi for 24th.

Bhartrihari's has said that politics is like a prostitute, but once in a while, it is also like a dead body blocking the path. Guruji also got an experience of this kind. For some unknown reasons, Bihar's Chief Minister and his advisors had decided to create big news by arresting Guruji somehow. Therefore, claiming that there were possibilities of communal riots in Hazaribagh on 22nd-23rd of March, administration imposed Section 144 there. As a follow-up, permission given to the Sangh for use of loudspeakers was cancelled; so also was the permission for the conference. But, after the meeting with local officials, permission was given for a small meeting in an enclosed place. A meeting of swayamsevaks was held accordingly in Munakabagh. That was 23rd evening. That same day, two representatives of District Magistrate met Guruji at his place of stay in the morning with two police officers. They demanded that Guruji should cancel his programme for visiting Ranchi the next day. Guruji told them, "My job is to awaken Hindu society. For this, I go to different parts of the country. I don't encourage violence. There has been no such experience wherever I have given my speech. Therefore, I do not think that the situation in Ranchi would deteriorate if I go to Ranchi. And, another point: swayamsevaks would be coming to Ranchi from all over the district. It is my job to meet them. Therefore, I will have to go there to meet them. I will go to the next destination after meeting swayamsevaks. I am not insisting on giving a public speech. If there is no permission, I will not give speech. I speak because I have to speak. I am not too keen about it."

After finishing Hazaribagh *baitha*k, Guruji proceeded to Ranchi after his evening prayers. His personal assistant Dr. Thatte and state Prachaarak Madhukar Dev were also accompanying him. Just as Guruji's car crossed the city limits of Hazaribagh, policemen standing at the check-post stopped the car. One officer handed over a paper written in English, 'Shri M.S. Golwalkar be arrested and detained in Hazaribagh Central Jail till further orders.' Order was from Chief Minister's office. Guruji came out of the car carrying items of regular worship and a set of clothes. He asked the police, "And, where?" "Should I also keep his hold-all?" asked Dr. Thatte. Police office said, "Yes." Guruji stopped Dr. Thatte and said, "No, no, my entire responsibility lies with these people." He went and sat down in the police jeep. On reaching jail, officers there asked him, "What are your requirements?" Guruji's answer was, "One mat and a jug of water." Nobody knows what happened behind the scenes, but on 24th itself, Guruji was released before even 24 hours had elapsed. Truth was that this sad drama was enacted with shameful intent of Muslim appeasement. Guruji did not offer any reaction. When journalists asked him about it, he said, "You have been misinformed. Please ask this question to the person who gave me one day of compulsory rest."[4]

Guruji evaded journalists with this response, but his views about this incident were clear. He did not hide them from his colleagues. He had received many letters immediately after his arrest. He responded to all of them, as was his nature. He wrote to Anna Bhambhre of Yeola, "The paradox of considering one's own as others and others as one's own, friend as enemy and enemy as friend, considering a murderer enemy to be a close-to-heart friend – this is a proof of hunger for illusory power. That is what I would call the incident I faced in Bihar state. It is not that a few patriots and I will have to bear the result of this state of mind. I can foresee signs of entire national life being threatened by severe disasters. Our swayamsevaks should not get upset at such a time. It will be only apt that our swayamsevaks should put in their all to expand our work that builds up true strength of our nation with great speed and present it as an invincible power that can defeat all internal and external threats."[5]

Giving indications about the harmful effect of such confused mentality, he wrote to Bharatiya Mazdoor Sangh worker, Mahadev Sane, "My experiences of Bihar state are not worth paying any special attention. Looking at the way, current rulers think, it seems that people who wish for pure patriotism would face such situations. There is such kind of mindless thinking in Orissa and Bengal too. They may imagine that non-Hindu society will feel contented with such actions. Long-term effects of such thinking would be same that were seen earlier and being seen now. In the past also, high-ranking people were put in prisons, still non-Hindu society's audacity and attacks did not cease. In fact, they only increased and we had to suffer what happened in East Bengal now. There will only be one outcome of this policy that we shall have to face severe situation within a short time and the face of our nation will be blackened with disgrace."[6]

Guruji did not go to Ranchi after his release. Due to compulsions of his onward programmes, he went to Chakradharpur from Hazaribagh and reached Nagpur after catching a train on 27th. His meeting with Vinoba Bhave at Pawnar Ashram had been fixed for 2nd April. These great people met on that day. Nearly one-and-half-hour of dialogue was carried in their mother tongue, Marathi. This was the first dialogue between the two. There was no specific purpose behind this time, nor any specific problem for this meeting. Relations build with dialogue, according to Kalidas, (*samabandhmabhashanpoorvamaahuh*; *Raghuvansh*-2) and this was the only purpose. Many subjects came up during discussions. Naturally, there was no clear thread in them, but there was sweetness all through. Subjects like Hindu, Muslim, Buddhists, aborigines, tribals, Catholics, Protestants, exclusiveness, tolerance, Sangh, Congress, humanity, etc. came up during the discussions. Finally, both of them got up. Vinoba ji said, "I felt very good that you came, could speak enough and openly", and added jokingly," if somebody comes and bores me, I (*touching his hearing aid with his fingers*) shut it." Guruji also said in the same mood, "Was it shut so far?" Both laughed aloud heartily, even the followers joined in.[7]

Guruji's next tour was of U.P. 13th April programme was in Almora that lay in the laps of Himalayas. The Municipal Corporation had taken a unanimous decision to give a civic reception to Guruji. Two sentences in the citation were, "A divine spiritual personality, named Swami Vivekananda, had come to this Himalayan region in 1899. Today, after 65 years, another divine personality from the same tradition is coming here to bless us….." At 10:30 a.m., the highest-ranking leader of Kumaon region, Shobhan Singh, President of Municipal Corporation, Mohanlal Verma and all other councilors welcomed Guruji. The official reception was in the evening. The meeting place was packed to capacity. On the second day, this disciple of Swami Akhandananda visited Mayawati Ashram. He went into an emotional trance on seeing Swami Vivekananda's staying place, painting of Swamiji in *samadhi*, etc. After this he went around the whole campus. On request of the chairman of Ashram, he wrote his comments in the visitors' book, "Today is a highly fortunate day for me as I have visited this sacred, calm place that has become most sacred with the presence of Swami Vivekananda and I have been able to fulfil my long cherished desire."[8]

Only after these incidents was Vishwa Hindu Parishad born in Mumbai on the pious day of Janmashtami. After this, Guruji got busy in preparing for the forthcoming Global Hindu Conference, coming up in 1966. Because of his perpetual touring of the country from the Himalayas to oceans, all the renowned saints-sages were well known to him. All of them thought of him as their own. Turning them favourable for the mission to create a Hindu society which was reformed from inside, was like walking on the edge of a sword. However, he was an expert in smoothening a path full of thorns as he was moulded by the working style of Dr. Hedgewar. He presented the subject to the heads of various temples and *mathams* through a letter. He wrote this letter in the fag end of 1964 on 20th December:

"Highly revered, my prostrate salutation at your divine feet.

Your hallowed self is aware of the disturbances in the society and instability and poor faith in *dharma* due to doubts created in the minds of people because to this situation. Everyone is aware that untouchability linked to specific castes inherited through generations has resulted in deep resentment and anger. Though many vested political interests have tried to create a catastrophic scenario out of this pent-up anger, even if one were not to pay attention to this factor, it is necessary to ponder over the increasing libertine behaviour and falling levels of religious and ethical behaviour in the entire society.

Dharma helps sustain a well-ordered society and makes it an organised power, capable of welfare of the people. Earlier teachers-*acharyas* had gone ahead to give up unnecessary or non-beneficial customs and establish new customs and traditions to bring about necessary changes in this *dharma*. Earlier, *gurus* and sages had given clear directions for future about rights of religious teachers and *acharyas* to think over the times and situations in the nation to avoid unnecessary or harmful traditions and rituals and accepting necessary customs.

Based upon these directions, respected *dharmacharyas* of Hindu society should think seriously about the current scenario in the country and give their verdicts about sustenance of the society and pass directions in their areas of influence to follow these verdicts. This is within their rights. It is beyond my jurisdiction to give my suggestions to your divine self about what decisions can be given. I am only requesting you humbly, now, whatever be the directive from your respected self, it will be acceptable to us. That is all."[9]

Year 1965 followed quickly. That year too proved to be good for religious awakening of Hindus. A notable incident took place in May of that year. Shankaracharyas of Puri, Dwarika, Shringeri *mathams* decided to celebrate Shri Shankaracharya's birthday together in his birthplace, Kalladi. Those days, post of the head of Badri *Peeth*, was vacant due to some dispute, or else, he too would have joined these celebrations. It was after centuries that heads of these *mathams* had shown such a spirit of togetherness. Hindu society, especially from Kerala, was very happy to hear this news. Coincidentally, the annual training camp of the Sangh was also being held at Shri Ramakrishna School in Kalladi. Guruji had been present in it for three days. Being aware of the coming together of Acharya trio, Guruji had also planned his tour during these days. He had planned to meet all the three *Acharyas*. But, the day Guruji reached there, Dwarika Shankaracharya had to rush back the same morning due to some unexpected urgent work. Guruji could meet the other two Shankaracharyas. The meeting was held at Shringeri Math's place at 8.30 in night. Three points came out in this meeting – 1) Vishwa Hindu Parishad – Shringeri Acharya told Guruji, "Some Apte had come to meet him from Pune." Guruji added promptly, "Yes, that is right. He is Shivram Shankar Apte. He had met you on my instructions." Acharya said, "Is it so? Then everything is fine, we shall give full co-operation." 2) Badri *Peeth* – Acharya, "See, that *Peeth* is vacant. Issue is in the courts, how insulting! Will we be able to correct it? Who will do it?" His words conveyed pain. Guruji's mood also changed. His face too was clouded with unhappiness. "May Lord give wise counsel to all," is all he could say. 3) Now, it was the turn of Guruji. He said, "I was of the view that participants of Sangh camp would be able to get blessings of all the three revered personalities, but, now they will be deprived of one. Will you two please come to the camp and bless these young people?" Secretaries of the *Acharyas* informed their available dates immediately and the head of the camp agreed to these. Upon confirmation of dates, Guruji said, "I will have to move out day after tomorrow. I have to reach all the camps taking place in the country. Our workers will make well-planned arrangements for your visit." Puri Acharya said with a smile, "Does Golwalkar have shortage of workers?" Response was, "This is all due to your blessings." The thirty-minute programme of divine blessings from *Acharyas* was over; the group came back after receiving *prasadam*.

Guruji's contact programme went on untiringly and continuously like this. He understood the limitations of raising an organisation through statements and pamphlets.

□

Endnotes

1. *Shri Guruji Samagra*, Vol. 1, pp. 67-69
2. Ibid, pp. 75-76
3. *Jeevan Prasang*, Vol. 1, pp. 353-357
4. *Jeevan Prasang*, Vol. 2 & *Memoirs of Madhukar Dev*, pp. 195-196
5. *Shri Guruji Samagra*, Vol. 8, pp. 297-298
6. *Shri Guruji Samagra*, Vol. 7, pp. 336
7. *Baba Talatule Sansmaran*
8. *Shri Guruji Samagra*, Vol. 6, pp. 101
9. *Shri Guruji Samagra*, Vol. 7, pp. 38-39

36

Prayag Religious Parliament

Guruji arrived in the third year Sangh Shiksha Varg at the end of May. He received heartbreaking news of the sudden passing away of his close friend and trusted lieutenant, Bhaiyyaji Dani. He had gone to Madhya Pradesh's Sangh Shiksha Varg to guide the participants, the first state where he went first as a Prachaarak for Sangh work expansion even after he had got married. He had died in Indore of heart attack at the age of 58. For Guruji, it was a big blow. Bhaiyyaji Dani had played a major role in the Sangh life for Guruji. He had a great understanding in matters of co-operation. His going away was a personal loss for Guruji. Still, Guruji kept his calm. He did not even mention this grievous news in his intellectual discourse of that day. He did not raise it during discussions. Nobody else had the courage to bring it up. We can get a little idea about his strong sense of grief in one of his letters, he wrote to Hanuman Prasad Poddar of Gorakhpur, who was like a brother disciples (*guru-bhai*) for him, "For me, with his death, it is as if ground had moved from under my feet."[1]

Non-stop travels, four to five programmes each day, open and endless sessions of discussions and advancing age led to weakening of Guruji's health. Dr. Abaji Thatte brought this to the notice of Sarkaryavaah Balasaheb Deoras. He took a decision to send Guruji to Kerala. He fixed the time and place after seeking advice from state Prachaarak Bhaskar Rao Kalambi. Accordingly, Guruji reached the residence of Pataykara Namboodiripad in west Edattaraa, about 6 kms from Palghat, in the first week of July. Shri Kuttancheri Aryan Moos was one of the practitioners from the eight famed traditional Vaidya families. Medical treatment was to be for 28 days.

On the first day of treatment, preparations were made for lighting the traditional lamp on instructions of Vaidyaraj. He called for the patient, Guruji, to light the lamp. On receiving this message, Guruji asked his attendant, "Why is the lamp to be lit before taking a bath?" The attendant said, "So that the treatment is successful." Guruji countered, "It is the job of Vaidya to cure successfully, what has that got to do with me? It is his job to light the lamp." The attendant said, "It is you who has to recite the prayer." Guruji said, "Me?

Oh friend, I have never prayed to God for this physical body. I have prayed a lot no doubt, but never for my body. (After two-three seconds) Doesn't Mother understand more about the demands of the child? For me, it is just *karishye vachanam tava* (carrying out thy orders). For everything else, I have faith in Him." Guruji did not get up from his easy chair. Vaidyaraj was waiting in the other room. The attendant informed him of the whole discussion. Vaidya was speechless! Only words that escaped his mouth were, "Noble soul." He told the attendant, "Is this medical treatment not for your Guruji? Your prayer will also reach the right place. So, you light the lamp." Which swayamsevak could have refused this privilege? He lit the lamp with reverence. A methodic treatment commenced after this.

After two to three days Yadavrao Joshi, Dr. Narasimhachari and two other swayamsevaks came to meet Guruji from Bangalore. Yadavrao had brought a thick manuscript of compilation of Guruji's thoughts. He handed it over to Dr. Abaji for Guruji's observations and corrections. Guruji finished the expected work in five to six days and handed it over to Yadavrao when he came to meet him again. An attendant, who had come from Mumbai, told him one day during the evening tea, "There is a serious need for such a book these days." Guruji countered him immediately, "Need is not as serious as you think. Howsoever great a book may be, it would not be correct to work on its basis. Would you be able to work by saying during intellectual training periods, for this, refer to Golwalkar's book? Will swayamsevaks receive right *samskaaras* from it? Actually, a book has limitations. Book speaks to everybody in the same way – new-old, boy-youth, friend-foe, without looking at the recipient. Education system of this nation is different. Here education is transmitted according to the differing qualities of the recipients. The teacher's voice is not wasted. A book does not measure up in this matter. Therefore, we do not lay stress on books in the Sangh, but more on *samskaaras*."

Guruji was a person who had read thousands of books and scriptures. He had a habit of reading with complete concentration. He would always write his views to the writer about a book that was gifted to him. This view about books comes from such a person! The only reason for this was that Guruji was not an avid intellectual; he was a successful builder of human beings. A book may, probably, help growth of personalities like Dr. Radhakrishnan, but will never be able to help the rise of people like Ramakrishna or Raman Maharshi. For that one needs God in heart. Guruji stressed this fact.

To make it easier for Guruji, a Shakha used to be conducted every evening in the compound of his place of stay. Shakhas of nearby areas would come there by a system of rotation. Guruji asked swayamsevaks after the Shakha one day, "What is the name of the game you played today?" Answer received was, "Extinguishing the lamp." Looking towards the Prachaarak, Guruji said immediately, "This name is not ideal for this game. Extinguishing a lamp is not considered auspicious in our tradition. Here we learn, 'Light up the lamp of knowledge'; this signals auspiciousness. It may be only the name of a game, but it conveys positivity." Next day, name of the game was changed to, 'Challenge' (*awahan*).

In Guruji's view, even games were a powerful tool for inculcating values. Here, we recall a sentence of world poet, Rabindranath Thakur, who said, "Not hammer strokes, but the dance of the water sings pebbles into perfection."

The same day Guruji took up this subject further after swayamsevaks had left. He said, "Storytelling should also be positive. It should never be negative." There was a little background to this. On a previous day, a worker had narrated a story. Its summary was – a boat capsized in the middle of a river due to one mistake and everybody died. Guruji said, "Essence of the story should be that everybody was saved due to good deeds of one person." Though it is true that "Everyone is destroyed because of the mistake of one person it is as correct as the conclusion that 'Good deed one benefits all.' What kind of thoughts should be instilled in Shakhas? This is an issue. Remember, positive *samskaaras* cannot flower in a poisoned mind."

One day, the topic of discussion was Kalari – martial art of Kerala. One person asked about Malkhamb of Maharashtra during the talks. The teacher inside Guruji came to the surface at that time. He started explaining, "Actually, '*mallastambh*' of Sanskrit became *malkhamb*. It is also a martial art like Kalari. By the way, Kalari is also from Sanskrit word *khurli*, meaning exercise of the brave. *Malkhamb* became very popular during Shivaji's time. It was very important for brave Shivaji for fighting in hilly areas. Its practice was useful for vertical climbs on steep hilly rocks, high walls of forts using everything like feet, hands, claws, fingers and twisting one's body. It is a 12-15 feet high wooden column made of well-seasoned wood and was very smooth surface. Once in a while, oil is also applied to make it more slippery. Practitioners of this art practice it on this column. In old days, it was part of military training in nearly all villages. But, today it has become a mere piece of exhibition like Kalari."

During this period of treatment, *Guru-pooja* festival also occurred on 13th July. It was celebrated in a big room because of the rains. Intellectual discourse was by a local Sangh official in the local language. Guruji sat listening to it very attentively, and after the programme, he said he could understand the essence of the lecture well.

Guruji went to Nagpur from Chennai in the first week of August after four weeks of treatment. Within a few days of this, Pakistan attacked Bharat. Bharat was facing it successfully. Still Prime Minister called a meeting of political leaders on 6th September in the capital to draw a flawless plan from national perspective. Guruji was on a tour of Maharashtra at that time. On 6th September, he was taking post-lunch rest in state Sanghchaalak Kakaji Limaye's home. At around 2-2:30, a message came from Prime Minister's Office on neighbour Bapusaheb Pujari's telephone, "Golwalkar may please contact Prime Minster at the earliest." Guruji interrupted his rest and went to Bapusaheb's home and contacted the given number. Dialogue went on like this:

Prime Minister: "You know about the war already. I want support from all the leaders. I have called leaders of all the political parties tomorrow at 10 a.m. You please also be present in it."

Guruji: "Thank you, Shastriji, but I am not leader of any political party. I am just a worker of an organisation."

Prime Minister: "Well, the nation is going through a tough time, I need your co-operation."

Guruji: "Accepted, but how do I reach Delhi tomorrow morning from such a long distance?"

Prime Minister: "Please reach Mumbai immediately. Arrangement will be made from there. I am sending instructions there."

Guruji: "I will definitely try; we shall meet."[2]

Everything went well. Guruji was present at the all-party meeting on 6th September. He gave a statement on 8th. He sent out an appeal, "Thus, I appeal to all the countrymen, especially brother swayamsevaks that they should co-operate with the government in resolving any problems that arise in these times. Work like serving the injured and the sick, order and peace, citizens' security can be done on non-government basis. Special attention will have to be paid towards keeping the morale of people high, awakening high sense of national pride and resolve to fight on firmly till the final victory. We are fighting for truth, honour and indestructible unity of our motherland. Our victory is assured."[3]

Guruji did not tell the journalists anything as he came out of the all-party meeting. Even in programmes or discussions later on, he did not talk of anything but national duty. Finally, war was won. The situation also calmed down. During this time, the nation experienced grievous untimely death of highly popular Shastriji. More than four years had passed, when he narrated a sour incident to the workers in a meeting of Nagpur workers, held in March 1970.

"When there was a war with Pakistan in 1965, Prime Minister had called for an all-party meeting to seek co-operation in war efforts from the top leaders of different political party. He had requested me to be present in this meeting, though I was not head of any political party.

"In that meeting, a gentleman asked the Prime Minister to elaborate the objective of that war. One leader was using the term 'your army' again and again. I interrupted him time and again and said, 'Say our army'. Even then when he did not relent, I told him, 'What are you talking about?' Only then did he come back to his senses and used the term 'our army'.

"I said in that meeting, I will speak of only one thing, that is, we have to win this war. For this we should be ready to put in whatever efforts are required. There should be no political groupism. Saying 'your army' is treating the army, that is defending the country, as outsiders. Even when it is clear that we have to defend ourselves when we are at war with the aggressors, it is astonishing to say, 'let us define our war aims'. Let those who attack us define it. We don't need to. Our 'objective' is very clear. That is to gain victory while defending our honour and teaching right lessons to the aggressor. Making worthless statements creates hurdle in our fervour during war'.

"I felt the people present in that meeting were so distant from each other, it seemed as if they were from different countries or different lobbies. So, they were sitting opposite each other as adversaries. There was no common thread between them."[4]

Guruji stayed in Delhi for three to four days after that all-party meeting. He made arrangements after consulting senior workers like Sanghchaalaks, Kaaryavaahs, etc. for preparing strong plans so that co-ordination should not falter while asking for or offering co-operation. He went to the border state of Gujarat, straight from Delhi. His speech was broadcast on 19th September from Akashwani station of Vadodara. Summary of the speech was, "So far the results of the war are honourable for our forces. Its glory has brightened greatly... Ruling and other leaders have the ability to fight this righteous war with firm resolve and also to search for the path of peace... All the knowledgeable brothers should keep up the moral fortitude of society... It is my request to all the countrymen that we should wish for victory, pray for victory, work ceaselessly and make sacrifice of the highest order. You should exhibit courage and fortitude."[5]

Guruji went to the second border state of Punjab. He spoke before the Army Jawans in Ambala cantonment on 15th October. Army officers were also present at that time. He met Prime Minster the second time on 12th November. He also met Defence Minister Yashwantrao Chavan. He spoke on 14th from Red Fort grounds in a public meeting organised by the Sangh. He said, "Our people say we should hate sin. Destroy sin, but forgive the sinner. Only someone who is a great person, a divine soul, a saint or God can do it. It is not possible for a normal person. Even the greatest and best of people whom people consider God, that Bhagwan Ramchandra, could not destroy sin by separating it from the sinner; keeping the sinner alive and transforming that sinner into a pious soul. If he were able to do so, why would he kill Ravana?"

"Evil nature is not manifest. It is not possible to attack it. If one were to attack it, one would have to destroy the very foundation on which that evil nature finds life. This is the only way; there is no other way."[6]

Bilateral summit was to be held with Russia as a mediator, or rather to be held on its insistence. Shastriji was to go there to take part in this proposed summit. Guruji sent his comprehensive views about the possible accord in writing to Shastriji. He did not do this as a political leader, but as a worker dedicated to the nation. So, he did not distribute it to the journalists. After this, he went for Assam tour as per his pre-planned schedule. He received the news of the sudden death of Shastriji. He rushed to Delhi the same day from Guwahati to pay his floral tributes to the last remains of the departed soul. He met the President on 13th January and expressed his own and his organisation's condolences.

Sarsanghchaalak went to Prayag from Delhi. Preparations were underway there for the proposed World Conference during the Kumbh Mela under the stewardship of Prof. Rajendra Singh ji. Guruji stayed with the workers for two to three days and gave the required directions to them. Finally, the much-awaited conference took place on 22nd, 23rd and 24th January. Religious parliament was organised at 'Dharma Nagar' on the huge Saikati banks of holy Triveni Sangam. One Religious Parliament had been organised in the times of King Harshvardhan in A.D. 680, nearly 13 centuries back. After that, the Hindu society, chained in slavery for a long time, could not even think of such an attempt. The era was undergoing a change now. Glow of renaissance could be seen on the eastern horizon. Sacred winds of transformation were blowing. Jagadguru Shankaracharyas of all the four *peeths* were present with other saints and a*charyas* of different sects. Governors of Uttar Pradesh, Bihar and Bengal had come. Delegates had come from 20 countries of five continents. This was truly a Global Hindu Conference (Vishwa Hindu Sammelan), as the name indicated. Eleven resolutions, related to Hindu society and religious sects belonging to Sanaatan Dharma, were passed in the conference. Of them, the most important resolution was about reconversion to original faith (*paraavartan*). Second name of *paraavartan* was 'returning home' (*ghar vapasi*). When Swami Vishweshwarteerth, head of Madhav sect of Udupi, declared, "*Na Hindu patito bhavet*" the large congregation sitting in front of him announced its positive support to it by pronouncing '*Aum*' loudly. Intellectual penance of Guruji that had begun in 1956, had concluded successfully on that day. From that day, this thought had become the thought of Hindu society.

In the concluding session of the conference, Guruji had to give his closing speech on insistence by the head of Dwarkadheesh *Peeth*. He presented the whole history of massive efforts looking back from Chinmayananda's Sandeepani Ashram to the present in front of the religious heads and the thoughts behind it.

"All religions and sects are mine, all castes are mine, people living in hills and forests are mine. If they are unhappy, then it is only because of our weaknesses. Our tribal society, lying neglected because of a big section of Hindu society that considers itself wise, is my inalienable part. I will do whatever is necessary to correct the wrongs perpetrated over years, awakening within all this a kind of strong resolve. The Hindu society will stand up in a unified way; a strong society that would stand in its place of birth, in its own land from Himalayas to oceans with its head held high in the world."[7]

"I feel this period of two-and-a-half days is worth writing in letters of gold. For us it is a moment of great fortune. Our destiny that was asleep for so many years has finally turned sides... Great people like Revered Swamiji Vivekananda traversing the world had told us that our flag shall flutter on the face of earth – there is no doubt that that day is not far now."[8]

Guruji was highly satisfied with the success of the conference. On return to Nagpur, he wrote to his close *guru-bhai* (brother-disciple) Amitabh Maharaj, that is, Swami Amoortananda ji, "I was present in Vishwa Hindu Parishad's conference on 22nd, 23rd and 24th morning. Programme went off very well from the point of view of number of participants, etc. Shankaracharyas of Dwarika and Puri, high-ranking personalities of Madhava, Ramanuja, Nimbark sects, many holy saints of Jain, Buddhist, and Sikh traditions were present. A large number of people present there were happy and satisfied with their blessings and guidance. We only have to see how this project moves ahead. My contribution to the programme was only that of a serving volunteer."[9]

After this, Guruji felt a little relieved. The thought of completing the balance part of tour abandoned half way due to the all-party meeting called by Prime Minister about four-and-a-half month back came to his mind. He went to Goa in the last days of January. It was his first tour of that state. There was a public meeting on 30th January in Panaji. The Sangh work there had started after it got independence from Portuguese rule. People had heard a lot about the Sangh. Many of their relatives from other parts of Maharashtra belonged to the Sangh, still the Sangh was something new for them. As a result, the public meeting turned out to be bigger than expected. After completing his tour, Guruji returned to headquarters and went off for a tour of Utkal state in the first week of February.

Guruji was in Baripada on 15th February. It was the auspicious day of completion of his sixty years (*shashthi purti*). It would have passed off as a normal unnoticed day like all other years. But, with Yadavrao Joshi's advance planning and instructions, one senior worker from each state had already arrived in Baripada that day. Apart from one or two exceptions, all the secretaries (*karyavaahas*) of various states were present. All of them sat with Guruji after breakfast. In that gathering, Yadavraoji submitted two copies of a book in his hands, saying, "Our offering on your birthday" and touched his feet. Dr. Abaji Thatte displayed the book that was dedicated to Guruji. It was *Bunch of Thoughts*. It was the same manuscript that Guruji had corrected and returned back during his *panchakarma* treatment last year. That evening the Sangh programme went off well as usual.

□

Endnotes

1. *Shri Guruji Samagra*, Vol. 7, pp. 258
2. *Shri Guruji Aplya Prantat*, pp. 36-37
3. *Shri Guruji Samagra*, Vol. 10, pp. 185
4. Ibid, pp. 207-208
5. Ibid, pp. 186-187
6. Ibid, pp. 202
7. *Shri Guruji Samagra*, Vol. 5, pp. 55
8. Ibid, pp. 54-55
9. *Shri Guruji Samagra*, Vol. 7, pp. 42

37

In Between Two Shashtipurti Celebrations

Guruji left for Calicut in Kerala from Baripada on the next day of his sixtieth birthday programme. According to plans drawn by the Sangh, Kerala was to have its first state-level camp after nearby two years of formation of separate Kerala state unit. Guruji reached Calicut on 18th February on Friday morning along with regional Prachaarak Yadavrao Joshi, State Secretary T.V. Anantan and Dr. Abaji Thatte by Chennai-Mangalore Mail. On reaching the camp site, Dr. Abaji told volunteers in charge of arrangements (*prabandhaks*), "Guruji is on Shivratri fast. He will have no food or drinks; only one cup of tea will be good enough in the evening after intellectual discourse." Actually, Guruji used to follow the ritual of fasting only on Shivratri and some days of Shravan. He did not fast on any other day like sixth day or *Ekadashi* day of the month, etc. Fortunately, the city's main Shiv temple was right opposite the house where Guruji was staying. He went for temple *darshan* after his morning bath and *pooja* rituals with two to three Sanghchaalaks. Two senior swayamsevaks from Karnataka also came along. After completing three-fourth circumambulation, Guruji said, "Stop," and then added, "Balance circumambulation is to be completed after turning around from here." Guests from Karnataka said mockingly, "What kind of Kerala custom is this?" Guruji did not say anything there. After completing *darshan* rituals, pointing out to that swayamsevak, he said, "It would be wrong to think it is a meaningless custom. Water offered to *Shivalinga* is considered to be holy Ganga and that is what comes out on the north side of the circumambulation path through a sculpture representing Gaumukh (mouth of River Ganga). Crossing it over is prohibited; it is said to be against Shiva, a-Shiv. Therefore, we have to turn back and complete the circumambulation from the point we started. We must understand that there is a reason at the root of every custom."

There was overwhelming enthusiasm in the camp because the number of participants was in excess of two thousand over the expected figure. There was a meeting of Prachaaraks in the night. There was an over-enthusiastic young Prachaarak who was always ready with answers to any question. Guruji asked him to stand up and asked him, "Are you in high spirits?" His answer was, "Yes, sir." Second question was, "Do you know spirit is highly volatile?" He did not grasp the meaning of this simile, still he responded enthusiastically, "Yes." Many people laughed. Then, Guruji asked another question with proper explanation of his words, "If spirit evaporates, then what will remain?" Actually, his remarks were directed towards all those present. Sarsanghchaalak had given his guidance that one should not lose one's sense of balance in times of enthusiasm and excitement.

Guruji went to Tamil Nadu after the Kerala camp. He toured 11 districts from 21st February to 3rd March. During the time he would get a telephone call made to Mumbai nearly everyday. Those were the days when Savarkar had gone into *prayopavesh* fasting (voluntary fast unto death). His health was turning critical with each passing day. At the end, that gigantic volcano turned calm on 26th February. Guruji was in Thiruvanvelli city of Tamil Nadu that day. Apart from sending a condolence message through telegram, he also wrote a letter of condolence to the son of the departed soul, Vishwasrao Savarkar, on the letter pad of his host, an ex-Prachaarak, advocate S.G. Subramaniam. About that fiery effulgent departed noble soul, Guruji wrote, "This self-willed end to a life satisfied with its work, a celebrated stormy life that exerted ceaselessly with devotion to the nation, is deeply painful for countless patriots. An incomparable national hero like Swaatantrayaveer Savarkar is rarely born in centuries."[1] As soon as programmes in Tamil Nadu were over, Guruji came to Mumbai to meet family members of Savarkar. He took part in the condolence meeting held on 5th March. His lecture was not about glorification. It was about bringing to light the illuminating life of that revolutionary soul for the grief-stricken audience present that day. It was an appeal to follow that action-filled life rather than sit down disconsolately in inaction, struck with grief. At the end of a 55-minute-long speech, Guruji said, "That life seems to be a blessing us from the horizon after leaving this earth. He will be happy seeing us go forward with more vigour, he will be thrilled."[2]

That same month, a national-level committee was formed to commemorate the memory of the late Rajendra Prasad ji. Its convenor was multi-dimensional, highly talented Kanyhaiyalal Munshi. It also included the name of M.S. Golwalkar in it. Guruji gave his assent with thanks.[3]

Guruji went to Delhi from Mumbai. Saints and holy men involved in cow protection movement were waiting for him there. Guruji met them at their own seats. Most of the saints in this group were in favour of a democratic non-violent agitation. Guruji was not in favour of confrontation with the government. He met Home Minister Gulzarilal Nanda to reach some compromise. During the discussions, other topics apart from the main topic also came up. At one point,

Nandaji, speaking in a well-meaning tone, said, "Guruji, once in a while you also make critical political statements." "Guruji also responded with a laugh, "It is not like that. In reality, the situation is different. I believe it is my duty to oppose any attempt to harm the nation's unity. If a political action goes against this spirit of unity, I will criticise that too."[4] What could Nandaji say about this basic approach to issues affecting the nation? His expression showed that he agreed with this feeling.

The month of May arrived, a season for training camps in the Sangh. Guruji reached Hyderabad in Andhra for its camp in second week of May. *New York Times'* reporter, Shri Lucas came to meet him there on 13th. It would not be a mistake if one were to imagine that this could have been something like a chase from Delhi to Hyderabad to take his interview. In those days, countries like America used to keep a special watch on Bharat. Those were the days when political monopoly of Congress over the country was weakening. In this scenario, political lobbies all over the world had started observing and studying political movements in Bharat. Naturally, a rising Bharatiya Jan Sangh led by a young leadership caught their eyes. From there they moved on to the source of its strength. Lucas may have come with that acute political understanding. Whatever be the case, the interview began with civil mutual respect in a cordial atmosphere.

Lucas: "We wish to publish an article about Rashtriya Swayamsevak Sangh and Jan Sangh in the magazine section of *New York Times*."

Shri Guruji: "Why are you putting these two together in one article? This way you will only increase the confusion created earlier on."

His response to the question about Sangh and Bharatiya Jan Sangh was, "Sangh swayamsevaks are free to join any political party. Till 1937-38, our swayamsevaks used to be in Congress and Hindu Mahasabha. Whatever be their political differences, they could work together quite well in the Sangh. The Congress shut its door on Sangh swayamsevaks later on. Hindu Mahasabha has become very weak and it does not even have a presence in many places. Therefore, those who wish to join politics, seem to get into Jan Sangh. But, the number of swayamsevaks who are not in any political party is substantially high. There is a reason behind it. Our work is cultural. Our policy is clear. It is our belief that our nation can progress only if the society is unified and organised in a thread of unity, and its ethical and spiritual association remains unbroken."

Speaking about establishing the Bharatiya Jan Sangh, Guruji told the correspondent, "It was founded as a regional party in Bengal by late Dr. Shyama Prasad Mukherjee. When he thought of expanding Jan Sangh in other states, he met many people. He also met me to get our co-operation. I gave some workers to him for this purpose and Jan Sangh grew expectedly."

"If I talk about the Sangh, I would say that the government has done grave injustice to us. All the doors to an understanding were shut. We had to labour hard to end the unjustified ban on us. If we had been left with no option, we would surely have set up a political party. But, this need did not arise. The ban was lifted. Sangh does not wish to control Jan Sangh, nor does it want to serve any political party. Such a situation would be harmful for both sides and the nation."*

"Lucas: I have heard that there are differences between Sangh leaders and Jan Sangh leaders.

Guruji's comments on this were, "Leaders of Jan Sangh are free to have any opinion. I can only speak about the Sangh. Our adversaries wish to create an impression in people's mind that we Sangh people cannot work easily with mutual co-operation. Let us accept, for a moment, that there are differences among Sangh. I wish to ask, how can there be objection to this? It is not necessary that everybody should have the same opinion about every issue. As long as we have a common view on fundamental objectives and we are on the right path, there is no need to worry. If there are some minor personal differences on small issues, skies would not fall. However, my view is that difference of opinion is natural and desirable. We should work together with the spirit of co-operation even if there are minor differences and this is the essence of an organisation."

"Lucas's next question seemed straight-forward but actually a searching question, What is your opinion about anti-West feelings prevalent in Bharat?"

Shri Guruji: "To an extent such feelings do exist. Primarily, these have been spread by Leftist parties. There are political reasons behind it. There are some other people too, who feel that Western interference is not desirable. Their opposition to West is due to cultural reasons. There is a natural feeling of resentment due to a very high influence of West. Those who oppose due to cultural reasons are nationalists. In my opinion, they are right.

"No nation can live in isolation. There is no way that it can remain unaffected by industrialisation and such similar developments. But, it is possible to achieve growth without sacrificing our national character."

Many questions were asked during the interview. They were all ordinary, routine, old questions. There was nothing new in them.

When Lucas got up to express his gratitude after this sufficiently-long interview, Guruji shook hands with him and expressing his happiness, said, "I greet you as per your custom."[5]

Guruji began his Bharat tour again after conclusion of the Sangh Shiksha Varg in August. The Vishwa Hindu Parishad convention in Guwahati, held in October, is worth mentioning here. Hindu leadership in Assam had organised

---

* It would be ideal to recall here the letter written by Guruji from Sivni jail to Deorasji and draft document shown by Bhaiyyaji Dani to Moulichandra Sharma about a proposed political party during the efforts being made to get the ban lifted. (pp.199-202)

this convention inspired by the historic Religious Parliament (*Dharm Sansad*) organised eight months back in Prayag. There was a historical background to the thought behind this. Activities of religious conversion by foreign missionaries were being conducted like a military operation even after Bharat gained Independence in 1947 without any hindrance. Missionary priests and Church establishments were trying in tandem to instigate local tribes to demand independent states. It must be especially noted that Foreign Services Department of Central Government was responsible for tackling problems of this region. Their condition for talks was that discussions regarding any accord should be held in a place outside Bharat. Their spokespersons were Michael Scott, a foreigner and Fizo.

On the other hand, for big religious preachers, who were ready to go to the UK and the USA in any and every season for religious and cultural sermons, this region of our own country was like Rishyamuk hills of Bali, which is very far off. It was region simply overlooked by celebrated saints. *Acharya* tradition established centuries back by Shri Shankaradev had lost its spirit. In short, the English saying, "Devil rushes where angels fear to tread," had proved to be true.

This is where the first regional convention of Vishwa Hindu Parishad had been planned. An auspicious launch of convention was done on 2nd October, Sunday, in Guwahati. Guruji was the Chief Guest. Dedicated leaders of the society had begun working tirelessly about four to five months before this event. As a result, more than 70 delegates took part from the foothills, forest and mountainous regions. There were representatives from tribes of Daflash, Aksa, Naga, Neka, etc. There were also brethren from Mikir, Jayantiya, Khasi and Kachari communities. It was after many years, perhaps for the first time, that 17 anointed disciples of Shri Shankaradev had come together.

As an organiser of society, Guruji understood that it would not be possible to meet people, get to know each other well, establish good relations, etc. during the formal activities of the convention. Therefore, he had met nearly everybody before the convention and discussed various subjects with them in advance. Main points of his speech as the Chief Guest were:

"The British had planned to break our society into pieces. Therefore, they labelled our brethren as indigenous, hilly tribes, civilised-uncivilised, high-low, progressive-backward, etc. that indicated separate identities. They called many people who worshipped inanimate objects or nature as non-Hindus. Actually all Hindus are nature-worshippers."

"Our philosophy is to envision unity in diversity. Therefore, Shankaracharya had weaved together all the prevalent sects into a unified thread through *panchaayatan upaasana* (worship of five elements). Hindu culture is all inclusive. Here, there is no division between believer and non-believer, but, it is not in our nature to bind everybody in a single form of worship or belief. Vishwa Hindu Parishad does not wish to create such a system, because the

Parishad itself will then become a sect."

"We will have to wipe out the accumulated sense of doubt and separatism between our religious leadership. People from outside a *math* do not come together inside it. There is an absence of close relationship between heads of *mathams* and their disciples. *Acharyas* of Shaiva and Vaishnav sects do not come together even in times of difficulties. In such a scenario, how will we face disasters like religious conversion?"

"In the recently concluded conference in Prayag, senior religious heads, teachers, scholars, Vedic and non-Vedic saints, etc., everybody sat together under a single roof. All of them discussed together the problems faced by society; something worth watching. A resolution to bring back our converted brothers and sisters into their mother society was passed unanimously. Religious conversions are harmful for our society. We shall have to embrace our brethren and bring them back to their original faith."

"Our entire work is based on reverence and faith in our *dharma* and it should never be reactionary. It should not be that Christians and Muslims have become active. So, we should also work for our society and *dharma*. It is true that a disease is cured by a medicine, but we should make the body healthy and strong so that it should not catch any disease. Therefore, I request you all that you should come out of your *ashrams,* and take lead in defending those who have strayed away from our *dharma* by moving around in the society."[6]

This exertion in northeast Bharat was successful from every angle. From a historical perspective, it was the beginning of Hindu renaissance in that part of our land. Guruji's first tour of Assam had taken place in 1950; 16 years had passed by now. Within this period, the hard penance undertaken by this ascetic had begun to show results.

Guruji stayed in Guwahati for two more days. After discussing ways and means of follow-up actions, he went to Mumbai via Kolkata on October 5. From there he went to Nagpur for Vijayadashami festival.

During his regular tour in November, he attended a programme to celebrate the sixtieth birthday (*shashthi purti*) of an acknowledged authority on devotional Varkari community, Dhunda Maharaj Deglurkar in Pandharpur on 20th November. He presented his respectful greetings to him in respectful words with all humility. But, his speech that day at this auspicious time is important from another point of view. He spoke, rather unexpectedly, about the spiritual side of his life. The audience was astonished and also happy to listen to it.

"I know Dhunda Maharaj, a highly dedicated devotee of Lord Hari for many years," and went on to add, "It is written in my birth-chart that I would enjoy the company of saints. Therefore, I get the chance to meet sages and saints regularly and receive their holy blessings. It has been happening with me since my childhood. I believe I could distance myself from personal and family related complications only due to having a divine *darshan* of holy people and their blessings. It happened for good, and it was also the ideal.[7]

"Normally, when one speaks of 'spirituality', it seems to be a complicated matter for a normal human being. There seems to be a generally misleading view that envisioning the Supreme Being and being blessed with his divine blessings is only for making this material world blissful. Since I never had this view, I never paid attention to this thought. Therefore, my mind was never confused about it."

"I got to read the literature of saints in my childhood. I got a chance to read out scriptures of divine people to my parents. I also recited the Gayatri *mantra* regularly. But, in practice, an urge to gain knowledge about these scriptures never awakened in me for a long time. Later, this opportunity arose when I began staying in Nagpur.[8]

"There used to be a great saint Gulabrao Maharaj in Vidarbha. He was blind by birth. I had good relations with his disciple Shri Babaji Maharaj Pandit. I used to visit him many times, and I do so even now. I just recalled an inspiring episode today. It was the beginning of *chaturmaas* – four months of monsoon. He had pledged to give discourses about *Gyaneshwari* as much as possible. He began by reciting, '*Om namoji adya*'. His scholarly and devotion-laced discourse went on continuously for four hours. I found that discourse highly scientific and logical. He made each '*sutra*' (line) very simple and clear by using different subjects as media to explain it. Even after this, he could not reach the second '*ovee*' (second stanza). While listening to him, it stuck me that if the first stanza is impregnated with so much meaning, how meaningful would *Gyaneshwari* be? Curiosity got awakened in my heart and I began reading Gyaneshwari in my own home."[9]

Dhonde Maharaj urged faithful devotional followers to pay respect to the divine presence of a devotee of the highest order. Sacredness of that auspicious moment – all this must have forced those words from Guruji's mouth due to some internal inspiration in that extraordinary atmosphere.

□

Endnotes

1. *Shri Guruji Samagra*, Vol. 7, pp. 262
2. *Shri Guruji Samagra*, Vol. 1, pp. 156
3. *Shri Guruji Samagra*, Vol. 7, pp. 136
4. *Smriti Parijat*, pp. 109
5. *Shri Guruji Samagra*, Vol. 9, pp. 150-163
6. *Shri Guruji Samagra*, Vol. 5, pp. 56-61
7. *Shri Guruji Samagra*, Vol. 1, pp. 176
8. Ibid, pp. 177
9. Ibid, pp. 177-178

38

From the Banks of Kaveri to the Peak of Badri

There was a state-level camp at Salem in Tamil Nadu on 30th-31st December, 1966 and 1st January, 1967. After staying there for all the three days, Guruji entered Bangalore in Karnataka state. He visited all the districts of Karnataka till 17th. Programmes that were organised were get-together of swayamsevaks on Sangh ground with intellectual discourse of Guruji and meetings with workers before or after them. It was mandatory to be present in the programme on time and insemi-uniform, i.e., *khaki* half-pant and white shirt. Work in Karnataka state was progressing well. The last programme was in Mangalore on 17th. That was the biggest programme in that state during this tour. Guruji went to Kerala and was in Kerala for nine days, from 18th to 26th.

He had to answer to one specific question many a time in all the southern states. Question used to be, "What is the condition of Prabhudatta Brahmachari and Puri Shankaracharya." Both the saints were on hunger strike in Vrindavan and Delhi respectively to press for a ban on cow slaughter. The government's strategy was to keep a dishonest silence. The entire Hindu society was worried. If something untoward were to happen, then nobody was sure what it could lead to. Guruji was most worried as the Sarsanghchaalak. One could sense it from what he spoke at various places. He was very unhappy with the government's approach.

A question related to this episode was asked in Thiruvananthapuram. Advocate Nedumangaad Keshavan Nair asked Guruji, "How can many religious believers be on a fast for very long periods?" Guruji replied, "It is possible. There is a science behind it. One has to keep the five sense organs clean with *yogic* actions or else the waste will become poison. Therefore, *jalvasti* (consumption and discharge of water) has to be done regularly as a rule. One has to drink water at regular intervals. Otherwise, the fast can prove to be fatal. I know a person well who has undertaken 111 days of fast. He is still alive. If somebody pushed food forcefully into his mouth, he knew a method of throwing it out.

His whole body was under his control."[1]

One can state that 1967 was a politically significant year. Many politically important developments took place during that year. The breakdown of unchallenged monopoly of Congress over power also began that year.

Guruji reached Delhi in February end. A meeting of Jan Sangh candidates had been arranged at Lala Hansraj Gupta's residence. Every candidate, whether he had won or lost, was expected. Nearly all of them were known to Guruji. After the initial formalities Guruji told them, "One should not take happiness or unhappiness of victory or defeat in election to one's heart. Criticism of the people you fought with, whether from your side or theirs – that chapter should be closed and fresh cordial relations should be established. Do not consider victory with personal ego even by mistake. One should only keep the thought in one's heart that this is people's blessing for you. There should be firm faith and belief that this victory is a result of keeping the Sangh work firmly in mind and growth of this fundamental work."[2]

Punjab's state-level meeting was also scheduled in Delhi on 22nd July. Gauging the atmosphere at that time, Guruji told respected Sanghchaalaks, Karyavaahas, Prachaaraks and other colleagues openly, "Many of our people have reached high and important posts in state governments in north Bharat due to results of the last elections. It seems natural to reach them for different jobs, reasons, and urge them to do so. But, my instruction is that Sangh workers should never go to them for personal or somebody else's work. If someone has to go, he should go after giving it a lot of thought. The Sangh work is paramount; it is most important and it is God's own mission. For its workers to stretch their hands in front of political workers for petty things is condemnable. And, our going to them to pursue them for personal work can also affect their honesty and impartiality. They should get ample opportunity to show their skills, capabilities and honesty to the people. And if there is any deficit in this, we should let them pay the price for it."[3]

It had been Guruji's endeavour to keep the Sangh away from politics. Still Bharatiya Jan Sangh was on the path of progress with the co-operation of swayamsevaks. However, Guruji was very alert that the average swayamsevak should not be politicised. He gave the required guidance through questions, counter-questions, humour, jokes, etc. to see to it that the working system of the Sangh, its policies, etc. should not influenced by politics. Atmosphere in all such matters of guidance used to be lighthearted.

Vishwa Hindu Parishad had made a place for itself in matters of religion in the country after Prayag Conference of 1966. Its general secretary, Dada Apte, was moving in the desired direction. It was pleasant for him to note that many religious scholar teachers (*acharyas*) were ready to consider Parsis as *Sanaatani* brethren. He wrote a letter in this regard to Guruji to get his view. In response to that letter, Guruji wrote, "...in the life of this nation, Parsi brethren have become one with the nation's aspirations a number of times with proud mention of people like Shri Dadabhai Naoroji, Pherozshah Mehta, Madam Cama and others. Therefore, there is no need to think of them as separate now. In reality, they are Hindus and it is justified to call them better Hindus in view of their nationalist nature. I had said so publicly. With this view in mind, I had invited my close friend Shri Jaal P. Gimi to inaugurate the camp of Baal swayamsevaks. He had graced the inaugural programme as its chairman."[4]

The 19th International Vegetarian Congress was held in Delhi on 23rd November. More than 40 delegates from Switzerland, Israel, Sweden, Germany, Norway, the UK, the USA, etc. were present in it. Guruji addressed them on a special request of organisers.[5]

"There has been comprehensive and deep thinking in Bharat about compassion for living beings...in all our religious scriptures, we have been told to follow non-violence... But, if one were to follow non-violence literally, then it will mean end of human beings. Therefore, use of vegetables has been allowed so that human beings can live their lives. While living one's life, one should not think that the universe has been created only for himself."

"According to Hindu thought, each individual has three qualities – *sattva* (spiritual) *raja* (action oriented) and *tama* (lower desires)... it has been said that an individual can attain his ultimate goal by developing *satogun* (spiritual qualities)."

"A human being is affected by the food he consumes. A person depending on violence for food will surely be violent in practice. *Sattvik* food will make a person *sattvik* too. After many types of experiments our wise practitioners have come to a conclusion that cow milk, fruits, vegetables, etc. make people pure, self-controlled and help them progress towards spiritual growth, so that they can merge into the supreme soul (*atma tattva*). A person taking such food does not consider only human beings as his brothers and sisters, but, he also has a feeling of kinship with the entire living world. This is true not only for this country but for other countries too. We know about Saint Francis and Theroux in the present times. They are living proofs of vegetarianism."

"From the food that he eats, he extends his relationship to countries, entire humanity and finally to entire universe. As a result the human being becomes one with nature. Thus, vegetarianism is necessary for purifying the soul and build a feeling of all-enveloping affection for the entire animate and inanimate world."[6]

After the session, many delegates told Guruji that they had received a new vision. They were unaware of the scientific philosophy behind vegetarianism. Their vegetarianism was only an opposition born out of a feeling of mercy for violence against animals. Only after Guruji's lecture did they become aware that there was a spiritual basis to it. Foreign delegates thanked the organisers for inviting Guruji to the conference.

Guruji was in Doddaballapur in Karnataka on 2nd-3rd January, 1968, for its divisional camp. Deendayal Upadhyay and Nanaji Deshmukh arrived in the camp on the 2nd, unannounced. There were four to five workers with them. Deendayal ji had been elected the all-Bharat president of Bharatiya Jan Sangh only a week back in the annual conference of Jan Sangh that had taken place at Calicut in Kerala. Driving over the Sahyadris, he had reached there to receive the sacred blessings of Guruji at the very commencement of his new responsibilities. All of them sat together in Guruji's tent and were having discussions. Chief of intellectual programmes entered the place to inform Guruji about the programme of the day. As soon as he saw him, he said, "Today's intellectual session will be taken by Deendayal ji," even before he looked at the paper. He smiled as he looked towards Deendayal ji, and that is how it happened. Deendayal ji spoke that day. There was not a trace of politics in his speech; it was completely a Sangh-related speech. But, what a misfortune! It proved to be the last intellectual discourse of Deendayal ji and last meeting of Guruji and Deendayal ji. Deendayal ji's abandoned body was found in the Mughal Sarai railway yard in Uttar Pradesh after 40 days of this meeting on 11th February. Some unidentified people had murdered him in the Lucknow-Patna train. Guruji was in the Prayag division's camp. Dropping out of the camp programme, Guruji left for Varanasi to have a last glimpse of his colleague who was dearer than life to him. On seeing that lifeless body, the only words that came out of his lips were, "Oh! What has happened…." Caressing that still, lifeless face with his right hand, he looked at his face once again, the last time in life, turned back and went away. When *Organiser*'s editor, Malkani asked for his condolence message, he expressed his inability and apologised. His short letter of apology indicates a deep sense of anguish in his heart. In it, this grieving soul wrote, perhaps with blood oozing from his heart, "Wound is deep, very deep. I do not know when will it get healed. I have no words to express my heart's feelings. Due to acute grief, I am unable to feel pain. I do wish to write, but I cannot. Please forgive me. Let the wounds heal a little. Please do not scratch them."[7]

Guruji's March-April tour was of Punjab-Himachal Pradesh. Senior workers took him to have a *darshan* of Jwalamukhi temple in between the programmes. Goddess Durga is worshipped in the form of an eternal flame in this temple. There is no other idol there. As Guruji was returning from the temple blissfully after the worship, gentleman manager presented the visitors' book to Guruji, who wrote happily, "I am feeling highly fulfilled for having the great fortune to have *darshan* of Jagadamba Bhavani Shri Jwalamukhi. I am feeling very happy at the successful efforts of the managing committee to keep the atmosphere clean and calm. People, bound by many kinds of bonds of the world, can have the divine view of the highly divine flame in this calm environment. I pray humbly at the feet of most kindhearted Bhagawati Jagadamba Shri Jwalamukhi that she give such heavenly inspiration and experience to human beings suffering from this world. I express my gratitude to the managing gentlemen with salutations."

Maa. Sa. Golwalkar, 16th March, 1968.[8]

From Jwalamukhi, Guruji and his compatriots climbed even higher in North. Let us listen to this experience personally from senior Prachaarak Anantrao Ramchandra Gokhale, who was with him, "From Mandi we reached Manali in the morning. Shri Guruji was very happy. On seeing the temple of Shri Manu, he expressed his wish to get it revived and reconstructed. He went to Vashishth village and had a divine view of Lord Vashishth temple; he also saw Hidimba temple. The incomparable beauty of Himalaya's high peaks that towered over each other, reflected in rain the showers at one moment and in sunrays in another, was worth viewing. Looking at Deodar trees touching the skies, Shri Guruji recited a few lines from the poem in *Raghuvansha* of great poet Kalidasa and said, "I don't feel like returning from here."

On the next day, Guruji began his speech in the evening public meeting in Kullu thus, "I had been studiously avoiding coming to the Himalayas. These great mountains, River Vyas and beauty of forests all around created by Supreme father like God attract one greatly. The heart says that one should keep gazing unceasingly at God's divine play keenly in this solitary and heart-warming atmosphere. The heart is filled with bliss. But, God has put before us another duty that we have to do."[9] Guruji's indication was towards the Sangh work. Finally, Guruji got down to that subject.

Here, we take a slight diversion in the narrative. Manali of present times is the ancient Manavalaya, that is, Manu'alay or home. The desire expressed by Guruji to get the temple renovated was fulfilled after some days. Current Manali is about 4-5 kms away from original Manavalaya.

Delhi Municipal Corporation had decided to honour Vedmurti Pandit Shripad Damodar Satavalekar on completion of his 100 years on Sunday, 14th April, 1968. For this, a committee had been formed with Mayor Lala Hansraj Gupta as its chairman. The committee had invited Guruji as the Chief Guest for the programme. Lieutenant Governor of Delhi, respected Adityanath Ojha, presided over the function. The meeting was to be held in a football stadium outside Delhi gate. Vedmurti, born on 19th September, 1867, reached the place before the desired time of 6 p.m. without support of even a walking stick. The programme commenced on time. Guruji gave detailed introduction about Vedmurti. "Birth in east Konkan in Sawantwadi a century back on the birthday of Sant Gyaneshwar, study of Sanskrit and English languages with his own efforts, establishment of Sanskrit-speaking institute, creation of book *Vedic Raashtrageet* (Vedic National Anthem), facing opposition from British because of it, carrying the responsibility of Aundh district Sanghchaalak, witnessing destruction of his invaluable library built over years of labour by misguided Gandhi devotees as a reaction to Gandhi murder, establishment of Vedic Swaadhyaay Mandal again in Gujarat at Pardi, writing of more than 420 books and their publication, carrying on activities like a young man even at this age – Guruji went on recounting all these qualities. And concluded it with, "I humbly salute this great soul who is forty years elder to me" and went back to his seat. Guests could grasp the stature and excellence of the felicitated personality because of this introduction given by Guruji.

Actually, Guruji's relations with Vedmurti Satavalekar were quite deep and old. Therefore, he had decided to be a part of the felicitation programme as his bounden duty. He had taken part in two similar programmes earlier too. He was the chief guest of the scholars' meeting held in Pardi Swaadhyaay Mandal when Vedmurti was entering his hundredth year on 6th October, 1966. Nine days before that, Guruji was chief guest in his felicitation function organised on 28th September in Ahmedabad. Gujarat Governor Nityanand Kanungo was chairman of the programme and chief guest was Justice Bhagawati. In the eyes of Guruji, Vedmurti was an ideal swayamsevak, who had deep faith in the Sangh. In all the three felicitation programmes, Guruji's presence was because of the wishes of Vedmurti that he be with him. It was not possible for Guruji to evade his insistence either in body or spirit. So close was their deeply heart-felt relation.

Guruji came to Kerala Sangh Shiksha Varg from Delhi via Nagpur. From there he gradually moved northward, reaching Rajkot in Gujarat by middle of May. In between, he came to Mumbai by air on 17th May, Friday. A release function of the collection of the late Pandit Deendayal Upadhyay's articles titled *Political Diary* was to be held there on 17th May, Friday. In his speech, Guruji happily complimented the celebrated politician, Dr. Sampoornanand, who had written the preface of the book with an open heart inspite of his political differences. He openly appreciated this healthy tradition. Talking about analytical clarity, incisive insight, highest form of idealism, civilised language, etc. in the essays, he highlighted Deendayal ji's incomparable personality. Guruji's speech that day was surcharged with emotions. He mentioned emotionally, his close heart-to-heart relationship with Deendayal ji. In conclusion, expressing his unshakeable faith in indestructible spirit of eternal Sanaatan, Mother Bharat, he said, "We should think; let us not grieve about one who has gone. How does it matter, if one individual is gone? Our Mother Earth is capable of giving birth to many a jewel-like people. Our society has produced extraordinary personalities, one after another. Deendayal is not the last. He was such a divine soul that it gives us faith that people like him can come again. Let us move ahead with firm focus, faith in mission with our own efforts; with this assurance and faith in our heart that more and more workers, each better than the other, will stand up once again. Thinking workers will arise. People who will leave aside worries about one's own family and social life, people with strong hearts who will think only of nation as their family, and those whom we may not call ideal pictures of sacrifice, but who could be looked upon as people filled with feeling of sacrifice, such people will rise. Our first duty is to put in efforts to this end. We should move ahead with such a strong belief."[10]

Guruji went to Sirsi in Karnataka for Ayurveda treatment after completing Sangh Shiksha Vargas of May-June and the Central Committee meeting after that. Period of treatment was of 15 days, from 27th July to 10th August, and the person imparting this treatment was Dr. Ganapatirao Patwardhan.

Sirsi experience was similar to that of Pattaambi and Palghat. Many swayamsevaks came to meet Guruji. Different subjects came up based on differing inclinations and views. Once, divisional Prachaarak of Dharwad, Babu Desai, asked a question about religious life of Maharashtra, "Samarth Ramdas created excellent book like *Daasbodh*, provided great leadership to the society and established hundreds of *mathams* at many places, nominated their heads, but all that has withered away. At the same time, Varkari community has not weakened and is growing over time. What is the reason behind it?" Guruji told the keen swayamsevaks, "Are you aware what kind of disciples Ramdasji had? All of them were loyal like Kalyanswami and hard working. Many disciples made hundreds of copies of Shri Samarth's *Daasbodh* and *Manaanche Shloka* by hand – only-hand-written copies were possible those days – and distributed them amongst devotees, and as you noted they also established *mathams*. But, Shri Samarth's views were not re-analysed and represented as per changing times. There was no capable person who could do it.

"Varkaris' story is different. The Varkari sect had also weakened after samadhi of Yogeshwar Gyaneshwar. This state of affairs continued for nearly two-to-two and half centuries. Then, came Eknath Maharaj who resuscitated it. He laid stress on the pledge (*vaarivrat*) of going on Pandharpur pilgrimage in *Ashaadh-Kartik* months. He inspired followers, devotees, saints and believers in Pandharinath to recite *bhajans*, *kirtans* and offer sermons. He asked them to publicise Sanaatan Dharma after completing their '*vaari*' pilgrimage. This is how Varkari sect blossomed. Ranks of socially committed volunteers also swelled. To make the mission simple and easily acceptable, he also wrote a collection of songs called, *Bharud*. These songs reverberated throughout Maharashtra during the time of pilgrimage. Eknath wrote many devotional songs and songs for worship (*aarti*). Many devotees of Vithoba presented lives of saints in poetic drama form. They also created an invaluable poetic religious scripture called *Eknathi Bhagwat*, through which they presented original thoughts similar to *Nam Mahatmya* and *Triputi* principles. A series of celebrated saints rose over a period, such as Namdeo, Tukaram, *Gorakumbhar*, *Saavatamali* and others. That series of saints is still alive with successive saints like Mama Saheb Dandekar, Vaaskar Maharaj, Dundhe Maharaj Deglurkar. Because of all these developments, Varkari sect could survive and grow too."

After a pause, he added another point, "For a sect to survive, there is another condition. The process of training of workers has to be continuous. Varkaris have this process in place. Therefore, they keep getting new workers."

Vibhag Prachaarak's question was about spiritual activities, but Athani's Sanghchaalak Anantrao Deshpande's question was about psychology. He asked a question based on his own experience about a friend of his, "I have a friend, whom I know quite well. He has taken *diksha* from a highly enlightened guru; he performs *pooja* twice a day, but in practice he is highly irritable, and like Sage Durvasa in his speech. Why is it so…?"

Guruji's answer was, "Do not worry about this. The path of spirituality is a path of progressive evolution. There is sustained movement during progress. It is called motion in English. There are many definitions of motion. One of this is, 'Loss of balance regained is motion'." Explaining this idea further, he said, "When an individual picks up motion, that is, takes a step forward, his balance is disturbed immediately. If somebody pushes a leg in his path when he is walking or running, he falls down. In this state of imbalance, that individual balances self by pushing his other leg forward and keeps up his motion. Thus, he gradually moves ahead while keeping up his motion. This principle at gross body level applies itself even at micro-level in case of efforts being made to move ahead intellectually. Possibility of gaining this balance is higher at the intellectual level. Arjun had said, '*Chanchalam hi manah Krishna*' (Krishna, mind is unsteady.) Therefore, one has to be highly conscious about this problem of imbalance in case of movement in *'sadhana'*. Only then can path of *sadhana* (spiritual practice) become a path of growth without hurdles. "Guruji did not talk about Sanghchaalak's friend, but, he explained well enough about the paradox and about imbalance in behaviour.

A young swayamsevak sitting there had a curiosity after listening to Guruji's explanation. He asked, "Some people speak about incidents that take place in the past or will possibly happen in future. Is it possible?" Answer was, "It is possible. Invention of cinema is an example. The audience in a cinema can see only the scenes that are being projected presently on the screen. He does not know what is going to come up. But, the operator of the projector knows about the scenes that are to follow later. Similarly, the assistant sitting next to him also has the information. Thus, the operator of this world also knows about the incidents that happened in the world in the past or will happen in the future. Similarly, a person living close to him also knows about it. Some seekers who have progressed on this path of spiritual studies, get in close communion with God. But, such people are very rare."[11]

Guruji went to Pune after completing his treatment. Just as he reached there, he received the sad news of passing away of his long-time friend and colleague from Nagpur, Balshastri Hardas. Guruji went to Mumbai. The main objective of the visit was to meet Saint Tukdoji Maharaj, who was suffering from cancer. He went to Bombay Hospital on 18th August and met the saint. Seeing his dear Golwalkar, the saint became highly moved. Once the atmosphere turned calm, Guruji informed him about modern medical science and informed him that his days were numbered. The saint accepted this information with a sense of neutrality.

The next programme of his pilgrimage to Badri is worth mentioning. It was the third week of September. Professor Rajendra Singh, popularly known as Rajju Bhaiyya, was the skilled person in charge of this programme. Let us listen to his fluid narration about this tour:

"Respected Shri Prabhudatta Brahmachari had a strong desire that Guruji should visit Badrinath temple. Guruji's close friend and *guru-bhai* Swami Shri Amoortananda gave great support in planning this pilgrimage in accordance with this wish. Shri Swamiji had also told Guruji many a times to make time for this pilgrimage. But, why would Guruji go there inspite of the inclination in his heart? There had to be some concrete reason for going to Badrinath. Generally, Guruji's programme used to be made only at places where there was a Shakha and swayamsevaks and he had to meet these swayamsevaks. Therefore, Shri Prabhudatt Brahmachari ji found a way out. There is a shortage of *dharamshalas* (pilgrims' low-cost rest houses) in Badrinath. So, Maharaj ji built a building, Sankirtan Bhavan, for the purpose through his organisation. He decided to have this building inaugurated by Guruji once it was ready and he sent his insistent persuasive invitation to Guruji in the July month itself."

"At the same time, Swamiji also insisted upon Guruji to take one week out in September for this pilgrimage. When Guruji's yearly tour plans were being finalised after the central meeting of July, I had also kept one week free. April-May-June months are preferred for Badari-Kedar pilgrimage or September-October months after the rains. Due to the Sangh training camps in summer months, it was not possible for Guruji to go at that time. So, the pilgrimage plans were made for September."

"Shri Guruji, Dr. Abaji Thatte, Swami Amoortananda ji, Lala Hansraj ji – all of us and young workers of the region were there. Shri Maharaj ji came directly from Vrindavan in his car and we met him in Rishikesh. A meeting of Vishwa Hindu Parishad had been organised in Haridwar at that time. A person asked Guruji in Haridwar, 'How did you think of Badrinath pilgrimage?'

Shri Guruji said, 'When can I get free time to go on pilgrimage? But I have been forced to go.'

"There was a sermon by Guruji in front of residents of the *ashram* of Divya Jeevan Sansthan of Swami Shri Shivananda of Rishikesh. We had to reach Srinagar the same evening where swayamsevaks had organised a small programme. We had an Ambassador car, a Jeep and an Impala for Guruji belonging to Dehradun Sanghchaalak. But Impala car began breaking down as soon as the road began to climb. We felt that a foreign car did not wish to go on a domestic pilgrimage. Thus, we returned the car. Passengers of that car were distributed in the remaining two cars. I sat in Shri Maharaja's car and we reached Srinagar."

"Motorable road to Kedarnath is not available till the temple. Last ten to twelve miles have to be covered on foot, on horse or in a palanquin (daandi). The climb of last five to six miles near Kedarnath is quite tough. Guruji had not been following the practice of walking on foot since some time. For a person not habituated to riding a horse, this ride is as tiring as walking. Back, shoulders and thighs start aching within first two to three miles. We wished to take Guruji on a palanquin, but he firmly refused to ride on the shoulders of a fellow human being. He really wished to walk, and if it proved too much, take a horse. But, we knew how difficult it would be. When we pleaded with him, he said clearly, 'I have decided to ride on people's shoulders only for my last journey, i.e., *Maha yatra*.' We requested Maharaj Shri to persuade Shri Guruji to complete the journey in a palanquin. We suggested that he should find some example in scripture that could prove that it is not objectionable to ride on somebody's shoulder. When Maharaj ji talked about it, Shri Guruji only conceded that he shall talk about it when they reached there. But, we never got a chance to go to Kedarnath. The road had been blocked at many places due to landslides following rains. Pilgrimage to Kedarnath could not be completed due to breaking down of the road to Kedarnath. We had to wait at Rudraprayag even to reach Badrinath to get the road cleared. We went to Badrinath directly from Rudraprayag. If a vehicle broke down on the way, Guruji would also join us in pushing it.

"It is very cold in the mountains and Guruji does not wear anything except *dhoti*. I had taken a new pyjama made of handspun cotton for Guruji that could be worn under the *dhoti*. It was done so that Guruji would not face any difficulty in the cold weather. But Shri Guruji did not use that. Guruji doesn't wear socks and shoes too, but we had made arrangements for them. Shri Guruji did not use them either, saying, 'There are many people in the mountains who manage to live without special clothes to ward off the cold, then why should I need so many clothes to protect myself from cold?' Shri Guruji loves drinking tea, but he had stopped eating anything with tea for many years. He would not take dinner in the evening or milk in the night. He used to take food only once in a day and that too very little. We were very worried that how such small quantities of food could provide enough strength and warmth to protect him from the cold. Thinking on these lines, we had taken along some dry fruits, some *laddoos* made with *munakka* (dried berries), etc. I told him that it is necessary in the mountains to eat something with tea. I forced him to eat one *laddoo* one day, but saying that sweet gets stuck in his teeth, he did not eat *laddoo* again nor did he take any dry fruits. Shri Maharaj ji knew that Guruji insisted on pure *ghee*, so he had specially got *moong laddoos* made in pure *ghee*, but we workers had to eat those *laddoos* too. Shri Guruji followed his regular habit of taking food once in the day and his regular tea."

"The Kedarnath pilgrimage could not be done but we got an opportunity to stay in Shri Badrinathregion for five days. Shri Guruji performed proper puja with all the rituals with great devotion. He also followed the ritual of '*pind daan*' (offerings to departed forefathers) for his mother, father and other forefathers. Not only this, he also did his own '*shraaddha*', rites generally performed after death by one's offspring. He tried hard, to best of his ability, to keep information about his own *shraaddha* to himself. Apart from other programmes, Shri Guruji also went to Mana village, the last village on Bharat's border. He collected young children together in Mana village and asked them questions about the nation and religion and also arranged to distribute sweets to them. There is a waterfall called *Vasudhara* about three miles from Shri Badrinath. Shri Guruji thought of going to Vasudhara. He went by Jeep till Mana but from there, one had to talk. Shri Guruji walked one-and-a-half mile somehow but then began losing his breath. Vasudhara was only 1.5 miles from there. Since he could not walk further, he had to return. On his return, he told Maharaj ji, "I realised today that I am growing old. It proved too much for me to walk 1.5 miles after Mana."

Shri Guruji had gone to Mana and Vasudhara without informing Maharaj ji. Shri Maharaj ji was very upset about it. He said, "You should have told me before going. I too would have gone with you. We could have arranged for horses from Mana. We could have made all the arrangements."

Shri Guruji said, "That is why I did not tell you. If I had told you, you would have surely come. You would have suffered pain."

There was a meeting of all the priests of the temple and other smaller temples of that area one day. In this meeting, Guruji asked all of them, how much did they know about various rituals. Shri Guruji suggested that without worrying about what kind of offerings people get in South, all the priests of various temples should work and follow complete rituals as per the Scriptures. Only with this could faith of Hindu society remain strong. Priests of Shri Badrinath temple are called Rawal and the tradition is that these Rawals come from Namboodiri Brahmin community from Kerala. The Rawal of the temple those days was a person who had heard Guruji as a young student in Kerala. He knew well about the Sangh too. Guruji had discussions with him and he took tea with him. He also met and talked with other citizens of Badrinath. He told all of them to follow their religion with faith and maintain strong bonds of affection with fellow brethren.[12]

On all the five days, there was a religious discourse by Maharaj ji on religious scripture *Bhagwat* in the afternoon. People used to gather there on their own like bees flocking to a flower. Guruji also used to sit along with them and enjoy the lecture with devotion.

For Guruji, this pilgrimage of Badri was as important as was his pilgrimage to Sargachhi. On that day, on 13th January, 1937, Wednesday, day of Til Sankranti, he had said, "I am no more, what I was a few moments back." Similarly, on that day, 18th September, Wednesday he offered '*pind daan*' and he was no more what he was till then. There was a difference in Guruji who went to Badri and Guruji who returned from there. There was a difference in the two. He had received an unbeatable mission statement in Sargachhi, '*naaham tu hi, naaham tu hi*' (Not me, only thou). And, as a result of today's Brahmakapal shraaddha of self, he became 'not me' in true sense and was left with 'only thou'.

□

Endnotes

1. *Smriti Parijat*, pp. 233-234
2. Ibid, pp. 75
3. Ibid, pp. 75
4. *Shri Guruji Samagra*, Vol. 7, pp. 348
5. *Smriti Parijat*, pp. 78
6. *Shri Guruji Samagra*, Vol. 5, pp. 70-71
7. *Shri Guruji Samagra*, Vol. 7, pp. 350-351
8. *Shri Guruji Samagra*, Vol. 6, pp. 102
9. *Jeevan Prasang*, Vol. 1, pp. 35-36
10. *Shri Guruji Samagra*, Vol. 1, pp. 190-191
11. *Baburao Desai Smritiyan*
12. *Jeevan Prasang*, Vol. 1, pp. 39-43

39

Hindavah Sodarah Sarve

1969 is a year that is specially memorable in Guruji's life from the point of view of social harmony. But, it had begun on a negative note. Editor of daily, *Navaakaal*, had taken an interview of Guruji. After seeking his views on problems of minority community, the methodology for bringing people back to their mother faith, the necessity of changing customs that had lost their relevance, etc., he asked Guruji, "Is it not necessary to change the fourfold caste system (*chaturvarna* system)?" Guruji's answer to the question is worth paying attention. He countered it with his question, "Are you drawing reference from article of Shankaracharya ji in the *Kalyan* monthly magazine and the questions raised in Parliament in this regard?" Upon receiving a 'yes' as an answer, he added, "Question-answers that were exchanged in Parliament were based on complete ignorance. My opinion is that people who asked those questions had not even read the article, and if they had read it, then they did not understand it. Similarly, the person who gave the answer had also not read the article or he did not understand it after reading it." There was further dialogue on the subject after this. Topics about casteism, untouchability, need to remove it, etc. came up and the editor published the whole interview in his newspaper.*

In the delicate Brahmin-non-Brahmin environment of Maharashtra the Sangh opponents and clever political leaders with evil designs tried to take advantage of its wrong presentation. They raised a storm against Guruji and RSS in a planned manner. Guruji had reached Kerala by then. Maharashtra's Prachaarak Moropant Pingle met him on 2nd February regarding this issue. Guruji understood the matter of this disturbance completely from him. He sent his clarification to newspapers on 4th February from Ernakulam. At the end of this statement, he noted, "Background to that interview was an academic discussion. Such discussions have been taking place routinely. I have no complaints that the caste system is not seen in practice currently. I do not wish that it should be pushed on to the society. It is my view that what is scientific and eternal truth will not be destroyed."[1]

---

* Complete interview is available in *Shri Guruji Samagra*, Vol. 9 on pp. 163–173

Other points in this clarification were about reiteration of philosophy of the Sangh work. In short they were:

1. From towns to villages and from hilly regions and forests to plains, the Sangh mission is to bring together every member of Hindu society without thinking about one's caste, poverty-wealth, literatecy-illiteracy, intellect, etc.
2. It was not my view that some people in our society are untouchable. There is no need to tell people that the Sangh does not think in terms of untouchability and touchability.
3. If there is anger within Harijan brethren about the situation today, then they are not to be blamed for it. Our behaviour with them should be such that bitterness in their heart is removed and they should consider themselves to be proud organs of the society.
4. Behaviour of the society has been changing with changing times. Law has to change with times and has to throw out something that has proved not to be useful anymore; this has always been the experience. In this, the important point is that when a change is brought about, it should not break the thread of continuity of original traditions.[2]

Actually, it was an attempt in Maharashtra to create a mountain out of a molehill, but, provocateurs had to get disappointed. Even opponents of the Sangh who knew the Sangh and Guruji from close quarters, did not fall prey to this attempt. But, one must concede that it was an evil attempt to present the Sangh in poor light.

Guruji went to Madhya Pradesh from Pune. He was present in Raipur for the inaugural programme for celebration of Swami Vivekananda's birth anniversary organised by Shri Ramakrishna Mission Vivekanandashram. Senior swayamsevaks feel Guruji's speech that day was longer than usual. In Swami Atmananda's view, "Guruji's thoughts were flowing with high emotions from the depths of his heart." He closed his speech with his heart's wish that, "Let it be proven once again that fulfilling their lives each, ignited with Swami Vivekananda's brilliance, every son of Bharatmata is capable of imparting the knowledge of Truth to the entire world.."[3]

This disciple of Swami Akhandananda spent his next 20 days travelling from Vivekanandashram at Raipur to Shri Narayanguru's Shivgiri Math in Kerala. After concluding a successful programme on 21st January in Thiruvananthapuram, he left for Kollam in the morning, next day. On way, there is a *samadhi* (memorial) of Gurudev in Shivgiri near Varkalaa. Guruji stopped there for some time to pay his homage to him. Swami Nijananda and Swami Poornananda welcomed the guests and took them to the *samadhi* temple. Guruji paid floral tributes to Shri Narayanguru's idol, circumambulated the temple and paid his respect by lying prostrate before it. From there, he went to highly celebrated Sharada temple founded by Gurudev. While he was taking *prasad* from the priest with bowed head, he exclaimed, "My great fortune that I could come to this sacred religious place, my heart is overwhelmed." Swami Nijananda requested him to write his opinion in visitor's register. Seated there, Guruji wrote, "Today, I was fortunate to have a divine view of Shivgiri Math. I spent some time in this divinely calm and inspiring atmosphere. It is my humble prayer at the revered feet of God that his workers may spread his powerful message of unity of human beings once again in Bharat and overseas with his sacred blessings. Because of the work done by him, peace, pure love for animate and inanimate and complete dedicated devotion toward ultimate eternal truth may become powerful in today's world, suffering from conflicts."[4]

From the early days as a Prachaarak, Pandit Deendayal Upadhyay had close relations with Barrister Narendrajeet Singh's family. That family, specially mother of the family, had a strong wish to begin a school in memory of this soft-natured soul dedicated to the mission. That family donated land and required funds for this purpose. On the wishes of the family, Guruji came to Kanpur on 23rd February, 1969 Sunday to lay the foundation stone of Deendayal UpadhyaySanaatan Dharma School. Guruji offered a garland to the oil-painted picture of the late Deendayal Upadhyay in a public function held on the occasion. Kanpur's Vibhag Prachaarak Ashok Singhal rendered the song soulfully that had opening lines, *"Bharat ke bhaal par kumkum ke sath lagaa akshat asamay hi jhar gaya"* (sacred rice put with vermillion on Mother Bharat's forehead has fallen off untimely). Guruji spoke after that. He began, "I have been a teacher as a family tradition. Being in the education field by tradition, it is but natural that I should feel happy on construction of a new school. Another reason for this happiness is that it has been resolved to run this school in the name of Pandit Deendayal ji." About the late Deendayal ji, he said, "The secret behind his greatness, gentleness, scholarship and notable humility was that in whichever field he worked, he kept his spirit of swayamsevak awakened. He never allowed his heart or nature to wander."[5] In his emotional mood, he said, "How wonderful it would have been, if I had not sent him to the political field." Eyes of all those present turned moist.

In the month of March, Chandigarh division Sanghchaalak, advocate Babu Dilipchand was present in Akhil Bharatiya Pratinidhi Sabha. He requested Guruji's presence at a personal function during that time. His submission was, "On completion of sixty years (*shashthi purti*) in *Vaishakh* month, I wish to take *sannyas* from law and work for the society in my remaining life." He wished Guruji to be present in the get-together of friends in the programme planned on that occasion. Guruji was in agreement with this idea and was happy with his plans. He agreed to be present for this function.

The day chosen for this new kind of *vaanprasth* by Dilipchand ji was sacred *Vaishakh*, 13th April. Dilipchand ji's taking leave of his profession was a surprise, both for lawyers and his clients.

It was beyond their imagination that such a busy lawyer would retire with such an easy frame of mind. Therefore, all the invitees, which also included judges, were present there out of a feeling of respect and wonder. Supporting this approach that was worth emulating, he said, "We Hindus have a tradition. When a person finds that his son and grandsons have become adult, he immediately surrenders his responsibility as the head of the family life and dedicates himself to social service. Third phase of life is, in a way, preparation for the fourth phase."[6] It is a matter of joy that the number of such socially-oriented *vaanprasthis* (who have given up family responsibilities), doing social service is growing substantially.

Guruji visited Sangh Shiksha Varg in Kerala at Pandalam at the end of the same month. While returning from there to Ernakulam, he stopped at Changanasheri where he dropped in at the home of Shri Mannat Padmanabhan who was on last leg of his life's journey due to old age that had ravaged his health. He was All Bharat President of Vivekananda Rock Memorial Committee and founder of Nair Service Society. As soon as he saw Guruji enter his room, he called out in a weak voice, "Swami", and waved is hand. (Shri Mannat ji always used to call Guruji, Swami Golwalkar.) Holding his hand and speaking in a loud voice, albeit slowly, Guruji said, "You have accomplished all your work in every aspect." (*Aap sarvavidhen poornakam hain*) This social worker, though ignorant about English or Hindi, could understand the full meaning and his face lit up with satisfaction of fulfilment. Here, words were scarce, face and eyes were speaking. Taking both the hands of the sick gentleman in his, he took his leave. This was their last meeting.

In May end, revered Jain Muni Sushil Kumar Maharaj contacted Guruji just as he reached Delhi, and requested him to join Bhagwan Mahavir Nirvaan Shatabdi Samiti as its member. Guruji accepted the request with pleasure and also offered his active co-operation later on.[7]

Guruji was in Nagpur for the third-year Sangh Shiksha Varg in the first week of June. Generally, Sarsanghchaalak used to stay there throughout this training camp and avoid other outside programmes. There used to be some exceptions on the rarest of occasions. This time such an exception came up on 6th June 1969, Friday. It was the seventieth birthday of highly respected Appaji Joshi. Appaji's life was totally dedicated to the Sangh. He was the one who had declared most revered Dr. Hedgewar the Sarsanghchaalak on 10th November, 1929 on Mohite Grounds of the Sangh. He had also presided over the meeting held in 1940 in Akola, in which the decision to nominate Guruji as the successor to most revered Doctorji was made. Appaji was always an undeclared but important and integral part of the Sangh. Kalidasa talks about, '*Anarthee prarthanavah*', meaning 'No desire for self, but always satisfying desires of others'. Appaji truly reflected this nature. Guruji attended this seventieth birthday function whole-heartedly. All the old and new officials of Vidarbha state came to Wardha. After receiving blessings from Appaji, Guruji presented his auspicious wishes that carried deep meaning, "Appaji was the person who was close to Doctorji's life like his breath. Doctorji used to seek his advice on every important issue. When the subject of nominating Sarsanghchaalak came up, it was Appaji who gave him advice. Actually, if Appaji had even an iota of any ego or desire for power, he could himself have become Sarsanghchaalak; he could have worked hard in any responsibility he was entrusted with. This, truly, is the treasured heritage of Rashtriya Swayamsevak Sangh, for which all the credit goes to Appaji. Such a spirit is required to build an unconquerable nation. May Appaji be blessed with such active 100 years."[8]

Guruji's training camp programmes ended by June end. After this he went to renowned Vaidya Pandit Ramnarayan Shastri in Indore for one week of rest. His *guru-bhai* Amoortananda Swami came there from Mohipura to meet him. Both of them embraced each other when they met, as was their habit. But today, much against his nature, a suppressed cry escaped Madhu's lips. During embrace a small boil on Madhu's chest got pressed by a pen in the pocket, and natural reaction to it was that suppressed cry. Recovering himself immediately, he began his discussions. Later, applying the medical paste given by Shastriji, he got busy with other programmes.[9]

Actually, this boil under the left breast was like a comet that gives a forewarning about a looming disaster. This was an advance intimation of an advancing cancer. But, whether that highly aware personality had grasped its significance, God alone knows. It did not seem so from his conduct.

The president of International Guru Nanak Trust, Bakshi Jagdev Singh met him in September and requested him to be a patron of the trust. Explaining his limitations, he said, "There is no meaning in taking up a post as a decorative jewellery. I have no interest in it. You know my busy schedules. Most of my time goes in the Sangh work. I am left with very little time. Keeping this in mind, I can offer every possible co-operation. This work is for Nanak Dev. Please tell your colleagues about my limitations. After that, you can inform me about your expectations from me." Jagdev Singh heard him out and said with a smile, "Guruji, we have decided to have your name on our committee" and laughed aloud. Guruji too joined in.

1969 was the centenary year of Mahatma Gandhiji. Entire Bharat was immersed in his sacred memories. All government and non-government organisations were conducting various kinds of programmes in his memory. During those days, Guruji's tour programme was planned for western Maharashtra from 27th September to 11th October. Many influential people of Sangli came to know that he was to visit their city. They decided to invite him to the centenary celebrations. With this purpose, Bapusaheb Pujari and Baba Potdar met chairman of the Centenary Committee, Vasantdada Patil. After getting his assent, Sangli's president, Rajaram Bhonsale went to Guruji's place of stay and invited him for the meeting to be held on 6th October.[10]

News that Guruji Golwalkar was going to take part in Gandhiji's centenary function spread in Sangli. Curiosity ran high in citizens of the city. Older generation remembered well that Guruji had to face strong opposition in the same Sangli, exactly 20 years back on 5th October. The younger generation recalled that Guruji had to go from Sangli to attend a war-related meeting on request from Prime Minister Shastriji four years back on 5th September. Even if it were for a brief time, politics took back stage, memories of Gandhiji and Guruji merged together and people were agog. As a result, people's participation was worth seeing. Chairing the meeting was famous Congress leader, Dhondiram Nana Patil. Both Patil and Guruji garlanded Gandhiji's picture; and after the formal programme, Guruji gave his speech. Summary of the speech is given below:

"We have come together for an important and sacred occasion. Mahatma Gandhi's birth took place like any normal person's, but with his duty-bound action and love in his soul, he reached the pinnacle as a person of highest order. We should follow his life to the best of our abilities.

"We have an old tradition of reciting *praatah smaran*. We remember sacred deeds and great people of our nation in this *praatah smaran*. For centuries, addition of new names in *'praatah smaran'* had stopped. Sangh has restarted it again and created Bharat *Bhaktistotra* by including names of great people to date. Mahatma Gandhi's name is clearly mentioned in the list of revered people.

"Gandhiji used to say, 'I am a die-hard Hindu, therefore, I love not only human beings, but all living beings.' The prominent place that truth and non-violence got in his life and politics on the principle of '*na hinsyat sarvabhootani*', was only because of his hardcore Hindutva.

"Gandhiji had the highest respect for Shri Ramakrishna Paramhamsa. While writing preface to his biography, he wrote, 'This character is a living image of truth.' Shri Ramakrishna Paramhamsa had loved the entire living universe as a die-hard Hindu. I believe an individual, who has pure feelings for Hindutva, one who cannot tolerate any impurity in it, only that person can have this kind of love; it is not possible for any other individual.

"Swami Vivekananda has said, 'Like we say, *Matri devo bhav* (Mother is equivalant to God), *Pitri devo bhav* (Father is equivalent to God), *Atithi devo bhav* (Guest is equivalent to God), we should also say '*Agyani devo bhav*' (Illiterate is equivalent to God) to banish ignorance of poor people. We should open doors to treasures of knowledge for all.' Swamiji's directions and Mahatma Gandhiji's practical behaviour – both are but same.

"He has expressed his views about the future of Hindu *dharma*, about which we speak so much, in his book *Future of Hinduism*. In that book he says, 'Hindu *dharma* means that which is unstoppable, that moves ahead with conviction, a path for search of truth.' Today we feel that this *dharma* seems to be a bit tired, not one that can help inspire people to move forward. The reason for this is that we are tired; *dharma* is not. When we get over our exhaustion, that very moment Hindu *dharma* will burst forth with all its strength, like never before in past. Hindu *dharma* will dazzle and impact the world with a huge strength. It is our responsibility to fulfil Mahatmaji's prediction."[11]

Newspapers of Mumbai and Pune reacted positively to this meeting and his speech. Response of the common people was good, except for one or two exceptions. Title of one letter to the editor was, 'Gandhi Followers, Beware!' And another was titled, 'Hijack of Gandhi by Golwalkar.' It is not surprising; such things happen. There is a saying in Malayalam, 'A mosquito sitting on cow's udder drinks blood, not milk!'

Another extraordinary programme after this was Karnataka state's Vishwa Hindu Parishad Conference in Udupi on 13th and 14th December. Guruji was felicitated on the first day by the Udupi Municipal Corporation. The number of delegates surpassed all expectations and crossed 15,000. When the planned facilities proved inadequate, the city's citizens came forward with enthusiasm. Doors of all the families were open for totally unknown Hindu brethren. Even before the resolution was passed, there remained no high or low caste, no touchable or untouchable.

Guruji was present from the beginning till the end of conference. Religious heads and scholars of more than 40 sects such as Shaivism, Vaishnav, Lingayat, Jain, Buddhist, Sikh, etc, were present. There were more than 100 *sadhus* and saints. The Speaker of Assam Assembly was the Guest of Honour. It was a grand *Dharma Samsad* (religious parliament) in every possible sense, reminding one of *Naimisharanya* of ancient times.

Guruji inaugurated the conference. He laid stress on social dimensions of *dharma*. His words were, "In our *dharma* equal importance is given to material prosperity and spiritual bliss. If we pay attention only to the latter goal, then it would be an incomplete viewpoint about *dharma*. In fact, a human being's spiritual progress is not possible in absence of peace and security. How is it possible for great souls to take birth and work for spiritual growth of society without a strong base for social life? Therefore, the first condition for *dharma* is that social conditions should be conducive."

Talking about prevailing conditions in the society, he said, "We have forgotten that we have to live as a unit of an organised society. We have become isolated, forgetting our immense human strength. Many people doubt whether we can stand up as an organised unified society with so many castes, sub-castes, sects, languages, traditions, way of dress, types of food, etc. But, we should not forget that there is an inner river of unity that flows through us inspite of our superficial differences on the surface."

Expounding on the practical aspect of *dharma*, "Our problems will not be solved by talking with high-sounding words. We shall have to absorb their principles in our lives. The principle of liberation of poor and exploited is gaining strength. But, the truth is that nowhere else is the feeling of empathy and self-sacrifice as strong as that prevails in our *dharma*. Our scriptures have declared, 'One who accumulates more than his daily requirement is a thief. He should be punished for theft'.

"However, the question is how much of this have we absorbed into our lives? When we take food, do we think even for a moment about our brethren in our neighbourhood who may be going hungry? If we do not do this, then all our great speeches about *dharma* are baseless and meaningless."

The second aspect of *dharma* is to lay stress on unified and organised life. Our scriptures pronounce, "Think together, speak together, work together and march ahead together. Only then will you achieve heavenly prosperity.' We have to mould our lives according to principles of our *dharma* and stand up as a united and proud society."[12]

Just as *veena* is tuned to match the pitch of a sacred recitation, similarly hearts and minds of all the delegates were tuned for a positive discussion about social reforms after listening to Guruji's guiding discourse. The second session was historic. A resolution to eliminate untouchability was to be passed in that session. The chairman of the session was retired I.A.S. officer from Scheduled Caste background, Shri R. Bharanaiyya. After discussions held in the background of social spirit of oneness, equity and unity, when the resolution was passed unanimously with the resonating sound of '*Aum*' the head of Madhav sect *math*, Swami Vishweshwar Teerth stood up and raising both his hand, pronounced, '*Hindavah sodarah sarve*', that is 'All Hindus are born from the same mother', meaning, they are brothers. The assembly echoed with salutations to all the religious heads. Bharanaiyyaji, overwhelmed with emotions and shedding tears of happiness, said, "Guruji, all this is due to you…" Guruji promptly said, "No, no, all this has been due to all of us and mother-like society's willpower." According to Yadavrao Joshi, who was witness to that moment, it was a moment of ultimate joy in Guruji's life.

No doubt, this was a moment of supreme joy, but it would not be right to limit this moment to Udupi as its source. To understand this, one would need to go back to the episode mentioned at the beginning of this chapter about chaos that *Naavaakal* interview had created. During that period Shirubhau Limaye was promoter of Gandhian socialism and president of 'Jat Pat Todak Mandal, Pune' (Organisation for Breaking Caste System). When we examine that dialogue, we can realise in which direction was the mind of Guruji working.

Shirubhau: "You claim that you have suggested an easy way to end untouchability. But who is untouchable? In my view, who has given rights to these religious heads to purify untouchables? We do not recognise them as religious heads."

Guruji : "We shall have to pay special attention to a few things. Untouchability is not just a question of only untouchables. It is in nobody's hand where a person is born. Nobody can say that he will be born in a particular family. Therefore, untouchability is a name given to narrow-minded thinking of high castes. Thus, banishing untouchability means banishing this narrow-minded thought. Similarly, it has nothing to do with whether you or I recognise religious teachers or not. Those who believe in untouchability also believe in their religious gurus. So, this problem can be solved through these religious gurus. Apart from this matter, I have had close relations for the past many years with many religious gurus and Shankaracharyas. So, I can say that religious gurus will surely do this work. Actually, many people have worked for abolishing untouchability. Mahatma Gandhi has played a major role in this. I too have tried to contribute in my own way in hundreds of experiments for removal of untouchability."

From this, we can realise that the joy Guruji felt on passing this resolution was not just an emotional upheaval; for him it was a moment of seeing the realisation of his efforts. Behind it were his skill in managing people's psychology and a long period of hard work with readiness to forget and forgive. Dragging the heads of various *mathams* out of their fortressed mindsets was akin to milking a tigress. So, achieving this feat successfully gave a rare feeling of joy.

However, this episode does not end here. This successor of Dr. Hedgewar was not going to be satisfied with just the passing of a resolution. Sense of organisation ablaze in his heart shone out immediately and he wrote a long letter to the chief organiser of the conference, Shri Suryanarayan Rao: "Karnataka state conference of Vishwa Hindu Parishad was successful beyond expectations... But, we should not sit back in inaction born of satisfaction. There is need for sustained hard work. It will not be wise to think that the situation will change like magic."

Putting his finger on limitations of the resolution passed in the conference with much enthusiasm and pride, Guruji wrote: "This resolution about untouchability authorised by scholars, religious gurus, heads of *mathams* and other saints will not become a part of our lives so easily and simply. Beliefs that have taken firm roots over centuries will not be uprooted simply by words or resolutions. We shall have to publicise it by contacting people, cities to cities, villages to villages and house to house…."

Drawing attention to the soul of the resolution, this revolutionary philosopher wrote: "We wish to transform hearts, religious and emotional transformation through contact and practical behaviour. Our goal and work is not only for achievement of economic and political equality. We wish to see the right kind of change, we wish to envision the spirit of unity...We shall have to blow outdated orthodox views to smithereens with hard blows."

Giving directions about work, this accomplished leader wrote: "We shall have to take these enlightened views across the country... We shall have to take it to jungles, caves and plains... we shall have to expect conflicts, opposition and hurdles... We should not expect show of gratitude... any miracles! Please give up this expectation also... We shall have to work untiringly with clear understanding of harsh realities with extreme compassion."

While ending the letter, he wrote about the true, positive vision of a truly dedicated social worker: "Many workers blame others for problems. Many people see a problem in distorted politics. Many people put blame at the door of Christian, Muslim and other religions. Our workers will have to keep free of such mentality. We shall have to work for our *dharma*, for our brethren with the right vision. We shall have to reach out and work where there is pain and poverty. We should not see differences in human beings when serving them; we should not look at their religion or sect… service to humans is not a feeling of pity by looking at a person from head to toe, but, it is a worship of Supreme God residing in them... This is the teaching of our *dharma*... We have to work with this sense of surrender."

Guruji had sent this letter to Suryanarayan Rao on the *Makar Sankraman* day of 1970. Thus, it was a message for transformation, a positive revolution, from Guruji – a message on *Sankranti* for a complete revolution – a contemporary message forever!

□

Endnotes

1. *Shri Guruji Samagra*, Vol. 9, pp. 175
2. Ibid, pp. 173-175
3. *Shri Guruji Samagra*, Vol. 1, pp. 91
4. *Smriti Parijat*, pp. 154,
   Shri Guruji Uttar Pradesh Mein, pp. 73
5. *Shri Guruji Samagra*, Vol. 1, pp. 191-197
6. Ibid, pp. 198
7. *Smriti Parijat,* pp. 79
8. *Shri Guruji Samagra*, Vol. 1, pp. 201
9. *Aarti Aalok Ki*, pp. 274
10. *Shri Guruji Aplya Prantat*, pp. 96
11. *Shri Guruji Samagra*, Vol. 1, pp. 208-215
12. *Shri Guruji Samagra*, Vol. 5, pp. 85-87

40

Cancer Patient with a Heart of Steel

Swami Amoortananda used to meet his guru-bhai, Guruji, once or twice in a year wherever possible and used to invite him to his Mohipura Ashram every time. And Guruji used to evade it every time, saying, 'Some time later'.'Some time later' due to his busy schedules. Finally, a day dawned when both could fulfil their wish to be together in Swamiji's *ashram* and Guruji reached Mohipura Ashram on 18th March, 1970. Dr. Abaji Thatte and a few other state-level officials accompanied Guruji. Soon on his arrival, both of them went down to sacred River Narmada that flowed past the *ashram*. After bathing, both of them sang hymns in praise of Narmada and then worshipped Mother Narmada. Many common people from the village and tribal brethren standing near the banks of the river atfive-six metersheight above the river were witnessing this rare scene, proclaiming, *'Narmada mata ki jai!'*. On completing his rituals, Guruji collected all these people around him and sat down to converse with them. Those poor people did not know much about hallowed rituals, worship, lectures, sermons, etc. For them, having *darshan* of *sadhus* and blessed by their touch as their blessings was all they desired. Guruji began his dialogue with them in an informal rural style. There is hardly a need to note that all the questions carried some underlying meaning and purpose. They would respond with enthusiasm from wherever they were sitting, in a high voice joyfully, guilelessly. Any person hearing them could easily conclude that they were far ahead of so-called civilised city dwellers, who were self-proclaimed progressives in terms of understanding of *dharma,* religion. Witnessing their progress in the'test' Swamiji too was feeling contented. Most of the people had heard about Rameshwar, Kedarnath, Badrinath, Dwarika, etc., and they also knew that these were centres of pilgrimage. Taking this thread forward, Guruji explained to them, "All these places were in our own Bharatvarsh and this great land is our mother who blesses us with spiritual liberation." These discussions were followed by partaking of *prasad*. All of them sat down in rows in the compound, and both *guru-bhais* shared food with them after worshipping Goddess of this Universe. After resting in the afternoon, Guruji left for Timarani and stayed with Bhausaheb Bhuskute that day.

In the second week, Guruji reached the land of River Brahmaputra. Vishwa Hindu Parishad's state-level conference was slated for 27th, 28th and 29th at the Culture Centre in Jorhat town. Guruji was present there on all the three days. Not only delegates from Assam but delegates from other northeast states were also present in it. Leading lights of society, such as head of Shri Shankaradev's Vaishnav sect, respected Queen Guidinlu, famous litterateur Mitradev Mahanta, Neelamani Phukan, Anand Chandra Baruah, Nalini Baladevi and others graced the programme. Head of Udupi Pejawar Math of revered Madhavacharya sect, Swami Vishweshwarteerth, came specially for the occasion. Secretary General of Vishwa Hindu Parishad, Dada Apte, known for faultless planning was there much earlier. Thousands of people living in forests and hills and town-folk had begun their trek two to three days earlier to reach there on time. This was a heartwarming coming-together of people akin to a *Kumbh Mela* in the beautiful surroundings blessed by Goddess Kamakhya Devi. Organisers of the conference, with a creative foresight, had brought in waters from Krishna, Kaveri, Narmada, Godavari, Poorna and 45 other rivers to sanctify the conference centre as a pilgrimage site. Swami Vishweshwarteerth mixed these waters together and created a pilgrim centre with the confluence of these holy rivers. Many faithfuls took this blessed water to their homes as *prasad*.[1]

The Jorhat conference was inaugurated with a pious sermon by highly-revered head of Shankaradev sect on 27th March, Friday. Special aspect of this programme was that Guruji met different types of people in smaller groups. He provided required guidance to different people after understanding their background, situation, problems, compulsions, capabilities etc., Guruji's concluding lecture was on 29th, Sunday, and the subject of this simply worded lecture was 'Our National, Religious and Social Problems': "We should not forget that we are facing China and Pakistan on our two sides." Quoting Swami Vishweshwarteerth, he said, "*Hindavah sodarah sarve* – we Hindus are brothers. Wicked foreign rulers made attempts to sow the poisonous seeds of divisiveness and claimed that tribal people are not Hindus but worshippers of nature. Actually, all Hindus are nature worshippers. Hindus consider Tulsi, *bilwa*, pipal etc. to be sacred and worthy of worship. Similarly, snake is worshipped all over the nation. There are huge temples of snake-god in distant South."

Guruji requested all the tribes that they should register themselves as 'Hindu' in forthcoming census. He warned, "Otherwise, just as the apathetic approach of Hindus prior to the Partition led to many Hindu-majority areas going to East Pakistan, we would make the same fatal mistake again." At the end, invoking confidence in the delegates, he said, "If all of us can build structured unity in this region, we shall see that we are be able to stand up as a very strong, powerful society, changing the complicated situation that obtains now. Every type of non-Hindu power will be defeated and this region will stand up as a powerful organ of Mother Bharat."[2]

Well-known traders, owners of tea estates and landlords had also come to this conference. In a special meeting with them, reminding these wealthy gentlemen of their duties, Guruji told them, "Such activities also require money. If we wish to improve the lot of our brethren living in very miserable conditions, then we would need money to provide them with different types of education and employment. Therefore, we should pledge to provide funds for this work. Whatever funds we give for such work, reaches God because this is, but, God's own work."[3]

Queen Guidinlu, who graced the dais, was specially felicitated by Guruji himself. He presented the revered goddess-like queen an idol of Lord Krishna holding a flute, made of elephant tooth.[4]

The conduct of Guruji in that conference was not that of a leader, who had come from outside, it was that of an active worker. He was fully alert about all the programmes taking place in the conference. Here is a small example: Delegates had come together to discuss resolutions to be passed that day. A gentleman presented a resolution to build a hostel for tribal students at a certain place. Everybody was in agreement, in spirit. However, working president, Shri Teerthnath Sharma ji suggested that a line, namely, 'to end the influence of Christian missionaries' should be removed. The proposer was not ready for this change. Not only this, but he became angry and the tempers in the session also began to rise. There arose doubt that the core point of the resolution would be lost in this debate. Guruji rose slowly at that time, took the mike and just spoke one sentence, "Respected gentlemen, all your feelings and ours are the same; what we want to express is also same. The only suggestion is that these words should not be there in the resolution." The atmosphere turned calm immediately. Resolution was passed unanimously with this amendment.[5]

In brief, there was a visible difference between the conference held in Guwahati in 1966 and the present conference. Awareness and spirit of brotherhood, equity and co-operation was definitely growing. Living proof of this was the Jorhat conference.

From the north-east, Guruji's next leap was to the southern region. Sangh Shiksha Varg had commenced there on April 1. He reached Palghat to stay there for three days. Formal salute to Sarsanghchaalak was to be conducted that evening. All the participating students came together on Sangh ground in well-prepared uniforms. All of them stood up for Sangh prayer after the salute. Suddenly, the sky was overcast with dark clouds and there began a heavy downpour. Everybody, without exception, got wet from head to toe. After dinner, when the instructors got together for the evening meeting, Sanghchaalak of Palghat, advocate Easwar Menon enquired from Guruji about inconvenience in the evening. Guruji answered with a smile, "It is my duty to get everybody wet during Sangh Shiksha Varg in Kerala." In fact, he was right. Guruji had similar experiences twice or thrice earlier on too. Last year, the special exception was that rain had begun before people could reach the Sangh ground; even then he was present on the ground without umbrella.

From Palghat, Guruji went to Chennai and then left for Nagpur by G.T. Express, reaching there on 6th April. He had to take part in *Varsh Pratipada* festival (Hindu new year day). But, what happened was quite different from what people expected. Breaking the tradition of last 30 years, he did not speak, and let his voice rest. His condition had deteriorated very badly. He used to lose balance while walking. He stood just still, in attention, unmoved by torrential rains but today he was not able to stand even in that normal atmosphere. There was no fever when he was examined. Doctors could not find anything unusual. Finally, they concluded that the patient had reached this state due to unrestrained labour and insufficient food over many years. For the time being everybody felt reassured and Sarsanghchaalak's tour for training camps began again. After South, his tours of North began. In every camp he had five programmes and sometimes six. To be present in Sangh assembly in the morning and evening, one intellectual discourse every day, two meetings in the day to get introductions of the participants, meeting with instructors of the camp and enquiries with them about their work, meeting with people managing the camp, meeting with well-wishers and officials, once in a while. Tour that began on 28th April ended on 27th June at Kolkata.

Now, we need to turn back to the incident about his boil that we talked of in the last chapter. Guruji was in the Pune camp on May 3rd-4th-5th. Famous homeopath doctor, S.S. Namjoshi came to examine Guruji on instructions of his personal assistant, Abaji Thatte. Discussions between the two took place in camp-in-charge's room. Both of them went to advocate Baba Bhide as decided between them. After doing his medical checkup, the doctor's attention was drawn to the large boil of the size of an *amla* (gooseberry). He was shocked to see it. On touching it, he found it was highly painful and problematic. His question was, "Since when did it develop?" Patient's answer was, "I do not know. I had suddenly felt pain when embracing a friend eight to nine months back, only then did I realise about it." Doctor Namjoshi was very sure that it was a cancerous boil. 'Guruji has cancer!' Doctor, himself a swayamsevak, was speechless. He only muttered, "We shall have to check it again, tomorrow." That same night the doctor expressed his fears to the senior people concerned. Next day, on 4th May, he did a minute checkup of the patient and after recovering himself, he told, "Guruji, I think it is cancer." There was not a trace of anxiety on Guruji's face. "Ok, let all the camps be over. Where is the time till then? Let us think about it in July." This was the reaction. Till then, he took some medicines from Dr. Namjoshi and left for other training camps.[6]

Guruji reached Mumbai during his tours on 18th May. Dr. Ajit Phadke and Dr. Shrikhande had planned to get Guruji examined by cancer specialist,

Dr. Prafulla Desai. He was examined accordingly and it was confirmed that it was a case of cancer. Guruji asked Dr. Desai, "Doctor, how far has it spread? Is it possible to cure it?" Doctor's answer was, "We can tell about it only after the operation; postponing it would be dangerous. My honest opinion is that you should not postpone it." Guruji paused a little, then said, "Let us do it after completion of the training camps by June end." It was decided to get the operation done on July 1 and Guruji commenced his training camps-related travels again from May 19. Tours began from one camp to another, as if the Sun was moving from one planet to another planet.

From Mumbai, Guruji had to go to the Indore camp. He reached there on 20th May. The cycle of programmes began again. There was a student participant in the introduction meeting. It came out that he was the son of an old swayamsevak, Shri Ram Kotwani. He asked Ashok immediately, "What number?" Answer was, "Fourth." Next question was, "Your father had got a tooth broken; have you broken one or not yet?" Everyone laughed. There was a story behind it. There had been a training camp 16 years back in 1956. During a *lathi*-practice session, one morning Ram Kotwani had lost one tooth. Guruji was present on the ground at that time. After ground exercises were over, he called the state Prachaarak Rajabhau Paturkar and told him, "Ram had brought all the thirty-two (teeth) from home. We should send him back in same condition." Paturkar followed these instructions. Guruji had reminded the son of that story about his father.[7]

While he was studying for exams in Varanasi, he had told others once, "Scorpion has stung me in the foot, but I am studying with my brain." With the same impersonal emotions, Guruji completed his tour from Indore to Kolkata through all the camps. Same happiness, sweetness and same effulgence. Nobody could guess even for a moment from his physical appearance that he was suffering from the highly fatal disease of cancer.

The nation's political environment was getting vitiated at the time. After the split in Congress, all powers of governance had passed into the hands of Indira Gandhi. She was busy strengthening it further and in finishing the opposition. She also saw the Sangh as her enemy. So, the idea of ban on the Sangh was floated. Old stale arguments that the Sangh was responsible for communal riots were played out again like stale tunes from an old flute, but, Guruji was unmoved. His appeal to all participants was to double the number of swayamsevaks. "The Sangh is an organisation that is not influenced by conditions. It is not reactive; it is active. Increase or decrease in temperature according to the temperature outside is a characteristic of inanimate objects. A living being keeps his temperature stable inspite of rise or fall in temperature outside." This was his guidance.

He reached Delhi on 11th June. He decided to meet journalists there. A good number of journalists turned up at Lala Hansraj's home. Press conference went on for nearly 50 minutes. Responding to a question about ban, he said, "Such a threat would not work. Such an action would prove to be dangerous for them. Let them remember their earlier experiences." He was speaking softly but with unbeatable fighting spirit. The title of the news next day was, 'Threats Will Not Work' – Golwalkar Roars.

After reporters had left, many senior journalists and editors came. Amongst them were D.A. Mankikar and Girilal Jain from *Times of India*, Kuldip Nayyar from *Statesman*, Ratanlal Joshi from *Dainik Hindustan*, Akshay Kumar Jain from *Navbharat Times*, G.G. Mirchandani from *U.N.A.*, K. Subramanyam from *P.T.I.*, Sadgopalan, Indrajeet, Anand Vidyalankar, Ramanujam, Haridatt Pathak, N.B. Lele and others. Conversation went on till 8:30 in the night. Guruji explained to them the work of the Sangh, its programmes and its working methodology in detail. He analysed the political activities of the time. He also shared some jokes about the prevailing situation.[8] When the people left after this programme, one was sure that none of them would have imagined that the person sitting in front of them, with whom they talked for 90 minutes, was going into an operation three weeks hence.

We may recall that Guruji met Dr. Namjoshi on 3rd-4th May and Dr. Prafulla Desai on 18th May. During this time he went to have *darshan* of world-renowned Jain guru, Acharya Tulsi on 11th May, Monday in Nagpur. This was a meeting that had taken place after 20 years. Both of them recalled the wonderful moments spent together. Dialogue between the two went on in a joyous mood, in a spiritual atmosphere for nearly 90 minutes. Muni Shrinathmalji was accompanying Acharyaji while Professor Bapurao Varhadpande accompanied Guruji. There were three to four devotees and two to three swayamsevaks also. Acharyaji and Guruji were of the unanimous opinion on nearly all the subjects. It could be seen that tone, tenor and thoughts were on the same wavelength. Both were in favour of giving up orthodoxies that had been corrupted by passing times. Both had similar thoughts about abolishing untouchability from the roots and providing equity, respect and prestige to backward brethren. Both were of the opinion that many heads of *mathams* and religious teachers were not ready to pay heed to the demands of the times. Still, there had been improvements, even if slowly. After meeting and reasoning, the society was getting changed in the desirable direction; on hearing about such recent experiences of Guruji, Acharyaji was happy. Acharyaji talked openly that in these matters, sometimes, he had to face opposition from his own disciples; and at that time, it was the duty and desirable action of *guru* to explain them and give them right vision. Guruji appreciated his views. When Acharyaji said that understanding at the top is easy, difficulty lies at lower rungs, Guruji told him of a story he had heard from another person. Once there was an occasion when forces of Lord Rama and Lord Shiva were about to clash. Both of them stood in front of each other and began threatening and throwing challenges. Hearing about it, Lord Shiva and Lord Rama came there. Since both of them were devoted to each other, they came forward and embraced each other while monkeys and ghosts began fighting with each other. Hearing this story, everybody laughed together. Acharyaji's opinion was: "Power is for the well-being of all. If religion is given up in Bharat, that is highly spiritual, what would we be left with? Today there is a need to pay special attention to people who have firm faith in *dharma*." Guruji showed his acceptance of this view and told him, "We have to work together in the coming days." People listening to these discussions realised that there was enough commonality between the *Anuvrat Andolan* of Acharya Tulsi ji and Rashtriya Swayamsevak Sangh of Guruji. After completing the dialogue, Guruji paid respects to Acharyaji and took his leave.[9]

After finishing the tour of training camps on 28th June, Guruji had his preliminary tests done on 29th in the Tata Cancer Hospital. He was admitted to the hospital on 30th and was operated on July 1 under anesthesia. The operation went on for nearly three hours and the doctors removed all the affected glands with acute care as far as possible. The patient was brought out at one in the afternoon. He took tea at 3:30 p.m. Tubes attached to the body were removed on the third day. People taking his care never felt that he was in pain; his face was calm and blissful.

He sat up on his bed on the second day. After four to five days, as his physical condition improved, he started moving around and commiserating with patients in neighbouring beds and assuring them. It was as if he had commenced his tour now within the hospital itself. People close to him began coming to meet him. Swami Hiranyamayanandaji from Shri Ramakrishna Ashram came and gifted *prasad* to his *guru-bhai,* who had also been ordained at one time. State secretary of Tamil Nadu, Dakshinamurthi, and state Prachaarak Ramagopalji came to meet him. Guruji told them in a low voice, "Go, meet the person lying at the other end. He will return to Chennai in two to three days." Both of them met him and came to know that he was a relative of a swayamsevak, whom Ramagopal ji knew well. He told them, "Guruji came to my bed half an hour back and reassured me that his problems had been totally resolved." He looked quite assured. Both of them came back to Guruji and informed him of their conversation. The lesson that the Sangh founder had given to swayamsevaks was about keeping in touch with people. This unwell Sarsanghchaalak had kept afresh even in hospital.[10]

A meeting that used to take place post-training camps in Nagpur, was shifted to Mumbai this year, keeping in mind the operation that Guruji was to undergo. All the expected officials had arrived for the meeting to be held on 10th-11th-12th July. They used to come to hospital one by one and meet him. Sarkaryavaah Balasaheb Deoras used to come with two to three colleagues every day and inform him of the discussions held that day.

The meeting that year had special significance. The government had moved in the direction that Guruji had visualised, when he had called for a press conference 20-25 days earlier in Delhi. Delhi government had banned holding of Shakhas in public grounds. There was a news that a bill to ban the Sangh would be presented in Lok Sabha. State offices of the Sangh began receiving notices from income-tax department that *guru dakshina* would be taxed. Not just a conspiracy, but open efforts were being made to corner the Sangh somehow. The Sangh leadership was forced to work out strategies to counter this policy. This was the background of the meeting held in Mumbai. Guruji had to be admitted into hospital during such a situation. But, colleagues like Balasaheb Deoras knew about the strength of Guruji's resolve with their earlier experiences. Therefore, they did not feel embarrassed to seek Guruji's advice even in the condition he was in. Guruji thought about being present for a little time in the meeting on the last day. When he sought Dr. Prafulla Desai's permission, who had become quite close to him by then, the doctor said with a laugh, "Do not run away from there." In the same vein, Guruji too replied, "What is this, doctor? Do I look like a cheat who will run away?" He was present in the closing session of the meeting and came back to hospital after dining with everybody.[11]

Guruji had been in hospital for three weeks. Doctors were satisfied with his progress. After the wounds dried up, he had to undergo deep X-ray treatment on his chest and back. After getting released from hospital on 26th July, he went to Vedprakash Goel's house in Sion and stayed there till he returned to Nagpur. Barrister Wankhede, Shri Sherrif Maharaja of Sangli, Revered Shankaracharya of Dwarika, Swami Chinmayananda and others came to meet him at Vedprakashji's home. One of those days, the Goel family organised a *sahasravartan vishesh Vishweshwar pooja* for his long, healthy life. One has to offer 1000 *modak* sweets in this *pooja*. Mothers and sisters of swayamsevaks of nearby area came to prepare these *modaks*. Many families came to take part in the ritual and take *prasad*. Actually, *prasad* and worship were an excuse to have *darshan* of Guruji. While returning from an evening Shakha one day, where he had gone for Sangh prayer, he went to Ramakrishna Ashram in Khar. Swami Hiranyamayananda ji welcomed him. He offered his salutations with folded hands (*namaskar*) that day to the idol of Shri Shri Thakur since he could not bow down those days. Swamiji requested him to stay in the *ashram* for some days. "I will accept your wish that is like a command to me, after Raksha Bandhan festival of Nagpur. 2nd August, a Sunday, was the day suitable for people of Mumbai. Swayamsevaks arranged for a *Sarvajanik Satyanarayan pooja* in Vanita Vishram hall in Dadar West. More than 20,000 brothers and sisters took part in it. Guruji left for Nagpur the next day.

It is said, where there is devotion, nothing else works. As if to prove this saying, on hearing about Guruji's travel plans from each other, swayamsevaks and their families gathered in large numbers at all the major stations on the way. Guruji used to stand at the door of the bogie to meet them. In this wave of devotion and love, people forgot about rest that the patient recovering from his sickness needed. And the recuperating patient too forgot about his rest in his affection for all.

Guruji reached Nagpur on 4th August. The Sangh brethren were waiting at the station with eager eyes, moist with happiness. No garlands, no slogans, just silent smiles and glad hearts – that is how they welcomed the angel of their hearts; just as Savitri might have welcomed her Satyavaan on his return from the jaws of god of death. Sanghchaalak of Nagpur, Babasaheb Ghatate took Guruji to his home.

The wound that resulted from surgery had to be cleaned and dressed every day. Dr. Ramdas Paranjape, a swayamsevak, used to come for it. While dressing work was going on, on one side, Guruji could be seen gossiping pleasantly with the family members. One day, a little flesh got pulled out along with cotton and a little blood oozed out too. The doctor uttered a suppressed cry. As he turned around, the patient told him, "Do not be afraid, Ram. I have pulled back my consciousness from that part. I am not feeling any pain at all; keep the dressing work on."

When the astonished family members told about it to Abaji Thatte, he told them, "A similar thing has happened earlier too. It seems he has achieved some special expertise to pull back his life force from any part of his body. Many years back, we had gone for treatment of his left hand that was in pain. Treatment was given by an expert called Siddha Vaidya. His treatment consisted of pressing a red hot wire on critical spots from shoulder to wrist. Heeding to senior colleagues' advice, Guruji agreed to it. With four to five brandings every day, he received about 32 brandings. One could smell the burning flesh all round every time. I could not bear looking at this scene. But, Guruji would sit at ease, with his hands spread comfortably, as if the treatment was being done on somebody else's arm."

This reminds us that such incidents are also mentioned in the lives of Swami Turiyananda, a close disciple of Shri Ramakrishna Paramhamsa and Shri Ramana Maharshi.

Guruji had to deliver a speech in Ghatateji's bungalow one day for Hindus, who had come from the U.K. Shri Krishna Janmashtami, the day of Bhagwan Krishna's birth, was nearing. Hindus of UK had built a Krishna temple in London. Sacred installation ceremony of the temple was slated for the auspicious day of 24th August. They wished to receive his message in the form of a speech for the assembly of devotees that sacred day. Heeding their wishes, Guruji got his speech recorded on a tape recorder and sent it to London through a swayamsevak, who was going to London. Thus, Guruji had his speech heard in London, sitting in the bungalow of Ghatate.

Raksha Bandhan festival was on 17th August. The final *guru dakshina* programme of Nagpur Shakha was also to be held on the same day. Guruji was present in it and he spoke for 35 minutes there, standing. People, who were present that day, recount that speed of his speech was a bit slow, but everything else was just like earlier times. Seeing him in this condition, swayamsevaks collected there feeling highly contented.

The car Guruji was travelling in while returning from the function reached a traffic island near Patwardhan Ground. When Ghatate's son Krishna tried to avoid the traffic island and turn right directly, Guruji spoke up promptly, "Please drive properly." He had also noted that there was no policeman at that traffic island. Guruji told Krishna, "Brother, not following rules is a sign of cowardice. Breaking rules in absence of police is not a matter of fortitude. Whether somebody watches us or not, we must follow rules. It may result in a little inconvenience, but bear with it; this is fortitude. Rules are made for society. Nobody in society has a right to break it."[12]

True to his promise to Swami Hiranyamayananda, Guruji left Nagpur on August 20 and reached Mumbai on 21st morning. From Dadar station he went directly to Ramakrishna Ashram. That year, he celebrated Janmashtami in the *ashram*. He stayed there till 25th evening.

While at *ashram,* he met Dr. Prafulla Desai on 22nd and went through medical checkup again. He had a little fever, but he did not pay attention to it. Guruji used to go for Sangh prayer in one or the other Sangh Shakha nearby. Taking advantage of the occasion, swayamsevaks of Goregaon Shakha invited him for attending their local *saanghik* one day. They had also decided to invite many new swayamsevaks. Guruji was present on Sangh Ground inspite of fever. During the prayer, Guruji's body was losing balance. Ever-alert Abaji Thatte ran forward and gave him support. Guruji lost consciousness at that moment. After some time he was alright. After returning to *ashram,* he noted that his dried wound had developed puss. When it was brought to the notice of doctor, he commented, "There is nothing to worry, it is perhaps a radio nacrotic ulcer developed due to deep X-ray therapy. It will get cured with medication." And so it happened.[13]

Guruji left for Indore on 25th after happily enjoying the company of *sadhus* in Ramakrishna Ashram. He had stayed there for nearly a month till 23rd September, at Pandit Ramnarayan Shastri's home for rest and medical treatment. During this time, Swami Amoortananda Maharaj from Mohipura used to drop in to share old experiences and memories with him. The stay at Indore was beneficial from this very aspect. Guruji regained his health to a great extent. His complete right arm was swollen without any cause. When doctors told him that it was a sign of a successful operation, Guruji quipped, "My obesity is going to start from this arm." This swelling lasted till the last day of his life.

Guruji was having his tea with swayamsevaks of a morning Shakha one day. He noted, "Today is the day – both of us (indicating towards Shastriji) had to be in Kanyakumari, but we are locked in here." When swayamsevaks seemed lost, he opened up his heart, "His excellency, the President, is inaugurating

Vivekananda Rock Memorial today." The date was 4th September, 1970. There was definitely the ache of being infirm. The painful story behind construction of the memorial to the builder of new Bharat, Swami Vivekananda, must have passed through his heart and mind.

Guruji came to Mumbai from Indore again on 4th September and met Dr. Desai. He was satisfied with the condition of his patient, but he advised that he should get himself checked wherever possible, during his tours. He did not raise any objections to his travel plans. However, that day, Guruji asked him bluntly, "Doctor, how long will it go on like this?" The answer was equally frank, "At least three years." "Good enough. I will be able to do a lot," was his answer. He returned to Nagpur on 26th September.

After many months, the room of Sarsanghchaalak in Dr. Hedgewar Bhavan became alive with activity again. Apart from resting time in the afternoon, there was no restriction to anybody walking in without prior permission. There was no restriction at all for children and young swayamsevaks. The atmosphere was nearly back to normal. Still, swayamsevaks, on their own, showed some restraint due to their own understanding.

However, the atmosphere outside was a little disturbed. Many people were bent upon vitiating it. 'A mouse and a polluter always try to find a hole.'* Proving these Sanskrit words of wisdom true, many self-manufactured rumours were floated by opponents. Running theme of all these rumours was common—Sarsanghchaalak on deathbed, tug of war within the Sangh for the post'.

Vijayadashami came up in this environment. The view of swayamsevaks was different. Their god-like heart had come out unscathed from the embrace of the black serpent of Kalindi. With great enthusiasm in their hearts, they resolved to make this festival more grand and beautiful than all the earlier ones. Worship of weapons (*shastra poojan*) was to be done on 9th October and Vijayadashami festival was to be held on 10th. Retired personal secretary of Sardar Patel, V. Shankar was to preside over the programme. In his speech, after the worship of weapons, Guruji said, "Internal situation is not reassuring. When threats have encircled us from all sides, efforts are afoot to create anarchy. At such a time, there is no other way but to awaken strong *samskaaras* of pure patriotism to halt evil ideas that wish to break our nation and society. Therefore, we should carry on our work with full vigour."

Taking note of rumours around him, he quipped, "Sarsanghchaalak may be on deathbed, but there is no tug of war for his succession. There can be pulls and pressures if there is any selfish interest. If one were to get some assets, some wealth, or one could build mansions, there could be some pulls. But, here one does not get anything. Even in this scenario, people deliberately spread propaganda. Such misleading propaganda will keep running, efforts will be made

---

* *Chhidraanveshee cha sarvatra dooshako mooshako yathaa.*

to blame somebody or other.But work firmly and tirelessly to build our nation, that is, build a life full of pure character for each human being without paying attention to all this. We should just think that only this will help our nation."[14]

On the evening of Vijayadashami, hundreds of swayamsevaks families turned up at Dr. Hedgewar Bhavan to offer *sonpatra* (a special kind of leaf in shape of a heart) for *seemolanghan* (a custom in and around Maharashtra, meaning crossing the borders, signifying victory). Each and every one of them met Guruji and spoke a sentence or two with him. Guruji, of course, knew all of them personally. Nobody touched his feet as per instructions passed earlier.

Sarsanghchaalak left for his organisational tours again on 23rd October. He took part in Vishwa Hindu Parishad's central committee meeting held under chairmanship of Maharana Bhagwant Singh ji of Mewar on November 15. He reached Delhi from there on 21st. There was a large get-together of swayamsevaks on 22nd November, Sunday, in the morning at 8:30 in Ramlila Grounds. People were strictly prohibited from coming late. Guruji stood up and gave his lecture in front of 14,000 swayamsevaks. Swayamsevaks could not sense any change in his voice or speech. So, they were very happy. There was a civic reception in the evening. The programme that day had been organised after due permission from Sarkaryavaah. The objective behind it was to firmly bury all the senseless rumours in the air. People had turned up in large numbers. When chairman of the reception committee, Diwan Anand Kumarji, said, "We have come to felicitate highly revered Guruji, who has come after getting free from a fatal disease with God's blessings," everybody clapped heartily to acknowledge this. Guruji began his speech on request of the chairman. Clarifying the objective of the meeting, Guruji said, "As it is, I come to Delhi every year. Therefore, there was no reason for organising my felicitation. But, for the last few months there had been a lot of discussions around my health. This programme today is in this background."

Sharing his views about imminent death with an experience he had earlier on, he said, "One of our workers had fallen sick in Nagpur. He was admitted to a hospital. Whenever I went to Nagpur, I used to meet him. Once it so happened that I went meet him just one day before I was to leave Nagpur. As soon as I saw to him, I had a feeling that he will not live for long now. I asked him, 'Brother, how are you feeling now?' He responded, 'Medicines do not seem to work.' I told him, 'You are right, you do not have much time left to live. But, do not worry. We have served God like a society on directions of God himself. We have never worked for the self; we have not done bad to anybody. We have thought about good of others. We have so much of positive *karma* with us. Therefore, there is no need to fear death. Be ready for death with a calm and happy mind. You will not be there by the time I return to Nagpur. This is our last meeting today." And it happened that way.

"There is another point about worrying about death," saying so, he added,

"Our Sangh work is not dependent on any individual. It is true that I have been made to sit here as its head. All the people working today take my name. They even seek my advice. All this is alright, but work is not dependent on a particular person. This work is, but the fruit of collective strength of many a worker, their common emotions, the deep sense of enthusiasm they carry in their heart for serving the nation; or else, what can one person do?... When countless workers sacrifice their lives, only then this work is accomplished."[15]

Lala Hansraj expressed his thanks at the end of this felicitation meeting. It was followed by light refreshments. Guruji kept refreshing old contacts during this time.

Next day, on 24th, Tuesday, Jain Muni Nagaraj and his 10-15 disciples came to Lalaji's bungalow to meet him. Topic of discussion was a controversial book called *Agnipariksha,* written by Acharya Tulsi.[16]

Towards the end of that year, on 5th-6th December, there was going to be a state-level conference of Vishwa Hindu Parishad's Maharashtra unit. The site was at the king of pilgrimage centres in Maharashtra, Pandharpur. Maharashtra had been leading the country in movements for social reforms since last the two to three centuries. The urge of dedicated seers for social reforms here was very strong. The conference of Pandharpur was very critical in this background. Then, how could Sarsanghchaalak of Rashtriya Swayamsevak Sangh keep himself out of it? More than 25,000 delegates turned up from far corners of Maharashtra and Goa. State level committee was also formed at that time. The guiding speech in the conference was delivered by Guruji. The summarised form of his flowing speech in Marathi of nearly 60 minutes is given below:

"Our Hindu society, its *dharm*a its culture and its traditions – the root of all these is Bharat. If we can keep its roots active, Hindu society spread across the world in the form of its branches and sub-branches will be able to live comfortably. It would be able to absorb its principles of life within itself. If we were to forget our life force and turn its roots hollow and worthless of action, then our pronouncement of unifying the world will not benefit anybody.

"We should accumulate such power that nobody should have the courage to attack a Hindu. We have to build that strength. Only by building up the feeling of unity in our hearts will this power grow.

"We have to bring up our neglected brethren with us on the foundation of love, making proper arrangements for their education and worldly knowledge. We have to help such groups rise. Taking everybody along, creating a pure and great atmosphere of love, it is our duty to make this society organised, woven together with strong discipline into an undefeatable, unbeatable powerful entity. The day we are able to create such a power, that very day, heads of Hindus across the world will be held high."[17]

Vishwa Hindu Parishad was born in 1964 in Mumbai in The Sandipani Ashram. It had grown into a pan Bharat organisation gradually by 1970. Guruji's contribution in this entire exercise was invaluable. He had every right to feel a sense of gratification as he glanced back. Just as Adi Shankaracharya had established four *mathams* in four corners of Bharat; in the same way Guruji had given new direction, new vision and goal to a newly awakened Hindu society in six years from Prayag in north, Udupi in south, Jorhat in east and Pandharpur in west. To regain what was lost, to retain what is in hand, to make something as one's own what is not in hand by extending one's hands – this seer dedicated to a mission lit that spark of confidence in this society.

□

Endnotes

1. *Vishwa Hindu Parishad Vikas Yaatra*, pp. 46
2. *Shri Guruji Samagra*, Vol. 5, pp. 112
3. Ibid, pp. 109
4. Ibid, pp. 106
5. *Smriti Parijat*, pp. 141-142
6. *Jeevan Prasang*, Vol. 2, pp. 313-317
7. *Shri Guruji Madhya Bharat Mein*, pp. 10-31
8. *Smriti Paarijaat*, pp. 80
9. *Shri Guruji Samagra*, Vol. 9, pp. 248-255
10. *Aarti Alok Ki*, pp. 278-279
11. Ibid, pp. 280
12. *Jeevan Prasang*, Vol. 2, pp. 122-123
13. *Shri Guruji Samagra*, pp. 12-23
14. *Shri Guruji Samagra*, Vol. 5, pp. 260-261
15. Ibid, pp. 16-117
16. *Smriti Parijat*, pp. 81
17. *Shri Guruji Samagra*, Vol. 5, pp. 119-124

41

Idealist Man of Action

In the felicitation meeting in November 1970, Guruji had said, "As far as I am concerned, I can assure you that my health today is better than what it was in the past 10-15 years."[1] The year 1971 proved him correct. That year, none of his programme had to be cancelled. There was no deterioration of his health during the programmes too, but, medical check-ups were carried out regularly. That year, too, he went to all the Sangh Shiksha Vargas to give guidance to the trainees. But, as centrally planned, the method of conducting Guruji's programmes was modified from this year onward. Instead of him moving from district centre to another when visiting state-after-state, an assembly of workers was organised for two to three days at state level at one centre. In the same way, big gatherings of swayamsevaks were planned instead of large public meetings. For example, there was an RSS workers' camp in Rajasthan that concluded with a get-together of swayamsevaks in full uniform. 5,000 swayamsevaks attended that programme.

One more noticeable thing may be mentioned. People close to him tell us that Guruji had become more eager to meet *sadhus* and saints in later days, but, it did not mean that he had lost interest in other programmes. He had same incisive eyes to observe them closely. He was in Bhopal for that year's Makar Sankraman celebrations.

He was in Kolkata on 29th-30th January. Dr. Saifuddin Jeelani met him on 30th for an interview. Dr. Jeelani was originally from Iran. He had settled down in Bharat long back. He was an expert on Islamic and Hindu philosophies. He was a columnist by profession, had come into contact with K.R. Malkani in that role and began writing a column for *Organiser* weekly. He got to know about Guruji from Malkani. He was very keen to meet Guruji after his surgery. He was able to fulfil this wish in Kolkata through his contacts. This interview of Guruji by Jeelani is important from a historical perspective. It states views of RSS lucidly about Muslim society since it has been enunciated by RSS Sarsanghchaalak himself. This interview can satisfy questions raised by both the supporters and opponents of the Sangh. It is available in *Shri Guruji Samagra*

(Vol. 9, pp. 186-195). Diffident that it may take too much of space, only the last part of this interview is being quoted below:

"Dr. Jeelani: You have presented your views very succinctly. No thinking and well-meaning person would disagree with you. Don't you think that time has come to arrange for a meeting between you and Muslim leaders with your co-operation, that could end communal disharmony in this country? Would you like to meet such leaders?"

"Shri Guruji: Why will I not like it? I will welcome such a meeting."[2]

Dr. Jeelani wrote about this extraordinary interview, "This meeting with Shri Guruji proved to be a highly inspiring and unforgettable incident in my life. I have met all the big personalities of world, from Hitler to Col. Nasser, but I have not come across any person as pleasant, confident and impressive as Shri Guruji. I honestly feel that Shri Guruji is the only person who can provide the desired guidance to solve the Hindu-Muslim problem."[3]

Guruji and Jeelani had become good friends with this very first meeting. This friendship grew closer in later days, but, in less than two years Mr. Jeelani expired on 17th November, 1972. Pained with this separation from a friend, Guruji wrote to Dr. Sujit Dhar of Kolkata, "I was deeply hurt on hearing the news of passing away of our dear friend Dr. S. Jeelani on 17-11-72. I was informed that he was not keeping well, so he had to be taken to hospital. I met my other colleagues in the last week of October and first three days of November in Mumbai, but I am surprised that I did not receive this information from either my friends or you."

"This incident has already taken place. Now, you have to fulfil one duty on my behalf – the duty of expressing our sympathies to the bereaved family, his wife and children. May God bestow peace and blessing upon him. I hope that we shall be able to maintain equally strong relations with his sons."[4]

February-March travel plans of Guruji also went off without any hitch. During the time, news came through All India Radio that the founder of Gorakhpur Gita Press had passed away on 22nd March. Poddar ji and Guruji were not only for friends but also co-workers. Guruji had high respect for him and he used to address him as '*Bhai*'. Guruji never disregarded any of his requests and Guruji's articles, though rare, used to appear in *Kalyan* monthly. On the very next day of Bhaiji's death, Guruji wrote to his colleague Radheshyam Banka, "Now assimilating the ideals of his life in our lives, we should strive to take forward his work of religious awakening to the best of our ability and efforts."[5] When Guruji received a request from Gita Press office to send an article to be published in a memorial souvenir, he sent his answer, "I have a serious difficulty, that separation of those for whom I have unlimited respect and love, leaves a deep wound in my heart. This wound deepens further when an occasion to speak or think about them arises. Pain of this wound becomes unbearable. Then, I cannot find words. Thoughts wilt. Heart is overpowered by an indescribable agony...Therefore, I seek pardon from everyone. It is possible that I may be able to control my heart's feelings enough as time passes, then I can put my heart's feelings in words and dedicate them to the memories of revered Shri Bhaiji. Today, emotions are too strong. Thoughts and words have stopped. What can I do? I seek your forgiveness again and again."[6]

Akhil Bharatiya Pratinidhi Sabha assembled at Nagpur in month of March. Guruji sat through all the sessions on all three days and gave his guidance in the concluding session. He went on a tour of Orissa after this. He received the sad news of the death of the son of Pandit Ramnarayan Shastri of Indore. He went to Indore immediately on completion of his tour and shared the grief of the family. After Sangh Shiksha Vargas, he returned on 20th July and stayed with them till 3rd August.

During the time of training camps of that year, Guruji had to take up an odd kind of responsibility in Coimbatore, that of inaugurating Dr. V.V. Giri Hall. The occasion was Sangh Shiksha Varg being held in G.D. Naidu's institution. Shri Naidu was a very special personality. Original thinker, inventor of extraordinary things, beyond politics, fearless businessman, founder of educational institutions, Shri Naidu was an enigma for the common man. He had given his institution for the training camp. He had a different kind of nature. He had built two assembly halls in his huge campus. He named one as 'Periyar Ramaswamy Naicker Hall' and second one, 'Shri Shankaracharya Hall.' He invited Shankaracharya to inaugurate the Periyar Hall and a D.M.K. minister to inaugurate Shankaracharya hall. Both of them backed out at the final moment. It was this background in which he had invited Guruji to inaugurate V.V. Giri Hall. Inauguration was done on May 6. Giving his welcome speech, Naidu said, "Based on my old experiences, I had doubts whether Guruji Golwalkar would come or not. He has come. I appreciate his commitment to his words, straightforward nature, natural approach, commitment to ideology and fortitude. These are true qualities of leadership." Guruji complimented Naidu's business intelligence and social welfare-related activities and mentioned about his relations with the Sangh. The function lasted for about 20-25 minutes. Naidu took a photograph of Guruji and his other colleagues with a 'button' camera. Such a small camera was a rarity in those days. Guruji took it in hand with curiosity to have a closer look at it. He had seen it for the first time. Everybody was quite happy. And Sangh Shiksha Varg-related activities also went on with his active co-operation.[7]*

After finishing with training camps across Bharat, Guruji presented himself to Dr. Desai for routine medical check-up. The doctor was quite satisfied with his health. The central meeting took place at Nagpur in August. It was decided to celebrate the birth centenary of Shri Aurobindo as a public event. On request from everybody, Guruji released a public appeal for publication in media. He noted in it, "Birth centenary programme of this great visionary commences on

* Photographs taken from that camera appear on pp. 123 in *Chitraanjali*

15th August, 1971. Come, as countrymen indebted to him; let us try to understand his teachings and spread his philosophy throughout Bharat and celebrate this occasion in a right manner; and believing in his futuristic spirit, take a sacred pledge that we shall put in intense efforts to realise his vision and will not rest till we achieve that goal."[8]

Eight years after celebration of Swami Vivekananda birth centenary, a good opportunity arose without any opposition to spread the principle of, in the words of great sage Aurobindo, 'a Hindu *rashtra* based on *Sanaatan Dharma*'. But, the government was not in a mood to participate in it with an open heart. The reason was that Aurobindo Ashram was not ready to be made a sacrificial animal for distorted secularism of the rulers. The *ashram* refused to accept a government suggestion of removing a map of 'Spiritual Bharat' exhibited in the *ashram* that represented an undivided Bharat. They were not ready to modify literature of Maharshi even by a fraction. Their faith was that these were the words spoken by the sage. Therefore, pseudo-secular government turned cold to the project to translate Shri Aurobindo's literature in regional languages. The Sangh organised celebration committees till the level of villages in entire Bharat. Shri Aurobindo's speech given in 1909 May in Uttarpada was translated and published in nearly all regional languages. Shri Aurobindo centenary was celebrated far and wide throughout Bharat, from Himalayas to the oceans.

Guruji reached Kolhapur during Maharashtra tour on 4th October. He had to perform a personal task apart from programmes of Shakha. Amba Bai is their family deity. He had been there for her *darshan* that same year on 12th February. But, now, he had to perform a special duty. It was his heart's desire to offer his dear mother's traditional inherited jewellery at the feet of the family deity. Sensing the God of Death knocking at his door, this celibate thought that right to this property inherited from his mother was that of the mother of Universe, Amba Bai and he wished to be free of this debt at the earliest. He went to the temple with two to three Sangh officials and returned after fulfilling his desire. This was the last contribution from the family tree of Golwalkars.

Guruji reached Ratnagiri on 5th October. He also had to fulfil a long-cherished wish to have *darshan* of Swami Swaroopananda of Pawas. One has to cross Gautami river from Rajibada to reach Pawas. Swamiji stayed in Anant Niwas there. Whoever be the saint, Guruji used to experience joy that went beyond this material world. But, there was another reason for this inner urge to see Swaroopananda ji. Swamiji was the ordained head of Nath sect. Guruji's mother too had taken *diksha* from this sect. Guruji was accompanied by Bapurao Patwardhan, state Sanghchaalak Kashinath Limaye, Vasantrao Bhide and Gopalrao Deshpande. Only Vasantrao Bhide was with him when he met Swamiji. Swami ji asked Guruji to sit on a high seat, but Guruji did not sit in front of Swamiji, but kept on standing. Conversation between the two began in subdued voices. Swamiji handed over the scripture *Sanjeevani Gatha*, written by him, as was his nature, to Guruji and asked him to open it. On this occasion, pp. 123 containing *stava* (canto) opened up. On being asked to read it, Vasantrao Bhide read it while Swamiji and Guruji listened to it. Sentences of *stava,* translated from Marathi, were:

"Bear pleasure and pain for your ideals
Sacrifice happiness and life for your ideals.
Drop selfishness for truth,
Push away material life.
Donate everything for God,
Break the bonds of ego, Swami says,
Dedicating self for ideals, become an image of ideals."

Everybody who knows Guruji's life would unanimously agree that these lines did full justice to him. It is true that people over whom God extends his blessed hand, receive their *prasad* accordingly.

Guruji dedicated a silver idol of Lord Ganesh to Swamiji; Swamiji placed it back in the hands of Guruji as his prasad. Accepting it, Guruji placed it on his forehead. Offering their salutations, all of them returned by boat.[9]

Pakistan rained bombs on airports in north-west Bharat at midnight on 3rd December, 1971. Thus, began the second Bharat-Pakistan war. But, as an action preceding this event, Pakistan had started throwing out Buddhist-Christian-Hindu brethren from East Pakistan into Bharatiya borders on false pretences since many months earlier. According to official sources more than seven million refugee brethren had already come into Bharat. According to information received by the Intelligence Bureau, massive preparations for attack from both East and West wings of Pakistan were afoot. In this complex scenario, much before the declaration of war, an emergency meeting of Central Committee, presided by Sarkaryavaah Balasaheb Deoras and attended by Sarsanghchaalak, was called at Lala Hansraj Guptaji's bungalow. Keeping the looming danger in mind, a resolution to awaken the people, maintain their morale and keep them ready to face the danger was passed. Resolution spoke of unconditional support and co-operation to the Central Government.[10]

Keeping in mind the difficult situation mentioned in the resolution, Guruji went on a tour of bordering states of the north-west from Delhi. He took part in meetings of Prachaaraks of the region from 17th to 20th October. He advised the Sangh to be 'ever ready'. He went to Punjab after this on 20th-21st. It was an emergency-like situation. Therefore, an emergency get-together was called on 22nd in Delhi. Guruji came from Punjab to Delhi to take part in it. The venue was jam-packed. In that get-together, Guruji said, "Enemy is all around us. On western and eastern borders, a nation created after cutting up this very country, is getting ready to attack us...It is fine for leaders to give a warning, but the question that arises is what are the plans for this? Increasing the strength of Army is one of the parts of that plan. Second part is to provide our forces with good quality arms... Even as these two things are fine, third point that is of utmost important is to awaken the entire society emotionally to defend the nation and build a well-organised power. If we were to think about it, then we shall grasp the importance of the Sangh work."[11]

From Delhi, Guruji went to Jammu. He addressed a massive public meeting in Jammu, but, the theme of the speech was different from that in Delhi here. What Guruji said in that heated atmosphere was something no other leader had said so far. It was a psychological issue. He opened up his heart, "One cannot deny that one can see a sense of fear in so-called big leaders of the country. They feel we have no friends in this world. Our treaty with Russia has been signed in this background. Actually, there can be treaties between different countries of the world. If China is keen for a treaty, we should sign it with them. But, what saddened me was that as soon as the treaty was signed, our leaders began dancing with joy of relief. Announcements are being made all around that we are not alone anymore; we have found a friend. We should give it a thought that just as we have signed the treaty with Russia, Russia has also signed this treaty with us; then why are not the people there dancing insanely? People here are going insane with happiness as if with signing of this treaty something unheard of has happened; something that has never taken place before in this world. The reason for this is that there is no realisation of inner power of this country. Therefore, leaders feel that it is a great blessing of God that we have found a friend. It cannot be called a reaction of someone powerful but a cry of someone powerless."[12]

From Jammu, Guruji went to South Bharat via Delhi. He cautioned swayamsevaks during his tour of Kerala, "It will be wrong to think that danger is only in north-western parts. It will be wrong to overlook the fact that the enemy can smuggle arms through seas. We shall have to be alert day and night."

From South, the sentinel of Bharat went to Kolkata for two days to meet select senior workers. He evaluated the scenario with facts gathered from them. From there, he went to two other border states – Gujarat and Rajasthan. His tour in Rajasthan was from 24th to 30th November for one week. He presented the situation prevailing in country everywhere, specially in the meeting held in Jaipur. Readers will recall that he was the first person to give information about Chinese attack to the nation. Therefore, people were listening to him attentively. Guruji's speeches in Gujarat and Rajasthan were more or less like that in Delhi.

When Guruji left from Ahmedabad for Udaipur after finishing his tour of Gujarat, he stopped for *darshan* of Lord Rishabhdev. This place is a famous pilgrimage centre of Jains, about 65 kms from Udaipur on the western National Highway. In practice, this pilgrimage centre belongs to all faiths. Groups of tribal people come in large numbers to seek fulfilment of their wishes. Village-dwellers call it 'Kaladev', perhaps due to the fact that the idol is carved in black stone. Jain brethren recognise as Rishabhdev's idol,the originator of Jainism,.

The offering sandalwood is the accepted way of praying for a boon.

Younger sister of Ashok Singhal ji, Usha Jain, had been a favourite of most of the well-known Sangh leaders since childhood. When she heard that Guruji was suffering from cancer, she sought a boon in Rishabhdev temple by offering of sandal paste for protection of Guruji's life. It was only in deference to the request of this sister that Guruji had come to Rishabhdev temple. It was a rule of the temple that the person for whom the boon was sought should enter the temple by only wearing a *dhoti* and a sheet on the top. Since Guruji's health at that time did not permit him to dress like this, Usha Jain had to honour her promise in the name of Guruji that day. Guruji stood meditatively during the *pooja*.[13] Guruji entered Rajasthan after Rishabhdev's *darshan*.

Guruji's warning proved to be correct. Pakistan declared war on 3rd December. Guruji was in the *praathamik varg* (primary training camp) in Nagpur. He gave a statement based on the resolution passed by Sangh's Central Committee. The war ended after 13 days. East Pakistan became Bangladesh. Guruji sent out letters of congratulation to Defence Minister Babu Jagjivan Ram and Prime Minister Indira Gandhi. He wrote to Prime Minister on 22nd December, "There is ceasefire now, but danger has not passed. It is necessary that the awakened power of nation should always be ready. I believe you are paying your full attention to this fact... Now with liberation of Bangladesh, it would be ethically correct to have such arrangements that refugees thrown out for the last 24 years should be able to return to their homes, their confiscated property be returned to them and they should be able to take part in the progress of the newly independent country with enthusiasm. The assurance given by you in this regard from time to time may be fulfilled at the earliest and may you have the fortune to accept gratitude of millions of unfortunate affected people...Today, I offer you and your team of ministers, heartfelt congratulations for the success that has raised the glory of the nation and salute the unbeatable Armed Forces."[14]

With liberation of Bangladesh, the psyche of the entire nation had undergone a transformation. Guruji stayed from 31st December to 2nd January, 1972 in Kolkata in such an atmosphere. The atmosphere there was, naturally, joyous. Guruji was also in a pleased mood. During a discussion, a mischievous swayamsevak asked Guruji, "What is the meaning of '*saavdhaan*' in the Sangh?" Guruji answered, "Be cautious." Picking up that thread, Guruji took the talk further, "In the life of our nation we should be cautious. Fervour should not overpower us, nor should we overpower fervour. Do not forget that Bangladesh is that land where Muslims are in majority. When Vijayanagar empire was prosperous by virtue of its own strength, five Muslim states surrounding it had come together to attack and destroy it. Possibly, in future, two enemy nations instead of one may confront us."[15] This was the Guruji's analysis done within two weeks of Bharat's victory!

Pakistan's attack of 1971 was the last national calamity in the life-time of Guruji. He had to go through five national calamities since he became Sarsanghchaalak in 1940. 1. Partition of his dear motherland and resulting inflow of refugees, 2. Pakistan's attack on Kashmir just at the dawn of Independence, 3. Attack by expansionist China in 1962, 4. Pakistan's attack in 1965, and 5. Pakistan's attack in 1971. Scrutinising Guruji's life in the background of these five incidents, the truth that emerges clearly is that he used to be the first to jump into the arena of calamity. It was the mental makeup of this serene person of fortitude to jump into the whirlpool of any flood. He was a living example of the fighting spirit of '*yuddhe apalaayanam*' – not running away from a battle – that *Gita* talks about. Even after a life-threatening operation for cancer, this nature of his remained as sharp. A small letter written by him on 2-12-71 proves this point clearly:

"Respected Shri Amitabh Maharaj,

Starting from Nagpur on 6-12-71 I will stay in the state of Andhra till 12-12-71. After this, I have to go to Bengaluru and from there I have to reach Madras on 16-12. I will go from Madras to Kolkata by air on 17-12 and after going to Assam from 18 to 24, there is a state-level camp at Cuttack in Orissa on 25-26-27. Then, there is Uttar Pradesh tour till 14-1-72, and I will return to Nagpur on 22-1-72. Then, after visiting Nasik-Mumbai, I will travel to Trivandrum on 22-1-72 to tour Kerala state. I plan to reach Kanyakumari on the morning of 1st February, 1972. I have thought of staying there for one week. Then I have to go to Madras and from there to Nagpur."[16]

Sitting in a corner, if one were to account for all this, in two months from 6th December to 6th February, a tour of nine states – Kerala, Tamil Nadu, Karnataka, Andhra, Orissa, Bengal, Assam, Maharashtra, Uttar Pradesh, four types of weather of south-north-west-east – all this by a sixty-six-year old traveller who had come out of an operation of cancer! Inspite of all this, to keep walking like the wind, without stopping, without tiring, to keep flowing like a stream, without stopping, without drying up! Of what kind of elements of earth was this mission-driven courageous man of action made?

□

Endnotes

1. *Shri Guruji Samagra*, Vol. 5, pp. 118
2. *Shri Guruji Samagra*, Vol. 9, pp. 195
3. *Jeevan Prasang*, Vol. 2, pp. 152-153
4. *Shri Guruji Samagra*, Vol. 7, pp. 157-158
5. Ibid, pp. 302
6. Ibid, pp. 304
7. Report – V.V. Giri Hall Inauguration
8. *Shri Guruji Samagra*, Vol. 1, pp. 94
9. *Guruji Aplya Prantat*, pp. 41

10. *Rashtriya Swayamsevak Sangh Resolutions*, pp. 67-68
11. *Shri Guruji Samagra*, Vol. 10, pp. 208-209
12. Ibid, pp. 209-210
13. *Jeevan Prasang*, Vol. 2, pp. 321-324
14. *Shri Guruji Samagra*, Vol. 7, pp. 149-150
15. Memoirs of Kalidas Babu of Kolkata
16. Nagpur Letter Register (1971–72), pp. 167

42

Preparations for the Return

Guruji went to Jhoosi, on the other side of Prayag, on 5th January on persuasion of revered Prabhudatt Brahmachaari. The purpose of his visit was to release *Bhagwat Vyakhyaan*, a book written by Brahmachari ji. Brahmachari ji did not want anybody other than Guruji for this divine task. The friendship between the two was founded on spirituality. They respected each other, but would also share lighthearted banter with each other. Brahmachari ji had, once, invited Guruji to inaugurate the Cow Protection Conference in Vrindavan. At that time Guruji had said, "There are door-keepers outside mansions of big people; they open the doors, perform inaugurations. I am also your door-keeper, hence I am opening these doors."[1] But, Guruji did not speak in such a light vein while releasing *Bhagwat Vyakhyaan*. Based on his own experience, he believed this lecture series had been done by one of the topmost exponents of *Bhagwat*. Once, he wrote, about it, "I was fortunate to stay at the divine feet of Badrinath for five days when I went there. I could enjoy boundless bliss at that time, listening to some parts of *Shrimad Bhagwat* from the sacred lips of Maharajji. The way he described the condition of grief-stricken milk maidens, *gopis*, especially emotionally distraught figures of father Nand and mother Yashoda when Lord Krishna left for Mathura, was a brilliant presentation of the tragic scenario that could melt the heart of even a stone."[2] Therefore, pull from Prabhudatt Brahmachari on one side for releasing the book, and push from Guruji's own heart resulted in Guruji reaching Satsang Bhavan inspite of his poor health. He told Prof. Rajendra Singh, "Please request them to complete the programme in half an hour." When the programme got over in 25 minutes, Guruji quipped, "Maharaj ji left even us behind." When convener Ramanuja was about to thank him, interrupting him, he stood up and said, "See, do not talk of formalities; there are no formalities at home. This is my home. If you talk of such formalities, I will not come again." Maharaj ji told him, "Let us take tea before you leave." Both of them laughed easily. Saying, "I know how to prepare tea," he went to the kitchen stove himself, prepared tea, distributed it, had it himself and went ahead to attend another programme.[3]

Guruji went to Agra on 15th January, Saturday, for Makar Sankranti festival. As soon as he arrived, the local secretary handed over the list of programmes for the entire day. After reading it, he asked, "Brother, are we not to go to Purohit's house? When is it possible?" Manohar Purohit was an Army *jawan*, who had become a martyr a month back in war. The schedule to visit his home was not mentioned in the programme list, but, Guruji had made a note in his heart about it when he landed up in Agra. It would not have been possible to go for this visit later once he got busy with scheduled programmes. Thus, on Guruji's instructions, it was decided to make this visit immediately and Guruji reached Purohit's house at 9:30 in the morning with other officials. Daughter-in-law of the family began crying when she saw Guruji. He went up to her and putting his hand on her head, he spoke in an affectionate way, "Be calm, dear daughter, you are wife of a brave person." It was as if the whole grief had been taken upon himself by Guruji, as the newly-wed became calm. He, then, commiserated with each member of the family individually. Others came to know only later that this girl's father was known to Guruji as a young baal swayamsevak in Nagpur.[4]

Completing his programmes, as noted in his letter to Amitabh Maharaj, Guruji reached Kanyakumari on 1st February. This was his first visit after inauguration of the Vivekananda Rock Memorial. Shri Eknath Ranade had made a comfortable faultless arrangement for Guruji's stay in Vivekanandapuram. Guruji was going to stay there for full seven days. A meeting of Central Committee had been planned from 1st to 7th February at Kanyakumari. Sarvashri Balasaheb Deoras, Babasaheb Apte, Madhavrao Muley, Ramnarayan Shastri, Bapurao Moghe, Prof. Rajendra Singh, A. Dakshinamurthi, Yadavrao Joshi, Moropant Pingle, Bhaurao Deoras, Bhaurao Bhuskute, and Suryanarayan Rao had already reached there. Amitabh Maharaj had also arrived to stay with Guruji.[5]

The entire team visited and took a round of the Rock Memorial on the evening of February 1. Honouring the request of Vice President of Vivekananda Kendra, Shri Vaswani, Guruji and Ramnarayan Shastriji wrote their views jointly, "Definitely, the great soul whose self-sacrificing life awakened the slumbering nation and gave birth to an enlightened Bharat; whose soul-stirring and visionary views gave strength to break away the chains of slavery, whose brilliant words inspired Hindu *dharma* to envision its own self and who with miracle of intellect of sages of Bharat unfurled the triumphant flag of Hindu *dharma* – this memorial on the rock of self realisation gives the message of a great liberator of this nation, Swami Vivekananda. May it enlighten the entire world eternally. This is our pious wish."[6]

During one of those meetings, Guruji went with all his colleagues to have *darshan* of Goddess Kumaridevi in her temple. He noticed the board kept outside the temple that read, 'Entry only for followers of Hindu religion.' After return from the temple, it became a topic of discussion. When Guruji began speaking about it, everybody else sat listening to him. Guruji's view was, "There can be no objection to any visitor being allowed to enter the temple. But, we should not forget one thing. This temple of Hindus is a place of worship. Those who wish to enter the temple should accept this fact. A common Hindu believes that a church or a mosque is also a place to worship God. Therefore, when he enters those places, he closes his eyes and focusses upon his deity. This, possibly, may be a reason why his entry is not prohibited in their places of worship. Now, let us look at the other side. What is the thought in a Muslim or a Christian who wish to enter a temple? Will he worship his own deity with reverence when he comes here? Will his heart be agreeable to it? If yes, then there is no problem with his entering a temple. But, history is witness to the fact that their conduct is contrary to this. Broken idols present in many temples are proof of this. Look at Shuchindra Temple 5 kms from here. Have you seen the broken noses, eyes of the idols there? In their hearts, they feel that a temple is worth breaking down. If this is the reason behind the thought that idol breakers should not be allowed entry, what is wrong in it?"[7] Point to be noted here is that this viewpoint was based on social psychology proven through history and practical experience of this behaviour.

The Working Committee meeting of Kanyakumari went off properly as planned. Planning of this meeting was under the supervision of joint Prachaarak of southern region, Suryanarayan Rao. When arrangements for the meetings were being made, Guruji called Suryanarayan Rao and told him, "All expenses of this meeting are to be borne by the Sangh. We should keep Vivekananda Kendra free from incurring any expense. Before you leave this place, you should settle their account." Suryanarayan Rao followed the advice. "Though more than one organisation or institution may look inseparable and similar, as per law and their constitution, they are different, their working methodology is not same and they are separate entities. We should conduct ourselves in matters of accounts etc. this way. We undoubtedly need transparency between us, only then is it possible to have long term co-operation and relations without friction." This was Guruji's incisive approach.[8]

Guruji had to reach Tamil Nadu's camp in Kadampakkam from Kanyakumari on 11th-12th-13th February. He went to Pondicherry for two days on 9th-10th in the time available during this travel. He went to Aurobindo Ashram, saw the entire campus of *ashram*, saw the map of unified (*akhand*) cultural Bharat, then sat in front of divine *samadhi* of Shri Aurobindo in meditation. Finally, he had *darshan* of the living vision of enlightenment, Shri Mother. Both of them just gazed at each other without batting eyelids. Both of them still, silent. Indescribable bliss on both their faces. After some minutes, Shri Mother gifted a red rose to the visitor. This was the silent conclusion of this episode. Lord has said in the Gita, *"Maun, aatmavinigraha, manahprasaad, saumya, bhavasanshuddhi"* – this is intellectual *tapas* or penance. Was it not this intellectual penance that was seen there?

Let us hear about it from Guruji himself. In a meeting to celebrate Shri Aurobindo centenary in Indore on 18th August, he says, "I had gone to Pondicherry some days back. I had *darshan* of Shri Mother. I did not say anything. She also did not say anything. Both of us kept looking at each other in full peace and gravity without batting eyelids."

"After some time had passed, I felt that she has ordered me in silence to be active, perform *karma*. This directive is not to work while stuck with selfish motive, worldly competition and envy, but a directive to move ahead performing pure action."[9]

Now straight to Uttar Pradesh. Three years back, Barrister Narendrajeet Singh's family had got the foundation stone laying ceremony performed by Guruji for Sanaatan Dharma Vidyalay to be built in memory of Pandit Deendayal Upadhyay in their city, Kanpur, on 23rd February, 1969. This school had been built subsequently and was running successfully. Later on, this family made plans to install a gigantic beautiful idol of *Atulit Bal Vikram Jitendriya Buddhimatam Varishtha Ramdoot*, Hanuman in the school. The family wished to get the consecration ceremony of this idol performed at the hands of Guruji. With a school in the name of Deendayal, the family of barrister, consecration of idol of Bajrang Bali – how could Guruji refuse! He reached the barrister's home a day earlier on 21st February. In the evening, the whole family sat together to discuss the next day's programme. When idea that Guruji should be the host for *yagna* was brought up, Guruji opined, "This is not correct; the head of the family should be the host for such a ceremony." Barrister's wife spoke up promptly, "What? Are homes of lakhs of swayamsevaks not your home? You are head of all our families. You are going to be the host." Guruji accepted defeat with a smile and said, "How can I refuse a mother's orders?" Everybody laughed together. Guruji was the host of the ceremony on 22nd February.[10] The topic of Guruji's discourse that day was, 'Complete Human Being'. The basis of this speech was Deendayal's Integral Humanism.*

From Kanpur, Guruji came to Mumbai and proceeded to Sawantwadi district of Konkan and Goa. Between 26th and 28th February he went to Ponda, Kawale and Dicholi in Goa. He took part in the oath-taking ceremony of select swayamsevaks in Kawale. This author was fortunate to search out and meet 3-4 senior swayamsevaks personally, who said, "I was fortunate to offer my salutation that day to Guruji personally, who was standing there as the senior official." Among the people who took oath of the Sangh that day, one was physically handicapped. He had been fitted with an artificial hand. Guruji had observed him, offering his salutation with that hand. After the programme, Guruji called him closer and said, "Normally, pranaam is given with right hand, but in

---

* *Shri Guruji Samagra*, Vol. 5, pp. 124-132 contain the full text of this speech.

an unavoidable situation, it is not wrong to give it with left hand."[11]

After this oath ceremony, Guruji went to the *math* of ancient Gaudpadacharya Kawale of Gomantak Sansthan. Officials of the *math* welcomed him with full-fledged decorum. He complimented them about studies and training in Sanskrit, Ved-Vedanta, philosophy, worship rituals, etc. He expressed his good wishes and said, "Wealthy believers of society should support such a pious work." He expressed the same views in visitor's diary.[12]

Coming to Ponda from Kawale, he stayed at Shantaram Sarjyotishi's home. Ponda is a temple complex in Goa state. There is a long history behind it. When Portuguese Roman Catholics landed on port towns like Teeswada, Bardesh, etc. and began breaking down temples unabashedly, persecuted Hindus carried idols of their gods across the river in boats and settled down in Ponda. Ponda was under a different ruler at that time. When swayamsevaks in Goa came to know of Guruji's arrival, they asked for a boon of healthy life for Guruji in temples of Shri Shanta Durga and Shri Mangeshi. Shantaram Sarjyotishi had made special arrangements with temple authorities for the purpose. Guruji went to both these temples and performed worship rituals etc. He went to Dicholi Shakha in the evening. There he announced the appointment of Dr. Balkrishna Sawaikar as Sanghchaalak. He also delegated responsibilities to some other swayamsevaks. After returning to Nagpur, he wrote a letter that provided guiding advice to Sanghchaalak. His expectations from him were, "You should use wide contacts that you have in your area to bring in more brethren in day-to-day Shakha work and expand our work. Also, keep encouraging present swayamsevaks.."[13]

Guruji stayed in Nagpur till April end. During this time, Varsh Pratipada festival, Akhil Bharatiya Pratinidhi Sabha and other scheduled programmes went about smoothly. His tours in connection with training camps began at April end from Palghat. His tour programmes linked to training camps, had begun two years prior to 1938. Leaving aside two years of the Sangh ban, this was his 33rd tour for this purpose. But, nobody would have imagined that this was to be his last training camprelated tour, such was his conduct during the camps. There was just one difference though. He had stopped going to Sangh ground during the morning drills. Still it seems that in his heart he had started preparing for his return from this world. There is an incident in Andhra during these camps that gives an indication about it.

Guruji left Hyderabad to reach the training camp at Tenali in the first week of May. In those days, transport services had come to a standstill due to an undesirable violet turn to Telangana agitation. Guruji and his team members had to turn back half way. He was sitting at night, at around 2-2:30 a.m. a little worried.. He tried to feel a little better by writing a letter to trainees in Tenali. In the regular central meeting that took place in Nagpur after the training camps, he said, "I could not reach Tenali as scheduled. At that time it seemed all roads are closed. But, after rethinking over it, I think I could have reached, perhaps, by another route. I could not carry out the responsibility given to me. I am the culprit. I seek pardon from all of you... It seems this body is not capable of doing this work now." [14] Last sentence of his self-confession was heart-rending.

Sarsanghchaalak came to Gwalior camp of Madhya Bharat on 25th May. Varg Sarvaadhikari head of the camp – Ramratan Tiwari presented him the newly published book, *Rashtra Raksha ke Morche Par*. This book was an illustrated book containing details of services performed by swayamsevaks during Bharat-Pakistan war. On understanding the contents of the book, he said in a serious tone, "I will not accept such a book." The book was sent back. Ram Ratan ji told him in a subdued voice, "Facts presented in the book can become material for history in future and such literature will also be able to publicise Sangh work." Answer was in the form of a question. "If a son serving his mother publishes his services as news, would that be considered creditable? That was his natural duty; where was the need to publicise it?"[15] Everybody says, 'We are sons of Mother Bharat,' but, only someone who has lived his life virtually breathing this truth can express such an opinion.

This year too, Guruji went for medical treatment and rest after Central Committee meeting to Indore to stay at Pandit Ramnarayan Shastriji's home. He stayed there from 25th July to 18th August, for 25 days. He spoke at *guru-puja* festival of Indore Shakha on 26th July. News about demise of Babasaheb Apte from Nagpur was received on 26th July. And, with this, one of his longest-standing colleague had left him. There was no trace of change in Guruji's expression, nor did he speak a word. There was a condolence meeting next day, a Sunday, organised by Indore Shakha. He spoke in it. His words pierced one's heart. He wrote nearly the same words in a letter he sent to Acharya Vishwabandhu of Hoshiarpur, "Shri Babasaheb Apte's departure from this world is a massive blow. He was an unending source of inspiration in creation of skilled workers right from the beginning of life of a pure seer, and always a guide for everybody because of his vast study and being a treasure house of knowledge. Even his leaving his body can be said to be extraordinary. He was not present, as he used to be, on 25-7-1972 in the morning. Therefore, worried about this, people entered his room from a ventilation window. He was found unconscious. Doctors rushed in and he was also taken to a hospital. All the wise doctors tried best of their knowledge and skills, but there was no result. Breathing was going at a very low pace. If one were to say that his face and body glowed, it would not be an overstatement. It seems that he merged his life's glow into the supreme glow of his own will. His low breathing stopped in the first part of the night on 29-7-1972."

"There are very few studious, idealist, action-oriented people; people who have sacrificed their all with full commitment for achieving the goal with their mind-body-soul. Within such a small number, absence of even one number can mean a major loss. This is what has happened. We are facing a major disaster in

Rashtriya Swayamsevak Sangh. Now, that father of the universe, the Supreme Being, with whose blessings this work is going on, should give us fortitude to make us capable to fill up this void. This is the prayer on our lips."[16]

Shri Aurobindo centenary programme of Indore city was to be held on 18th August. The keynote speaker was Guruji. Guruji had made it sure that the programme would begin with complete national song, '*Vande Maataram*.' His speech that day was a systematic narration of Shri Aurobindo's life. Just as the story of Lord Shri Rama is narrated, he narrated the history of Shri Aurbindo's life. He spoke about his experience of his silent meeting with Shri Mother, as quoted above, at the fag end of this speech.

Guruji went to Delhi on 19th August. Nanaji Deshmukh and his team were waiting for him on 20th for inauguration of Pandit Deendayal Research Institute. Guruji was the host of the *yagna*done before the formal inauguration and senior leaders such as Lala Hansraj, Atal Behari Vajpayee and Jagdish Prasad Mathur were present there. The bust of Pandit Deendayal Upadhyay was also unveiled at that time.

That same day, there was an interview with editor of *Motherland* newspaper. The subject was Common Civil Code that was being discussed intensely those days. Answering the editor's questions, Guruji said, "That Uniform Civil Code is a necessity to nurture nationalist sentiments, I don't think so. You and many others may be surprised with this view and I must say what I see as truth... harmony and uniformity are two different things. Uniformity is not necessary. There have been countless differences in Bharat, still this nation has remained powerful and united in its lengthy life. For unity, harmony is required, and not uniformity... There have been countless scriptural directives (*samhitas*) since ages, but they have not harmed us in any way. Till recently, Kerala had matriarchical culture. What was wrong with it? All ancient and new legal experts are unanimous that traditions are stronger than laws, and this is how it should be."[17]

What Guruji said at the beginning of this interview was correct. This view of Guruji was quite unexpected in political camps. It was a generally held belief that he would be a staunch supporter of Common Civil Code, but, his root inspiration was that of a philosopher. It came from Hindu culture that confirmed the view of unity in diversity. His stand was that differently coloured cows providing delicious milk look uniformly black only in the darkness of night. As a principle nobody opposed it.

Like 1971, eight months of 1972 till August were also favourable for Guruji. All his work went on uninterrupted. But, another boil on the left side was detected in September. All his colleagues got anxious. Dr. Abaji and Guruji had no doubt that it was the hood of the black serpent of cancer slithering and growing inside the body. Guruji's direction was, "Keep driving the vehicle; let us see how far does it take me." From 4th to 8th October, there were two day workers' camps in Ajmer, Jodhpur and Jaipur. Sarsanghchaalak reached the Ajmer camp on 4th. He fell sick during the third programme while he was in the Jaipur camp. In the words of Dr. Abaji, "It was the first time in his life that he could not keep his in balance during a fever. There was disorientation in his speech. Finally, the meeting was halted. He was back to normal after three hours."[18] He went to meet an important leader of Bharatiya Jan Sangh, Shri Bhairon Singh Shekhawat in hospital even in that condition and told him, "Get well soon, young man; you still have to do a great deal of work."[19] He came to Mumbai by air from Jaipur on 10th and went back to Nagpur for Vijayadashami festival.

Guruji came to Mumbai after the function and met doctors in Tata Hospital. Doctors told that this boil is recurrence of the same disease and radiation therapy would have to be done immediately. Guruji agreed to radiation therapy, but after 21st-22nd October. He had to be at Sidhpur in Gujarat where the first Vishwa Hindu Parishad conference of that state was to take place. Guruji even managed to reach there. Nearby 1,50,000 delegates turned up as against estimated 40,000. Swami Chidaanand, head of Divya Jeevan Sangh of Rishikesh, inaugurated the conference on 21st at 10 a.m. The keynote address was by Guruji. Laying a strong stress on liberation of neglected brethren, he said, "It is but natural and expected that our attention be drawn towards these brethren, called Dalit and work hard to bring them at par with us. But, while doing so, one would have to take care of one thing. Sometimes, such efforts become unnaturally artificial; it should not be so. If one tries to make special efforts for them, then such a synthetic feeling creeps in and the natural feeling about considering them as organs of our society starts getting weakened. It cannot nurture unity...Social unity cannot be achieved through the political field. This work can be accomplished only through the religious field. We will have to do this work on the basis of religion, culture, unity of hearts within each other, affection and co-operation."[20]

In that radiant conference of Sidhpur, a large number of *sadhus* and saints were present on the dais and also in the assembly. Guruji criticised undesirable mentality rising within religious leadership of Hindu society and recounted his experience quite frankly, "I will tell you about an incident. We have many different sects. Vishwa Hindu Parishad organised a conference to create some harmony between them. Some workers met heads of various sects to invite them for the conference. When they presented the invitation to one such head, he accepted it and asked immediately, 'What is the seating arrangement?' When workers informed him about the arrangement, he said, 'How can I come? Will all others sit with me? What kind of arrangement is this? After all we too have certain protocol with limitations and a concept of senior and junior. Therefore, make arrangements accordingly, only then will I come'.

"This fact was brought to my notice. I thought, this is indeed very strange that a person who has sacrificed everything, has taken to saffron clothes; he has not been able to get rid of petty thinking about honour-insult. Therefore, when an opportunity to meet him came up, I told him, 'Maharaj, did you say that how can you make us sit with junior people?' He said, 'Yes, I did say so.' I told him, 'Please take off your saffron clothes. I am ready to give you my *kurta*, please wear it. Then talk like this. I am not even ready to listen to you in these clothes. I have never accepted the fourth *ashram* (sanyaas). But, my life has been spent among *sadhus*. It has been spent in the company of such divine souls about whom one can say, '*Guruh sakshat parabrahma*'. On the basis of that experience I am asking you to get rid of your saffron clothes."

He was a great soul. He was not upset. He looked at me for a moment and said, "Brother, what you say is correct. We people were busy only taking care of customs and protocols of our institutions and priesthood. We left behind our *sanyaas-dharma*. Your view is right." Later, he took part in the conference quite enthusiastically."[21]

It is clear that Guruji's words in that open assembly were directed towards *sannyasi* delegates and not household people. Adi Shankaracharya had perhaps talked of such people when he had said, "*Kashaya ambara abahukritave shah.*" But, it strengthens a view. That Guruji's had an imposing standing within *sadhus*-saints, heads of *mathams*, *Mahamandaleshwaras* and they used to listen to his views with respect and were ready to think over them seriously. Sometimes they used to come to him to resolve problems within themselves. A couple of examples have been mentioned earlier. It would not be an over-statement to say that Guruji's impressive personality played an unmatched role in growth and nurturing of Vishwa Hindu Parishad.

The conference ended on 23rd October and Golwalkar, the patient, presented himself to Dr. Prafulla Desai for radiation therapy.

□

Endnotes

1. *Sukhad Sansmaran*, pp. 21
2. Ibid, pp. 32
3. Ibid, pp. 26
4. *Jeevan Prasang*, Vol. 1, pp. 227-228
5. *Chitraanjali*, pp. 60
6. *Shri Guruji Samagra*, Vol. 6, pp. 103
7. *Madhavan Adhichyuvattil*, pp. 211-212
8. Ibid, pp. 213
9. *Shri Guruji Samagra*, Vol. 1, pp. 108
10. *Shri Guruji Uttar Pradesh Mein*, pp. 50
11. *Avismaraneey Guruji*, pp. 60-61
12. *Shri Guruji Samagra*, Vol. 6, pp. 103-104
13. *Shri Guruji Samagra*, Vol. 8, pp. 388
14. *Avismaraneey Guruji*, pp. 119

15. *Jeevan Prasang*, Vol. 1, pp. 6-7
16. *Shri Guruji Samagra*, Vol. 7, pp. 306-307
17. *Shri Guruji Samagra*, Vol. 9, pp. 195-197
18. *Shri Guruji Samagra*, Vol. 12, pp. 23
19. *Shri Guruji Rajasthan Mein*, pp. 35
20. *Shri Guruji Samagra*, Vol. 5, pp. 133-135
21. Ibid, pp. 135-136

43

Last Intellectual Workshop, Last Diwali

Central Committee meeting that used to be held after Sangh Shiksha Vargas every year in July-August, was held in 1972 under the chairmanship of Sarkaryavaah Balasaheb Deoras. It was resolved in this meeting that a special intellectual study workshop will be conducted that year at a suitable time. This type of workshop was last organised at Indore 12 years back. In this passage of time, different dimensions of Sangh movement had grown in multiple ways, and on the other side, Guruji's condition was becoming a point of worry. Keeping all this in mind, everybody felt this workshop must be held. It was also decided that this workshop should not be limited only to Prachaaraks but people involved in different fields should also be invited. Thus, keeping the convenience of all concerned in mind, the workshop calendar was finalised for 28th October to 3rd November as it was a period of Diwali festival holidays. Realising the possibility of deterioration in the delicate health of Guruji, the meeting was planned at Mumbai. There was no doubt that this workshop was going to be bigger than the earlier workshops of Sindi and Indore and arrangements were done accordingly. Tatvagyan Vidyapeeth of revered Pandurang Shastri Athavale was finalised as the venue.

As mentioned earlier, the time for treatment of Guruji with radiation therapy was fixed after the Central Committee meeting. And this period was decided keeping this workshop in mind. Personal assistant Dr. Aba Thatte and Guruji had mutually decided that other programmes would be conducted after radiation therapy in the morning at Tata Memorial Hospital. Apart from morning Shakha, other sessions included presentation on a subject by Guruji, team wise discussion on this subject, clearing of queries and doubts by Guruji and finally, conclusion of that topic. Thus, Guruji was supposed to be busy for four hours every day. This programme went on till 3rd November, that is, going from Thane to Mumbai, getting radiation therapy, return and the workshop. Inspite of this, Guruji never seemed exhausted. His face reflected same happiness, his voice had same sweetness, his presentations had same logical clarity and his conclusions carried same sharp intellectual prowess. The only difference was that he spoke in a sitting posture and bouts of cough used to disturb him once in a while. One night, after dinner, revered Pandurang Shastri addressed the workshop participants and he was present there too.

In the opening session of the workshop, he said, "All of you present here are mature with experience. I have nothing new to say; my duty is only to remind you about those ideas once again, the rest you know well enough." It was, indeed, correct. Guruji's submissions were about Hindu, Hindu nation, Sangh Shakha, Swayamsevak, creating Prachaaraks, growth of work in different fields, dedication, etc. – all old subjects. Apart from these, he also analysed other issues like democracy, socialism, communism, social systems, libertine permissive groups and responded to participants' doubts too.

Speaking in his first discourse about the word 'Hindu', he threw light on facts that were beyond doubt and said, "This nation of ours is Hindu nation – *rashtra*. We wish to rebuild its paramount status and a sovereign, prosperous life for it. We are striving to this end only and this exercise will continue till we are successful in this endeavour."

"It is true that people try to create confusion about the word 'Hindu'. In many places, motivated by selfish motives, a Hindu is shown as being anti-Muslim, anti-Christian and now even anti-Sikh, anti-Jain, anti-Harijan. People perpetrating such propaganda do not do so with proper information. They have their vested political interests. It is not that they make these statements after studying *dharma*, culture and history.

"Hindu philosophy and the systems of living one's life have been present in this country, when Islamic and Christian communities did not even exist in this world. One may ask then, how can Hindu mean anti-Muslim? Similarly, Sikh and Jain sects, etc. come within the purview of Hindu. If one were to carry a sentiment of opposing them, when one speaks of 'Hindu', it would be akin to cutting one's own limbs. Then, how is a Hindu against them? Undoubtedly, these allegations are borne out of petty mentality and confusions resulting from it. There is no truth in this. All these are falsehoods. 'Hindu' is not against anybody. This is a completely emotional thought, not against anybody at all."

"Therefore, we must assert with complete resolve that yes, we are Hindus. This is our *dharma*, our culture, our society and built from all this is our nation. That is all. Our birth is only to build a powerful, capable, grand, radiant sovereign life for it. It is paramount to have such a strong belief in our hearts. Therefore, we must motivate many people towards this purpose. There is no need to be embarrassed or be afraid to broadcast this belief."[1]

"We have to take work of our organisation to each and every district." He laid stress on the approach of co-ordination and co-operation required to achieve this. "Sangh's work is omnipresent, but how is it omnipresent? There is an example. Light is omnipresent, but it does not accomplish all the work by itself. It dispels darkness and shows the way to everybody. We must understand this fact. Then, there will be no blunder."

"There are different fields in national life. We say that there is need for this work in every field, therefore, whosoever does this work, should work in those fields. Our only insistence is that understand the principles properly and work on that basis. People in different fields should move ahead this way. Think of the nation's progress. Work for multi-dimensional prosperity of the nation.

"It is not our job to provide readymade or ready to use material to people who are working in different fields of this nation's life. People working in different fields will have to think and find ways to remain steadfast to principles and bring them into practice."[2]

A deer does not enter into mouth of a sleeping lion, reminding this truth the action-oriented sage said, "This work will not be accomplished with talks. Expanding slowly and steadily, such people should stand up at the earliest in each small area of cities, smallest settlements in a district; people who will be able to resolve all difficulties of their areas successfully by putting in all the strength of their lives. It has been oft repeated in our organisation that building human beings is the most important task and problems will get resolved depending on the quantum with which our work grows."[3]

"Full-time workers are required for this purpose. Therefore, special attention would have to be paid to creation of more Prachaaraks. Bringing this to the notice of participants he said, "We are talking about expanding this work to every nook and corner of the entire country. For this, we need workers whom we call 'Prachaaraks'. The question is whether we shall get Prachaaraks in sufficient numbers without exerting? Sangh has many senior workers. They are busy with Sangh work, renouncing all thoughts about personal family life. We cannot say that special efforts were made for them at that time. It just happened easily at that time, but it is not possible that such a thing will happen that easily in today's scenario. We need to understand that special efforts would be required over those whom we wish to make into Prachaarak. One would need to equip each person by explaining all the issues to him and analysing the current scenario for him. One will have to inform them well about various hurdles that come up in this exercise of nation's upliftment. There are many attractions in life at different junctures. One has to go through many calamities. One is buffeted by adversities and one has to bear with them. Desires to receive honours rise within; one has to strain oneself to suppress them. Occasions arise for popularity and prestige, called 'attractions of exercising leadership'. It is necessary to be on guard against them. Inspite of these and many other hurdles, one has to accomplish this mission. We shall have to strive hard to awaken the challenge for this work in each heart."[4]

His view about modern permissive behaviour or permissiveness with reference to social structure and systems was, "As far as the matter of 'permissive society' is concerned, it is harmful from every angle. Situations arising out of absence of rules of conduct are also described in our *Puranas*. There were no regulations in ancient times, but people realised that immoral acts were on the rise due to it. It was then decided that rules should be framed and every human being should behave in accordance with them. Thus, it is our experience since ancient times that talk about permissive society will only give rise to immoral behaviour that can lead to human beings becoming each other's enemies and leading to annihilation of life. Today, people may say anything about it, but it would not be proper to drag human life based on just an experience of last 50-100 years. It must only be decided on the basis of in-depth thinking about what is beneficial or harmful for human beings."[5]

Carrying the same thought process and analysing it more clearly, he said, "In our nation, thought was given to the fact that running after unlimited lusts and desires and their fulfilment will not lead to happiness. Therefore, it was thought necessary to bring in self-restraint in life. This restraint is important for the individual as well as society. It is quite clear that it is difficult to have restraint at social level. Therefore, our people have thought of fourfold action plan for life, that is, four '*purusharthas*'. All these four *purusharthas* are defined to build up such a life of restraint. Thought should be given to duties of both individual and society. Both should be under the authority of *dharma* and then work for and worship the *purusharthas* of wealth creation and desires through this life controlled by *dharma*. That is, consumption, power, wealth, prosperity, instruments of luxury, etc. – all these should be guided by *dharma* and urge for liberation (*moksha*) would complete this control so that one should be able to experience the real form of genuine happiness. This same urge, that is fourth *purushartha -moksha*, has been put before us. It does not make any difference whatever name you give to this fourth *purushartha*. But, this fourth *purushartha* was presented before us so that desire to achieve our original enlightened personality should remain alive within us.

"Our life should be directed through the first and fourth *purusharthas*. Consuming, acquiring means of consumption, enjoying luxuries, etc. should be under the sway of these two *purusharthas*. Like waters of a river that flow between its two banks so that everyone can use them properly; otherwise that water creates havoc if it breaks banks and it cannot be used as it wastes away, flowing in various directions. Therefore, it is a happy situation that the river of enjoyment should flow between two banks. Directing the life's flow through the first and the fourth *purusharthas*, thought should be given to how to provide all kinds of material enjoyments at individual and social levels for human beings. Idea about organising our social system that can provide this level of satisfaction in material enjoyment has been worked out."

"I feel the above idea can provide happiness to human beings. Competition etc. result in conflicts. Stopping competition and avoiding the harm that it could inflict upon the society, enjoying every kind of material happiness but still keeping restraint and keeping focus only on the ultimate goal of life will result in real happiness to an individual. As an individual and a society, it will result in satisfaction and happiness in life in both ways."[6]

About democracy he noted, "Of all the types of systems of governance in the world, it is accepted that democracy has the least shortcomings. The entire populace gets representation in this system. But for the system to succeed, it is mandatory that the common people should be well educated. Not only well educated but they should have good knowledge about economics, politics, international relations, etc. so that they are capable of selecting the right representative. If it does not happen this way and the common people are illiterate and have no information, then they can chose ineligible representatives due to some selfish motive or inducements. Then such a society repents for next five years, wondering what has it done. Lack of education and awareness of voter means a bleak scenario for democracy as capable representatives are not elected. There are other negative fallouts too because of this and then the basic thought about democracy is lost."

"Such difficulties arise in a democratic structure. How can we find a way out of these? One view that comes up in this regard is that the current system is to elect people, territory and population based on Census, etc. This can be kept as it is and in addition, a system of having representatives of industry and other segments should be followed. All other professions and businesses should be represented in a structured manner this way. It is called 'functional representation' in English. It is already implemented in some countries. If it can be linked to the present electoral system, then the assembly which is made up of uninformed people and takes responsibility of running the government will also have some knowledgeable people. They would be able to provide novel thoughts about any subject when required."[7]

There was a session of questions and answers; questions that day were about Socialism and Communism. Persons asking those questions were mostly responsible Bharatiya Mazdoor Sangh workers. One of the questions seemed a little out of place. Many people thought that it was not a question that needed to be asked from Guruji. Looking at Thengadiji, Guruji asked, "So, Dattopant, have you heard the question?" Dattopant stood up and said, "Question is right, but address is wrong." The whole assembly area burst into a laugh. Guruji's laugh could be heard through the microphone. Tension in the atmosphere simply melted away. Now, Guruji asked a question directed towards all, "Have you read the book, *Sukhdayak Rajyaprakarani Nibandh*?" Nobody stood up. Guruji, then, began telling about the said book. "This is a Marathi book written by Shri Vishnubua Brahmachari in 1867. As the name indicates, it is an essay about a system of governance that would result in happiness. Vishnubua had sent out 10,000 copies of the translated book in English in 1870 within and outside Bharat. The book became a subject of discussion everywhere. It was also translated in Hindi and Gujarati. The same year also saw publication of Karl Marx's *Das Kapital*. It is beyond imagination that both of them could have met by any chance. Still their direction of thinking and conclusions are quite close to each other. Surprisingly, both are original and revolutionary books about political, economic and social thinking. Both sages give directions about the progress of human society with their own intellectual prowess. But, the only difference in their presentations is that Brahmachaari took both material and spiritual aspects into account, therefore, accepting *dharma* as the power that holds a society together. Marx said that religion is opium of the mind. He found it obligatory to criticise religion and he did so successfully. There was solid reason behind it. It was not possible for him to think of *dharma* the way this concept is understood in Bharat. What he had in front of him were outdated Semetic forms of religions. On the other hand, Vishnuji was a follower of Dattatreya sect. He was a celibate. Because of this background, his analysis was based on Bharatiya experience and ethics. This scripture of Vishnubua being inspired by *swadeshi* thought, can be more valuable and helpful for the labour movement in this country."[8]

This question raised by Guruji and more than that, this answer of his was a matter of curiosity for everybody. Information that Guruji gave aroused the curiosity of the people about the subject and they met him during the tea-break that evening. Satisfying their inquisitiveness, Guruji spoke like a teacher then, "All this information is about a person and does not relate much to our subject. Therefore, I left it half way. There is a limitation of time too." Proceeding from this opening remark, he said, "Complete name of this *brahmachari* is Vishnu Bhikaji Gokhale. Bhikaji, his father, was a village priest in Raigarh district. It is said that Vishnu envisioned Lord Dattatreya at the age of 20. He became a *sannyasi* in Nasik at the age of 23. I do not know the name of this *sannyasi*. He wrote *Rajyaprakarani Nibandh* at the age of 42. His earlier creation was *Vedokta Dharmaprakash*. He had done deep study of the *Vedas*. He did not get stuck in mere meanings of the words. Thus, he was not caught in hollow rituals."

"He wished well for all and became a progressive thinker as per the norms of those times. He was a strong opponent of priests and *mahants* and their orthodox views as they had turned into brokers buried in temples of gods. He had the firm belief that untouchability is nonsense and unnecessary; that the caste system is baseless and meaningless. He supported women's education and widow remarriage by quoting *shlokas* from *Vedas*. In his view, there was nothing like *malechh* (a fallen person).

Therefore, he used to have food in Christian and Muslim homes without hesitation. But, he was a bitter opponent of conversions attempted by foreigners. He was a combative thinker. There is an episode of those times. There was a Christian missionary named John Wilson. It was his hobby to publish literature in the name of *Tract Society* that tried to undermine Hindu gods and beliefs and distribute it. Vishnu and Wilson confronted each other once. Vishnu challenged Wilson for a scientific debate. Both of them met at Chaupati Beach of Mumbai in the presence of a large gathering. There were arguments and counter arguments and Vishnu outclassed Wilson. Unfortunately, he died at a young age of 46. Last year was his centenary year. It would be useful to study his personality and his work."[9]

Thus, Thane's intellectual workshop was highly inspiring. The thought that this would be Guruji's last guidance was swirling in mind of each participant, but no one spoke about it. Everybody went back to his field of work after conclusion of the workshop on 3rd November, but, Guruji's treatment continued. His place of residence was shifted from Thane to Chembur at the residence of Mumbai city secretary, Anantrao Deshpande. November 4 was the Diwali day and it was one of the happiest days for Deshpande family. It was the first Diwali when they had the rare company of Guruji. And who knew, this could be his last Diwali? Guruji stayed there for one more week till 11th November. It was impossible to stop people in an organisation built on family relations from trickling in to see a father figure like Guruji personally; it was only possible to control it. So, from the beginning, visiting hours of 4 p.m. to 6 p.m. was fixed for the purpose. Many young and old swayamsevaks came and met him with their families. Nearly all old swayamsevaks were well known to him. He used to speak a word or two with each of them. Day after day went on like this. One day, a person who came to meet him, was wearing a white shirt and *khaki* half pants. After he went back, Guruji said, "Ananta, it seems he does not go to Shakha every day; he came in the afternoon in half pants just to show off." It was a correct observation as the city secretary Anantrao knew this person well.

During those seven days, Guruji used to go to a pre-appointed Shakha. He used to converse with swayamsevaks for four to five minutes after the conclusion of Shakha. He went to a village Shakha in Turbhe, about 5 kms from Chembur. The whole settlement belonged to fishermen and nearly each family had a swayamsevak. The day Guruji went there, 1,000 swayamsevaks were present. All of them felt fulfilled by just catching a glimpse of Guruji. Next day, he was to go to Mahul village. His experience there was similar to that of Turbhe. The satisfaction that he could go to homes of his brethren during Diwali was reflected on Guruji's face.

Editor of *Illustrated Weekly*, Khushwant Singh came to meet him on November 8 at 10 a.m. It was not a day for radiation therapy in the hospital. He would probably have come after making enquiries about it. As soon as Khushwant entered, Guruji held both his hands to welcome him and asked him to sit beside him. The conversation was mostly introductory in nature, a few general questions and answers too were general.But, he liked Guruji's style of conversing very much. He too began talking in an informal manner. He asked Guruji for a copy of *Bunch of Thoughts*, but in a very interesting way. He began,

"My father, Sir Shobha Singh, is an expert in town planning. I have seen your autographed copy of *Bunch of Thoughts* on his table. I too want such a copy. It may probably lead to a fight between father and son." Clapping on Singh's palms, Guruji said with a chuckle, "I will arrange for it very soon. Why should I be the reason for a fight?" The atmosphere turned joyful. Khushwant took leave. The next week, Khushwant Singh wrote a beautiful article in his weekly magazine about this meeting.

People came to meet Guruji even on 9th. The president of All Bharat Wadar Samaj, Shri Dhotre came to meet him at 4 p.m. The *mistry,* that is artisan community involved in building-related profession is regarded as a backward community in Maharashtra. Their topmost leader, Dhotre, was a gentleman who had risen in society through hard work. The Sangh work was also growing well in his community. Deeply hurt with the low social status of his fellow-brothers, he asked Guruji a solution that would help them rise. Guruji's answer was, "Contributing education and imparting *samskaaras*. After these two are accomplished, plans for economic upliftment can be drawn. In the absence of these two, wealth alone will result in the society going down the immoral path. You can give right direction and motivation with your own example."[10] The Maharana of Mewar, a descendant of Maharana Pratap and all Bharat President of Vishwa Hindu Parishad at that time, came to visit him the same day. Freedom fighter of Goa, Mohan Ranade also came the next day. During the conversation, he told Guruji, "I was able to master Portuguese, Spanish and French languages during my long imprisonment in Portuguese jails." Responding to it, Guruji said, "In these days of international diplomacy and foreign affairs, it has become necessary to learn and speak as many number of languages as possible. Not only youngsters, even children should be encouraged in this direction. But, overriding commitment to our nation is undoubtedly required. One should be ready for any sacrifice if the situation arises."[11]

Thus, many a brethren came to Anantrao Deshpande's house and met Guruji. Information of Guruji's stay in Chembur was not released anywhere, but it was not even kept a secret. Just as the family members know about a sick person in the family, something similar happened here too. Of their own accord, relatives from the large family that Guruji had, came to see him. There was no register to make a note of their names and their work or purpose of visit. Finally, that wandering seer got into a car on 11th at 4:30 p.m. On the way, he stopped at Laxmi Hospital where a sick swayamsevak from Nagpur was being treated and reached the station on time. After finishing his last intellectual workshop and celebrating his last Diwali, he reached Dr. Hedgewar Bhavan on 12th, Sunday, just as a grazing cow returns home at twilight.

□

Endnotes

1. *Shri Guruji Samagra*, Vol. 2, pp. 281-283
2. Ibid, pp. 283-284
3. Ibid, pp. 314
4. Ibid, pp. 320-321
5. Ibid, pp. 300
6. Ibid, pp. 300-301
7. Ibid, pp. 304-306
8. *Aarti Alok Ki*, pp. 264-265
9. Diary of author
10. *Avismaraneey Diwali – Ekta Diwali issue*, 2001 (Marathi Complete Information about Chembur Stay
11. *Shri Guruji Samagra*, Vol. 9, pp. 202

44

Final Offering of Self-Sacrifice

Guruji's conduct during the workshop in Mumbai that showed him to be physically fit, was actually a sign of his steely resolve and fortitude of Mother Earth. This fact is verified by succeeding events that unfolded shortly. Within two days of this workshop, he told Anantrao Deshpande's family that he was finding it difficult to swallow any solid or liquid food. The food he took with his colleagues sitting in rows with them on the auspicious occasion of Diwali was only for namesake. His condition deteriorated further by the time he reached Nagpur. Writing to his colleague in Pune, Baba Bhide, on 16th November (remember that he had reached Nagpur on 12th) he noted, "Results of the treatment taken in Mumbai give pain even now. Pain in throat, inability to eat or drink anything (I drink water or take food under immense pain), problem with voice, not being able to speak at all – all this is happening with me. There are no signs that I will be able to come out of this pain in the coming 15 days."[1] Looking at Guruji's condition and understanding its gravity, Appaji Joshi and Baba Bhide had seen to it that all the programmes in Vidarbha and Maharashtra were cancelled. Mentioning this, he wrote in the same letter, "If I were to attend these programmes, I would have made a laughing stock of myself; you have saved me from this precarious situation."

On insistence of Pandit Ramnarayan Shastri and Dr. Abaji Thatte, Guruji stayed at Shastriji's house on 13th for treatment. As a result, it was possible for him to swallow again. After return to Nagpur, he had taken these medicines for another 15 days. Swayamsevaks kept him free from any programmes. He used to go to Mohite Shakha every day for Sangh prayer. Inspite of all this, there was a pre-planned programme for him on 27th December which he could not avoid – it was unveiling of life-size statue of Dr. Munje in Sitaburdi. Guruji was the chairman of its organising committee. Guruji wrote letters to many dignitaries, requesting them to attend this programme. Those were the days when political untouchability was not practiced like the present times. Aware of the close relations between Chakravarti Rajagopalachari and Dr. Munje, he made a special request to Rajagopalachari to put his signature on a joint appeal for raising funds for the project. Rajaji told Sanghchaalak of Chennai, "Generally, I do not affix my signature on such appeals, as I have a bitter experience. But, Golwalkar has put his signature at the top and I know that he is steadfast in truth. I will sign on it." Similarly, Guruji was also able to get support from Babu Jagjivan Ram. This unveiling on 27th was an outcome of all these efforts.

There was another motive behind this – to repay his organisation's debt. Dr. Munje had given the whole-hearted support to Dr. Hedgewar when he founded the Sangh in 1925. Many people used to think for a long time that Dr. Munje was the founder of the Sangh. Dr. Hedgewar considered him his elder, a great person and one of his own. After becoming Sarsanghchaalak, Guruji also gave the same reverential respect. But, we can call it only a misfortune that when this great supporter of the Sangh died on 3rd March, 1948, neither Guruji nor any other Sangh official could offer his tearful floral tribute to the lifeless body of the brave soul at that time. The Sangh had been banned and Sarsanghchaalak was in prison. To make amends for this failure, to perform one's duty on which one had no control, an opportunity came up after 25 years in this form. People of Nagpur took care to make this an event a success. Retired Chief of Army, General Cariappa, was the chief guest and he unveiled the statue. The function was a grand success. Guruji himself took the respected guest to Dr. Munje's home, Dr. Hedgewar, his memorial and other places of significance for the Sangh. It may be noted that this successful programme was the last public programme attended by Guruji![2]

After a gap of one day, Guruji left for his circumambulation of Bharat yet again on 29th December. After completing this 75-day-long tour, he returned back to his centre on 14th March. On that day, Supreme God ultimately gave the final relief from his travels to this seer, the ascetic of unending travels. He did not leave Nagpur after this day. He was in the worker's camp on 29th December in Ahmedabad. He provided guidance to Maharashtra state's workers on January 10 at Nasik. He went to Amravati for Vidarbha state meeting on 12th-13th. He took part in Makar Sankraman festival on 14th in Nagpur, toured Punjab from 21st January to 1st February for 12 days. From the land of five rivers he flew into the state of River Kaveri on 1st February. Bangalore city was all agog, waiting for Sarsanghchaalak's programmes planned for 2nd-3rd-4th February. All the programmes had been organised with a spirit of courage and triumph. Prachaarak of South region, Yadavrao Joshi, made a touching comment during a committee meeting of this programme, "Brothers, this may be the last programme of our living idol." Thus, every atom of swayamsevaks was fired with zeal. Workers began working as if to beat back death.

The first programme on 3rd was a press conference in Madras Woodlands Hotel in the afternoon. The conference went on for 70 minutes. Subjects that came up included federal and unitary form of governance, war mongering by Pakistan, Muslim problem, Kashmir problem, creation of Bangladesh, Bharatiya

Jana Sangh, caste system, growth of Sangh, etc. For many journalists it was the first 'press conference of Golwalkar'. Therefore, many fresh young enthusiastic journalists, carrying no past baggage, were in full form. It was a time when Communists, the ruling party, intelligence agencies, news media had run the propaganda that "Golwalkar is on his deathbed and there is tug of war between top RSS leadership." In this background, one journalist asked, "Who, after Golwalkar?" Countering it with his own rhetorical question, Guruji asked with a smile, "Why not you?" Journalist asked, "On Guru's seat? It is not that easy." Guruji added, "It is true, it is not easy. But, it is possible by imbibing right *samskaaras*. Now, this problem does not arise in our organisation. If there was some compulsion, it would have been a problem. The Sangh has not built its organisation like this. And whosoever comes up, will fulfil his responsibility, what else?" The press conference went off in a cordial atmosphere. One journalist noted, "Golwalkar is quite fine."[3]

There was a public gathering of swayamsevaks on 4th February, Sunday, at 6 in the evening. Swayamsevaks in thousands had contacted people on a massive scale in all corners of the city and distributed invitations. In that massive densely-packed meeting, Guruji stood up and spoke for 50 minutes in English. Speed, flow, style of the speech was just like that of the earlier days, but, he had to take help to climb down from the stage after the speech. There was a meeting of workers of Karnataka state on 5th February. This programme also ended on a happy note, but older workers who participated in such meetings of Guruji earlier, could detect some difference and they were a little distressed. Finally, in the list of 'final' programmes, the final programme too got included – it was the last public meeting of Guruji on 4th.

He was in Bengal on February 24th-25th. He went to Kashi on instructions of revered Prabhudatt Brahmachari on 28th. Let us understand the reason behind this in Brahmachariji's words, "Some people had shown his birth-chart to an astrologer belonging to Bhrigu Samhita school. It came out clearly that this 66th year of his life was highly inauspicious for him, that is, it signified death. We decided that we should perform *Rudrayagna* to calm the planets. He did not wish that 'something should be done for me or other people should worry about me'. Brothers like Madhav ji Deshmukh, Bhaurao Deoras and others arranged for *Rudrayagna* at Madhavji's house in Kashi. This*yagna* went on for nine days. In my letter I had asked him to come to Kashi for its concluding ritual (*poornahuti*). He was on a tour of Assam, Orissa and Bengal. He came to Kashi for *poornahuti* from Kolkata for a few hours. I too went to Kashi. He had reached there by that time. Wearing a clean, freshly washed *dhoti* and a yellow coloured cotton shawl with Ram's name written over it, he sat for the *pooja* like a true believer. Madhav ji accompanied by his wife, was helping him. He performed worship following proper rituals and performed *poornahuti*."[4]

28th February happened to be Guruji's birthday. The whole programme was managed in such a way that he would perform the final parts of rituals himself on this very day. In the same period, an important significant incident took place. It had nothing to do with this *yagna*, but it related to the special bond that connected these two divine personalities. It would be ideal to quote it in Brahmachariji's words, "Once, his 51st birthday was being celebrated as a public programme. At that time, there was a felicitation programme in Kanpur and a gift was being offered to him. I was presiding over that meeting. I wore a cotton sheet with a saffron hue. I gifted him a similar sheet made of cotton (its colour being a natural saffron), a short length sheet for waist, one small towel, sacred thread and *multani mitti* (a kind of natural bathing soil). Accepting these clothes respectfully, he had said with a laugh, *Maharaj ji*, you will not leave me alone till I become a *sadhu'*.

"I told him laughingly in the same vein, 'Maharaj, you are a born *sadhu*; who can make you into a *sadhu*? These clothes are not dyed in saffron, they are naturally saffron. It is their natural colour."

"Whenever he came to meet me, I used to gift him some cloth. When he came to our 'home of cows' – *gaushala* – in connection with cow protection movement that he was to preside, I presented him a new cotton sheet before he left. At that time, he spoke with great devotion, 'Maharaj ji, please do not give me fresh cloth; give me a sheet used by you as a *prasad*.'

"Those were winter days. I gifted him the blanket I was using and said, 'It is torn at one place.' He said, 'It is fine. I will be happy with anything.'

"After some days when he met me, he told me with great joy, 'See, Maharaj ji, I have completed the entire travel this year with this blanket.'

"This time when he came to Jhoosi, he did not tell me anything, but told Ramanuj Pandey, secretary of our Sankirtan Bhavan Dharmic Nyas, 'Maharaj ji always gives me a sheet, but never gifts a loin cloth. This time I will request for a loin cloth (*langoti*)."

"Within us *sadhus*, *langoti* is given only to *sadhus* who have become unattached from the world. This time when I went to Kashi, I took along a sheet, short waist-cloth and also a loin cloth and told him, 'This time I have brought you a *langoti* too.'

"On hearing this, he was highly pleased. How would I know that by wearing this *langoti*, he was preparing to take leave from all the programmes of the Sangh?"[5]

Guruji returned to Kolkata from Kashi and restarted his tour of the north-east. There was a state-level workers' camp in Bihar on March 10th-11th. He had to suffer great physical pain during that programme. On 11th evening, he came to Ranchi station to board Ranchi Express for Kolkata. He was in acute pain as he tried to alight from a car and had to take help. As he walked towards the train taking support of Vibhag Prachaarak Shrishankar Tiwari's shoulder, he muttered in a weak voice, "Shrishankar, what has happened to this body? It seems it is worn-out." What could poor Prachaarak say? He just wiped off his own tears silently.[6]

On 12th Guruji got into Kolkata-Nagpur flight with Dr. Abaji Thatte. He was returning to his nest after two-and-a-half month of tour. But, it seems there was still some debt left in his travel account. The plane landed in Mumbai due to fog in Mumbai that day instead of Nagpur. Similarly, the plane travelling to Nagpur ended up in Kolkata again instead of Nagpur! Finally, he landed safely in Nagpur from Kolkata. A car brought him to Dr. Hedgewar Bhavan from the airport.[7] With this, his sustained unbroken travel across the country, first as Sarkaryavaah in 1939 and then as Sarsanghchaalak from 1940 to 1973 finally came to an end after 34 years. Coincidentally, the number of times he had traversed and circumambulated Bharat was same as his age at that time. After this, he never left Dr. Hedgewar Bhavan. Yes, he used to take part in Shakha that used to run on Mohite Sangh Ground in the compound. This was also only till 26th March.

The day he arrived and went to the Sangh ground for prayers, Sanghchaalak of Nagpur city Bapurao Varhadpande saw him walk from one end. Knowing him for years, he recognised his walk well. He found something amiss that day. He called Dr. Balasaheb Pendse immediately and got him examined. Dr. Abaji Thatte took his X-ray on 16th to Mumbai and met Dr. Desai. According to him, cancer had reached his lungs. The patient's weight went on decreasing after this and weakness went on increasing.

Even a week had not passed yet and Akhil Bharatiya Pratinidhi Sabha (All India Delegates' Meet) was to be held from 22nd-25th March. Entire arrangements for this were to be made by the Central office. There was enough space for it during those days. All the delegates coming from across Bharat were anxious about Guruji's health. Guruji heard the entire proceedings sitting there. On the last day, 25th, Sarkaryavaah Balasaheb Deoras requested him to speak a few words of guidance. He began his speech sitting in a chair. He knew that this concluding speech was going to be the conclusion of his speech. It was very painful for him to speak. He would be breathless after speaking one or two sentences. Frequent bouts of cough gave a lot of trouble, still, he had spoken for 40 minutes, as was his nature.

"When I had said on the first day of Thane meeting that the Sangh work is to be carried on by others now onwards, I have no role to play in it now, at that time many colleagues had come to me and told me that I should not have said this. I told them, 'I spoke what was true.' …it means that whether a person lives or not, the organisation is not going to lose out in a big way. Actually, history of our country is that organisations run well for a few days, then there are personality clashes...But we have taken a path to unite and organise, not to divide. We shall never allow division... We have to organise the entire society and take our work to the entire society with a feeling of co-operative living. We carry the responsibility of this gigantic task. Therefore, whatever situation we might face, we should not allow any ill feeling to come between us... Now we shall have to think even harder at this stage of organisation because our workers are working in different fields like student, politics, labour, etc. The set-up of these organisations, their constitution, rules, style of functioning are all different. Still our swayamsevaks go to those organisations with the same commitment of this organisation and try to establish it there. All of us should take care whether such an attempt is being carried out or not... our mission to empower our nation with everlasting power may take time for people to understand, but as we come in touch with people one by one, as we keep working, we should keep explaining this to them. All these different forms of work have the same objective and that is, this country, society and nation are all ours and work in different fields is being carried out to build a supreme life force. The nation is our deity. Every work of ours is dedicated to its service…some people will say that if we speak about our views on Hindu nation, many people will not agree with it. However, it does not matter if some people do not agree with this pronouncement. Our vision should be clear and we should have full faith in it. Then propounding it with persistence will result in people accepting it. This has been our experience… In our society, we have been told about the ideal of pure character. We have attempted to build a national character in social life. We have seen success to some extent... We should keep our conduct pure in different kinds of tasks that we have to accomplish... We should also keep in mind always that we shall not be able to do these different tasks without the Shakha. Wherever our Shakha is working well, we can take any work in hand and definitely make that successful. Therefore, we should pay attention to programmes of the Sangh Shakha, its working methodology, conduct of its swayamsevaks, nature of its swayamsevaks, improvement in their qualities and work with full focus to expand the Shakhas and strengthen them."

"If we do this much, we shall achieve victory in all the fields. The more this work is done with conscience and strong effort, more will we see victory all across. I say this with full belief... Delegates from all over the country have come here; they will work with whole-hearted efforts in their respective fields. I wish to say only this much for now. Who knows whether God gives me a chance to speak again or not next time!"[8]

We do not know whether Guruji felt that he had taken a load off his heart. From the next day, Guruji's health began deteriorating further. It became difficult to take a bath by himself. It became nearly impossible to come to the Sangh ground. Arrangements were made for Sangh salutation and prayers in the next room. Habit of chatting with swayamsevaks after Shakha was carried on but, intelligent swayamsevaks gave him very few chances for this. A dedicated swayamsevak, Vishnupant Muthal was appointed to take his care. His condition got worse. Guruji found it difficult even to stand. Ingestion of food or liquid became very painful.

There has been a tradition in Nagpur and Vidarbha states that appointments of the Sangh workers is declared on Varsh Pratipada festival day. Activities for next year, too, begin that very day. Varsh Pratipada that year was on 3rd April. Guruji wrote his thoughts on a paper on the last day of the passing year on 2nd April, Amavasya Day on official stationery carrying his name. Putting it in a sealed envelope, he called the officer in-charge of administration, Pandurang Pant Kshirsagar in his room and handed it over to him. After handing over the letter he said, "Please open it after my soul abandons this body." His colleague for a long time, Kshirsagar ji had no doubt that it would be a review of his work through his life. His hand and heart trembled as he picked up and carried it.

It was a coincidence or God's will, the same night at 9:30 p.m. Kanchi Kamkoti Peeth head, Shri Shankaracharya Jayendra Teerth Saraswati climbed up the stairs of his room to meet him. He had started on his feet from Kanchi to perform pilgrimage of four holy centres in the Himalayas. He had reached Nagpur a day earlier. His relations with Guruji were very old. On hearing about the worrisome health of Guruji, he walked straight from one end of city to Mahal area and was face to face with Guruji in his room. Guruji was waiting for his divine feet. On having *darshan* of Acharya swami, he said, "I wish to offer salutation lying prostrate but this body does not allow me to bow, inflicts unbearable pain." Acharyaji's consoled him in Sanskrit, blessed him, drank a little of cow's milk from Sangh office and returned back. While going, he did not forget to tell Guruji, "I am going to be present for Varsh Pratipada festival tomorrow." Guruji immediately thanked him happily with folded hands and said, "All our swayamsevaks are fortunate to receive your blessings."

Ramnarayan Shastri's medical treatment was going on to reduce the impact of the disease and one could see its curative effects. During this time, upon instructions from Guruji, advocate P.N. Sontakke prepared the Last Will of Guruji, on which Guruji signed as 'Sadashiv Golwalkar's son Madhav Golwalkar in the presence of witnesses, W. K. Thatte and S.B. Motlag, on 19th April. According to the will, his house in Ramtek was donated to Bharatiya Utkarsh Mandal.[9]

On the second day, on 20th April, he sent his utensils of *pooja* to his paternal cousine Vasudev Ramchandra Golwalkar through Dr. Sitaram of Jashpur. Items were a collection of memorabilia of Swami Akhandananda like a signed full-length picture of Swamiji, a little ash from his funeral pyre, three to four small pieces of bones, some hair, woolen sheet, socks, footwear, spoon, silk *dhoti* worn during *pooja*, two handkerchiefs with prints of his holy feet – all of this laid out properly in a sandal box that had the famous swan seal of Shri Ramakrishna Ashram.*

---

* On the request of the author, Vasudev Golwalkar showed him these articles himself.

Only after writing a letter and seeking his permission had he sent these articles of worship to his elder brother as sacred heirloom. He had also informed him how to keep them, "Please offer one set*bilwa* leaves and light an incense stick every morning and in the evening, just light the incense stick. This is enough, nothing more needs to be done."[10]

He had sought his *guru-bhai* Swami Amoortananda's advice on this matter about one-and-a-half years before this in November 1971. It is worth remembering that one month prior to this, he had donated all the jewellery of his respected mother at the feet of family deity, Ambaji. When one strings together all these incidents, one realises that Guruji had begun efforts to free himself slowly of worldly debts one-by-one from September 1971 itself. Surrender of mother's jewellery, donation of father's house, transfer of artifacts of Gurudev in a proper place – accomplishing all these tasks, he completed his life's surrender to God (*padmapatramvaambhasa*), and freed himself too.

He was left with two objects now – one- pocketwatch that had Swami Akhandananda's name inscribed at the back, signifying a stable mind, second – a *sadhu's* pail (*kamandalu*) signifying non-attachment as a *sadhu*. And Lord has said, "I always love my devotees who are of stable mind and unattached."*

All the swayamsevaks of Nagpur had been busy collecting funds for drought relief for nine days from Varsh Pratipadaa till Ram Navami. Renowned and outstanding singer of *Geet Ramayana,* Shri Sudhir Phadke had also arrived for his recital to be held for this purpose. He came to the Sangh office to be with Guruji on 7th April before his public concert at Chitnis Park. He sang four to five songs at Guruji's request. When the episode about Bharat's departure for Chitrakoot came up, tears flowed down the eyes of that *sthitpradnya*. Words in very low voice came out of his lips, "Bharat! Father is gone, he leaves his mother, he leaves behind his monarchy, leaves behind his dear ones, he is coming to forests to bring back his brother. Oh, what a love! How deep is this love!... You have set its tune so well."

Tears flowed again! Offering his prostrate salutation, an emotionally moved Sudhir Phadke departed from his room.[11] What kind of God's play was it, one does not know. Guruji's condition began improving from 10th April. He could stand for four to five minutes, could go to the next room on his own; his voice also became a little clearer! Dada Apte of Vishwa Hindu Parishad came to meet him on 18th April. He presented Parishad's story of growth without Guruji's query. Guruji seemed to be highly pleased. After this, taking advantage of his closeness and old relations, he asked Guruji, "Guruji, have you decided what could be theme of your life?"

Guruji: "Theme? I have decided to flow with the current."

Another question: "Does it mean, just sit idle in the current?"

---

* *Aniketahsthirmatirbhaktimaan me priyonarah* (Gita 12)

Guruji: "No, no. To flow with the current. Not moving out of current. Not even get finished by sinking inside the current; why should one go against the current? Not even to just see the flow of the current standing at the banks. Being thrown aside by the current, not even this. God has told us, *Kurya advidvanstatha asatkash chikeerushurlokas angraham*, that is, people who lead the world should not look different from ordinary common people. This is the theme of my life."[12]

Prabhudatta Brahmachaari came to know that Guruji's condition was improving. He invited Guruji to Jhoosi for recuperation. Explaining practical problems in this, Guruji wrote a long letter in his own hand. Last part of this highly readable letter is, "I think, I have expressed my inability well enough about my condition and reason for not accepting this virtuous suggestion. My health is improving. I am experiencing *Achyutanandgovindan-amasmranam bheshajam. Nashyanti sakalah rogah satyam satyamvadamyaham.* A little before and after Shri Varsh Pratipadaa doctors had doubts that my condition was very critical. But, now the situation is not the same and my colleagues have breathed a sigh of relief. A doctor had come. He had lot of suggestions about using some medicines. I just gave him a short answer, *'Hoi hai soi jo Ram rachi rakhaa'*, then where is the reason to worry or to be sad?"[13]

Third year training camp of Nagpur commenced on 13th May. During that period, Guruji's condition was such that he could sit for about 10-15 minutes. Balasaheb Deoras and Bapurao Varhadpande recalled the time 33 years back when Doctorji was on sick-bed at Ghatate's home and participating students were bereft of his company in Reshim Bagh's camp. Keeping his physical condition in mind and more importantly his strong desire, they arranged an introduction programme for all the participants. Arrangements were made accordingly, for participants to come in groups of 25-30 to Hedgewar Bhavan and receive his guidance. For people who could not attend any other camp this year, this arrangement was like a sip of nectar. Keeping the list of students in hand, he would speak to each of them for a minute or two. At the end of the scheduled 15 minutes, he would speak four to five sentences in a thematic way and then stop for his rest. Meetings of third-year participants finished on 28th May. Now, was the turn of first-year and second-year students of Nagpur. In the last meeting in this series, the leader of the group gave order of '*uttishta*' (rise) as Guruji entered the room. First question Guruji asked was, "In the order given for rising up, is it alphabet '*t*' of '*gat*' or '*th*' of *nishtha*'? Everybody took note of the mistake. Instructor answered, '*th*' of '*nishtha*'. With a smile, he told, "Whether it is an order or prayer, pronunciation should be correct, chaste." He was firmly alert all the 24 hours that life of a swayamsevak and his conduct should be faultless. Literally, a person with steely resolve.[14]

Just as the sea gets into low tide as moon goes down, in the same way Guruji's health deteriorated immediately after the introductory meetings with student participants were over and the speed of this deterioration increased from June 1. Still, people kept coming in to meet him. June 1 was the day of *Amavasya* (dark phase of moon). He tied up all his scriptures he read regularly with proper care and kept them in the cupboard, cleaned his wooden sandals and stored them too. Rashtra Sevika Samiti founder Mausi Laxmibai Kelkar came to meet him on 3rd June. On enquiring about his health, the short answer Guruji gave was, "Preparation for leaving has been done," and there was a light smile on his face. Mausi ji was stunned into silence and she left after offering her *namaskar*. 4th June just dragged on. Then came, 5th June, Tuesday *Jyeshtha Shukla Panchami*. Guruji, who used to get up at 4 a.m., but got up at 3:45 a.m., shut off the cooler, completed his morning ablutions and began holy chanting sitting in his armchair. He took his tea at 5:45 a.m. as usual. He told Abaji standing next to him, "Aba, bell is ringing." After taking bath with help of Baburao Chauthaiwale at 7, he entered his room, shut the door and began his morning spiritual practices. As he came out at 8, he saw that Atal Behari Vajpayee was sitting there, waiting for him and so were four to five other friends, one of them being the doctor. Easy conversation began. Guruji was speaking, others were listening. Question about his health came up. In response, he shared a joke, "There was an adamant patient. He went to the doctor. Doctor asked him, 'What is the problem? Please tell me the whole story.' Patient said, 'If I have to tell you about my sickness, how can you cure me? I need a doctor who can tell about the sickness without me telling him.' Doctor kept quiet for a moment, then said, 'I will call another doctor for you.' After the other doctor came, he introduced him and said, 'This is your doctor. He can understand without telling anything.' He was a veterinary doctor!" The room of the patient was filled with hearty laughter.[15] Guests went back at 8:30. Guruji had got very tired by then. Breathing became difficult and he had to be given oxygen immediately. He had to be administered oxygen like this many times in the day. He took a little curd milk and rice at 11:45 and took rest till 2:30 p.m. He could take only two to three sips of tea, that too with great difficulty. Breathing became more difficult by 6 p.m. Doctor Mukundrao Shastri and Doctor Bhagwat were called. When they talked of giving an injection, he told them, "It is not required. Why waste medicine?" Still due to affectionate persuasion, he gave permission to the doctors. Still, as he had predicted, breathing did not improve inspite of administering injection. Dr. Abaji got worried. 'Fowler's bed' was brought into his room. Guruji was asked to lie down on it after it was set up. Refusing with a wave of his hand, he said, "We shall see about it later." Sangh prayer was due at 7:15 p.m. He could not tie his *dhoti*, as his hands were trembling. Attendants brought a chair and said, "Please recite your prayer in the sitting position. There is no need to go to the other room." "Will I have to listen to the orders from the ground and prayer from here?" was the next question. "We shall make arrangements for it," came the reply. Prayer began at 7:10 after salutation to *Bhagwa dhwaj*. Dr. Abaji Thatte stood behind Guruji. Shakha was disbursed. Generally, Guruji used to take tea with colleagues after Shakha, but that day he said, "No" to it. Difficulty in breathing was still there. In the meanwhile, there was a phone call in the office below and Abaji went down to receive it. Baburao Chauthaiwale and Vishnu Muthal ji stayed behind. Guruji asked for water and suddenly stood up after taking two to three sips. It was time for evening prayers. He went to the bathroom for a wash. During washing his hands, he just froze. Baburao caught him. He fell into his arms. Both of them brought him into his room and put him on his armchair. He just lay still there, at rest. "Guruji, Guruji," Vishnu called out two to three times. There was no response, breathing was on. It was 8 p.m.; team of doctors – Mukund Shastri, Ramdas Paranjape, Balasaheb Pendse and Inda Pawar – went into action. Injection was given; oxygen was given. It was found after some wait that there was no result. Patient was just lying still like a still flame of a lamp. Heartbeat sank gradually. 9:05 p.m. – the body finally fell calm. Madhav Sadashiv Golwalkar's body became lifeless; soul had left for the ultimate destination.

There was an epilogue to this life; it was the envelope that he had handed over saying, "Open it when my body turns cold." Only after disclosure of the contents written in it, could completeness of his life be considered concluded. Pandurangpant Kshirsagar presented that envelope with reverence in the emergency session of Central Working Committee. It contained not one, but three letters! It was decided to read out all the three letters to the people who had collected in Hedgewar Bhavan campus. Babasaheb Bhide read out the first letter. It was addressed: "To all swayamsevak brothers." It said, "The Sangh work will, ofcourse, proceed as per its constitution. Based on that very constitution is the issue of planning for appointment of new Sarsanghchaalak. Members of Akhil Bharatiya Kaaryakaari Mandal with whom I could meet and discuss, all of them are very senior, with very long experience and Sanghchaalaks, taking care of various states. After talking to them and listening to their views, it is my duty to present the essence of their decision as the current Sarsanghchaalak.

"Fulfilling this duty, I am pronouncing my decision that after I leave this body, a person known to all, Shri Madhukar Dattatreya Deoras, that is, Balasaheb Deoras will take up the responsibility as Sarsanghchaalak."[16] In that letter the then Sarsanghchaalak expressed confidence, "All young and old swayamsevaks will keep working with heart, body and soul under the guidance of new Sarsanghchaalak to complete the Sangh mission and work will achieve its goal soon." It is clear that Guruji completed his constitutional responsibility with this letter. Second letter was more personal, but was going to provide necessary guidance to swayamsevaks for times to come. Newly appointed Sarsanghchaalak, respected Balasaheb Deoras, read it out. It said, "Our work worships nation, worships our ideals; there is no place in it for personality worship… Sangh's goal and Sangh founder who envisioned that goal for us, apart from these, it is not necessary to give more importance to any other person as a personality, nor is it necessary to build any memorial for him."[17]

Third letter was completely personal; it was the last adieu, a symbol of a great divine soul's innermost feelings that were bereft of any pride and represented the highest level of selflessness, egolessness. The manner of address itself said it all, "My dearest respected swayamsevak brothers," Balasaheb Deoras could somehow read this, though with choked voice, "Highly revered Dr. Hedgewar left his body on 21st June, 1940 and enormous responsibility of Sarsanghchaalak fell on my shoulders as per his wish. I did not know of anything. Still all the elder workers co-operated with love, guided me and I could carry this weighty responsibility for 33 long years... In this long period, due to my peculiar nature or due to other shortcomings, the hearts of many workers must have been hurt. I seek their pardon with folded hands."[18]

It was time when the sun had set, time for bidding final good bye to Dr. Hedgewar Bhavan. At 9 in the night, the scenario at Reshim Bagh – a body abandoned by the soul earlier in the day, a chariot abandoned by its driver, was offered to God of fire by member of Golwalkar clan, Shri Vasudev Golwalkar, in the presence of Dr. Hedgewar's idol as a witness to this event.

□

Endnotes

1. *Shri Guruji Samagra*, Vol. 6, pp. 258
2. *Jeevan Prasang*, Vol. 1, pp. 183-185
3. *The Guidelines, Bengaluru*, pp. 16
4. *Sukhad Prasang*, pp. 38
5. Ibid, pp. 39-40
6. *Kisankunj* – Lucknow, pp. 51
7. *Nagpur Patra Register* 73 - Letter No. 579 (20-3-73)
8. *Shri Guruji Samagra*, Vol. 3, pp. 84-90
9. *Vaseeyatnama* – Nagpur Documentation Centre
10. *Shri Guruji Samagra*, Vol. 6, pp. 260
11. *Jeevan Prasang*, Vol. 1, pp. 66-67
12. Ibid, pp. 57
13. *Shri Guruji Samagra*, Vol. 6, pp. 262-263
14. *Shri Guruji Samagra*, Vol. 3, pp. 138
15. *Jeevan Prasang*, Vol. 1, pp. 367
16. *Shri Guruji Samagra*, Vol. 6, pp. 264
17. Ibid, pp. 265
18. Ibid, pp. 265-266

45

A Few Observations

Arjun had asked Lord Krishna three questions to understand the personality traits of *Sthitpradnya* (a balanced, calm personality – transcendentally situated) "*Kim prabhaashet, kim aaseet, kim vrajet*?" meaning, "How does a '*sthitpradnya*' speak, how does he sit and how does he walk?" Observant readers would have found answers to these questions while reading about Guruji Golwalkar's life and views in the preceding pages. Still, it would be a good idea to know a little more about his day-to-day conduct in practical life. With this in mind, the author is mentioning a few of the facts collected from his near-and-dear ones and one's own experience.

Guruji's speech used to be professorial. He never followed an unnatural style of greeting people in their regional language or speaking two or three sentences in regional language when he went to a particular state or region. His voice would be very low at the beginning of a speech, and would reach middle pitch in another two to three minutes. Later, the lecture would move on in the same flow without highs and lows like a smooth flowing river. But, there would definitely be a variation in the words and stress on them, depending upon seriousness of a point that he was putting forth. If some jokes or anecdotes came into his narrative, the audience would be laughing, not the speaker. *Bhagwad Gita* talks of '*anadvegakaram vaakyam*' – words that don't incite emotions – such would be his words. But, his sentences used to be long, specially concluding sentences of a lecture. If he spoke of an incident, he would never name the person concerned and would only talk about 'a famous poet, or a big leader'. That way a common swayamsevak would not be biased about that person. He used to speak in *aaram* or 'at ease' posture of physical drill of the Sangh, and raising his arms or waving them around was an exception. He never drank water during his speech. He would speak in same style, whether he spoke in Hindi, Marathi or English. Most of the times, his speech would be over in 50-60 minutes. But, in a get-together of well-wishers, he did not speak for more than 20-25 minutes, and spent the remaining time in getting to know people personally.

His style during meetings with workers (Sangh *baithaks*) was quite in contrast as compared to his lectures. It was more like a conversation during spiritual gatherings. He used to analyse the work and worker through queries, humorous interaction, quips and comments. Guidance about each and every point would be provided there itself. There would be no speech at the end of a *baithak*, only 5-10 minutes of talk offering guidance. In those short concluding remarks, the subject of criticality of Sangh work, qualities required of a *karyakarta* (worker) and demand of times – these would definitely be highlighted in a brief manner. Sentences in these meetings used to be short. It did not matter whether the meeting was of 30 people or 300. All meetings would be like an exhortation and blessed offering. Each swayamsevak would come out of his meeting in a joyful mood.

While sitting on ground, Guruji would squat in yogic posture with straight spine. He used to sit in the same posture even for his food. Even if there was a supporting pillow at the back, he would never take its support. This habit may, perhaps, be a result of his practice of yoga. He always sat on the left side of the driver in a car. If owner himself drove the car, he would keep the conversation flowing with him. He read books during travels too. Nobody ever saw him taking a nap in the car; he did not have this habit. He insisted on following all the traffic rules.

By nature he loved taking walks. He may have inherited this trait from his father and mother. He always used to walk from Dr. Hedgewar Bhavan to his home. It generally used to take him 20 minutes for a distance of 10 minutes as he stopped on way, asking about well-being of people he knew and met on the way. He would even walk to the homes of swayamsevaks in Mahal locality. However, when he walked alone, he walked very fast. It was while seeing him walk briskly at a function in Calicut that the chief correspondent of daily *Mathrubhoomi* had noted, "He is a 'goal walker' who 'walks' towards his 'goal'."

It was his habit to reach any programme, whether it was Sangh's or somebody else's, in time. Therefore, participants used to arrive at his programmes on time. Visitors also used to come at the appointed time to meet him.

It was his nature to go home and touch his mother's and father's feet before he left Nagpur for any tour. Father used to ask him about his tour programme and the son would provide complete details of his travel calendar to his satisfaction. Therefore, father would always be aware about the place his son would be in, on a particular date.

Guruji used to wear wooden sandals at home. There was a designated place for them. Presently his wooden sandals are kept in his grand-nephew Sarwate's place of worship at his home. His grand-nephews tell us, "Nanaji used to take bath with hot water, pour the left over water from the pail over his head. He would always push up his *rudraksh-mala* on his forehead near his hair while doing so." While chit-chatting with his mother at home, if an awkward topic came up during a conversation, the son used to start humming '*Shri Krishna Govind hare Muraare, hey naath Narayan Vasudeva*', clapping and laughing easily. His understanding mother would close the subject then.

Guruji treated all the seven days of the week in a uniform manner. He had no favourite or special day. He used to take his food only once every day before 12 noon. Apart from this, he used to take tea twice before noon and twice after noon, with no snacks, etc. in between. A doctor in Kolkata, who knew him personally, did his medical examination there once. On hearing about his food habits and quantity he took, he joked, "According to our medical science, you should not be alive now." "But, I am alive," was Guruji's response. On directions from his *Vaidya*, he used to take only cow's milk as his nutrition during the last phase of his life. He used to fast only two days in a year, *Mahashivraatri* and *Shraavan Poornima*; he practised no other fast apart from these. Surely, as a lifelong vow, he would not leave any food particle served to him in his plate as a rule, because he believed, 'food is God, it is not right to insult it'. Therefore, the role of an ever alert Dr. Thatte, as his personal assistant, used to be infinitely important in these matters.

Guruji used to wear only *swadeshi* clothes. Even within this, he never wore silks. When the owner of a silk factory, Shri Ramarao presented him silk fabric, he handed it over to local swayamsevaks to dye it in saffron and use it for making *bhagwa dhwaj* (saffron flag of Sangh) for Sangh Shakha.

He used to be specially uncomfortable about getting himself photographed. Many a times he used to get angry because of this. Therefore, no worker would even try to photograph him. However, he had to bear with this issue during family programmes. In his long innings as Sarsanghchaalak, only one photograph with all his colleagues is available. This has been clicked at the time of Central Working Committee meeting on 6th February, 1972, at Vivekananda Rock Memorial in Kanyakumari. Regarding the practice of accepting a garland, he carried on with the tradition of Dr. Hedgewar. He did not allow anybody to garland him. This tradition was put on hold only during the mammoth public programmes organised after lifting of ban on the Sangh in 1948 and during the functions to felicitate him on his 51st birthday. Otherwise, this tradition was followed till the end. There is a custom in many temples to garland a distinguished guest when he visits a temple and usher him to have a *darshan* of the presiding deity in the same state. Guruji did not accept this practice. He never went inside a temple wearing a garland like this. His view was that only the presiding deity had the right to wear a garland in the temple, nobody else; and he steadfastly stuck to this stand.

There was another thing many people were not aware of. Guruji would not drink or eat anything in a house where he went to see a sick person. There is a belief in many parts of Bharat that one should not bid a formal goodbye in a patient's room and should come out without doing so. Guruji believed in this tradition. He also believed that one harms a patient's age by eating something at a patient's home. He had bound himself in this matter. Dr. Abaji Thatte and very few close colleagues knew about this habit and they used to take care about it when Guruji went to meet a sick person.

He never used to wear a cap. His Sangh uniform was also without its black cap. He even entered a *gurudwara* in Punjab without covering his head. Jathedaars gave him special permission for this and also honoured by offering him *saropaa*. Nobody knows the purpose behind this condition Guruji had imposed on himself. It seems that it may have something to do with his spiritual practices.

Guruji always used to call out swayamsevaks with their first names like Ram, Govind or their pet names like Baba, Bapu, etc. He avoided calling people by their surnames like Trivedi, Tiwari, etc. He never had any difficulty in this regard due to his extraordinary memory. Swayamsevaks, too, used to feel closer to him this way.

His view was that responding to letters was a duty that was something beyond a mere social protocol. He used to send answers himself even to invitations. Only his correspondence with government used to be typewritten; all his other letters were in his own neat handwriting. Understanding the mother tongue or language that an addressee preferred, he used to write in Hindi, Marathi or English. Depending on the length of his answer to a letter, he chose postcard, inland or envelope. He kept on writing his letters while conversation flowed in his room in Nagpur. Therefore, regular swayamsevaks would not feel awkward to keep on conversing with him even as he wrote letters. There was nothing novel about this style of Guruji for old swayamsevaks of Nagpur. People who knew him, tell us that he preferred blue ink to black ink.

Such were a few of his habits and behaviour as an individual. It is also possible to understand a person through his habits. Just as habits develop one's nature, in the same way, one's nature also evolves into a certain behaviour. Nevertheless, it is true that habits give a measure of an individual. This measure of a person proves to be correct, when a person is alone. Guruji was a kind of personality who had purity of thought, purity of spiritual essence present in full measure. Transparency was like an alternative name for his life. Therefore, there was no difference in his being whether he was alone or with many others, just as fragrance of sandalwood is the same whether there is darkness or light. We have highlighted his habits based on our own experience. There is no doubt that this information would be helpful in understanding this divine personality from within and outside. When one thinks of such a saintly personality, one recalls the lines of a famous poet:

"Tulsi aaye jagat mein,
Jagat hanse tum roye,

Aisee karanee kar chalo,
Aap hanse jag roye."

Meaning: O Tulsi, whence you came unto this world, world laughed while you cried. Such should be your actions that when you leave this world, world may cry while you laugh.

□

Appendix-I

Physical Structure

- RSS has a highly federal structure that is defined clearly in its constitution. Though the policies are controlled centrally, the execution of different ideas and plans is left to the regional, state or local level depending upon the scale of a plan.
- Shakha is the basic unit of the organisation. An RSS swayamsevak is the basic cell of this huge network of the organisation. Shakha is headed by a kaaryavaah (secretary) and mukhya shikshak (chief instructor or teacher).
- Groups of shakhas are organised at the level of 'tehsil' in rural areas and 'mandal' that form part of a 'nagar' in case of urban areas. In the upcoming re-organisation, 'basti' or locality of approximately 10,000 citizens will be the smallest unit in cities and towns.
- The next level is district (zilaa)-level committees, followed by state (praant) and region (kshetra). District-level committees are important units of an organisation that help execute organisational plans, guide and support the shakhas under their areas.
- National-level policy-making body is Kendriya Karyakarini (Central Working Committee). It is nominated from the Akhil Bharatiya Pratinidhi Sabha (All India Delegates Council), the apex body in RSS. ABPS has ex-officio members of central committee and elected members who have been elected by senior local shakha members within a district. Their numbers depend on size and population of respective states.
- Organisational units from Tehsil or Mandal to Central level have Kaaryavaah (Secretary) as the executive head of the team and in-charge of overall activities. Committees at all the levels have members for physical training, intellectual training, social service, co-ordination for other associate organisations and a few other members assigned to some responsibility depending upon the size of the organisation and other related activities in that area.
- Regular elections are held every three years for the election of Sanghchaalaks at district and higher levels. Member delegates to ABPS delegates are also elected during these elections. These members then vote for the post of General Secretary (Sarkaaryavaah). People elected to ABPS need to have

a good record of organisational work to qualify as delegates.

- The guide and philosopher at tehsil level onwards is 'Sanghchaalak' (Chief of Organisation of a particular area). He is the public face of RSS in his area. Sanghchaalak commands high respect and his word carries weight, though he has no executive powers in day-to-day working of the Sangh.
- The post of Sarsanghchaalak (Chief of RSS) is non-elective. As a convention and part of its accepted constitution, he is nominated by his predecessor after due discussions with the most senior members of central committee (Kendriya Kaaryakaarini). So, it is not one man's decision, though he carries the final responsibility of this nomination.
- Resolutions passed in the Pratinidhi Sabha truly reflect RSS views of various issues facing the nation and Hindu society at a given time. A serious student of RSS should read these resolutions that are made public immediately after they are passed and sent to media for publication.
- There is a structured way a communication or an instruction passes from HO to a local shakha or from state-level or district level to the local-level organisation. It is an unwritten protocol that any directive or information must pass through the designated organisational structure. There is no short-cut from top to bottom or bottom to top.
- There are formal and informal systems of information-sharing that flows both ways. This two-way flow of information and feedback helps the organisation and its leaders firmly grounded about social and political issues from local to national or international level. Communication in any particular region generally happens in the local language.

□

Appendix-II

Glossary of Terms used in Rashtriya Swayamsevak Sangh

Sarsanghchaalak	:	Mentor or guide of the Sangh
Sarkaryavaah	:	Topmost office-bearer to be elected
Sanghchaalak	:	Guardian of local activities and local volunteers
Prachaarak	:	A person who dedicates his entire life for the Sangh without expecting anything in return
Vistaarak	:	The full-time worker who dedicates a brief period (less than a year) for the Sangh
Shakha	:	Daily assembly or gathering for imparting (Sangh) culture
Upashakha	:	Various Shakhas in the same area
Mukhya Shikshak	:	The one who is responsible for conducting regular Shakha activities
Karyavaah	:	Leading person in the purview of a Shakha
Gatnaayak	:	Team leader of a small area which falls under the purview of the Shakha
Karyakarta-Karyakram	:	Worker-programme
Baithak	:	Meeting for discussing, deliberating and decision-making
Pravaas	:	Visiting and staying in other places as a part of Sangh work
Sampata	:	Command given for arranging Swayamsevaks in a specific manner before the commencement of a programme
Danda	:	Lathi
Veekira	:	Command given at the end of a Shakha programme
Bauddhik	:	Intellectual exercise programme, (intellectual) discourse
Samataa	:	Physical training programme for self-discipline
Chandan	:	Joyful gathering for having snacks
Sahabhojan	:	Gathering for having homely meal

Saanghik : Congregation of Swayamsevaks belonging to more than one Shakha

Ekatrikaran : Gathering of various Shakhas, gathering of main workers

Sangh Shiksha Varg : Training programme for teaching Sangh programme scheduled over three years

Shivir : Camp

Rakshak : Security in-charge of Shivirs

Prabandhak : In-charge for looking after the programmes conducted by the Sangh

Saarvajanik Samaaroh : The public programme at the end of Shivir and Varg

Deekshant Samaaroh : (Special Convocation) Special programme for the trainees at the end of Varg

Vividh Kshetra Sangathan : Other organisations not inspired by the ideals of the Sangh

□□□